Turnover = Sa...

$$\frac{Net\ Profit}{Capital} \times \frac{100}{1} =$$

Chap. 35, 36, 37.

PRACTICAL BOOKKEEPING
AND ACCOUNTS
(DECIMAL EDITION)

BY
A. J. FAVELL, B.Sc.(Econ.), A.C.I.S.
Late Principal of the Hammersmith Commercial Institute

Also in Two Parts:

Part I. Comprising a complete elementary course.
Part II. Intermediate course.

A KEY to the book is also available.

UNIVERSITY TUTORIAL PRESS LTD
9-10 Great Sutton Street, London, EC1V 0DA

PREFACE

Practical Bookkeeping and Accounts explains the methods and principles on which accounts are based. Though not restricted to the requirements of any particular examining body, the book covers Ordinary Level of the various G.C.E. Boards, and the elementary and intermediate examinations of the Royal Society of Arts and the London Chamber of Commerce.

In the present edition the chapters on Records of Sales and Purchases and on Control Accounts have been revised. A chapter on Mechanised Accounts has been introduced with the help of British Olivetti Ltd; the charts at the end of the book are reproduced with their kind permission. The chapters on Company Accounts have been amended to take note of the Companies Act 1967.

The following examining bodies are thanked for permission to use examination questions: the University of Cambridge Local Examinations Syndicate, the University of London School Examinations Council, the Universities of Manchester, Liverpool, Leeds, Sheffield, and Birmingham Joint Matriculation Board, the Oxford Delegacy of Local Examinations, the Associated Examining Board, the College of Preceptors, the London Chamber of Commerce, the National Union of Teachers, the Northern Counties Technical Examinations Council, the Royal Society of Arts, the Union of Educational Institutions, and the Union of Lancashire and Cheshire Institutes. In some questions amounts were converted from £ s d to decimals with the consent of the examining bodies concerned, sometimes using a third decimal place.

Published 1935
Sixth Edition (Decimal) 1969
Reprinted 1970, 1971, 1973, 1974, 1975 (twice),
1976 *(with minor corrections)*

ISBN: Complete   0 7231 0674 6
        Part I   0 7231 0675 4
        Part II   0 7231 0676 2

Printed in Great Britain by **The Burlington Press**, Foxton, Royston, Herts SG8 6SA

CONTENTS

PART I

Contents

PART II

PRACTICAL
BOOKKEEPING AND ACCOUNTS

PART 1

CHAPTER 1

INTRODUCTORY

Bookkeeping is the recording of the financial transactions of a business in a methodical manner so that information on any point in relation to them may be quickly obtained. The method of procedure is based upon definite principles which are discussed and illustrated in the chapters that follow. The kind of information which a trader may desire to have and which is readily available is summarised below.

The trader may discover—

(a) The value of his purchases.
(b) The value of his sales.
(c) His expenses.
(d) The amount of cash in the office or at the bank.
(e) The sums owing to him by customers.
(f) The sums owing by the business.
(g) The recorded value of the property and things owned by the business.
(h) The profit made during a particular period.
(i) The financial position of the business on any given day.

The ultimate purpose of business is to make a profit, and, as every transaction plays its part in determining the final profit for a trading period, accuracy in recording is essential. Such accuracy is no less essential for the smooth running of a business as customers may be irritated and custom and money lost through inaccurate records of transactions. A bookkeeper, therefore, should cultivate accuracy and carefulness and should be able to make good figures and to write legibly.

The Business and the Owner

The first important point in the study of the principles of book-keeping is to distinguish and separate the business from the owner. The bookkeeper records the transactions from the point of view of their effects on the business. The owner may personally attend to the buying and selling, but he must be regarded in such a case as acting on behalf of the business and not in his personal capacity, and the sales and purchases must be recorded as sales and purchases by the business. This distinction should be borne in mind as the following chapters are studied.

Accounts as an Aid to Management

The owner of a business naturally wishes to run his business as efficiently as possible. One of the main purposes of keeping accounts is to enable him to do this. His accounts should tell him the exact cost of what he is selling, the exact amount of each expense which is involved, and the exact revenue of the business. With such information the owner of the business can make comparisons from year to year, comparing the profit this year with that of preceding years and investigating the cause of any difference by making comparisons of the amount of each cost and each expense. By studying his accounts in this way the business man is able to formulate a business policy. He may, for example, decide to raise or to lower prices, to advertise more, to change the method of delivery of his goods, or to change the organisation of the office work.

EXERCISES 1

1. Why is it necessary for a business to keep accounts? Give as many reasons as you can.

CHAPTER 2

THE LEDGER

The book required for a proper record of the transactions of a business is called the Ledger, though it will be shown later how the recording is assisted, in certain circumstances, by the use of other books. A suitable Ledger may be purchased from a stationer who usually has a stock of Ledgers of various sizes and thicknesses to meet the special needs of customers. The Ledger may be recognised by the ruling of its pages, and a specimen page, unused, is shown for this purpose below.

Specimen Page from the Ledger

It is not invariable that Ledgers are ruled in this way. With the growth of mechanised accounting Ledger cards are increasingly used and are usually ruled as follows:—

DATE	DETAILS	DEBIT	CREDIT	BALANCE

3

A sheet of paper ruled similarly is called Ledger paper. It will be observed that there are twelve columns on a Ledger page, six of which fill half the width of the page and are repeated again on the other half. A page in a Ledger is called a folio, and the pages are numbered consecutively for reference purposes.

A Business Transaction

To show the particular use made of the columns and to make a start in the actual use of the Ledger, it is proposed to deal with the following example:—

Example 1.—M. Redman begins to deal in second-hand bicycles, starting with £20 in cash
On 1st January he buys a lot of 4 bicycles for £12, paying cash down.
He sells 2 bicycles on 8th January for cash at £6 each, and the remainder on 10th January at £5 each.
He pays £1 for advertising.

This example comprises several transactions which will have to be recorded in the Ledger, and they may be summarised as below—

(1) Redman separates from his private funds the sum of £20 for business purposes.

(2) The purchase of bicycles on 1st January and the payment for them in cash.

(3) The sale of bicycles on 8th January and the receipt of cash.

(4) The sale of bicycles on 10th January and the receipt of cash.

(5) The payment of the advertising charges.

These transactions are entered in the Ledger by the bookkeeper as they occur, and the page in the Ledger will then appear as below. Reference numbers, as above, have been inserted to enable the student to trace the respective entries.

Dr.					Cash Account				Cr.
19..			£		19..				£
Jan. 1	Capital (1)	..	20		Jan. 1	Purchases (2)			12
,, 8	Sales (3)	..	12		,, 3	Advertising			
,, 10	Sales (4)	..	10			charges (5)..			1

			Capital Account (M. Redman)				
				Jan. 1	Cash (1)	..	20

			Purchases Account			
Jan. 1	Cash (2)	..	12			

Dr.	Sales Account				Cr.

19..		£	19..		£
			Jan. 8	Cash (3)	12
			„ 10	„ (4) ..	10

Expenses Account

Jan. 3	Cash (Advertis-				
	ing) (5) ..	1			

The student should have this completed Ledger page before him as he reads the following explanations of its use.

First, it will be observed that the respective columns have special uses—the first column for the date of the transaction, the second for the particulars of the transaction, the fourth, and fifth for the money value. The third column is called the folio column and its use is explained later. The five columns repeated on the right-hand half of the Ledger page have similar uses.

Formerly debit entries were prefaced by the word "To" and credit entries by the word "By." This is no longer considered to be necessary.

The *third* observation is that five cross-headings have been inserted on the Ledger page—Cash Account, Capital Account, Purchases Account, Sales Account, and Expenses Account. Each of these covers a statement of things relative to its heading. For example, records of transactions involving the movement of cash have been grouped into a statement or account called the Cash Account, and the records of sales have been grouped under the heading Sales Account. It is obvious that each item was first classified and then entered in its appropriate group or account. Further accounts are opened as may be necessary according to the range of the transactions to be entered.

The *fourth* observation is that there are ten entries in the Ledger, though the list on page 4 shows five transactions only. It should be apparent that there are two entries for each transaction, and it should be further apparent that one of the two entries is on the left-hand side of an account, and the other, or corresponding, entry is on the right-hand side of an account.

This brings us to the basic principle of the system of double-entry bookkeeping with which this book is concerned. Every transaction may be viewed from two aspects and both aspects of each transaction are recorded in the accounts. This fact becomes clearer as the transactions are analysed in more detail below.

Having made these observations, it remains to discuss the basis of classification of the items in the example and the respective entries in the accounts. The student is advised to have before him a properly-ruled sheet of Ledger paper, and to make the entries as each transaction is dealt with.

Transaction 1.—Redman starts the business with £20 in cash. His private means are diminished by this amount. Though he manages the business and appears to have no separate premises in which to work, this sum of £20 must be regarded as no longer available for his personal needs.

The cash now belongs to the business, and as a check against the actual coins and notes wherever they are kept, a record must be made of the receipt of cash, of its expenditure, and of further receipts as business operations take place. All dealings with the cash are recorded in the Cash Account, and whenever cash is received or paid away the amount must be entered in this account.

The first entry, therefore, is to record that the business receives £20 from Redman, and it is made in the Cash Account—"Jan. 1. Capital, £20"—on the left-hand or debit side of the account.

The left-hand side of all accounts is called the debit side, and an account is always debited—that is, the entry is made on the debit side, with all value that comes into that account whatever form the value takes.

One aspect of the transaction has now been entered, but there is the other aspect to be recorded. The receipt of anything implies a giver. The business receives £20 from Redman, but this implies that Redman gives £20 to the business, and this second aspect of the transaction must be entered so that the financial relationship of Redman to the business is on record.

Reference to the Ledger page will show that the entry is on the right-hand, or credit, side of the Capital Account,—"Jan. 1. Cash, £20."

The right-hand side of every account is called the credit side, and the account is credited—that is, an entry is made on the credit side, with all value that goes out from that account.

Had the Capital Account been headed "M. Redman's Account" it would doubtless have been more obvious to the student why the entry was made in that account since, under such a heading, it should contain all entries affecting M. Redman. The Capital

Account is the name given to the personal account of the owner of the business, and it shows how he stands financially with the business. By making the credit entry of £20, it is recorded that he has parted with that sum and is to that extent a creditor of the business, that is, a person to whom a debt is owing.

What the trader invests in the business is termed its capital. It may be money or money's worth in goods or other form of property or both money and money's worth. Whatever form it takes, that is the original capital of the business and remains as owing by the business to the proprietor.

The two-fold aspect, therefore, of the first transaction in the example involves a debit entry in the Cash Account and a corresponding credit entry in the Capital Account.

Transaction 2.—This is the purchase for cash of four bicycles for £12. The two aspects of this transaction are (*a*) that cash to the amount of £12 leaves the business, and (*b*) that bicycles to the value of £12 come into the business.

Remembering what has been discussed under the first transaction, it is obvious that the first entry must be in the Cash Account and on the credit side as the sum of £12 is paid away. The credit entry is "Jan. 1. Purchases, £12."

The second entry is to record the receipt of goods value £12. As the goods are received it must be a debit entry. A special account is kept in which to record purchases made to provide a stock of goods for sale. This is called the Purchases Account, and the second entry of *transaction 2* is to the debit of this account—"Jan. 1. Cash, £12."

The record, therefore, of the two-fold aspect of cash purchases of goods for sale is made by a credit entry in the Cash Account and a corresponding debit entry in the Purchases Account.

Transaction 3.—This is the sale of bicycles for £12 in cash on 8th January. The two aspects are (*a*) that £12 in cash was received by the business, and (*b*) that the business parted with bicycles to the value of £12.

The receipt of cash is entered on the debit side of the Cash Account—"Jan. 8. Sales, £12."

The sale involved parting with goods from stock to the value of £12. All such sales in the ordinary course of business are grouped in the Sales Account. As the goods go out from the business a credit entry in that account is required—"Jan. 8. Cash, £12."

In this case the two aspects involve a debit entry to the Cash Account and a credit entry to the Sales Account.

Transaction 4.—This is the sale of bicycles for £10 in cash on 10th January. It is similar to *transaction 3*, and similar entries are made. See the Ledger page.

Transaction 5.—This is the payment of £1 for advertising.

It is evident that one aspect of this transaction is the payment out of £1 in cash, and that the entry required is to credit the Cash Account—"Jan. 3. Advertising charges, £1."

The other aspect is what the payment was for, namely, £1 worth of advertising services. This demands a debit entry. It will be seen on the Ledger page in the Expenses Account. This account contains a record of all expenses incurred by the business. The £1 of services received for publicity, looked at from a profit-making point of view, is a loss, since the profit it is hoped to make from the sale of the bicycles will be less by £1 paid for advertising.

Debit the amount to the Expenses Account—"Jan. 3. Cash (Advertising Charges), £1."

The entries, summarised, are—a credit entry to Cash Account, a debit entry to Expenses Account.

All such expenses or losses are debited to the Expenses Account.

Double Entry

The two aspects of each transaction have been entered in the accounts. The student will have observed that the recording of the two aspects has involved a debit entry and a corresponding credit entry, but not in the same account. An essential point, therefore, to bear in mind is that every transaction must be entered in its two-fold aspect, and that this results in a debit entry and a corresponding credit entry in the accounts.

The bookkeeping record is made for reference purposes. It derives its value from the fact that it is a classified record and that the information it contains is readily available at any time. This is evident even in the above simple example where it is possible to ascertain at once the total sales or the total purchases for the period, as may be desired, by reference to the Purchases Account or Sales Account.

Again, the Cash Account gives full particulars of the cash received and the cash paid out and, by simple subtraction, it is possible to ascertain the amount of cash that should be in hand. This provides a check against the actual cash and makes available the information without the necessity of counting up the coins and notes.

Checking the Entries

One benefit the bookkeeper derives from the principle of double entry is that it enables him to check the arithmetical accuracy of his work. As every debit entry has a corresponding credit entry it follows that the total of all the debit entries should equal the total of all the credit entries. This is not a complete check since it will not disclose that an item has been omitted altogether, if such is the case, or that the same wrong sum has been entered on both sides. Further, though the totals agree, an amount may have been entered to a wrong account. The value, however, is to the careful worker who ordinarily avoids such mistakes.

The checking of the entries for the example given above is as below:—

	Debit Entries £	Credit Entries £
Cash Account	42	13
Capital Account ..		20
Purchases Account ..	12	
Sales Account		22
Expenses Account ..	1	
Totals	£55	£55

As the totals of the debit and credit entries agree, it may be assumed that, given careful work on the part of the bookkeeper, the entries have been made correctly.

EXERCISES 2

1. F. Watson begins to deal in typewriters, starting with capital of £140 in cash.

Jan. 10. He purchases four portable typewriters at £18 each, paying cash down.
„   14. He sells one typewriter for £27.
„   16. He sells two more typewriters for cash at £30 each.
„   17. He buys another typewriter for cash £20.
„   20. He sells the two remaining typewriters for £50 the two.
„   21. He pays £15 cash for advertising and other sundry expenses.

Make the necessary entries to record these transactions in F. Watson's Ledger.

2. T. Williams started to sell record players, putting aside £175 in cash for the business. On 1st October he purchased for cash 16 portable record players at £10 each and sold them all at £16 each, the customers paying cash. He sold 4 on 3rd October, 2 on 4th October, 4 on 5th October, and the remainder on 7th October. His advertising and other expenses amounted to £10 which he paid in cash on 10th October. He intends to continue his business, but meanwhile, you are asked to show how he should have recorded the above transactions in his Ledger.

3. J. Dunbar starts to trade in wireless sets with £300 in cash. Make the appropriate entries in his Ledger for the following transactions:—

On 1st June he paid £200 for ten portable sets, and on 5th June he purchased for cash three battery sets for £48. His cash sales amounted to £150 by 8th June and the following day he sold the remainder of his stock for £160. He paid sundry expenses and delivery charges amounting to £4 on 10th June.

4. J. Bennett began to deal in travelling and cabin trunks with £70 in cash as his capital. The following transactions took place:—

					£
Dec.	1.	Bought for cash trunks costing	..	..	55
,,	6.	Sold four trunks for cash	..	..	20
,,	8.	Sold four more trunks for cash	..	..	24
,,	12.	Paid cartage expenses	..	..	2
,,	14.	Sold remainder of trunks for cash	..	..	25
,,	15.	Paid man for help rendered	..	..	5

Show the record of these transactions in Bennett's Ledger.

5. Open the Ledger Accounts to record the following transactions:—

H. W. Harrod started business as a dealer in furniture with £56 in cash as his capital. On 1st April he bought sundry articles for cash, £40. On 3rd April he paid £5 in cash for a further quantity. He paid £2 for repairs and £3 for cartage on 4th April. His sales for cash were—8th April, £6; 10th April, £8; 14th April, £22; and for the remainder of his goods, on 19th April, £24.

CHAPTER 3

THE QUESTION OF PROFIT. TRADING AND PROFIT AND LOSS ACCOUNTS, AND BALANCE SHEETS

In actual practice it is usual for a trader to find the profit he has made in a definite period of trading, taking six months' or a year's trading as the basis.

In the example given in Chapter 2, M. Redman may be anxious to know his profit from that particular group of transactions. It is a simple matter arithmetically, and this is a suitable example to illustrate the bookkeeping method of ascertaining and recording the profit.

Gross Profit

The practice is first to find the gross profit which is the amount by which the selling price exceeds the buying price. The information from which this may be ascertained is contained in the Purchases Account and the Sales Aecount. The Sales Account shows that the sales, in total, brought in £22, and the Purchases Account discloses that the Purchases, in total, cost £12. The difference, £10, is the gross profit.

The bookkeeping method is to transfer the information from the Purchases Account and Sales Account to a new account, called the Trading Account, used specifically for the purpose of finding the gross profit.

Once the information has been transferred from the Purchases Account and Sales Account these two accounts have served their purpose and are closed, new accounts being opened for the purchases and sales of the succeeding trading period. The transfers and the closing of the accounts are shown below:—

Dr.			Purchases Account			Cr.
19..		£	19..			£
Jan. 1	Cash	12	Jan. 10	Transfer to Trading A/c.		12

11

Dr.   **Sales Account**   Cr.

19..		£	19..			£
Jan. 10	Transfer to Trading A/c.	22	Jan. 8	Cash		12
			,, 10	,, ...		10
		£22				£22

Dr.   **Trading Account**   Cr.

19..		£	19..			£
Jan. 10	Purchases ..	12	Jan. 10	Sales		22
,, ,,	Gross Profit ..	10				
		£22				£22

The double-entry principle is carried out.   The credit entry of the transfer of the total purchases is in the Purchases Account and the corresponding debit entry is made in the Trading Account.   The debit entry of the transfer of the total sales is in the Sales Account, and the corresponding credit entry is in the Trading Account.

The difference between the totals of the two sides of the Trading Account is the gross profit—provided, of course, that the selling price exceeds the buying price.   Had the goods been sold for less than they cost then a trading loss would have resulted, being shown by the debit side of the Trading Account being greater in amount than the credit side.

The gross profit having been ascertained, it is entered in the Trading Account as shown.   Both sides of the account then add up to the same amount and the totals are inserted and the account ruled off.

The cash columns of the Purchases Accounts and the Sales Account are added and ruled off.   As there is one amount only in this instance on each side of the Purchases Account it is not necessary to do more to close the account than to rule double lines.

Net Profit

The second entry for the debit of gross profit (£10) in the Trading Account has not yet been made.   The corresponding credit entry is made in the Profit and Loss Account which appears as below:—

Dr.   **Profit and Loss Account**   Cr.

19.. Jan. 10	Expenses (Advertising) ..	£ 1	19.. Jan. 10	Gross Profit from Trading A/c... ..	£ 10

The Profit and Loss Account is a summary of all the profits or gains on the one side and all the losses or expenses on the other side. The main item of profits, which are credited, is gross profit. Losses which are debited consist of the various expenses of the business. The corresponding credit for expenses is on the Expenses Account, while the debit for Gross Profit is in the Trading Account.

The Profit and Loss Account is then balanced and the balance—the difference between the two sides of the account, is entered on the debit side and the account is closed.

It is possible for expenses to exceed the gross profit, that is, for the costs of selling to be greater than the profits on sales, in which case a net loss is made and will appear as the balance on the credit side of the Profit and Loss Account.

The entry of the balance in the Profit and Loss Account is but one entry of the net profit and is on the debit side of the account. It remains to make the corresponding credit entry. First, however, consider the question of profit. It arises from the trading activities exercised by the owner in the business. His capital and his efforts, either in person or through paid employees, have met with financial reward in the form of profit, and such profit belongs to the owner.

The Capital Account is the owner's account, showing his financial relationship with the business. It contains already an entry showing the owner as a creditor of the business for the initial capital invested, and the credit entry of the net profit is made to the Capital Account as a record that the business holds £9 net profit on the owner's behalf in addition to the original capital.

The Profit and Loss Account and the Capital Account will appear as below.

Had a loss and not a profit resulted from these dealings, the business would owe the owner the original capital less the amount of the loss. As the net loss would appear on the credit side of the Profit and Loss Account, the corresponding second entry would be to the debit of the Capital Account, thus showing, when balanced, a smaller sum due to the owner.

Dr.			Profit and Loss Account			Cr.
19.. Jan. 10	Expenses (Advertising) .. Net Profit transferred to Capital A/c.	£ 1 9	19.. Jan. 10	Gross Profit from Trading A/c.	£ 10	
		£10			£10	

Dr.			Capital Account			Cr.
19.. Jan. 10	Balance carried down ..	£ 29	19.. Jan. 1 ,, 10	Cash .. .. Net Profit from Profit & Loss A/c.	£ 20 9	
		£29			£29	
			,, 11	Balance brought down	29	

The transfer of the net profit from the Profit and Loss Account to the Capital Account is the concluding entry on double-entry principles for the period of trading under review. It remains for the Cash Account to be balanced and closed, and the balance representing the cash in hand to be carried down to the opposite side to start the new Cash Account for the next trading period.

The Ledger page is now given with all the accounts, including the Cash Account, shown as completed on the lines discussed in this chapter. It will be seen that it contains a record of all the transactions and the entries required to record the financial results of the trading for the period.

Dr.			Cash Account			Cr.
19.. Jan. 1 ,, 8 ,, 10	Capital .. Sales .. .. Sales	£ 20 12 10	19.. Jan. 1 ,, 3 ,, 10	Purchases .. Advertising expenses .. Balance carried down ..	£ 12 1 29	
		£42			£42	
,, 11	Balance brought down ..	29				

Dr.	Capital Account (M. Redman)			Cr.
19..		£	19..	£
Jan. 10	Balance carried down ..	29	Jan. 1 Cash	20
			Net Profit from Profit & Loss A/c... ..	9
		£29		£29
			,, 11 Balance brought down ..	29

Dr.	Purchases Account			Cr.
19..		£	19..	£
Jan. 1	Cash	12	Jan. 10 Transfer to Trading A/c.	12

Dr.	Sales Account			Cr.
19..		£	19..	£
Jan. 10	Transfer to Trading A/c.	22	Jan. 8 Cash	12
			,, 10 ,, ...	10
		£22		£22

Dr.	Expenses Account			Cr.
19..		£	19..	£
Jan. 3	Cash (Advertising) ..	1	Jan. 10 Transfer to Profit & Loss A/c. ..	1

Dr.	Trading Account			Cr.
19..		£	19..	£
Jan. 10	Purchases ..	12	Jan. 10 Sales	22
	Gross Profit ..	10		
		£22		£22

Dr.	Profit and Loss Account			Cr.
19..		£	19..	£
Jan. 10	Expenses (Advertising) ..	1	Jan. 10 Gross Profit from Trading A/c... ..	10
	Net Profit to Capital A/c.	9		
		£10		£10

The Balance Sheet

It will be observed that most of the above accounts have been closed by the transfer of the balance to another account. The balances of the Cash Account and the Capital Account, however, have been carried down to commence the new accounts for the succeeding period. There will be Purchases Account and Sales Account for the next period of trading, but they will be new accounts without any starting balance from the last period.

The balance of the Cash Account brought down represents the amount of cash in hand at the date of balancing the account and available for subsequent trading. The balance of the Capital Account is carried down as it indicates the amount to the owner's credit at the date of balancing and at the beginning of the new trading period. From the point of view of the business the cash balance of £29 in hand represents a valuable possession, whereas the balance of the Capital Account is the amount to which the business is in debt to the owner. In short, the cash is an *asset*, and the balance of the Capital Account is a *liability* of the business, the term Asset being applied to all forms of property and possessions which the business holds, including all debts due to the business, and the term Liability to all sums owing by the business. Assets and liabilities may take forms other than those disclosed in the above example, but these are discussed in succeeding chapters.

Should Redman desire to know the financial position of the business at the date of balancing the accounts, all that is necessary is to trace the assets and liabilities and to set them down in customary form. The statement is called the Balance Sheet and comprises all the balances on the Ledger after the appropriate transfers have been made in the preparation of the Trading and Profit and Loss Accounts. All such remaining balances are either assets or liabilities, and the statement is compiled by placing the liabilities on the left-hand side and the assets on the right-hand side:—

Balance Sheet

as at 10th January, 19..

LIABILITIES	£	ASSETS	£
Capital	29	Cash in hand ..	29

This is the simplest form a Balance Sheet can take, but it illustrates the principles underlying its compilation. The Balance Sheet is not a Ledger account; it is a statement only of the outstanding balances. It would be equally valuable as a statement of the financial position if the sides were reversed, but it conforms to the usual practice in England to have the liabilities on the left-hand side and the assets on the right. In Scotland, except in the case of limited companies, the reverse form is used.

It happens that the items in the above Balance Sheet do not differ, except in amount, from the items which would have appeared in a Balance Sheet prepared immediately after the business was started and before trading commenced.

This would have been as below:—

Balance Sheet
as at 1st January, 19. .

LIABILITIES	£	ASSETS	£
Capital	20	Cash in hand ..	20

A comparison of the two Balance Sheets shows that one of the results of trading has been an increase in the value of the business assets but, concurrently, the amount owing by the business, in this case to the proprietor, has been increased by a similar sum. How and why this takes place is an interesting and valuable point for the student's observation as he proceeds in his study of the subject.

The two sides of the Balance Sheet agree in total. The fact that they should do so provides a further arithmetical check on the accuracy of the entries in the accounts and on the preparation of the Trading and Profit and Loss Accounts.

The Trader's Drawings

The profit from the series of transactions remains at present in the business. There is now the sum of £29, as against the original £20 as capital invested in the business. The owner may decide to leave the profit in the business as additional capital to finance further transactions or, requiring money for personal needs, he may decide to withdraw all or part of the profit. Should he draw out £5 in cash on account, the business will, in that case, be indebted to him to an amount less by the £5 so drawn, and the cash balance will be £5 less.

The two aspects of the withdrawal of profit are that cash is paid out and that Redman receives the cash. It follows that a credit entry would be made in the Cash Account, "Drawings, £5," and a debit entry in the Capital Account, "Cash, £5."

The reasons for these entries should now be apparent. The Capital Account would appear as below, showing £24 only as due to the proprietor.

Dr.   **Capital Account**   Cr.

19..		£	19..		£
Jan. 10	Cash (Drawings)	5	Jan. 1	Cash	20
,, ,,	Balance carried down ..	24	,, 10	Net Profit from Profit & Loss A/c... ..	9
		£29			£29
			,, 11	Balance brought down ..	24

The entries are made on the assumption that the withdrawal took place before the Cash and Capital Accounts were closed. The withdrawal would affect the balances on these accounts and, necessarily, the figures in the Balance Sheet would vary from those given in the first Balance Sheet above, as that was prepared when no drawings had been made.

EXERCISES 3

Enter the transactions in the following exercises in the Ledger and check the double entry. Prepare the Trading Account and complete the Profit and Loss Account in each case to find the gross profit and net profit or loss for the trading period. Prepare also the Balance Sheet as at the date of the last transaction in each example.

1.   £

			£
Oct. 1.	G. Pearce commenced to trade in wireless sets with capital in cash of		84
,, 2.	He bought six receivers and paid cash		78
,, 4.	Sold three sets for cash		56
,, 6.	Paid in cash advertising charges		3
,, 8.	Paid in cash printing and postage expenses		1
,, 9.	Bought for cash three more receivers		37
,, 10.	Sold remaining six sets for cash		113

2. On Dec. 15th J. Leatherhead set aside £145 from his private means as capital for a business deal in fancy leather goods.

			£
Dec. 15.	He bought a job line of leather goods for cash		140
,, 17.	Paid for printed bills of special offer		1
,, 18.	Sold a quantity of the goods for cash		125
,, 20.	Sold the remainder for cash		50
,, ,,	Paid travelling and other sundry expenses		2
,, ,,	He withdrew cash for private use		15

3. On 10th January John Watt began business with cash in hand £30. The same day he purchased a quantity of electrical equipment for £27.

			£
Jan.	12.	He sold part of the goods for cash	12
,,	14.	He made a further purchase for cash	10
,,	18.	He sold the whole of his remaining stock of goods for cash ..	30
,,	19.	He paid cartage and other expenses in cash	5

4. On April 10th J. Steering set aside £900 in cash from his private means as ✓ capital for a business deal in motor cars.

			£
Apr.	12.	He paid in cash for a second-hand car	290
,,	,,	He sold the car the same day for cash	350
,,	15.	He bought two second-hand cars for cash	400
,,	17.	He sold one car for cash	260
,,	18.	Paid haulage charges in cash	45
,,	20.	He bought another car for cash	140
,,	22.	He sold the remaining two cars for cash	460
,,	23.	He withdrew in cash all profit for private use. £195.	

5. J. Taylor began business as a dealer in furniture on 1st May with capital in cash of £150. On 2nd May he purchased a quantity of goods at auction rooms for cash, £100, and a further quantity privately the next day for £35. His general expenses amounted to £4, which he paid on 4th May in cash. He made the following cash sales: 8th May, £30; 10th May, £26; 14th May, £35; 17th May, £31. On 21st May he sold the remainder of his goods for £72, paid as wages to an assistant, £15, and withdrew cash for private purposes on account of profit, £30.

CHAPTER 4

THE QUESTION OF STOCK

In the example in the preceding chapter the trader disposed of all his goods. This may happen in practice, but it is more usual to find that a quantity of goods remains in stock on the day to which the accounts are made up. Unsold goods must be taken into account when finding the gross profit for a trading period as the following example illustrates.

> **Example 2.**—M. Redman continues his business for a further period, from 11th January, his position on that date being shown in the Balance Sheet on page 16.
>
> The following transactions take place: all purchases and sales being for cash:—
>
> | | | |
> |---|---|---|
> | Jan. | 12. | Bought six second-hand bicycles at £3 each. |
> | ,, | 15. | Sold two bicycles for £6 each. |
> | ,, | 24. | Bought two more bicycles at £4 each. |
> | ,, | ,, | Paid £2 for lighting. |
> | ,, | 26. | Sold three bicycles for £18 the lot. |
> | ,, | ,, | Paid charges for delivery to customers, £2. |
> | ,, | ,, | Redman withdrew £8 on account of profits. |
>
> Trading and Profit and Loss Accounts are to be prepared for the period ending 26th January, and a Balance Sheet as at that date. Redman values the stock of goods on hand at 26th January at cost, £10.

The financial position of the business is known from the state of the Ledger at the close of business on 10th January. This appears on page 14 and discloses that there is a cash balance in hand of £29 and, from the Capital Account, that the sum of £29 is due to Redman as proprietor. The same accounts continue in use for the further period, and sufficient space would be allowed in practice between the accounts to permit of this—not less than one page of the Ledger being allotted to an account. The balances brought down—in this case on the Cash Account and Capital Account—provide the first items for the accounts for the new trading period. Where no balances are brought down, as in the case of the Purchases and Sales Accounts, the account for the new period will begin immediately below the account for the old period, the original heading to the account being sufficient in each case.

For exercise purposes, if insufficient room has been left to continue the accounts, new accounts may be opened for fresh transactions, but the balances brought down must not be omitted.

The transactions set out in the example should be entered in the manner already explained, and the arithmetical accuracy should be checked on the last entry being made for the period.

The new point is that of the stock of goods on hand. In Example 1, Redman sold all the goods, and the gross profit was easily calculated as the difference between cost and selling prices. In the present example the Purchases Account shows the total purchases as £26, and the Sales Account shows the total sales as £30, but bicycles to the value of £10 at cost price have not been sold.

The value at cost price of *all* the bicycles is £26. The value at cost price of the bicycles not sold is £10. It follows that the value at cost price of the bicycles sold is £16, and that as these bicycles costing £16 were sold for £30, the gross profit is £14.

This calculation is made in another form in the bookkeeping records.

The trader finds the value at cost price of the stock of goods on hand at the close of business on the last day of the trading period. In the example the value at cost is £10.

A double entry is made in the accounts for the value of the stock on hand; the debit entry is made in a new account—the Stock Account—and the credit entry in the Trading Account, as below. The sales and purchases are shown as already transferred to the Trading Account.

Dr.		Stock Account			Cr.
19..		£	19..		£
Jan. 26	Trading A/c. (Stock on hand) ..	10			

Dr.		Trading Account for the period 11th to 26th January, 19..			Cr.
19..		£	19..		£
Jan. 26	Purchases ..	26	Jan. 26	Sales	30
	Gross Profit ..	14		Stock at close..	10
		£40			£40

If there is any difficulty in understanding these entries let them be considered in the light of the following remarks.

The arithmetical solution proceeded by deducting the value at cost of the unsold goods from the value at cost of all the purchases.

The result was the value at cost of the goods sold. Taking this figure from the value of the total sales yielded the gross profit.

The Purchases Account shows the value at cost of all the purchases. It would be more on the lines of the arithmetical method if an entry were made which had the effect of reducing the full value of the purchases in the Purchases Account to the value of that part which was sold. The entry would be to credit the value at cost of the stock on hand to the Purchases Account instead of to the Trading Account. For example—

Dr.		Purchases Account			Cr.
19..		£	19..		£
Jan. 12	Cash	18	Jan. 26	Transfer to Stock A/c. being value at cost of un-sold stock ..	10
,, ,,	,, ...	8		Transfer to Trading A/c. being cost of goods sold ..	16
		£26			£26

Dr.		Stock Account			Cr.
19..		£	19..		£
Jan. 26	Transfer from Purchases A/c. being value of un-sold stock	10			

Dr.		Trading Account			Cr.
19..		£	19..		£
Jan. 26	Purchases ..	16	Jan. 26	Sales	30
	Gross Profit ..	14			
		£30			£30

The opening of a special Stock Account separates the unsold portion from the full total of purchases and sets it down clearly for future reference and use.

The only objection to the credit entry for the value of the unsold stock being in the Purchases Account is that the balance of the Purchases Account then transferred to the Trading Account is not a record of the total purchases made during the period. The owner probably sees the Trading and Profit and Loss Accounts separate from the other records, and it is preferable for purposes of comparison that the full total of purchases made should be evident in the final accounts. The practice, therefore, is to place the credit entry for the stock at close to the Trading Account. The arithmetical result is, of course, the same.

The completed Ledger Accounts for Example 2 will appear as below:—

Dr.				Cash Account					Cr.
19..				£	19..				£
Jan. 11	Balance	..	b/d	29	Jan. 12	Purchases	..		18
,, 15	Sales ..	..		12	,, 24	,,	..		8
,, 26	,, ..	..		18	,, ,,	Expenses	..		2
					,, 26	,,	..		2
					,, ,,	Drawings	..		8
						Balance	..	c/d	21
				£59					£59
,, 27	Balance	..	b/d	21					

Dr.				Capital Account (M. Redman)					Cr.
19..				£	19..				£
Jan. 26	Cash (Draw-				Jan. 11	Balance	..	b/d	29
	ings)	..		8		Net Profit	..		10
	Balance	..	c/d	31					
				£39					£39
					,, 27	Balance	..	b/d	31

Dr.				Purchases Account					Cr.
19..				£	19..				£
Jan. 12	Cash	..		18	Jan. 26	Transfer to			
,, 24	,, ..	..		8		Trading A/c.			26
				£26					£26

Dr.				Sales Account					Cr.
19..				£	19..				£
Jan. 26	Transfer to				Jan. 15	Cash ..	..		12
	Trading A/c.			30	,, 26	,, ..	..		18
				£30					£30

Dr.		Expenses Account				Cr.
19..		£	19..			£
Jan. 20	Cash (Lighting) ..	2	Jan. 26	Transfer to Profit and Loss A/c. ..		
,, 26	Cash (Delivery charges) ..	2				4
		£4				£4

Dr.		Stock Account			Cr.
19..		£	19..		£
Jan. 26	Trading Account (Stock on hand) ..	10			

Trading Account

Dr.		for the period 11th to 26th January, 19..				Cr.
19..		£	19..			£
Jan. 26	Purchases ..	26	Jan. 26	Sales		30
,, ,,	Gross Profit ..	14	,, ,,	Stock.. ..		10
		£40				£40

Profit and Loss Account

Dr.		for period 11th to 26th January, 19..				Cr.
19..		£	19..			£
Jan. 26	Expenses ..	4	Jan. 26	Gross Profit ..		14
	Net Profit ..	10				
		£14				£14

Tracing through the Ledger Accounts it is found that the Cash, Capital, and Stock Accounts remain open. The other accounts have been closed in the preparation of the Trading and Profit and Loss Accounts. The balance of each of these open accounts represents either an asset or a liability, and is an item for the Balance Sheet.

Balance Sheet

as at 26th January, 19..

LIABILITIES		£	ASSETS			£
Capital ..	.. ..	31	Cash	..	..	21
			Stock	..	..	10
		£31				£31

Stock at Start of Business

If the trader, M. Redman, continues his business his books will show that the new trading period opens with assets in cash, £21, and in goods, £10, with the capital liability to the proprietor of £31.

Example 3.—Redman continues his business for a further period, the following cash transactions taking place:—

Feb. 10. Sold two second-hand bicycles for £20.
,, 20. Bought four new bicycles for £40.
,, 24. Sold three new bicycles for £40.
,, 28. Paid sundry expenses, £4.

Trading and Profit and Loss Accounts are to be prepared for the period ending 28th February, and Balance Sheet as at that date. The stock of bicycles on hand on 28th February is valued at cost at £14.

As with Example 2, it is assumed that Redman has left sufficient room in his Ledger to continue his accounts for the further period so that on the balances being carried down the initial entries in the Cash, Capital, and Stock Accounts are already made.

The point of difference from the preceding period is that the stock at start must be taken into account as well as the stock at close. Where there is a stock of goods in hand at the commencement of a trading period it is more than probable that some, if not all, of this stock will be sold during the period. The stock of goods at start and the subsequent purchases are all available for sale, and the total cost of the goods sold can be found only by deducting the cost price of the goods remaining on hand at the close of the period from the combined value at cost of the stock at start and the purchases—unless, of course, a record is kept as sales take place of the original cost of the articles sold.

Stock at start	..	..	£10
add Purchases	..	..	£40
			£50
less Stock at close	..	..	£14
Cost price of goods sold	=		£36

These goods were sold for £60. The gross profit is, therefore, £24.

In the bookkeeping record the stock at *start* is added to the Purchases by transfer from the Stock Account to the Trading Account as shown below. The Stock Account is thereby closed and a new account is opened for the stock at close.   The latter is treated as explained under Example 2.[1]

Dr.					Cash Account				Cr.	
19..				£	19..					£
Jan. 27	Balance	..	b/d	21	Feb. 20	Purchases	..			40
Feb. 10	Sales	..		20	,, 28	Expenses				4
,, 24	,,	..		40		Balance	..	c/d		37
				£81						£81
Mar. 1	Balance	..	b/d	37						

Dr.					Capital Account				Cr.	
19..				£	19..					£
Feb. 28	Balance	..	c/d	51	Jan. 27	Balance	..	b/d		31
					Feb. 28	Net Profit	..			20
				£51						£51
					Mar. 1	Balance	..	b/d		£51

Dr.					Purchases Account				Cr.	
19..				£	19..					£
Feb. 20	Cash	..		40	Feb. 28	Transfer to Trading A/c.	..			40

Dr.				Sales Account					Cr.	
19..			£	19..						£
Feb. 28	Transfer to Trading A/c.		60	Feb. 10	Cash	..				12
				,, 24	,,	..	..			48
			£60							£60

Dr.				Stock Account					Cr.	
19..			£	19..						£
Jan. 28	Trading Account (Stock on hand) ..		10	Feb. 28	Transfer to Trading A/c.					10
Mar. 1	Trading Account (Stock on hand) ..		14							

[1] The entries in the Trading Account may appear exactly as in the arithmetical example above.   This method is usually adopted as it shows clearly the cost price of goods sold.

Trading Account

| Dr. | for month ending 28th February, 19.. | | | Cr. |

19..		£	19..		£
	Stock at start ..	10		Sales	60
	Add Purchases	40			
		50			
	Less Stock at close ..	14			
	Cost of goods sold	36			
	Gross Profit ..	24			
		£60			£60

Profit and Loss Account

| Dr. | for month ending 28th February, 19.. | | | Cr. |

19..		£	19..		£
	Expenses ..	4		Gross Profit from Trading A/c... ..	24
	Net Profit to Capital A/c.	20			
		£24			£24

Balance Sheet
as at 28th February, 19..

LIABILITIES		£	ASSETS		£
Capital		51	Cash		37
			Stock		14
		£51			£51

Valuation of Stock

The valuation of the stock on hand at the close of a trading period must be carefully made, as undervaluation or overvaluation materially affects the accounts. It is usual to value the stock at cost price. If, however, market conditions are such that the current prices for similar goods have fallen considerably, then the value should be the current market price, that is the price the stock would cost at that date. On the other hand, a rise in market value does not warrant a marking-up of stock values, except under exceptional circumstances. The rise may be temporary only, and it is financially unwise to overstate profits and to allow inflated values to appear in the Balance Sheet.

The value placed upon the stock affects the profits of a business, and the aim of sound bookkeeping and accounting is to give an accurate statement of profit. It would provide a profitable exercise for the student to work again the above two examples with the stocks at close at lower values and again at higher values and to study the effect on the Final Accounts and the Balance Sheet.

EXERCISES 4

Open the appropriate Ledger Accounts and record the transactions given in the following exercises, checking the accuracy of the double entry in each case. Find the gross profit and net profit, and prepare a Balance Sheet as at the closing date of each exercise.

NOTE.—For Exercises 3, 4, and 5 leave sufficient space between accounts to continue them for a second period of trading.

1.   £

March 16.	J. Filmer began to deal in cameras with capital in cash	..	200
„ 16.	Bought 30 cameras for cash	..	135
„ 17.	Bought 6 tripods for cash	..	13
„ 17.	Paid sundry expenses	..	1
„ 19.	Sold 3 tripods and 10 cameras for cash	..	75
„ 20.	Sold 3 tripods and 15 cameras for cash	..	103
„ 20.	Paid messengers and other expenses	..	1

Stock of cameras on hand at 20th March valued at cost, £22.

2.   £

April 16.	J. Ribbon commenced to deal in portable typewriters with capital in cash	..	150
„ 16.	He bought 7 typewriters for cash..	..	126
„ 16.	Bought one second-hand machine for cash	..	15
„ 17.	Paid for advertisements	..	6
„ 19.	Sold 5 typewriters for cash	..	126
„ 20.	Sold the second-hand machine for cash ..	..	16

Stock of typewriters on hand at 20th April valued at cost, £36.

3.   £

Sept. 2.	J. Sharp began to deal in cutlery with capital in cash	..	100
„ 2.	Purchased quantity of cutlery for cash ..	..	80
„ 2.	Purchased further quantity	..	8
„ 2.	Paid carriage	..	1
„ 3.	Bought packing materials ..	..	2
„ 8.	Sold cutlery for cash	..	50
„ 10.	Sold further quantity for cash	..	40

Find the gross and net profit for the period and prepare Balance Sheet as at 10th September. Value at cost of stock on hand at that date, £36.

Continue the accounts for a second period.

				£
Sept. 11.	Bought more cutlery for cash	..	.. ..	70
„ 12.	Paid carriage	..	.. ..	2
„ 15.	Sold cutlery for cash	..	.. ..	52
„ 16.	Sold further quantity for cash	..	.. ..	60
„ 16.	Withdrew cash for private purposes		.. ..	20

Stock on hand at 16th September at cost, £26.   Find the gross and net profit for this period, and prepare a Balance Sheet as at 16th September.

4.

			£
Oct. 1.	J. Plater began business in hardware with capital in cash	..	100
„ 2.	Bought quantity of goods for cash	.. ..	60
„ 3.	Bought further quantity for cash ..	.. ..	32
„ 6.	Paid carriage and packing charges	.. ..	2
„ 12.	Sold goods for cash	.. ..	36
„ 18.	Sold further quantity for cash	.. ..	40

Find his gross and net profit (if any), and prepare Balance Sheet as at 18th October.   Stock on hand at cost, £17.

Continue his accounts for a further period.

			£
Oct. 22.	Bought quantity of hardware for cash	.. ..	50
„ 24.	Paid carriage and packing charges	.. ..	1
„ 29.	Sold goods for cash	.. ..	39
., 30.	Of goods sold on 29th October customer returned quantity as defective. Refunded cash, £5. (Credit Cash, Debit Sales Account.)		
„ 31.	Sold goods for cash	.. ..	38
., 31.	Withdrew for private use, cash	.. ..	20

Find the gross and net profit for the period, and prepare Balance Sheet as at 31st October.   Stock on hand at cost, £30.

5.

Nov. 1   J. Preston began to deal in clearance lines of motor car tyres with cash capital of £200.

			£
„ 1.	Bought quantity of tyres for cash..	.. ..	60
„ 2.	Bought further quantity for cash ..	.. ..	75
„ 3.	Bought further quantity for cash ..	.. ..	45
„ 6.	Paid advertising and other expenses	.. ..	13
., 8.	Sold tyres for cash ..	.. ..	216
„ 8.	Withdrew cash for private use	.. ..	15

Find his gross and net profit for the period, and prepare Balance Sheet as at 8th November.   Stock of tyres on hand at cost, £30.

Continue the accounts for a further period.

			£
Nov. 10.	Bought tyres for cash	.. ..	156
„ 12.	Paid advertising charges	.. ..	12
„ 15.	Sold tyres for cash ..	.. ..	90
„ 30.	Sold tyres for cash ..	.. ..	105
„ 30.	Paid cartage expenses	.. ..	6

Prepare Trading and Profit and Loss Accounts for the period, and Balance Sheet as at 30th November.   Stock of tyres on hand at cost, £48.

CHAPTER 5

THE QUESTION OF CREDIT

The transactions in the earlier examples have been cash transactions, the cash passing at once in exchange for the goods. Business transactions may be either for cash or on credit. In the latter case the goods are taken but payment is made later, after an interval of days, weeks, or months, according to the arrangements between buyer and seller. Most transactions in the retail trade are cash transactions, but between wholesaler and manufacturer and between wholesaler and retailer credit transactions are more usual than cash transactions.

Credit transactions create debts, and a record must be kept of the debts owing by or to another person or firm as a result of such credit transactions.

If Redman sells to Brown goods for cash, Redman records the sale of the goods and the receipt of cash. If, however, Redman sells to Brown goods valued £10 on credit, Redman parts with the goods but no cash passes at the time of sale. Payment is to be made later. Meanwhile Redman must record that £10 is due from Brown.

Similarly, Redman may purchase goods on credit, receiving the goods at once and being trusted to pay at a later date. He records the value of the goods coming in, and, also, he must record that he owes the supplier for the goods.

Credit transactions, therefore, involve the opening of personal accounts. Cash transactions, as a general rule, require no personal accounts to be opened as each transaction is completed on the immediate payment of cash in exchange for goods.

Example 4.—Redman continued his business from 1st March, the capital of the business then being £51, comprising Stock, £14, and Cash, £37.

The following transactions took place:—

March	5.	Bought on credit from Smith's Cycle Company, bicycles value £56.
,,	12.	Sold one bicycle for cash, £16.
,,	19.	Sold bicycles on credit to J. Dunbar, value £40.
,,	26.	J. Dunbar paid £20 cash on account.
,,	28.	Paid for packing materials, £2.

Prepare Trading and Profit and Loss Accounts for the month of March, and Balance Sheet as at 31st March.

Value of stock on hand at 31st March, at cost price, £40.

The transactions occurring on the 5th, 19th, and 26th March only require illustration.

The purchase on the 5th March is entered to the debit of the Purchases Account in the usual manner. The credit entry is in a new account:—

Dr.				Smith's Cycle Company's Account		Cr.
19..			£	19.. Mar. 5	Goods ..	£ 56

This follows the rule to credit an account with the value that leaves it and records that Smith's Company parted with these goods. In short, the company is Redman's creditor, that is, one to whom money is owed.

Later, when Redman decides to pay for the goods, the payment will be credited to the Cash Account and *debited* to Smith's Cycle Company's Account. The latter entry will have the effect of cancelling the debt on record in Smith's Account.

The sale on 19th March to Dunbar is entered in the usual way to the credit of the Sales Account. The corresponding debit entry is in a new account, to record the receipt of the goods by Dunbar.

Dr.				J. Dunbar's Account		Cr.
19.. Mar. 19	Goods ..		£ 40	19..		£

When, on 26th March, Dunbar pays £20 on account of the amount due from him the Cash Account will be debited, and Dunbar's Account will be credited as he relinquishes that sum. He remains a debtor, that is, one who owes, for the balance of £20 as is shown by his account on page 32.

Redman's Ledger will appear as below, the accounts in practice following on those from the preceding period:—

Dr.					Cash Account				Cr.
19..				£	19..				£
Mar. 1	Balance ..	b/d		37	Mar. 28	Packing materials			2
,, 12	Sales ..			16	,, 31	Balance ..	c/d		71
,, 26	J. Dunbar ..			20					
				£73					£73
Apl. 1	Balance ..	b/d		71					

Dr.   **Capital Account**   Cr.

19..			£	19..			£
Mar. 31	Balance ..	c/d	75	Mar. 1	Balance ..	b/d	51
				,, 31	Net Profit ..		24
			£75				£75
				Apl. 1	Balance ..	b/d	75

Dr.   **Stock Account**   Cr.

19..		£	19..		£
Mar. 1	Trading A/c. (Stock on hand) ..	14	Mar. 31	Transfer to Trading A/c. ..	14
Apl. 1	Trading A/c. (Stock on hand) ..	40			

Dr.   **Purchases Account**   Cr.

19..		£	19..		£
Mar. 5	Smith's Cycle Co. ..	56	Mar. 31	Transfer to Trading A/c	56

Dr.   **Sales Account**   Cr.

19..		£	19..		£
Mar. 31	Transfer to Trading A/c.	56	Mar. 12	Cash ..	16
			,, 19	J. Dunbar	40
		£56			£56

Dr.   **Smith's Cycle Company Account**   Cr.

19..		£	19..		£
			Mar. 5	Goods ..	56

Dr.   **J. Dunbar's Account**   Cr.

19..			£	19..			£
Mar. 19	Goods ..		40	Mar. 26	Cash ..		20
				,, 31	Balance ..	c/d	20
			£40				£40
Apl. 1	Balance ..	b/d	20				

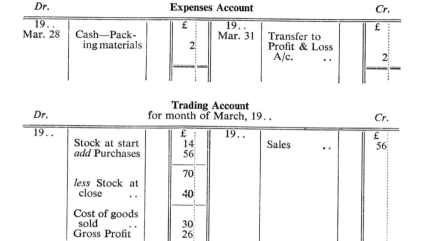

Dr.		Expenses Account				Cr.
19..		£		19..		£
Mar. 28	Cash—Pack- ing materials	2		Mar. 31	Transfer to Profit & Loss A/c. ..	2

Trading Account
for month of March, 19..

Dr.				Cr.
19..		£	19..	£
	Stock at start *add* Purchases	14 56	Sales ..	56
		70		
	less Stock at close ..	40		
	Cost of goods sold ..	30		
	Gross Profit	26		
		£56		£56

Profit and Loss Account
for month of March, 19..

Dr.				Cr.
19..		£	19..	£
	Expenses ..	2	Gross Profit	26
	Net Profit to Capital A/c.	24		
		£26		£26

Balance Sheet
as at 31st March, 19..

LIABILITIES		£	ASSETS		£
Capital ..	.. ..	75	Stock ..	.. ..	40
Creditors	.. ..	56	Debtors..	.. ..	20
			Cash ..	.. ..	71
		£131			£131

An additional point to be observed is the effect on the Balance Sheet of the outstanding amounts on the personal accounts. There are two more open accounts in this example than in the preceding examples. The accounts remaining open after the preparation of the Trading and Profit and Loss Accounts are either *real* or *personal* accounts. Real accounts are records of property—such as the Stock Account. Personal accounts are records of dealings with persons. The balances of these accounts are either assets or liabilities and, as such, as already shown, provide the material for the Balance Sheet.

The balance on Dunbar's Account is called a *debit* balance. The debit side is greater in amount than the credit side. The difference, or balance, is placed on the credit side to make the two sides equal in amount, and is brought down to the debit side for the next period. The Capital Account shows a *credit* balance. The credit side exceeds the debit side in total and the balance is inserted on the debit side, being brought down to the credit side of the account for the new period.

Debit balances of real and personal accounts are always assets. Credit balances are always liabilities. The accounts of creditors— those to whom debts are owing, always show a credit balance, whereas the accounts of debtors—those who owe debts to the business, show a debit balance.

The financial position of Redman's business at 31st March has altered from the position at the commencement of the new trading period. There is a new liability—the amount due to Smith's Cycle Company, and a new asset, the balance due from J. Dunbar.

The proprietor's capital is now £75, but it is not now so simple a matter to show how that amount is invested in the business. On 1st March it consisted of cash and stock. Now, at the close of the month, it comprises cash, stock, and book debts, less the amount due to a creditor.

This leads to the point that the proprietor's capital is best expressed as the excess of the value of the assets over the liabilities of the business, other, of course, than the capital liability to the owner. It follows from this that the insertion of the owner's capital in the Balance Sheet makes the two sides to agree in total.

EXERCISES 5

Enter the transactions given in the following exercises in their appropriate Ledger Accounts, and check the double entry. Find the gross and net profit or loss for the period, and prepare a Balance Sheet in each case as at the date of the last transaction. Transactions are on credit unless stated otherwise.

1. Jan. 1. J. White commenced business in motor car accessories with capital in cash, £100.

			£
Jan.	1.	Bought accessories for cash..	60
,,	2.	Sold accessories on credit to F. Lawson ..	50
,,	6.	Paid carriage charges	3
,,	16.	Bought goods on credit from Motor Equipment Company	90
,,	19.	F. Lawson paid his account in cash	50
,,	23.	Sold goods on credit to B. Coombes	70
,,	27.	Sold goods on credit to F. Lawson	72
,,	31.	Paid sundry expenses	5

Stock on hand at 31st January, £30.

2. May 1. J. Cade began to deal in tennis equipment with capital in cash, £240.

			£
May	1.	He bought racquets for cash	120
,,	2.	Bought sundry equipment for cash	52
,,	3.	Bought equipment and racquets from Lazenby & Sons ..	120
,,	8.	Paid cash for advertising and fares	16
,,	12.	Sold goods to L. White & Co.	200
,,	17.	Sold goods to B. Blackburn	30
,,	24.	Cash sales	80
,,	27.	Paid Lazenby & Sons their account in cash.	
,,	31.	Received cash from L. White & Co. on account	100

Stock on hand at 31st May, £60.

3. June 1. J. Shaw began to deal in camp stores with capital in cash, £170.

			£
June	1.	He bought tents and sundries from Camp Supplies Ltd. ..	150
,,	2.	He bought further equipment for cash	120
,,	4.	Paid for conveyance by rail	7
,,	10.	Sold tents to Smith's Stores Ltd. ..	140
,,	15.	Sold equipment for cash	119

Find his gross and net profit for this period, and prepare Balance Sheet at this date. Stock on hand, £84. Continue accounts for a further period.

			£
June	16.	Sold equipment to Smith's Stores Ltd.	100
,,	21.	Paid Camp Supplies Ltd., cash	150
,,	22.	Bought tents from Camp Supplies Ltd. ..	120
,,	28.	Received cash from Smith's Stores for their account to date	240
,,	30.	Paid sundry expenses	4
,,	30.	Drew cash for private use ..	40

Find the gross and net profit for the period, and prepare a Balance Sheet as at 30th June. Stock on hand, £140.

4. Sept. 4. J. Wright began as a furniture dealer with capital in cash, £264.

			£
Sept.	4.	He expended £240 on sundry articles for stock.	
,,	7.	Bought furniture from Shaw & Wood	300
,,	9.	Paid sundry expenses in cash	15
,,	12.	Sold furniture for cash	180
,,	14.	Sold furniture to B. Burns..	198

Find his profit or loss for the period and prepare Balance Sheet as at 14th September. Stock on hand, £210. Continue his accounts for a further period.

								£
Sept.	15.	Bought furniture from Shaw & Wood	..	..	..	..	150
,,	20.	Paid Shaw & Wood cash on account	..	..	..	..	180
,,	20.	Cash sales	..	..	..	..	130
,,	27.	B. Burns paid cash	..	..	..	..	198
,,	30.	Sold furniture to P. Hastings	..	..	..	..	240
,,	30.	Paid assistant's wages ..	..	..	..	..	3
,,	30.	Paid rent of premises	..	..	..	..	30
,,	30.	Withdrew for private use	..	..	..	..	45

Find the profit or loss for the period, and prepare Balance Sheet as at 30th September. Stock on hand at that date, £120.

CHAPTER 6

THE TRIAL BALANCE

The entries for the transactions in the examples already considered have been few so that the check upon the double entry has been simple. The possibility of error increases with the number of entries, and it is necessary to prevent the carrying of errors into the Final Accounts. A check by means of a Trial Balance is therefore made on the arithmetical accuracy of the entries after the last transaction of the trading period has been entered and before the preparation of the Trading Account.

The transactions from Example 4 in Chapter 5 are taken for illustration. The accounts are shown as they stood after the last transaction was entered.

Dr.			Cash Account					Cr.
19..			£	19..				£
Mar. 1	Balance	b/d	37	Mar. 28	Packing			2
,, 12	Sales		16		materials..			
,, 26	J. Dunbar ..		20					

Dr.			Capital Account					Cr.
19..			£	19..				£
				Mar. 1	Balance	..	b/d	51

Dr.			Stock Account					Cr.
19..			£	19..				£
Mar. 1	Stock	..	14					

Dr.			Purchases Account					Cr.
19..			£	19..				£
Mar. 5	Smith's Cycle Company		56					

Dr.			Sales Account					Cr.
19..			£	19..				£
				Mar. 12	Cash	..		16
				,, 19	J. Dunbar ..			40

Dr.			Smith's Cycle Company			Cr.
19..		£	19.. Mar. 5	Goods ..		£ 56

Dr.			J. Dunbar's Account			Cr.
19.. Mar. 19	Goods ..	£ 40	19.. Mar. 26	Cash ..		£ 20

Dr.			Expenses Account			Cr.
19.. Mar. 28	Cash—Packing materials	£ 2	19..			£

The fact that the double-entry principles lead to a debit and a credit entry for each transaction and that this permits the accuracy of the entries to be checked has already been referred to. A debit entry has a corresponding credit entry somewhere in the accounts for the trading period. A complete list of all the debits in the accounts should therefore equal in total a similar list of all the credits. Again, for the same reason, if the debits on each account are added and a list made of their totals, this should equal in amount a similar list of credit totals.

The Trial Balance, as its name implies, is, however, a trial of the balances of the accounts to check the accuracy of the entries. The use of the balances and not of the totals of the debit and credit entries saves much clerical work, and is, at the same time, equally valuable as a check as it is based on the axiom that if equals are taken from equals the remainders are equal.

In preparing the Trial Balance the balance of each account is ascertained and, if the debit side of the account is the greater, then the balance, being a debit balance, is placed in the column for debit balances in the Trial Balance. If the credit side is the greater, then the balance of the account being a credit balance, it is entered in the credit balances column of the Trial Balance. When all the balances are entered, the columns are added and the totals should agree.

On the opposite page is the Trial Balance extracted from the above accounts.

Sometimes the totals do not agree: the debit column may be greater than the credit, or perhaps, the other way round. In either

Trial Balance

	Dr.	Cr.
	£	£
Cash	71	
Capital		51
Stock	14	
Purchases	56	
Sales		56 *£.co*
Smith's Cycle Co.		56
J. Dunbar	20	
Expenses	2	
	£163	£163

case there must be an error or errors in the Ledger, or in extracting balances from the Ledger.

The errors, of course, must be found, and students would be well advised to follow the routine described below when they find a Trial Balance disagreeing. If (*a*) does not reveal the error then (*b*) should be tried, and so on.

- (*a*) Re-add the totals in order to be sure that the difference is not a matter of simple addition.

- (*b*) Check all figures from the Ledger to the Trial Balance in order to be certain that figures have not been overlooked when the Trial Balance was compiled.

- (*c*) If the amount by which the two sides of the Trial Balance differ is, say £14, look for amounts of £14 in the Ledger and be sure that the double entry for each amount has been completed.

- (*d*) If an amount of £7 was entered twice on the debit side in the Ledger, or twice on the credit side, instead of being entered once on the debit side and once on the credit side, then the amount of difference will be doubled, viz. in this case £14. So halve the difference between the two sides of the Trial Balance and look in the Ledger for entries of this amount and check the double entry to see that they have been carried out properly.

- (*e*) If the error or errors are still elusive, then go through Ledger and check all totals and balances to assure the accuracy of the arithmetic.

- (*f*) Finally, check the double entry throughout the Ledger.

aration of the Final Accounts should not be proceeded with until the error or errors that the non-agreement of the Trial Balance indicate have been discovered and rectified. If, however, it is necessary to prepare Final Accounts quickly while there is still a difference in the Trial Balance, this difference is placed to a Suspense Account. The Balance of the Suspense Account is shown in the Balance Sheet on the liabilities or asset side according to whether the balance is a credit or a debit entry.

The agreement of the Trial Balance does not prove that no errors have been made in the books.

Here is a list of types of error a Trial Balance does not disclose:—

(i) Errors of Omission.
(ii) ,, ,, Commision.
(iii) ,, ,, Principle.
(iv) ,, in the Original Entry.
(v) Compensating errors.

(i) *Errors of Omission.*—In the event of an invoice for goods purchased being lost, no entry would have been made on the debit side of the Purchases Account nor would there be an entry on the credit side of the Supplier's Account. The missing debit equals the missing credit so the Trial Balance would agree. This is an example of an Error of Omission.

(ii) *Errors of Commission.*—Entry of transaction in a wrong account of the same class.

If money were received from B. Jones the entries would be debit Cash or Bank Account and credit B. Jones's Account. But it is possible we may also have dealings with a W. Jones & Co. and if the credit were entered in W. Jones & Co.'s Account instead of in the account of B. Jones, this would of course be an error. The Trial Balance would not show it up because a debit (in the Cash Book) has a credit (in W. Jones & Co.'s Account). This is an example of an Error of Commission.

(iii) *Error of Principle.*—Entry of transactions in the wrong class of account. T. Edwards purchased some machinery for use in his business. His bookkeeper, seeing it as a purchase, made the debit entry in the Purchases Account. The only entries in the Purchases Account should be for goods bought for re-sale, so the debit in this case is wrong; it should have been made in an Asset Account, *e.g.*

Machinery. This is an example of an Error of Principle. This will be better understood after Chapters 11 and 12 have been studied.

(iv) *Error in Original Entry.*—Where an incorrect entry is made in a book of prime entry and the incorrect entry is posted to the debit and the credit sides of the Ledger.

This type of error can be understood only after the student has studied the use of journals in Chapters 9 and 12.

(v) *Compensating Error.*—Incorrect entries on the debit side are compensated for by equalising incorrect entries on the credit side.

Suppose the purchases were over-added by £15, then the debit side of the Trial Balance would be £15 too great. Suppose that the Sales Account by some coincidence had also been over-added by £15. This would mean that the credit side of the Trial Balance was also too great. Thus, although two errors have been made, the Trial Balance agrees. This is an example of a Compensating Error.

These classes of error would naturally be corrected only when they were discovered, and the method of correction will be found in Chapter 12.

EXERCISES 6

Enter the transactions in the following exercises into their appropriate Ledger Accounts. Take out a Trial Balance for each exercise as on the date of the last transaction.

Find the gross and net profit for the period, and prepare a Balance Sheet.

1. Dec. 1. J. Bentham began to deal in framed pictures with capital in cash, £90.

Dec. 1. Bought six pictures for cash at £6 each.
,, 3. Bought six frames at £3 each from J. Tobin & Co.
,, 7. Bought a lot of framed water colours at auction for cash, £45.
,, 8. Paid for packing materials, £1.
,, 10. Sold to J. Smith, framed pictures, £78.
,, 12. Sold to W. Wilkins, water colours, £36.
,, 17. J. Smith paid his account in cash.
,, 31. Paid sundry expenses in cash, £5.
,, 31. Stock on hand, £30.

2. N. Chambers began business on 1st July with £162 as capital in cash.

		£
July 1.	Bought quantity of rayon silk for cash	97
,, 3.	Sold rayon silk for cash	54
,, 7.	Bought further quantity of silk from Silk Weavers Ltd... ..	180
,, 10.	Paid Silk Weavers Ltd. on account	90
,, 15.	Sold silk to the following customers:—	
	J. Wesley & Sons	30
	H. Boyce	112
,, 17.	Paid for parcel post and carriers' charges.. .. .. ,,	2
,, 19.	H. Boyce paid £45 on account.	
,, 19.	Stock of goods on hand valued at £126.	

3.

			£
May 1.	J. Summer began to deal in sports goods with capital in cash..		42
,, 1.	Bought quantity of goods from Sportsman & Sons	.. ..	52
,, 3.	Bought goods for cash	.. ..	16
,, 7.	Bought goods from Fielding & Co.	.. .. ..	17
,, 8.	Paid for circulars and postage	.. .. ..	2
,, 12.	Sold sports goods on credit to—J. Park ..	.. .. ..	31
	M. Meadow	.. .. ..	14
	L. Field..	.. .. ..	21
,, 15.	Sold goods for cash	.. ..	33
,, 17.	Received cash from J. Park	.. ..	10
,, 18.	Received cash from L. Field	.. ..	10
,, 18.	Paid for assistance ..	.. ..	2

Stock on hand, 18th May, valued at £20.

4. The following Trial Balance shows all the balances of the accounts in J. Thorburn's Ledger. From the Trial Balance prepare the Trading Account, Profit and Loss Account, and Balance Sheet.

Trial Balance. 31st December

	Dr. £	Cr. £
Cash Account	21	
Purchases Account	84	
Sales Account		100
Expenses	5	
J. Wilson's Account	62	
M. Dover's Account	53	
T. Kent's Account		15
Capital Account		110
	£225	£225

The stock on hand at 31st December was valued at £24.

5. H. Williamson's Trial Balance shows the following balances on his Ledger Accounts as at 31st December. From the Trial Balance prepare his Trading Account, Profit and Loss Account, and a Balance Sheet as at 31st December.

Trial Balance

	Dr. £	Cr. £
Cash Account	48	
Capital Account		57
Purchases	104	
Sales		106
Expenses..	8	
B. Watson's Account	26	
F. Morgan's Account	19	
T. Young's Account		42
	£205	£205

Stock on hand at 31st December was valued at £30.

6. Give one example of each of the following kinds of error. State which will, or will not, cause a Trial Balance to disagree, giving reasons for your answer:—

    (*a*) Error of principle.
    (*b*) Error of omission.
    (*c*) Compensating error.   *R.S.A.*

7. The following balances were extracted from the books of S. Martin on 31st December, 19... You are required to prepare a Trial Balance therefrom, inserting the amount required to balance it as "Capital":—

	£
Purchases	8280
Cash at bank	1278
Drawings	612
Loan from J. Haylock	500
Loan to J. Smith	100
Stock in hand at 1st January, 19..	335
Returns inwards	63
Sales	13122
Furniture	80
Freehold property	2000
Sundry debtors	1316
General expenses	495
Discount received	41
Sundry creditors	1042
Carriage outwards	68
Plant and machinery	1412

R.S.A.

8. If a Trial Balance failed to agree, what steps would you take in order to find the difference?

9. What are the different types of error which are not thrown up by a Trial Balance? Give an example under each heading.

10. A Trial Balance was extracted from the books of V. Baker, and it was found that the debit side exceeded the credit side by £40. This amount was entered in the Suspense Account. Subsequently the following errors were discovered and corrected:—

    (i) The Purchases were over-added by £20.
    (ii) An amount paid to B. Simpkins was debited to his account as £98 instead of £89.
    (iii) The Sales were under-added by £11.

Write up and rule off the Suspense Account as it would appear in Baker's Ledger.

11. The Trial Balance of B. Clandon failed to agree because the credit side exceeded the debit by £19. The difference was placed to Suspense Account.

Later, the following errors were discovered and corrected:—

    (i) An amount received from T. Black was credited to his account as £52 instead of £25.
    (ii) An amount for Cash Sales £18 was entered in the Cash Account but was omitted from the Sales Account.
    (iii) The Sales had been over-added by £10.

Write up and rule off the Suspense Account as it would appear in Clandon's Ledger.

CHAPTER 7

THE TRADER'S BANKING ACCOUNT AND THE CASH BOOK

Few traders find it either safe or convenient to use coin and notes only to settle their transactions. If only for safe custody of cash a trader will open a banking account and, having such an account, he is able to make use of the other facilities that banks offer to their customers. An account is opened by the payment in of an initial sum of money. When the trader has to pay an account, he may do so by cheque, which is a written order to a banker to pay a stated sum of money to a named person on demand. The payment of this sum by the banker depletes the trader's banking account. On the other hand, if the trader receives cheques from customers in payment of their accounts, his bank will collect the sums due on the cheques and place them to the credit of his account.

By means of the cheque system the holder of a banking account has a simple yet safe means of making payments and of receiving payment. Cash surplus to immediate requirements may be paid into the account, and many traders pay their takings daily into the bank whatever form the takings are in, whether coin, notes, postal orders, or cheques, making all payments out by cheque.

The bank keeps an account in its Ledger of the money received and paid out for each customer and periodically sends a copy of the account to the customer. This copy is called a Bank Statement.

The trader also keeps a Ledger Account as a record and as a check upon the bank. Periodically he compares the bank's account, as disclosed by the Bank Statement, with his own account to satisfy himself that both are in order and complete.

It follows that the trader should now have two accounts to record his cash, one relating to the cash in the office and the other to the cash at the bank.

Example 5.—M. Redman continues his business during April, the position on 1st April being—

Cash in hand	£71
Stock	£40
Owing *by* J. Dunbar	£20
Owing *to* Smith's Cycle Company ..	£56
Capital	£75

The following transactions take place:—

April 1. Redman opens an account with the Counties Bank, paying in cash, £67.
„ 3. Received from J. Dunbar, cheque £20, in settlement of his account.
„ 8. Bought from Smith's Cycle Company, bicycles, value £100.
„ 15. Sold bicycles to J. Dunbar, value £120.
„ 20. Paid in sundry expenses in cash, £2.
„ 24. J. Dunbar paid his account by cheque.
„ 27. Sold one bicycle for cash, £15.
„ 29. Paid Smith's Cycle Company £156 by cheque.
„ 30. Paid assistant's wages in cash, £12. Stock at close at cost £64.

Note that the items dated 8th and 15th April are on credit. As credit transactions are more frequent in practice than cash transactions it is assumed that a transaction is on credit unless it is otherwise indicated. Compare the transaction dated 27th April.

The entering of the above transactions requires the continuance of the Cash Account and the opening of a Bank Account.

What the bank receives is entered on the debit side of the Bank Account. The sums it pays away are entered on the credit side of the account. If this is borne in mind no difficulty should be experienced with the first transaction. Redman takes £67 from the office cash and hands it over to the bank. The double entry is in the Cash and Bank Accounts—credit Cash Account, debit Bank Account, to record the change in location. At any time the trader may find more cash in the office than is needed. He then pays the cash into his Bank Account, making in his books entries similar to those required by the first transaction above. The converse would happen should the trader find himself short of office cash and cashes a cheque to replenish his supply. "Drew cheque for £5 for office cash," as it is often worded, would involve a credit entry in the Bank Account, since the bank parts with £5, and a debit entry in the Cash Account as the trader receives the cash.

Overleaf are the Cash and Bank Accounts as they would appear for the month of April. The double entries are not shown—except for the first item as they come within the two accounts—as these should now present no difficulty.

It is the usual practice of traders to pay in all takings daily. It may be assumed, unless the contrary is stated, that this is so in every case, and the cheques received should be debited direct to the Bank Account.

Dr.   **Cash Account**   Cr.

19..			£	19..			£
Apl. 1	Balance ..	b/d	71	Apl. 1	Bank ..		67
„ 27	Cash Sales ..		15	„ 20	Expenses ..		2
				„ 30	Wages ..		12
				„ „	Balance ..	c/d	5
			£86				£86
May 1	Balance ..	b/d	5				

Dr.   **Bank Account**   Cr.

19..			£	19..			£
Apl. 1	Cash ..		67	Apl. 29	Smith's Cycle		
„ „	J. Dunbar ..		20		Co. ..		156
„ 24	„ ..		120	„ 30	Balance ..	c/d	51
			£207				£207
May 1	Balance ..	b/d	51				

The balance of the Bank Account will appear among the assets in the Balance Sheet when that is drawn up. An exception to this is referred to in Chapter 17, and occurs when the bank allows a customer to draw out more than he has to his credit at the bank.

Balance Sheet

LIABILITIES		£	ASSETS		£
Capital (including net profit)		120	Stock	..	64
			Cash at bank ..	..	51
			Cash in hand ..	..	5
		£120			£120

The Cash Book

As the business grows in volume and the transactions increase in number a greater demand is made on the bookkeeper to keep the accounts entered day by day. Some suitable scheme must be devised to sub-divide the work, but the use of one Ledger only for all accounts sets a limit to any scheme, as the Ledger cannot be used by more than one person at a time. A step in the direction of sub-division of duties is to place one person in charge of the cash and the Cash and Bank Accounts, and for his convenience and the general convenience of the staff, to separate these two accounts from the other accounts in the main Ledger. The Cash and the Bank

Accounts, in such circumstances, are kept in the Cash Book—a book bound separately from the Ledger purely as a matter of convenience in the internal organisation of the business, and the Cash Book is placed in charge of the cashier. The accounts are still Ledger Accounts and the separation does not affect the double-entry principles already discussed.

Having made this separation, a second convenience is found in the adaptation of the Ledger ruling contained in the Cash Book. Instead of the Cash Account and the Bank Account being opened in different parts of the book, the account columns are placed together, enabling the cash and bank balances to be found on the one page. To effect this further convenience the Cash Book is ruled as shown herewith, where the debit column of the Cash Account is placed alongside the debit column of the Bank Account, and the credit columns of the two accounts are similarly placed. The transactions affecting the accounts are entered chronologically, but care is taken that the amounts are entered in the right money columns according to whether they affect the office cash or the banked cash. Though the accounts appear in conjunction they are balanced in the usual way.

The Cash Book should be compared with the Cash Account and Bank Account on page 46. It will be observed that there is no

Cash Book

Dr.

Date	Particulars		Cash £	Bank £
19.. April 1	Balance	b/d	71	67
,, 1	Cash			20
,, 3	J. Dunbar			120
,, 24	,,		15	
,, 27	Cash sales			
			£86	£207
May 1	Balance	b/d	5	51

Cr.

Date	Particulars		Cash £	Bank £
19.. April 1	Bank		67	
,, 20	Expenses		2	156
,, 29	Smith's Cycle Co.			
,, 30	Wages		12	
,, 30	Balance	c/d	5	51
			£86	£207

variation from the bookkeeping principles. The change is only in the formal ruling of the accounts and their separation from the Ledger. Should a customer pay or be paid his account, as the case may be, partly in cash and partly by cheque, the particulars have to be entered once only and the amounts paid entered side by side in the cash and bank columns on the appropriate side of the Cash Book.

EXERCISES 7

Enter the transactions in the following exercises in their appropriate accounts, using a two-column Cash Book. Extract a Trial Balance, and prepare the final accounts to show the profit or loss for the trading period. Prepare also a Balance Sheet in each case as at the date of the last transaction.

1. April 1. M. Rafter commenced business with capital in cash, £250.

			£
April	1.	Paid cash into bank	220
„	3.	Bought goods from B. Croydon	160
„	8.	Bought goods from T. Brighton	130
„	12.	Cash sales	52
„	13.	Paid cash into bank	50
„	15.	Paid expenses by cheque	7
„	21.	Sold goods to L. Sussex	10
„	22.	Sold goods to J. Worthing	200
„	24.	Paid cash for stationery	3
„	27.	Paid B. Croydon by cheque	160
„	28.	Received cheque from L. Sussex	10
„	30.	Paid rent by cheque	8
„	30.	Paid assistant in cash	10

Stock of goods on hand, 30th April, £120.

2.

				£
Oct.	1.	J. Pearce commenced business with capital—Cash at bank		400
			Cash in hand	20
„	2.	He bought goods from R. Southwark		300
„	3.	Bought goods for cash		18
„	4.	Cashed cheque for office cash		20
„	7.	Cash sales		57
„	7.	Paid cash into bank		60
„	12.	Sold goods to J. Fulham		150
„	17.	Paid sundry expenses in cash		4
„	24.	J. Fulham paid his account by cheque		150
„	27.	Paid R. Southwark by cheque		300
„	28.	Bought goods from R. Southwark		200
„	30.	Cash sales		35
„	30.	Paid one month's rent by cheque		20
„	30.	Withdrew cash for personal use		30

Stock on hand, 30th October, £310.

3. Dec. 1.   J. Mackintosh began business in fancy goods with capital of £500 consisting of—Cash at bank, £475; Cash in hand, £25.

			£
Dec. 2.	Bought job line of goods and paid by cheque	.. .. ..	200
,, 3.	Bought leather goods from Farmer & Co.	.. .. ..	250
,, 7.	Cash sales paid into bank ..	.. ..	70
,, 8.	Paid Farmer & Co. by cheque	.. ..	250
,, 10.	Paid sundry expenses in cash	.. ..	12
,, 12.	Sold goods to H. Benson ..	.. ..	340
,, 14.	Paid wages to assistant in cash	.. ..	6

Prepare Final Accounts and Balance Sheet as at 14th December.   Stock on hand, £170.

Continue the accounts for a further period.

			£
Dec. 15.	Bought goods from Farmer & Co.	.. .. ..	300
,, 20.	Sold goods for cash	.. ..	53
,, 22.	Sold goods to J. Wilson ..	.. ..	200
,, 22.	Paid carriage charges in cash	.. .. ..	2
,, 22.	H. Benson paid on account by cheque	.. .. ..	200
,, 24.	Sold goods to J. Wilson ..	.. ..	136
,, 28.	Paid assistant, cash ..	.. ..	6
,, 31.	Paid one month's rent by cheque ..	.. .. ..	8

Stock on hand, £90.

4.

			£
Feb. 1.	J. Harding began business in hardware with Cash in hand	..	20
		Cash at bank	.. 600
,, 2.	Bought goods from M. Cromwell	.. .. ..	325
,, 3.	Sold goods to B. Ward ..	.. ..	50
,, 6.	Paid M. Cromwell by cheque	.. ..	325
,, 6.	Paid wages in cash ..	.. ..	15
,, 8.	B. Ward paid in cash on account ..	.. .. ..	25
,, 10.	Bought goods from P. Pitt ..	.. ..	150
,, 12.	Cash sales ..	.. ..	75
,, 13.	Paid wages in cash ..	.. ..	15
,, 14.	Paid rent by cheque..	.. ..	10
,, 18.	Sold goods to B. Burton ..	.. ..	200
,, 20.	Paid wages in cash ..	.. ..	15
,, 21.	Cash sales ..	.. ..	20
,, 22.	Paid all cash, except £5, into bank.		

Stock on hand, 22nd February, £225.

CHAPTER 8

THE CLASSIFICATION OF EXPENSES

The written record of financial transactions is of the utmost value, but the scheme of classification by accounts is of equal importance. Any information that is required is readily accessible, and time is saved and the possibility of error is lessened by grouping related transactions under their appropriate headings. Moreover, as the system of bookkeeping is adaptable to special needs, accounts may be opened to record the information that a trader may wish to be available at any time. The Expenses Account, for example, contains the record of all the expenses or losses of a business, and that is the account to which the proprietor would refer if he desired to know the various expenses incurred in conducting the concern. Such expenses would take the form of wages and salaries, postage, stationery, rent, rates and taxes, lighting and heating.

Usually as trade increases expenses also increase, so that the proprietor of a progressive business would find the Expenses Account becoming a lengthy account and containing many repetitive items. Anxious to know his expenditure in any particular direction the trader would have to analyse the items in the account to find the total expenditure for the period. Wages, paid weekly, would, for example, occur fifty times during the year. To save the trouble of analysis and to have the information available at any time, accounts are opened in the Ledger for each form of expense, loss, or gain, and expenses and losses are debited and gains are credited to their respective accounts. At the end of the trading period the balances of these accounts are transferred to the Profit and Loss Account which then contains all the expenses and gains as hitherto shown but in summarised form. Such accounts for the expenses, gains, and losses of the business are known as Nominal Accounts.

Instead, therefore, of all items of expenditure being posted to the Expenses Account items belonging to a definite class are posted to a separate account for that class, while the Expenses Account, now called General Expenses, is used only for items such as office teas and gratuities which cannot be easily classified.

Example 6.—The following transactions took place during June:—

June 4. Paid assistant's wages, £6.
 „ 10. Bought for cash envelopes and other office stationery, £3.
 „ 11. Paid assistant's wages, £6.
 „ 18. „ „ „ £6.
 „ 25. Paid rent by cheque, £20.
 „ 25. Paid assistant's wages, £6.
 „ 27. Paid Fire Insurance Premium, £3.
 „ 30. Received from J. Whiteman cheque for £22 as commission on arranging the sale of certain goods for him.

The above transactions are entered in their appropriate accounts as follows. The transfer entry as at 30th June, the closing date of the period of trading, is also given in each case and is shown in the Profit and Loss Account that would then be prepared. The Cash Book entries are not shown.

Dr.			Wages				Cr.
19..			£	19..			£
June 4	Cash ..	..	6	June 30	Transfer to		
„ 11	„ ..	..	6		Profit & Loss		
„ 18	„ ..	..	6		A/c.		24
„ 25	„ ..	..	6				
			£24				£24

Dr.			Stationery Account				Cr.
19..			£	19..			£
June 10	Cash ..	..	3	June 30	Transfer to		
					Profit & Loss		
					A/c...	..	3

Dr.			Rent Account				Cr.
19..			£	19..			£
June 25	Cash ..	..	20	June 30	Transfer to		
					Profit & Loss		
					A/c.	..	20

Dr.			Insurance Premiums Account				Cr.
19..			£	19..			£
June 27	Cash ..	..	3	June 30	Transfer to		
					Profit & Loss		
					A/c.	..	3

Dr.		Commission Account				Cr.
19..		£	19..			£
June 30	Transfer to Profit & Loss A/c. ..	22	June 30	Cash— J. Whiteman		22

Dr.		Profit and Loss Account			Cr.
19..		£	19..		£
June 30	Wages	24	June 30	Commission Gross Profit (when ascertained) ..	22
,, ,,	Stationery ..	3			
,, ,,	Rent	20			
,, ,,	Insurance ..	3			

It is not practicable to give numerous items of expense as examples, but the above should be sufficient to indicate the use of specific accounts for expenses and how the Profit and Loss Account is built up from these details.

EXERCISES 8

1. J. Whitehouse began business with capital of £200, cash at bank. Enter his capital and the following transactions in his Ledger and Cash Book, using separate accounts for his expenses.

			£
Jan.	1.	Drew from bank for office cash	10
,,	2.	Bought goods from R. Nunn	60
,,	3.	Bought goods and paid by cheque..	130
,,	7.	Paid wages in cash	6
,,	12.	Sold goods to J. Dunn	75
,,	12.	Cash sales, paid into bank	38
,,	14.	Paid wages in cash	6
,,	16.	Paid postage and delivery charges	1
,,	20.	Cash sales	50
,,	21.	Paid wages in cash	6
,,	22.	Paid for packing paper	2
,,	24.	Paid R. Nunn his account, in cash £20, by cheque £40.	
,,	28.	Paid wages in cash	6
,,	31.	Paid rent by cheque	12
,,	31.	Paid lighting account in cash	5

Take out Trial Balance, prepare Trading and Profit and Loss Accounts, and draw up a Balance Sheet as at 31st January. Stock on hand, £90.

2. Enter the following transactions of J. R. West, who is dealing in accumulators, in his accounts, including a two-column Cash Book, and using separate Expense Accounts:—

			£
Dec.	7.	Cash in hand	24
,,	7.	Cash at bank	120
,,	9.	Bought 6-volt accumulators from Electricity Ltd. ..	84
,,	11.	Bought 12-volt accumulators by cheque	100
,,	15.	Sold accumulators for cash	42
,,	16.	Paid delivery charges	1

				£
Dec. 16.	Paid advertising charges in cash	.. ..	..	4
„ 18.	Sold accumulators for cash	.. ..	..	78
„ 19.	Paid delivery charges	.. ..	..	1
„ 19.	Paid cash into bank ..	.. ..	..	110
„ 24.	Cash sales, paid direct to bank	.. ..	..	80
„ 24.	Paid delivery charges	.. ..	..	2
„ 31.	Drew cheque for personal use	.. ..	..	20

Take out a Trial Balance. Prepare Trading and Profit and Loss Accounts, and draw up a Balance Sheet as at 31st December. Stock on hand at that date, £44.

3. R. B. Brooker began business as a stationer on 1st October. Enter the following transactions in his books, using separate expense accounts:—

			£
Oct. 1.	Cash at bank	..	220
„ 3.	Bought stationery from Johnson & Co. Ltd.	.. ..	150
„ 5.	Bought notebooks and pens and pencils from Wetherby & Co...		25
„ 7.	Cash takings, paid into bank	.. .. ..	42
„ 14.	Cash sales	..	38
„ 18.	Bought further goods from Johnson & Co. Ltd...	.. ..	130
„ 21.	Cash sales, paid into bank ..	.. .. ..	61
„ 25.	Paid rent by cheque ..	.. .. ..	10
„ 27.	Paid electric light charges in cash ..	.. .. ..	3
„ 28.	Bought packing paper and string for cash	.. .. ..	2
„ 28.	Paid rates by cheque ..	.. .. ..	20
„ 31.	Cash sales, paid into bank ..	.. .. ..	54

Take out Trial Balance. Prepare Trading and Profit and Loss Accounts and a Balance Sheet as at 31st October. Stock on hand at that date, £140.

4. The balances of the accounts of N. Shepherd at 31st December are shown in the following Trial Balance. From it prepare Trading Account and Profit and Loss Account and a Balance Sheet as at 31st December.

Trial Balance. 31st December

	Dr.	Cr.
	£	£
Capital Account		250
Cash balance	12	
Bank balance	212	
Stock at start	200	
Purchases	1200	
Sales		1720
Wages Account	100	
Lighting Account	10	
Telephone Account	9	
Rent Account	12	
Debtors, J. White	104	
J. Smith	137	
Creditor, B. Burt		26
	£1996	£1996

The stock on hand at 31st December was valued at £180.

5. At 31st December, 19.., J. Spalding's Ledger showed the following balances. You are required to prepare from them a Trial Balance in proper form, and from the Trial Balance a Trading Account and Profit and Loss Account for the period and a Balance Sheet as at 31st December.

The balances were: Capital Account (*Cr.*), £800; Sales, £3,000; Purchases, £2,250; Cash in hand, £18; Cash at bank, £542; Cartage Account, £10; Rent and Rates Account, £135; Insurance Premiums Account, £4; Wages Account, £150; Stock Account, 1st Jan., £460; S. Kemp (Debtor), £299; L. Lacey (Creditor), £68.

The stock on hand at 31st December was valued at cost at £500.

6. The following Trial Balance was extracted from the books of R. Heather. Prepare his Trading and Profit and Loss Accounts for the period, and a Balance Sheet as at 31st December.

Trial Balance. 31st December

	Dr. £	Cr. £
Capital Account		500
Cash in hand	10	
Cash at bank	350	
Stock at start	250	
Sales		1100
Purchases	700	
Wages Account	150	
Rent Account	100	
Rates Account	45	
B. Rivers	74	
J. Hills		79
	£1679	£1679

Stock on hand, 31st December, £260.

CHAPTER 9

RECORDS OF SALES, PURCHASES, AND RETURNS

The growth of a business is usually growth in the number of its transactions. The most numerous of these transactions are usually sales on credit. Purchases will have to be made in correspondingly larger quantities to meet the increased demand, but as these purchases will usually be in bulk the entries necessary are not so numerous as for sales.

The increase in sale and purchase transactions gives rise to the use of numerous invoices. An invoice is a document which gives details and prices of the goods sold and shows the customer how much he owes. These documents are used as the original material for the purpose of recording sale and purchase transactions. With a large number of such documents it would be most cumbersome to make an entry for each separate invoice in the Sales Account or in the Purchases Account as these accounts would be hopelessly overloaded with entries. It is necessary, therefore, to organise the material in such a way as to economise the number of entries which must be made.

Sales Records

When a sale on credit is made an invoice is sent to the customer. A copy of this invoice is retained by the firm supplying the goods and forms the basis of bookkeeping entries relating to the transaction. To deal with the numerous invoices arising from sale transactions they may be listed day by day on a Sales Record. An example of a hand-written sales record, known as a Sales Book, showing the amount of invoices sent to three customers might be as follows.

7   **Sales Book**

19..				£
Sept. 1	M. Tyburn	..	40	128
	J. Laxton ..	..	47	80
	T. Rose ..	..	33	87
	Cr. to Sales A/c. ..		14	£295

The copy invoices, containing details of the goods sold are filed and can be referred to if necessary.

The entries from the copy invoices would continue day by day for a definite period, usually one month. During the month each sale is debited to the customer's account and to indicate that this has been done the number of the Ledger page on which the customer's account appears is placed in the *folio column*. Note the numbers 40, 47, and 33 in the example. At the end of the month the Sales Book is totalled. This total is credited to the Sales Account and represents perhaps hundreds of individual items which have been debited to the personal accounts of customers. At the end of a year there will be twelve monthly totals in the Sales Account which gives, easily, the total sales for the year for transfer to the Trading Account.

The Sales Book on page 55 contains only three entries, but can be used for illustration purposes. In practice there would be many more entries and for a much longer period. The posting, as it is called, of the Sales Book on page 55 would be as follows.

40			M. Tyburn				40
19.. Sept. 1	Sales ..	S.B. 7	£ 128	19..			£

47			J. Laxton				47
19.. Sept. 1	Sales ..	S.B. 7	£ 80	19..			£

33			T. Rose				33
19.. Sept. 1	Sales ..	S.B. 7	£ 87	19..			£

Sales Account

19..			£	19.. Sept. 1	Sundries	S.B. 7	£ 295

The methods of assembling sales transactions illustrated above while useful for small businesses and for use in exercises and examination work by students is being increasingly superseded by methods which save labour and time by the use of mechanical aids.

With the aid of a simple adding machine the copy invoices may be totalled thus giving the total to be credited to the Sales Account. The entries to the personal accounts may be made direct from the copy invoices. A further development is the use of a simple accounting machine which makes the debit entry in the Personal Account on a Ledger card as shown on page 3, and prints the new balance on the account. The machine, at the same time, accumulates the amount of the individual entries to give the total of postings to be credited to the Sales Account. This is more fully explained in Chapter 29 on mechanised accounts.

The method of dealing with numerous sale transactions will also vary with the type of business. In a retail business dealing mainly in cash sales a cash register may be used which aggregates the amount of cash sales to each customer and at the end of the day gives the total cash sales for the day which should agree with amount of cash in the till of the register. This amount may be debited to the Cash Book in a special column, the total amount paid into bank being extended into the bank column. At the end of a specified period, say a week or a month, the sales column in the Cash Book may be totalled thus giving the amount to be credited to the Sales Account.

Where a retailer makes sales on credit each assistant may be supplied with a "bill" book. The customer is given the "bill" and a carbon copy remains in the assistant's book. These carbon copies may be used to post the amount to the debit of customers' accounts and the credit to the Sales Account by totalling the carbon bill copies on an adding machine.

In practice students may find a variety of methods in use for dealing with the multiplicity of sale transactions in various types of businesses, but all will result eventually in the same Ledger entries a debit to the account of a customer for a sale on credit or to the cash record for a cash sale and, in each case an accumulated total to be credited to the Sales Account.

Purchases Records

When a purchase is made from a supplier an invoice will be received. The amount of each invoice will be credited to the account of the supplier either direct from the invoice or from an entry made in a Purchases Book which is similar in form to a Sales Book. The total of individual credit postings will be debited periodically to the Purchases Account thus completing the double entry. This total may be obtained from the Purchases Book where it is in use or from an adding machine or accounting machine.

4 **Purchases Book** 4

19..			£	19..			£
Sept. 1	Speedway						
	Cycle Co.	15	126				
	Cycles Ltd.	22	36				
	Cycles Supplies Ltd.	27	13				
	Dr. to Purchases Account ..	15	£175				

15 **Speedway Cycle Co.** 15

19..			£	19..			£
				Sept. 1	Purchases	P.B. 4	126

22 **Cycles Ltd.** 22

19..			£	19..			£
				Sept. 1	Purchases	P.B. 4	36

27 **Cycles Supplies Ltd.** 27

19..			£	19..			£
				Sept. 1	Purchases	P.B. 4	13

Purchases Account

19..			£	19..			£
Sept. 1	Sundries	P.B. 4	175				

Folio numbers to indicate the posting of items are used in the same way as in the Sales Book.

Returns and Allowances Records
Sales Returns and Allowances

After a sale has been made, a customer may return goods as damaged or unsuitable, or it may be necessary to make an allowance to the customer because the goods are damaged, have been wrongly priced, or for some other reason. In such cases it will be necessary to reduce the amount of the invoice already sent to the customer. The amount of this invoice will have been debited to the customer's account. It will, therefore, be necessary to credit the account to reduce the amount already debited. That this has been done is indicated to the customer by sending him a *credit note.* This credit note shows details of the allowance made but is printed in red to distinguish it from an invoice.

The firm sending the credit note retains a carbon copy. The amount of each credit note may be credited direct to the customer's account and the total of all credit notes so credited, debited to a *Sales Returns and Allowances Account,* or the carbon copies may be entered into a *Sales Returns and Allowances Book,* in the same form as a Sales Book, and the Ledger entries made from that book. The total of the Sales Returns and Allowances Account will be transferred, at the end of the trading period, to the Trading Account and shown in that account as a deduction from sales.

Purchases Returns and Allowances

When a business returns goods or, for some reason, receives an allowance on goods it has already purchased it will expect to receive a credit note from the supplier of the goods. These credit notes may be entered into a *Purchases Returns and Allowances Book* and the necessary Ledger postings made from that book, a debit to the personal account of each supplier (the amount of the goods purchased will have been credited to the account) and the total credited to a *Purchases Returns and Allowances Account.* Alternatively the debit entries may be made direct from the credit notes and the total, ascertained by adding machine, credited to the Purchases Returns and Allowances Account. At the end of the trading period the total amount credited to this account will be transferred to the Trading Account and shown as a deduction from purchases.

Undercharges on Invoices

If, for any reason, goods have been undercharged, a *debit note* will be sent to the customer. This will be treated as an additional invoice and passed through the Sales Book, or will be debited direct to the customer's account.

EXERCISES 9

1. Sales transactions may be entered in a Sales Book from copy invoices and then posted to the personal account of debtors. Explain any alternative method of dealing with sales transactions.

2. Explain how a retailer may deal with a multiplicity of small cash sale transactions for bookkeeping purposes.

3. In working the following exercise use a two-column Cash Book and a Sales Book and Ledger. Extract a Trial Balance.

John Purvis began business with capital of £296, of which sum £40 was Cash in hand and £256 Cash at bank.

		£
Jan. 1.	Bought quantity of cutlery from Cutlery Manufacturers Ltd.	200
„ 7.	Bought six canteens of cutlery and paid by cheque	120
„ 10.	Paid special advertising expenses in cash	10
„ 14.	Sold to J. Beaumont—	
	2 canteens of cutlery at £31 each.	
	6 sets of carvers at £4 a set.	
„ 21.	Sold to W. Bishop & Sons—	
	3 canteens of cutlery at £31 each.	
„ 22.	J. Beaumont paid his account by cheque.	
„ 27.	Sold to A. M. Godfrey—	
	6 doz. table knives at £3 a dozen.	
	6 doz. table forks at £2 a dozen.	
„ 31.	Cash sales for the month	24
„ 31.	Paid one month's rent by cheque	16
„ 31.	Paid delivery and packing charges in cash	3

Prepare Trading and Profit and Loss Accounts and Balance Sheet as at 31st January. Stock on hand, £150.

4. Using a two-column Cash Book, Sales Day Book, and Ledger, enter the following transactions of M. Sinclair:—

		£
M. Sinclair's capital at 1st June consisted of—Cash in hand		16
	Cash at bank	84
June 2.	Bought record players, paying by cheque	60
„ 4.	Bought record players and records from the Star Recording Company	102
„ 10.	Sold to J. Welch—3 portable record players at £9 each.	
„ 17.	Cash sales	15
„ 23.	Sold to T. Palmer & Sons—1 console record player for £25.	
„ 25.	J. Welch paid his account by cheque	27
„ 27.	Sold to B. Fogg—2 table record players at £15 each.	
„ 28.	Paid sundry expenses by cheque	5
„ 29.	Paid stationery and printing charges in cash..	3
„ 30.	Withdrew cash for private use	10

Take out a Trial Balance. Prepare Trading and Profit and Loss Accounts and a Balance Sheet as at 30th June. Stock on hand, £82.

5. Enter the following transactions of B. Luscombe in his Cash Book, Sales Day Book, and Ledger:—

		£
Dec. 3.	B. Luscombe began business with capital—Cash in hand ..	15
	Cash at bank ..	160
„ 3.	Bought fancy leather goods and paid by cheque	63
„ 7.	Bought further supply from Hounsditch & Co.	150
„ 7.	Paid fares in cash	1
„ 8.	Paid postage and cost of circulars in cash	1
„ 12.	Sold to J. Platt & Co.—1 dozen handbags at £1 each and 1 dozen manicure sets at £1 each.	
„ 15.	Cash sales	55
„ 16.	Paid cash into Bank	55
„ 17.	Sold to B. Newton—1 dozen brush and comb sets, enamelled backs, at £6 each.	

£

			£
Dec. 18.	J. Platt & Co. paid their account by cheque.		
,, 20.	Paid Hounsditch & Co. their account by cheque.		
,, 24.	Cash sales		32
,, 30.	Paid transport charges in cash..		2
,, 31.	Withdrew cash for private use		30

Take out Trial Balance at 31st December. Prepare Trading and Profit and Loss Accounts for the month, and Balance Sheet as at 31st December. Stock on hand, £42.

6. Enter the following transactions in B. Bertram's books, using a two-column Cash Book, Sales Book, and Sales Returns Book, and Ledger Accounts:—

B. Bertram began business with capital of £400 in the bank.

£

			£
Nov. 1.	Drew cheque for office cash		20
,, 3.	Bought quantity of electrical equipment, paying by cheque		320
,, 4.	Bought further quantity from Electrical Supplies Ltd. ..		100
,, 10.	Paid cash for circulars and distribution		15
,, 15.	Cash sales paid into bank		175
,, 20.	Sold to B. Johnson— 6 lacquered case electric clocks at £10 each		60
,, 23.	B. Johnson returned one clock sold on 20th instant as defective.		
,, 25.	Sold to B. Beamish & Sons— 6 fancy dial electric clocks at £5 each. 6 electric kettles at £2 each.		
,, 27.	B. Beamish & Sons returned two electric kettles as not of kind ordered.		
,, 30.	Paid one month's rent by cheque		16
,, 30.	B. Johnson paid his account by cheque.		

Take out a Trial Balance as at 30th November.

Prepare Trading and Profit and Loss Accounts for the month, and a Balance Sheet as at 30th November. Stock on hand, £237.

Note:—For the following exercises bring into use as required a two-column Cash Book, Purchases Day Book, Sales Day Book, and Sales Returns Book.

£

			£
7.	Gordon Pearce began business on 6th June with—Cash in hand		21
	Cash at bank		399
June 7.	Bought from T. B. Smith— 6 badminton rackets at £3 each; 6 tennis rackets at £4 each		42
,, 8.	Bought by cheque racket covers, balls, and other tennis equipment		229
,, 17.	Bought from T. B. Smith— 12 badminton sets at £12 each		144
,, 17.	Sales for cash		75
,, 19.	Sales for cash		225
,, 19.	Paid cash into bank		270
,, 24.	Sold to J. B. Vincent— 3 badminton sets at £18 each; 3 tennis rackets at £6 each		72
,, 25.	Paid T. B. Smith his account by cheque		186
,, 27.	J. B. Vincent returned one tennis racket as defective; forwarded credit note to him		6

			£
June 30.	Paid lighting account in cash ..	.. ..	16
„ 30.	Paid one month's rent by cheque	.. ..	18
„ 30.	Paid sundry expenses in cash ..	.. ..	22

Extract a Trial Balance as at 30th June.

Prepare Trading and Profit and Loss Accounts and a Balance Sheet as at 30th June. Stock on hand, £105.

8. J. Riley began business on 1st January with capital, in cash £40, at bank, £400, and transacted the following business during the month:—

			£
Jan. 3.	Bought from Lynch & Co., stock of photographic papers and materials		120
„ 3.	Bought from Barnet & Hurst— 24 folding pocket cameras at £4 each. 12 „ „ „ „ £6 „ 6 folding tripods at £1 each.		
„ 6.	Bought from Essex Camera Company— 3 reflex cameras at £10 each.		
„ 12.	Cash sales paid direct to bank		200
„ 19.	Cash sales paid direct to bank		100
„ 26.	Paid Lynch & Co., Barnet & Hurst, and the Essex Camera Company their accounts by cheque.		
„ 27.	Customer returned goods purchased on 19th Jan., refunded cash		6
„ 28.	Cash sales		75
„ 31.	Paid delivery expenses in cash		5
„ 31.	Paid rent by cheque		30
„ 31.	Drew cheque for personal use		75

Draw out Trial Balance as at 31st January.

Prepare Final Accounts, including Balance Sheet as at 31st January. Stock at close, £90.

Note:—In working the following exercises bring into use as required a two-column Cash Book, Sales Day Book, Sales Returns Book, Purchases Book, and Purchases Returns Book.

9. J. M. Biggs began to deal in household furniture on 1st December with capital of £750, cash at bank.

			£
Dec. 2.	He bought from J. Townsend & Sons— 3 walnut bedroom suites at £75 each; 3 lounge suites at £60 each; 6 fireside chairs at £6 each ..		441
„ 2.	Bought sundry articles, paying by cheque		560
„ 2.	Paid one month's rent in advance by cheque		36
„ 7.	Cash sales		90
„ 10.	Sold to J. Burton— 2 bedroom suites at £96 each; 3 fireside chairs at £9 each		219
„ 12.	Cash sales, paid direct to bank		264
„ 12.	J. Burton returned one fireside chair as faulty in construction		9
„ 17.	J. Burton paid his account by cheque.		
„ 19.	Paid J. Townsend & Sons their account by cheque.		
„ 21.	Bought from J. Townsend & Sons— 2 oak sideboards at £36 each; 6 walnut bedsteads at £15 each		162

£

Dec. 23. Returned to J. Townsend & Sons one walnut bedstead, not
of design ordered   15
 ,, 28. Cash Sales, paid to bank   231
 ,, 31. Sundry expenses paid in cash   26

Take out Trial Balance as at 31st December. Prepare Trading and Profit
and Loss Accounts for the month, and a Balance Sheet as at 31st December.
Value of stock on hand, £510.

10. R. B. Thornton began to trade in silverware on 12th October. His
capital consisted of—

£

                 Cash at bank   600
                 Cash in hand   45

Oct. 12. Bought from Silversmiths Ltd.—
3 dozen hand-wrought silver table spoons at £24 a dozen;
3 dozen similar table forks at £24 a dozen   144
 ,, 13. Bought quantity of silverware including tea spoons and forks,
paying by cheque   300
 ,, 13. Bought further quantity for cash   24
 ,, 15. Returned to Silversmiths Ltd. as of wrong design, 6 table
spoons and 6 table forks   24
 ,, 18. Sold to Webb & Warings—
1 dozen silver table spoons at £36 a dozen.
1 dozen silver table forks at £36 a dozen.
2 silver soup ladles at £10 each   92
 ,, 20. Paid sundry expenses in cash   4
 ,, 20. Webb & Warings returned the 2 silver soup ladles, style not
as ordered. Allowed them   20
 ,, 21. Paid Silversmiths Ltd. their account by cheque.
 ,, 24. Bought from Silversmiths Ltd.—
2 dozen hand-wrought silver coffee spoons at £13 a dozen   26
 ,, 27. Sold to Swan & Lacy—1 dozen tea spoons at £16 a dozen   16
 ,, 31. Cash sales for the month paid into bank   375
 ,, 31. Paid sundry expenses by cheque   30

Take out Trial Balance and prepare Trading and Profit and Loss Accounts
for the month, and a Balance Sheet as at 31st October. Stock on hand, £150.

11. Allow sufficient space to continue the accounts for two periods.

J. B. Freeman began business on 1st May with capital of £300, consisting of
£200 Cash at bank and £100 Cash in hand.

£

May 1. Paid cash into bank   60
 ,, 1. Bought from Firestoves Ltd.—
4 electric cookers at £25 each   100
 ,, 2. Bought from Electric Supplies Ltd. ..
12 electric irons, list No. 44, at £1 each; 4 nickel-plated
electric warming plates at £6 each   36
 ,, 5. Bought from Firestoves Ltd.—
12 electric boudoir fires at £8 each   96
 ,, 7. Returned to Electric Supplies Ltd., the 4 warming plates at
£6 each and exchanged them for 4 polished copper warming plates at £5 each.
 ,, 14. Paid Firestoves Ltd. their account by cheque.
 ,, 24. Sold to Baring & Lee—
2 electric cookers at £32 each; 3 electric irons at £2 each ..   70

£

May 31. Cash sales for the month **40**
" 31. Paid one month's rent by cheque 16
" 31. Paid transport charges in cash.. 1

Prepare Trial Balance and Trading and Profit and Loss Account for the month and Balance Sheet as at 31st May. Stock on hand, £145. Balance the Ledger Accounts at 31st May, and record the following transactions:—

June 10. Sold to Warner & Sons—
    3 electric irons at £2 each; 2 copper warming plates at   £
    £6 each 18
" 12. Warner & Sons returned one electric iron as defective.
    Forwarded credit note for 2
" 30. Paid delivery charges in cash 1
" 30. Paid one month's rent by cheque 16
" 30. Received cheque from Baring & Lee for their account .. 70
" 30. Cash takings paid into bank 183
" 30. Drew cheque for private use 40

Prepare Trial Balance and Trading and Profit and Loss Accounts for the month of June, and a Balance Sheet as at 30th June. Stock on hand valued at £14.

CHAPTER 10

THE COLUMNAR SYSTEM OF BOOKKEEPING

A trader may be satisfied with the information provided by his accounts that the year's trading has yielded certain sums of gross profit and net profit. Other traders whose businesses are of a different nature or are organised on different lines may require further information. One business may deal in several distinct commodities. Another concern may be divided into departments. The proprietors may wish to have the trading results relative to each commodity or department in order that they may be in a position to determine future policy. Without analysis in some form it is impossible to discover whether each department is contributing its share to the general profits or whether the expenses and management costs of a department are disproportionate to the total costs and stand in need of revision.

In order that the accounts may yield the required information, all the items from which the Trading Account is built up must be analysed and the analysis should be in continuous form throughout the trading period. This will involve analysis of the purchases, sales, returns inwards and outwards, and it may be done by suitable alterations in the rulings of the subsidiary books.

The trader who deals, for example, in three distinct commodities may use subsidiary books ruled as below:—

Sales Day Book

| DATE | PARTICULARS | | SOLD LEDGER FOLIO | TOTALS | WIRE-LESS SETS | RECORD PLAYERS | RECORDS |
	NAME	IN-VOICE No.					
19..				£	£	£	£
July 9	J. W. Jackson	277	36	24	24		
,, 10	P. W. Jones	278	39	8		6	2
,, 12	L. Palmer	279	56	25	15	10	

The Purchases Book and the Returns Books will be ruled on similar lines.

It will be noticed that in the above Sales Book there is a column headed "Invoice No." This is a useful addition to any Sales Book. The copy invoices containing details of the goods sold to the customer bear numbers corresponding to the numbers on the original invoices. The copy invoices are filed and should they be required they are easily located by the reference number shown in the Sales Book. The same method may be adopted in the Purchases Book by numbering the invoices received from creditors before filing them.

To return to the consideration of the above example, the amount entered in the Totals column is posted to the personal account of the customer, and the Totals column also permits of the cross checking of the totals of the analysis columns. The personal accounts in the Bought and Sold Ledgers[1] are not affected by the analysis, but in order to make full use of the information given in the analysed subsidiary books it is necessary to extend the analysis to the accounts in the General Ledger.[1] The Stock Account,

[1] For fuller explanation see page 192.

Sales Account

Dr.

Date	Folio	Wireless Sets £	Record Players £	Records £	Total £
19..					

Cr.

Date	Folio	Wireless Sets £	Record Players £	Records £	Total £
19.. July 31 Total sales for July		39	16	2	57

the Sales Account, the Purchases Account, the Sales Returns Account, and the Purchases Returns Account, will accordingly be given similar analysis columns, and the periodical totals of the analysis columns of the subsidiary books will be posted to the appropriate columns in the Ledger Accounts. The Sales Account for the above example of a Sales Day Book will appear as shown alongside, the entries in the example being treated for the purpose of illustration as the total sales for the month.

The illustrations refer to distinct lines of goods. If the business is departmental and the purpose of the analysis is to ascertain the trading results of each department, the rulings will be as shown above, but the headings of the columns will refer to the departments and not to commodities. Where there are many departments it may be impossible to have sufficient additional columns in the Ledger Accounts without causing the Ledger to be unwieldy in size. The alternative method is to open separate accounts for each department, for example, "Dept. A. Stock Account," "Dept. A. Sales Account," and "Dept. A. Purchases Account," and similarly for each department.

To obtain the trading results for each department or commodity there must be separate Trading Accounts or one Trading Account with analysis columns. The separate Trading Accounts will be combined to form the general Trading Account for the business. Where an analysed Trading Account is used the totals column is the general Trading Account. For a business with three departments as illustrated on page 65, the analysed Trading Account would have the same form of ruling as the Sales Account there shown. The purchases, sales, and stocks of each department would be entered in the appropriate columns, yielding a department gross profit or loss as the case might be. The totals column would contain the combined figures and would show the gross profit or loss for the business as a whole.

The analysis will yield the turnover[1] and gross profit of each department or relative to each commodity as the case may be. In many cases the analysis is carried far enough when this point is reached. In other cases it may be necessary to ascertain the net profit earned by each department, as, for example, when the department manager is entitled to a percentage commission based on the

---

[1] Turnover is equal to net sales, *i.e.* sales less sales returns.

net profit. This will involve the analysis of the expenditure shown in the Profit and Loss Account. Separate Profit and Loss Accounts or a Profit and Loss Account with analysis columns may be used, but the apportionment of the expense items needs careful consideration.

Advertising, general administrative costs, and similar expenses may be apportioned on the basis of the turnover of each department. Special advertising or other charges for a particular department would be charged to that department. The items for rent and rates may be similarly apportioned or, as in some cases, apportioned on the basis of the floor space occupied by each department, but no one method of apportioning the expenses is applicable to all cases.

The portions of the various expenses to be carried to the respective sections of the Profit and Loss Account may be obtained from analysed expense accounts or the ordinary form of expense accounts may be used, and the analysis made on separate sheets of analysis paper.

Brief reference may be made to another form of analysed day book, namely, the Purchase Day Book with analysis rulings to provide for the usual entries of purchases of stock for re-sale and also for purchases of fixed assets and of sundries. The use of such a book simplifies the postings to the assets and expense accounts.

The purpose of the additional columns in the accounts and the subsidiary books is to provide information by continuous analysis that would involve much labour to obtain by other means. The method does not abrogate the principles of double entry; it is an adaptation only of procedure to meet special requirements as may be seen from the above examples, and in the analysed Petty Cash Book and Bill Books described in later chapters.

The illustrations given above have been concerned with the application of the columnar system to find the trading results for each of several departments or of distinct lines of goods. In some kinds of businesses the ordinary day to day records of transactions involve a system of tabulation to simplify the work of recording. Water, gas, and electric light companies, hotels, dairies, bakers, and similar businesses dealing in a few regular commodities or services for a large number of customers, find it convenient to keep their records on a tabular system of bookkeeping and to carry periodical totals only to the appropriate Ledger Accounts. A dairyman's record may take the form of large sheets in a loose-leaf Ledger, and a customer's account for a week may occupy one line across the page. With thirty horizontal lines the page would accommodate the weekly account of thirty customers. Vertical lines divide the page into the days of the week, and each vertical column for a day is subdivided to record the commodities sold. Vertical cash columns are ruled for each day to contain the sums paid by the customers, and additional cash columns are included in which the balance brought forward and the balance due at the end of the week are shown.

The Visitors' Ledger used in hotels usually shows each visitor's account in a vertical column. The page is divided vertically into columns for each visitor and bedroom number and the items are shown horizontally. The total at the foot of each column is the balance due from the visitor at the close of the day. The cross totals are carried forward from day to day, and at the end of the month the accounts brought forward are posted in the General Ledger.

The tabular system is applicable only to the kinds of business having uniformity from day to day in the services rendered or the commodities dealt in.

EXERCISES 10

1. Rule a suitable Sales Book for three departments, (*a*) wireless, (*b*) record players, (*c*) bicycles, and enter the follow sales:—

Jan. 2. To M. Keston, 3 A.C. "Trevor" receivers at £31 each.
„ 6. To G. Elton, 2 portable record players at £10 each, and 1 "Trevor" A.C. receiver at £31.
„ 7. To T. Edwards, 2 "Speedway" bicycles at £12 each, and 1 portable record player at £18.

2. D. Kettle & Co. are provision importers. They divide their business into three departments—(1) butter and eggs, (2) poultry and bacon, and (3) tinned or bottled goods. Rule a suitable Purchase Book and enter the following invoices:—

Nov. 12. M. Peterson. 50 cases of eggs at £1 per case;
30 cwt. of bacon at £8 per cwt.; and
20 gross condensed milk at £2 per gross.
„ 13. A. Merrick. 20 gross of "Amber" peaches in syrup at £18 per gross.
R.S.A.

3. A trader opens a shop dealing in cigarettes, sweets, and stationery. In order to ascertain separately the trading profit realised by each of these commodities he adopts, as far as may be necessary, the columnar system of bookkeeping.

Give suitable rulings for the Purchase Day Book and the Nominal Account(s) affected, and insert sufficient entries to make clear the working of the system.
R.S.A.

4. J. Whitehouse has two departments in his business—tools and gardening sundries. Rule a suitable Purchase Day Book and enter the following:—

July 2.   Bought from Steelmakers Ltd.—
              3 garden rollers, 16 inch, at £4 each.
„   3.   Bought from Watson & Sons—
              6 doz. table knives, stainless, at £1 a doz.
              6 doz. table forks at £1 a doz.
„   5.   Bought from Ironware & Co.—
              3 lawn mowers, "Reliance," 12 inch, at £3 each.
„   7.   Bought from Webb & Co.—
              6 sets of carvers at £3 a set.
              3 grass edging tools at £1 each.

5. J. Whitehouse is in business dealing in cutlery and tools and gardening supplies and equipment. He maintains separate departments, (1) for the cutlery and tools, and (2) for the gardening sundries. His financial position on 31st May was as follows:—

	£
Capital	1740
Shop fittings	120
Cash in hand	19
Cash at bank	260
Stock—Cutlery and tools ..	600
Garden sundries ..	800
Creditors—J. Smith	59

Open his books and enter the following transactions for June, using analysed subsidiary books and separate Stock Accounts:—

			£
June	2.	Bought cutlery from J. Smith	78
„	8.	Cash sales paid to bank—Cutlery	34
		Garden sundries	63
„	10.	Sold to C. Welchman—Cutlery..	16
		Garden sundries	26
„	12.	Paid carriage on sales in cash	1
„	15.	Sold to B. Wells—garden sundries	24
„	20.	Paid advertising charges by cheque	5
„	21.	Paid J. Smith his account by cheque.	
„	21.	Paid for stationery, cash, £1, packing materials, cash, £2.	
„	24.	Bought from J. Smith—Cutlery..	30
		Garden sundries	45
„	30.	Cash sales to date, paid to bank—Cutlery	86
		Garden sundries	150
„	30.	Paid wages in cash	5
„	30.	Paid rent by cheque	25

Take out Trial Balance. Prepare departmental Trading and Profit and Loss Accounts, and a Balance Sheet as at 30th June. Stock on hand at 30th June was valued, cutlery, £610, gardening sundries, £665. Expenses are to be apportioned, one-third to cutlery and tools, two-thirds to garden sundries.

6. A business is carried on in two departments, A and B. From the following Trial Balance prepare Trading and Profit and Loss Accounts in departmental form, and prepare also a Balance Sheet as at 31st December.

Trial Balance, 31st December

	Dr. £	Cr. £
Cash at bank ..	3526	
Capital		12000
Stock—Dept. A	4800	
Dept. B	2600	
Debtors	6724	
Creditors		2851
Purchases—Dept. A ..	5200	
Dept. B ..	4860	
Sales—Dept. A		9600
Dept. B		6400
Salaries	1256	
Rent, rates, and taxes	471	
Water and electricity	104	
Discounts	76	104
Postage and telephone	52	
General expenses	256	
Printing and stationery	144	
Carriage on sales	36	
Advertising	850	
	£30955	£30955

Value of stock on hand at 31st December, Dept. A, £4,620, Dept. B, £3,950. The expenses are to be apportioned between the departments on the basis of the sales.

7. Smith's Stores are owned by S. Smith. The stores are divided into three departments, A, B, and C. From the following Trial Balance prepare Trading and Profit and Loss Accounts for the year in departmental form, and prepare a Balance Sheet as at 31st December. The expenses are to be apportioned between the departments on the basis of their sales.

Trad. Acc.

Trial Balance, 31st December

	Dr. £	Cr. £
Capital Account—		
S. Smith..		4000
Drawings	600	
Stock, 1st January—		
Dept. A	1100	
„ B	500	
„ C	2400	
Purchases—		
Dept. A ..	3200	
„ B ..	2200	
„ C ..	5400	
Sales—		
Dept. A		4800
„ B		3200
„ C		8000
Cash at bank	1250	
Wages and salaries	850	

	Dr. £	Cr. £
Advertising	220	
Printing and stationery	20	
Postage and telephone	42	
[1]Fixtures and fittings	350	
Rent and rates	500	
Insurance	25	
General expenses	97	
Discounts		150
Sundry creditors		204
Sundry debtors	1600	
	£20354	£20354

The stock on hand at 31st December was valued at, Dept. A, £1,200, Dept. B, £630, Dept. C, £2,540.

[1] This item is an asset and will appear in the Balance Sheet.

CHAPTER 11 4 Noo.

KINDS OF PURCHASES: CAPITAL AND REVENUE EXPENDITURE: TYPES OF CAPITAL

A trader buys goods for his stock and continues to buy from time to time as he finds his stock needs to be replenished. These are the kinds of purchases which have been the subject of consideration in earlier chapters. They may be purchases for cash or on credit, but in every case the intention is to sell all such purchases in the ordinary course of business. It is not long, however, before a trader finds he must buy certain things to keep for use and not for his stock to sell in the ordinary course of business. He requires shop fittings, such as counters and showcases, and office furniture, typewriters, delivery cycles, and motor vans. He may consider it desirable to purchase the business premises. All such things are kept permanently in the business for use, and for that reason are differentiated from the goods bought for the purpose of selling again at a profit.

It has been shown that the entries of purchases for stock and eventual sale are made in the Purchases Account. This account is reserved for such purchases and cannot be used to record the purchase of things to be kept for permanent use.

The business premises, shop fittings, office furniture, and similar purchases made with the view of keeping them for use are counted among the valuable possessions, or assets, of the business, and, as it will be necessary to keep a record of their value, a special account is opened in the Ledger for each of such assets.

Example 7.—On Jan. 1 M. Redman buys his shop premises, freehold, for £4,500, paying by cheque.

The credit entry for this transaction is in the Bank Account in the Cash Book. The corresponding debit entry is made to a new account to record the asset of the value of £4,500 that the business has acquired which takes the place of the cash asset to that amount.

90

Dr.		Shop Premises				Cr.
19..		£	19..			£
Jan. 1	Cash Bank	4500				

On closing the books and preparing the Final Accounts, the accounts for these assets will remain open and their balances will be included among the items in the Balance Sheet. In the above example, Shop Premises, £4,500, will appear as an asset in the Balance Sheet. The total value of the firm's assets have not been increased by the purchase: there is only a change in the form of the assets.

The trader may, of course, purchase such assets on credit. That will involve no immediate change in the Cash Account, but the fact that an asset has been acquired must be recorded and, at the same time, a record must be made of the debt created.

Example 8.—On Jan. 10 M. Redman bought one showcase, £60, on credit from Mint & Company, Ltd.

94

Dr.			Shop Fittings				Cr.
19..			£	19..			£
Jan. 10	Mint & Co.	98	60				

98

Dr.			Mint & Company				Cr.
19..			£	19..			£
				Jan. 10	Shop fittings	94	60

Shop fittings will appear among the assets in the Balance Sheet. If payment is not made before the Balance Sheet is prepared the αebt due to Mint & Co. must be included in the item Sundry Creditors on the liabilities side. Notice that in this case the assets have increased in total, but the liabilities show a similar increase in amount. The payment of the account would extinguish the liability to Mint & Co., and at the same time the total assets would be diminished as £60 would be paid out from the office or bank cash.

Consumable Stores

From time to time purchases will be made differing from either of the kinds discussed above, such as office stationery, typewriter ribbons, ink, envelopes, packing materials, and postage stamps. These are consumable goods, being used up in the ordinary routine of business, and as such, must be treated as part of the expense of conducting the business.

Accounts will be kept for these forms of expense, for example, Office Stationery and Sundries Account, Packing Materials Account,

Postage Account. The balances of these accounts will be transferred to the Profit and Loss Account at the close of a trading period. The expenses will be debited to their respective accounts, the credit entries being to Cash Account, if bought for cash, or if bought on credit, to the personal accounts of the firms from whom they are obtained.

Thus it will be seen that a business purchases three different kinds of goods which must on no account be confused:—

(1) Goods bought for re-sale (or for manufacture for re-sale)— debit Purchases Account.

(2) Consumable stores—debit appropriate Expenses Account.

(3) Assets—debit appropriate Asset Account.

In addition to the above, a business will find, as we saw in Chapter 8, that it must spend money for which no return in goods is to be obtained. This fourth classification of out-goings will include expenditure on wages, postage, insurance, etc.

At the end of the Trading Period the expenditure on goods bought for re-sale is transferred to the Trading Account together with such items of consumable stores and expenses such as wages, etc., which directly affect the Gross Profit. At the same time the expenditure on consumable stores and expenses such as wages, etc. (other than those items referred to above which directly affect the Gross Profits) are transferred to the Profit and Loss Account. The expenditure on assets is left in the Asset Accounts concerned as balances which consequently appear on the Balance Sheet.

Capital and Revenue Expenditure

If we consider Trading, and Profit and Loss, as one account, it can be seen that all expenditure by a business would be either ultimately transferred to this account or retained in other separate accounts as assets. Those items which are transferable to Trading, and Profit and Loss Accounts are called Revenue Expenditure, and those retained in the Accounts as assets are called Capital Expenditure.

Sometimes there is some doubt as to which category an item of expenditure belongs. If, for example, extra machinery is bought, then clearly the value of the machinery in the business has risen and the extra machinery is a Capital Expenditure. But when the existing machinery is repaired in order to maintain it at its present book value, then the asset has not risen in value, and so the expenditure

on repairs is Revenue Expenditure chargeable to Trading, and Profit
and Loss Account.

Capital

When a man starts a business he usually begins with a sum of
money, which, let us say, is £5,000. He will probably open a
Business Bank Account and place this sum, called his capital, to it.
If we were asked to produce his Balance Sheet at the commmence-
ment of business, it would appear as follows:—

Balance Sheet

	£		£
Capital	5000	Cash at bank ..	5000

This position, of course, could not last long. We know that he
would spend money on the purchase of various assets. Before he
began trading, his financial position might be as follows:—

Balance Sheet

	£		£
Capital	5000	Machinery	1500
		Furniture and fittings	500
		Stock	2000
		Cash at bank	1000
	£5000		£5000

From this second Balance Sheet we can see that capital may be
not simply money, but the total of assets which can be converted
into money. The business still owes the owner £5,000; it can pay
him £5,000 after the machinery, furniture, fittings, and stock are
converted into money.

The assets which he purchases are of two kinds. Machinery and
furniture and fittings are acquired for use in the business over a
prolonged period. They are known as *Fixed Assets*. Assets such
as stock, sundry debtors, and cash in hand and at bank are known
as *Current Assets* as they are acquired for disposal in the course of
trade and will quickly be renewed again. Hence they are sometimes
known as circulating assets.

The liabilities of a firm may be of two types. *Current Liabilities*
are those such as trade creditors or a bank overdraft which will have

to be met within a comparatively short period of time. *Long Term Liabilities* may consist of loans made to the firm for a fairly long period of time, at least more than one year.

When the trader has been in business for some time his balance sheet might be as follows:—

Balance Sheet

	£			£	£
Capital	6400	*Fixed assets*			
Loan (7 years)—S. Gee ..	2000	Machinery	3300		
Current liabilities		Furniture and fittings	700		
Trade creditors	2100			———	4000
		Current assets			
		Stock..	3750		
		Trade debtors ..	950		
		Cash in hand and			
		balance at bank ..	1800		
				———	6500
	———				———
	£10500				£10500

The total of fixed assets is £4,000, the total of current assets is £6,500 and of current liabilities £2,100. The total of assets in the business is £10,500 but, of this amount, £2,100 must be easily available to pay the trade creditors. The difference, £8,400, is known as the *net value of the assets*. This net value is equal to the *capital employed* in the business. This "capital employed" may consist partly of funds contributed by the owner of the business known simply as "capital" and also of funds borrowed from other sources which will be avilable for a prolonged period. This is known as *Loan Capital*. In the above balance sheet the capital employed is £8,400 consisting of £6,400 due to the owner of the business and £2,000 due to S. Gee.

To illustrate these points the Balance Sheet may be set out as overleaf.

This form of balance is being increasingly adopted, especially by companies. Students are advised to use this form of Balance Sheet.

The figure £4,400 is an important figure. It is known as the *Working Capital* and is equal to the amount of the current assets less the amount of current liabilities. It is important because it is essential that a business should have a sufficient margin of current assets over current liabilities to not only meet its immediate liabilities but to carry on and expand its trading activities. If the working

Balance Sheet

	£		£	£
Capital	6400	*Fixed assets*		
Loan (7 years)—S. Gee ..	2000	Machinery	3300	
		Furniture and fittings	700	
				4000
		Current assets		
		Stock.. ..	3750	
		Trade debtors	950	
		Cash in hand and balance at bank	1800	
				6500
		Less current liabilities		
		Trade creditors ..	2100	
				4400
Capital employed	£8400	Net value of assets ..		£8400

capital was inadequate the business might not be able to meet its immediate liabilities and even if it could do so the margin might not be sufficient to enable it to quickly renew its stocks or to take advantage of trading opportunities. It is clear that a business would be in a very serious position indeed if it were compelled to sell any of the fixed assets to meet pressing and immediate liabilities. If a business has been buying large amounts on credit and has, perhaps, acquired a large bank overdraft it may, if it is unable to collect cash quickly from its debtors get into difficulties. This is known as overtrading.

EXERCISES 11

1. Enter the following transactions of J. Herbertson in his books. Take out a Trial Balance and prepare Trading and Profit and Loss Accounts for the period, and a Balance Sheet as at 17th March.

			£
Mar.	3.	J. Herbertson began business with—Cash at bank	6000
„	3.	He bought business premises and paid by cheque	3600
„	5.	Paid by cheque for shop fittings and fixtures ..	186
„	7.	Paid by cheque for automatic scales and cash register ..	72
„	7.	Cashed cheque for till money	30
„	7.	Paid by cheque for paper bags, string, and packing paper ..	13
„	9.	Bought from National Stores—	
		Provisions, £450; groceries, £750	1200
„	10.	Bought from Hudson & Co.—	
		Dry goods	300
„	17.	Cash Sales to date	258
„	17.	Paid boy's wages in cash	3
„	17.	Paid cash into bank	240
„	17.	Stock on hand valued at	1305

2.   £

B. W. Ward began business on 10th April with the following capital:—

Cash in hand	.. ..	10
Cash at bank	.. ..	680

April 10. Bought from J. Birmingham—

Cutlery	.. ..	100
Fancy silver goods	.. ..	350

,,	10.	Bought at auction old silver, and paid by cheque	300
,,	12.	Bought two showcases for shop, paying by cheque.. ..	80
,,	12.	Paid cash for stationery and wrapping paper	3
,,	15.	Sold to J. Bentley—	
		Cutlery and silver	50
,,	16.	Paid cash for polishing materials	2
,,	18.	J. Bentley returned part of cutlery order—allowed him ..	6
,,	23.	Cash sales to date, paid direct to bank	370
,,	30.	Paid by cheque for rent of premises	25
,,	30.	Paid J. Birmingham his account by cheque	450
,,	30.	Drew cheque for personal use..	50

Take out Trial Balance and prepare Trading and Profit and Loss Accounts for the period, and a Balance Sheet as at 30th April. Stock on hand, £500.

3. The following balances were extracted at 31st December from J. Wetherby's books. From them prepare a Trial Balance and from the Trial Balance prepare Trading and Profit and Loss Accounts for the year and a Balance Sheet as at 31st December: Purchases, £1,700; Sales, £2,700; Salaries and Wages, £400; Carriage on Sales, £10; Office expenses, £75; Office furniture, £150; Rent Account, £100; Sundry debtors, £800; Sundry creditors, £277; Cash in hand, £10; Cash at bank, £182; Stock, 1st Jan., £500; Stock, 31st Dec., £480; Capital Account (credit balance), £950.

4. From the following Trial Balance from B. Downing's books, prepare Trading and Profit and Loss Accounts, and a Balance Sheet as at 31st December:—

Trial Balance. 31st December

	£	£
Stock at start of year	350	
Purchases	1100	
Sales		2100
Wages	250	
Office expenses	90	
Carriage on sales	81	
Rent and rates	160	
Capital account		791
Sundry creditors		360
Sundry debtors	750	
Cash at bank	350	
Office furniture	120	
	£3251	£3251

The stock on hand at the close of the year was valued at £320.

5. From the following Trial Balance, you are required to prepare Trading and Profit and Loss Accounts, and a Balance Sheet.

Trial Balance. December 31st

	Dr. £	Cr. £
Stock on hand at beginning of year ..	326	
Purchases	879	
Sales		2248
Salaries and wages	596	
Office expenses	98	
Carriage on sales	87	
Rent and rates	157	
Capital Account (H. Dickson)		~~600~~ 1000
Creditors		321
Debtors	777	
Cash at bank	249	
Motor Van	~~450~~	
	£3169	£3169

The stock in hand at the end of the year was valued at £295.

R.S.A.

6. Distinguish carefully between Capital Expenditure and Revenue Expenditure.

7. Give a list under the two headings Capital and Revenue, of items of expenditure which might be made by (*a*) a riding school, (*b*) a chimney sweep, (*c*) a wholesale grocery and provision merchant.

8. Say, with reasons, whether the following transactions of a catering business should be classified as capital or revenue expenditure:—

    (i) Bought a new refrigerator to replace an old one which was both faulty and too small.

    (ii) Ordered and received 2 pails soft soap.

    (iii) Purchased on credit 12 doz. sets of cutlery for new dining room.

    (iv) Paid for <u>hire</u> of new coffee-making machine.

    (v) Bought and paid for 5,000 cigarettes.

9. T. S. Appleby gave you the following figures and asked you to prepare from them his Balance Sheet as at 31st May, 19... In addition, he wishes you to state the total capital employed in the business, the total borrowed capital, the working capital and the total capital due to himself. Cash in hand £24. Loan from his uncle V. Appleyard £750. Motor vans £1,200. Sundry debtors £2,376. Sundry creditors £1,850. Bank overdraft £90. Machinery £2,000. Loan from T. Garth and Sons £600. Furniture and fittings £350. Stock in hand £1,340.

10. The following balances remained in J. Ashworth's Ledger *after* he had prepared his Trading and Profit and Loss Account for the year ended 31st December 19...

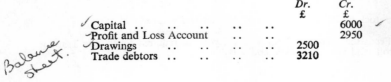

	Dr. £	Cr. £
Capital		6000
Profit and Loss Account		2950
Drawings	2500	
Trade debtors	3210	

	Dr. £	Cr. £
Creditors: Trade		4170
Expense		140
X.L. Loan Co. (10 year loan)		1000
Stock	4670	
Furniture and fittings	690	
Motor vans	1320	
Cash in hand and balance at bank ..	1870	
	£14260	£14260

Prepare Ashworth's Balance Sheet in such a way as to show *within the Balance Sheet*:—

(i) The total of fixed assets.

(ii) The total of current assets.

(iii) The total of current liabilities.

(iv) The working capital.

(v) The net book value of the assets.

(vi) The capital employed.

CHAPTER 12

CONCERNING THE JOURNAL AND ITS USE

It has been shown how the pressure of work and the need to subdivide duties among a larger staff led to the use of the subsidiary books known as the Purchase Day Book, the Sales Day Book, and Sales Returns and Purchases Returns Books. They are of proved worth as aids to efficiency in the counting house, but they do not diminish the importance of the Ledger, nor are they in substitution of any part of the actual double entry record the Ledger should contain. The subsidiary books are useful channels only, directing the flow of entries to their appropriate places in the Ledger Accounts. So great is their utility, however, as adjuncts to the Ledger that, where they are taken into use, it is made an imperative rule that no entry shall be made in the Ledger unless it has first been entered in its appropriate subsidiary book. The carrying out of this rule ensures that the information contained in the respective subsidiary books is complete and leads also to accuracy in the Ledger record, since the rule provides for an orderly system of posting to the Ledger. Interruptions cannot be avoided in practice, and to post to the Ledger from what are virtually lists of transactions avoids omissions in posting, as it is an easy matter to note on the list the last item dealt with before the interruption and to resume again from that point. The entry of the Ledger folios against the items in the subsidiary books is in itself an excellent method of indicating which items have been posted.

Because of the rule that transactions must be passed through the subsidiary books before being entered in the Ledger, the subsidiary books are known collectively as books of original, or first, entry. The term is applied also to the Cash Book. The four books referred to above contain classified records of transactions and provide chronological lists for posting to the Ledger. The Cash Book, though part of the Ledger and containing Ledger Accounts, is a separate book and contains entries of a particular kind, namely those affecting the firm's cash. It provides, therefore, a suitable record from which the entries may be posted to their respective Ledger Accounts. The Cash Book differs from the four subsidiary books as it is a substitute for the Cash and Bank Accounts in the

Ledger and is an integral part of the double entry record, whereas the other books of prime entry are not. The Cash Book contains, however, a record only of one aspect of each transaction, except in the case of transfers between office cash and bank cash.

The cashier enters in the Cash Book each transaction affecting the firm's cash, ignoring the other aspect, so that the Cash Book contains a specialised list of transactions from which the double entry may be completed by posting therefrom to the Ledger.

As the rule above referred to is extended to cover the Cash Book, the Cash Book is regarded as one of the books of original entry, but it cannot be classed with the others as a subsidiary book as it contains actual Ledger Accounts.

The Journal

In practice it will soon be discovered that transactions occur of a nature that cannot be passed through the books of first entry mentioned above, since these are limited to certain transactions, namely—

(a) Purchases on credit and any returns thereof.

(b) Sales on credit and any returns thereof.

(c) Transactions affecting the firm's cash.

If the rule that no entry should be made in the Ledger unless it has passed through a book of first entry is of practical use, then it is reasonable to assume that it should apply to all transactions. But transactions other than those above mentioned are usually not so numerous as to warrant special books for each class. One book is brought into use as a book of original entry for these items. This book is called the Journal. It has two cash columns on the right-hand side of the page, but the form in which the entries are made differs from the form taken in the other subsidiary books. Both aspects of each transaction are recorded, and, since the items relate to several kinds of transactions and the Journal is not reserved for any one class, an explanatory note, called the narration, is made immediately below each entry. The making of this note ensures that the nature of and reason for the entry are not forgotten.

One of the kinds of transactions passed through the Journal is the purchase on credit of fixed assets such as machinery, furniture, and fittings.

Example 9. On July 1 M. Redman purchased two office desks at £31 each on credit from the Hoxton Furnishing Co.

Journal					Dr.		Cr.	
19..					£		£	
July 1	Office Furniture Account	Dr.	29		62			
	To Hoxton Furnishing Co.		77				62	
	being the purchase of two office desks.							

Examination of the above entry will show that the debit and credit aspects of the transaction were first determined, and the appropriate entries made in a particular form. The account to be debited is entered first, with the abbreviation "Dr." at the end of the line. The amount is entered in the first cash column. The account to be credited is entered on the next line, usually starting a short space to the right and prefaced by the word "To." The amount is entered in the outer cash column. On the next line is the narration, and below this is ruled a line to separate this Journal entry from the next. The line is not continued across the cash columns. Sometimes these are added at the foot as a simple check to find that the two columns agree.

The following is the form the entry takes if the transaction affects two or more accounts:—

Example 10.—On July 1, M. Redman purchased on credit from the Hoxton Furniture Company one office desk at £30, and show case for shop at £60.

Journal					Dr.		Cr.	
19..					£		£	
July 1	Office Furniture Account..	Dr.	29		30			
	Shop Fittings Account		31		60			
	To Hoxton Furnishing Co.		77				90	
	being purchase of office desk and showcase.							

It must be stressed that the Journal entries, though recording both aspects of a transaction, are not part of the double entry record proper. They are entries in the Journal as a book of first entry, and are posted therefrom to the appropriate accounts in the Ledger. The fact that the twofold aspect is recorded in the Journal makes the posting a simple task. Note that the Ledger folios are entered against the items in the Journal. A similar entry of the Journal page is made in the folio column of the Ledger Account.

No entry, of course, would have been made in the Journal had Redman bought these goods for cash and not on credit. Also, the Journal and not the Purchase Day Book is used, as the Purchase Day Book is reserved for the purchase on credit of goods bought to sell again in the ordinary course of business. These goods were bought to keep for daily use.

Correction of Errors

Another use for the Journal is for the preliminary record of entries to correct wrong postings in the Ledger.

Example 11.—June 4.   Under this date goods, £10, were sold to J. Brown. The amount was debited in error to A. Brown.

The wrong entry made in A. Brown's account is not erased or struck through, as the reason for the alteration would not be apparent. A double entry is made. £10 is credited to A. Brown's account, as a set off to the wrong debit of £10, and a corresponding debit entry is made to J. Brown's account. This is the usual method of correcting all similar errors in posting. The usefulness of the Journal explanation of the entries is obvious.

		Dr.	Cr.
	Journal		
		£	£
19..			
June 4	J. Brown .. .. Dr.	65	10
	To A. Brown	69		10
	being correction of error in posting to A. Brown for J. Brown.		

On those few occasions when the Trial Balance does not agree and a Suspense Account is opened, the error or errors when subsequently discovered are also corrected by means of a Journal entry (see Example 12, next page).

The first entry, which is really completing the double entry of the debit in the Cash Book on 6th June by crediting S. K. Green's account, must, however, be debited to the Suspense Account, as in that account appears the £35 credit entry (part of the £75) which was made to agree the Trial Balance. The entry may be regarded as transferring the £35 from the Suspense Account to S. K. Green's account.

The second entry is not only a question of posting to the wrong account but also posting to the wrong side of the Ledger. A debit entry, or remembering that Purchases Returns are posted individually to the debit side of the creditor accounts, a total of debit entries is posted to the debit side of the Sales Returns Account.

Example 12.—July 21st.   M. Redman finds that the credit balance of £75 in the Suspense Account is accounted for as follows:—

Cash £35 received from S. K. Green on 6th June was not credited to his account.

Purchases Returns £20 for the month of June were posted to the debit side of the Sales Returns Account.

Journal

19..		Dr.	Cr.
		£	£
July 21	Suspense Account.. .. .. .. Dr. To S. K. Green .. .. .. being cash received from S. K. Green on June 6th not previously credited to his account.	35	35

„ 21	Suspense Account.. .. .. .. Dr.
	    To Sales Returns .. .. ..
	    „ Purchases Returns.. .. ..
	being correction of error in posting £20 Purchases Returns for June to the debit side of Sales Returns Account.
		40	20
			20

It will be seen that a credit is necessary in the Sales Returns Account to correct the debit entry of £20 and a further credit in the Purchases Returns Account is necessary to make the correct posting to that account.   The original error in the Suspense Account was in this case £40, twice the amount which was incorrectly posted.

The two entries could have been corrected as one Journal entry, but the matter is more clearly shown as two entries.

Opening Entries

The opening of a new set of books involves the entry of assets and liabilities existing at the time.   The financial position is summarised and a preliminary entry is made in the Journal from which the various assets and liability accounts may be posted.

Example 13.—Hugh Hurd, whose financial position on 1st January 19.. is as below, decides to open a set of books on double entry principles:—

			£
Cash in hand	..	..	10
Cash at bank	..	..	104
Shop fittings	..	..	50
Office furniture	..	..	60
Stock of goods	..	..	500
Debtors—B. Beaver	..	..	35
R. Weaver	..	..	24
Creditor—			
L. C. Smith	..	..	76

The trader's capital is the excess in value of the assets over the liabilities, and a simple calculation gives H. Hurd's capital at 1st January as £707.

Journal					Dr.	Cr.
19..					£	£
Jan. 1	Sundry Debtors—B. Beaver	..	..		35	
	R. Weaver	..	..		24	
	Shop fittings ..	..	..	..	50	
	Office furniture	..	..	..	60	
	Stock ..	..	..	..	500	
	Cash at bank ..	..	..	..	104	
	Cash in hand	..	..	Dr.	10	
	To Sundry Creditors—					
	L. C. Smith ..		..			76
	„ Capital (Hugh Hurd) ..	..	..			707
	being assets and liabilities at this date.				£783	£783

A Journal entry is made, as above, summarising the position and separating the assets and liabilities. In the journalising of the opening entries, an exception appears to the rule that no cash entries should be made in the Journal. If they were omitted in this case the summary would not represent the true financial position.

This summary of the financial position is on record in the Journal for reference at any time. The Ledger is opened by posting from this summary to the appropriate accounts, the assets being debited and the liabilities being credited thereto respectively. Not only is the summary of use in that it is a preliminary classification of the items, but it lessens the risk of omissions in the Ledger postings.

Closing Entries

A further use for the Journal is to record the closing entries in the preparation of the Final Accounts at the end of a trading period.

The example overleaf of such closing entries is taken from the transfers shown in Example 4 on pages 32 and 33. Reference should be made to those pages, and the Journal entries below should be traced in the Ledger Accounts.

It will be apparent that the transfers comprise the items required in the preparation of the Trading and Profit and Loss Accounts. The balances of the *personal* and *real* accounts are not transferred,

Journal		Dr.	Cr.
		£	£
19..			
Mar. 31	Trading Account .. .. .. Dr.	14	
	To Stock Account..		14
	being transfer of balance of Stock Account.		
„ 31	Trading Account .. .. .. Dr.	56	
	To Purchases Account		56
	being balance transferred.		
„ 31	Sales Account .. .. .. Dr.	56	
	To Trading Account		56
	being balance transferred.		
„ 31	Stock Account .. .. .. Dr.	40	
	To Trading Account		40
	being Stock in hand 31st March, 19..		
„ 31	Trading Account .. .. .. Dr.	26	
	To Profit and Loss Account		26
	being transfer of gross profit.		
„ 31	Profit and Loss Account .. .. Dr.	24	
	To Capital Account		24
	being transfer of net profit.		

such balances being carried down on the accounts for the new period.

Except for the first year of a business, when there is usually no stock of goods on hand at the beginning of the trading period, the closing entries will always include transfers from the Stock Account to the Trading Account and likewise from the Purchases and Sales Accounts. Between the Trading Account and the Profit and Loss Account the transfer is of the gross profit or loss as disclosed in the former account. Subsequent Journal entries are those required in the preparation of the Profit and Loss Account. The example given does not include many items, but in practice various forms of expenses, loss, and gains occur and are recorded in separate accounts. All *nominal* accounts are closed by the transfer of their balances to the Trading or Profit and Loss Accounts. The appropriate closing Journal entries and the transfers are made after the extraction of the Trial Balance.

The closing entries may not always be journalised, the entries being made direct between the accounts, but the journalising of them ensures that they are complete, and also facilitates the posting of them.

As a Journal entry is but the setting down of the two-fold aspect of a transaction, it follows that all transactions may be journalised. It was once the practice to pass every transaction through the Journal, but the use of subsidiary books render this unnecessary.

EXERCISES 12

1. Record the following transactions by Journal entries:—

Jan. 14. The purchase of a motor delivery van on credit from the London Motor Company for £675.

„ 17. The purchase of an office desk on credit from Shoreditch Cabinet Co. for £45.

„ 25. The purchase of a typewriter on credit from the British Typewriter Co., for £40.

„ 30. The purchase on credit of two showcases and other shop fittings from Mint & Co. for £165.

2. Record the following transactions of A. Bentley, furniture dealer, in Journal form.

Feb. 2. The purchase of a warehouse and showrooms for £10,000 from the Freehold Properties Company.

„ 6. The sale of a second-hand delivery van for £150 to Car Mart Auction Company.

„ 8. A. Bentley took for his private use a sideboard which cost £20.

„ 10. The purchase of a cash register for office use for £50, from the Office Furniture Supplies Company.

„ 12. The purchase of a new delivery van for £500 from the City Motor Company.

3. A. Burton's financial position on 1st January was as follows:—

	£
Cash in hand ..	27
Cash at bank ..	230
Stock on hand	750
Creditors—J. Bones ..	130
T. Smith ..	150
Debtors—Williams & Co. ..	20
Wilson & Sons ..	35
Capital ..	782

Make the appropriate Journal entries to open his books.

4. The following are the liabilities and assets of R. B. Graham, excepting his capital. Find his capital, make the appropriate Journal entries preparatory to opening a new set of accounts, and post the items to the respective Ledger Accounts.

					£
Cash	..	..	..	..	10
Bank	..	..	..	..	321
Stock	..	..	..	..	800
Office furniture		..	..	..	50
Delivery bicycles		..	..	..	10
Shop fittings	..	..	..	..	60
Debtor—Brown & Co.			..	..	204
Creditors—J. Westerby			..	..	87
R. Easter			..	..	31
B. Groombridge		..		..	8

5. The following Balance Sheet represents L. Chamber's financial position as at 31st December. Make the appropriate opening entries for the next year in the Journal from which the Ledger and Cash Book may be posted.

Balance Sheet. 31st December

LIABILITIES		£	ASSETS		£
Capital	.. .. ..	1180	Cash in hand		30
Creditors—R. Jones	..	240	Cash at bank		320
T. Lewis	..	120	Stock		530
			Furniture and fittings..		110
			Debtors—J. Neill ..		150
			R. Firth ..		380
			N. Tyson ..		20
		£1540			£1540

6. Ascertain M. T. Green's capital as at 1st January from the following list of his liabilities and assets, and prepare the appropriate Journal entry to open a set of books on that date. Post the items to the Ledger Accounts.

LIABILITIES		£	ASSETS		£
Creditors—B. Smith	..	44	Cash in hand		20
B. Brown	..	33	Cash at bank		169
B. Robinson		22	Stock on hand ..		750
			Shop premises		1200
			Delivery van		120
			Shop fittings		52
			Debtor—J. Winder ..		18

Enter Green's transactions—

									£
Jan.	3.	Sold goods to J. Winder ..	..	..	..	..	..		130
„	6.	Bought goods by cheque ..	..	..	..	..	..		50
„	7.	Paid wages in cash	..	..	..	..	..		6
„	9.	Bought petrol and oil for van in cash ..		..	..	..		1
„	12.	Paid B. Smith his account by cheque.							
„	14.	J. Winder paid his account by cheque.							
„	15.	Paid B. Robinson his account by cheque.							
„	17.	Bought new showcase on credit from Cabinetmakers Company Ltd.							100
„	17.	Stock on hand valued at							770

Take out a Trial Balance and prepare Trading and Profit and Loss Accounts for the period. Draw up a Balance Sheet as at 17th January.

7. The financial position of L. J. Lewis, a dealer in furniture, was as follows on 1st July, 19..:—

	£
Cash in hand	10
Cash at bank	800
Stock on hand	350
Shop furniture and fittings	150
He owed R. Jones ..	80
His debtors were—	
Smith's Stores ..	120
Benson & Co. ..	33

Journalise these items and his capital preparatory to opening L. J. Lewis's books. Post the items to the Ledger and Cash Book, and enter the following transactions:—

		£
July 2.	Sold goods to Smith's Stores	75
,, 6.	Bought furniture from R. Jones	180
,, 8.	Drew cheque for personal use	25
,, 10.	Paid rent for quarter ending 30th June	30
,, 12.	Benson & Co. paid their account by cheque	33
,, 14.	Paid R. Jones his account	260

Take out a Trial Balance as at 14th July. Prepare Trading and Profit and Loss Account for the period, and a Balance Sheet as at 14th July. Stock on hand, £480.

8. Show the Journal entries to correct the following errors in J. Sullivan's books:—

Sept. 2. Goods to the value of £20 were returned to B. Clark, but the item had been posted to J. B. Clarkson's account.

Sept. 10. The sale of one of the office desks for £10 in cash was wrongly posted to the Sales Account.

,, 13. The purchase of an office desk for £36 cash to replace the one sold was posted to the Purchases Account.

,, 17. A purchase of goods for £75 from R. Wilkinson & Co. was credited in error to R. Williamson & Sons.

9. Show in Journal form the entries required to correct the following errors made in R. Benson's books:—

July 3. £50 paid by R. Lewis was credited to R. Levy's account.

,, 28. A sale of goods for £25 to R. Jones on credit was debited to R. B. Jones & Co.'s account.

,, 31. The purchase of a typewriter for the office for cash, £15, was posted to the Purchases Account.

Aug. 6. The payment of £10 by cheque to B. Watson was debited to B. Watkinson's account.

10. Journalise the closing entries on the transfer of the following balances to the Trading and Profit and Loss Accounts on the 31st December:—

	£
Purchases	1600
Sales	2590
Stock at start	300
Wages	120
Expenses	47
Rent	150
Stock at close	400

11. There was a difference in the Trial Balance of A. Spencer at 31st August, 19.., which was transferred to the Suspense Account. Subsequently the difference was found to be due to the following errors:—

£10 cash received from A. Brown was correctly entered in the Cash Book but was debited to his account.

Sales Day Book for August was undercast by £10. The total sales should have been £2,060 not £2,050.

£25 paid to the landlord for rent on 28th August was entered in the Cash Book but not in any other account.

Correct the errors by means of Journal entries and state the nature and amount of the balance on the Suspense Account.

12. Give entries in the Journal proper to correct the following errors:—

(a) Feb. 1. A cheque received for £18 was posted to the credit of P. Dawson, though in fact it came from F. Dawson & Co. and should have been credited to them.

(b) „ 1. An entry for £10 goods returned was, in error, made in the Sales Book instead of the Purchase Returns Book.

(c) „ 1. A cheque for £5 paid to G. Law was debited to a personal account in his name. It should have been charged to Legal Expenses Account.

13. Prepare Journal entries to show the effect of the following transactions in the books of Peter Grimes.

Dec. 1 Sold to A. Butt for £100 goods belonging to G. Sykes. Commission £5.

„ 31. £56 has been included in the Wages Account and £63 in the Purchases Account which sums represent expenditure on an extension of the business premises.

Purchases Returns £5 had been posted in error to the debit of Sales Returns and the resulting difference in the books has been placed temporarily in a Suspense Account. The matter is now to be corrected.

One of the branch shops makes a net profit of £1,100 and it is decided to give the manager a commission of 10% of the amount of profit that will remain after the commission has been granted.

CHAPTER 13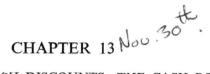

TRADE AND CASH DISCOUNTS: THE CASH BOOK

Trade Discounts

Traders who buy in large quantities from a manufacturer or wholesaler are generally given an allowance on the list price of the goods. This is known as *trade discount.* In some cases manufacturers recommend a retail selling price, invoice the goods at that price and allow the retailer a trade discount to cover his expenses and margin of profit.

The amount charged to the trader is the invoice price, *i.e.* the list price less trade discount and it is the *net* amount which is entered in both the subsidiary sales and purchases records and in the Ledger Accounts. When allowances are made on such goods the amount of the allowance will be the invoice price, *i.e.* the list price *less* trade discount.

Some wholesale houses provide catalogues of goods from which the retailer may order his supplies and which he may keep by him for reference purposes. The catalogue or trade list may be a costly production and, to avoid frequent reprints being required on any change in price levels, the price against each article is purposely placed at a high figure bearing little relation to current prices. The retailer is notified that present wholesale prices are the list prices less, say, 40 per cent. trade discount. At any change in the price level owing to changes in the cost of materials or labour or other cause, the percentage deduction may be altered and the retailers are informed of the fact.

The price to be paid to the wholesale house is the net amount after the deduction has been made. The trade discount is a means only of indicating the price to be paid. It is never entered in the Ledger Accounts, as it forms no part of the value of the goods or of the debt due for them.

Cash Discounts and the Cash Book

In the sale of goods on credit the advantage is with the purchaser, as he may sell the goods and may realise sufficient cash to meet his account and to yield a profit before the expiration of the credit period. In such circumstances his own capital requirements for buying stock are small, as he is making use of the capital of his wholesale supplier. The seller realises this and is willing, in many instances, to forgo something from the account if the purchaser will pay promptly and not take advantage of a longer period of credit. What he offers to a purchaser as an inducement to pay promptly is a specified percentage reduction called Cash Discount. To firms having sufficient capital resources to pay their accounts promptly the discount offers an additional profit and, in the course of a year's trading, may amount to a considerable sum.

The amount of cash discount offered for prompt payment is usually notified on the trade lists and on the invoices. For example, the terms may be stated as: $2\frac{1}{2}\%$ discount on monthly credit accounts. $1\frac{1}{4}\%$ extra for prompt cash. Whatever the terms of payment may be, the discount is granted only on payment within the specified period; thereafter the amount is payable without deduction.

Prompt Cash is payment within seven to ten days from the date of the invoice.

Trade Discount and Cash Discount must not be confused. The treatment of cash discount can never arise until payment is made as, until such time, it is not known whether payment is being made within the period during which the allowance may be claimed.

Discounts Received

The following example illustrates the treatment of discounts received:—

Example 14.—M. Redman buys bicycle accessories to the value of £40 from Cycles Supplies Limited, on 1st November. Terms of payment: $2\frac{1}{2}\%$, one month. He pays the account by cheque on 28th November.

The amount of the cheque is £39, being £40 less $2\frac{1}{2}\%$ cash discount. The sum of £39 will be credited by Redman to his Bank Account and debited in due course to the account of Cycle Supplies Limited. At that moment the latter account will appear as below:—

Dr.					Cycle Supplies Ltd.				Cr. 79
19.. Nov. 28	Cash	..	C.B.	£ 39	19.. Nov. 1	Goods	..	P.B.	£ 40

Cycle Supplies Ltd., however, by their terms of payment, indicate that in this case £39 settles the debt of £40 but the above account, as it stands, shows £1 outstanding. The entry of the amount of the discount on the debit side would close the account. The corresponding credit entry for the discount is made to a new account opened in the Ledger and called the Discounts Received Account. The discount received is regarded by Redman as a gain, and at the close of the trading period the balance of the Discounts Received Account is transferred to the *credit* of the Profit and Loss Account.

The Account for Cycle Supplies Ltd. and the Discounts Received Account will now appear as below:—

				£		19..	£			£	79
Dr.			**Cycles Supplies Ltd.**								*Cr.*
19..						19..	£			£	
Nov. 28	Cash	..	C.B.	39		Nov. 1	Goods	..	P.B.	40	
,, 28	Discount	..	14	1							

			£		19..			£	14
Dr.						**Discounts Received Account**			*Cr.*
			£		19..			£	
					Nov. 28	Cycle Sup- plies Ltd.	79	1	

Discounts Allowed

Similarly Redman may allow cash discount to his customers to encourage prompt payment.

> **Example 15.**—On Dec. 1, Redman sold bicycle accessories to the value of £20 to J. S. Smith on terms 5%, one month.
>
> Dec. 17. Smith paid his account by cheque.

When Smith paid his account the cheque received was for £19, being £20 less 5% cash discount, as he paid within the credit period of one month.

The amount of the discount must be credited to his account as otherwise the entry of £19 only will make it to appear that he still owes £1. The corresponding entry for the discount will be to the debit of a new account called the Discounts Allowed Account, as the amount of the discount is of the nature of a loss to M. Redman.

The balance of the Discounts Allowed Account will be transferred at the close of the trading period to the *debit* side of the Profit and Loss Account.

84

Dr.					J. S. Smith				Cr.
19.. Dec. 1	Goods	..	S.B.	£ 20	19.. Dec. 17	Cash Discount	.. ..	C.B. 16	£ 19 1

16

Dr.				Discounts Allowed Account					Cr.
19.. Dec. 17	J. S. Smith ..		84	£ 1	19..				£

The Three Column Cash Book

Cash discount occurs frequently in business, and the number of entries relating to discount is correspondingly large. The method of recording discounts presently described yields the same advantages as the subsidiary books, in that periodical totals are posted to the discount accounts instead of individual items.

The deduction for cash discount is made at the time of payment. It saves time and labour if, instead of turning at once to the appropriate Discount Account, a note of the discount is made alongside the entry in the Cash Book, and only periodical totals of the discounts allowed and of discounts received are posted to the respective Discount Accounts. To do this another cash column is added to each side of the Cash Book, making three cash columns on each side. The use of two of each of the three columns is already known. The third column on each side is to be regarded as a memorandum column only, wherein a note is made of the discount as it occurs. In this way the additional columns serve the same purpose of grouping like things for eventual posting to the Ledger as the subsidiary books do.

Example 16.—The following transactions took place during the first two weeks of January:—

Jan. 1. Balance at bank, £84.
  Cash in hand, £5.
  „ 2. Paid J. Jones his account for £80 by cheque, *less* 2½% cash discount.
  „ 4. Received cheque from R. Roberts for £39, being in payment of account for £40, less 2½% discount.
  „ 5. Paid B. Brown by cheque his account for £20, deducting 5% discount.
  „ 7. Drew from bank for office cash, £10.
  „ 8. Received cheque from G. Green for £11 in full settlement of account rendered for £12.
  „ 9. S. Smith paid his account for £20 by cheque, deducting 5% discount.

The above are typical transactions affecting the firm's cash, and would be entered in the Cash Book as shown. The personal accounts are not given.

Alongside is a simplified example of a three-column Cash Book. The Cash and Bank columns are added and balanced in the usual way. The Discount columns are added but not balanced, as they are not account columns but memorandum columns only. The addition is made at the time the Cash and Bank Accounts are balanced, usually weekly or monthly. The details of cash and discount are posted from the Cash Book to the respective personal accounts. The weekly or monthly totals of the discount columns are taken to the Discounts Allowed Account and Discounts Received Account. The double entry for the discount items in the personal accounts is then to be found in the appropriate Discount Account. The entries to the Discount Accounts are placed on the same side of those accounts as the totals are found to be in the memorandum columns in the Cash Book.

The balances of these accounts will be transferred

Cash Book

Dr.

		Discount Allowed £	Cash £	Bank £
19.. Jan. 1	Balance			153
„ 4	R. Roberts	1	5	
„ 7	Bank		10	
„ 8	G. Green	1		
„ 9	S. Smith	1		
		£3	£15	£153
„ 10	Balance b/d		15	46

Cr.

		Discount Received £	Cash £	Bank £
19.. Jan. 2	J. Jones	2		78
„ 5	B. Brown	1		19
„ 7	Cash			10
„ 10	Balance c/d		15	46
		£3	£15	£153

at the close of the trading period to the Profit and Loss Account.

16

Dr.		Discounts Allowed Account			Cr.

19..		£	19..		£
Jan. 10	Total discounts allowed ..	3			

Dr.		Discounts Received Account			Cr.

19..		£	19..		£
			Jan. 10	Total discounts received ..	3

There should be no difficulty in understanding the use of the three-column Cash Book if it is borne in mind that it is simpler in practice for the cashier to make a note of the discount when he enters the cash items, and for those notes of the discounts to be entered in total in the Discount Accounts in the Ledger.

The Bank Cash Book

This form of Cash Book is now widely used in business, as it is a means of preventing the occurrence of errors and discrepancies in the cash. The book is illustrated below, and its use follows on the enforcement of the rule that all money received, whether coins, notes, drafts, or cheques, is to be paid intact into the bank, and that all payments are to be made by cheque. Certain small payments in cash, as messengers' fares and telegrams, are necessary in any business, but where these occur they are reserved for payment out of petty cash, as described in Chapter 15, a cheque being drawn weekly or monthly to cover such payments. These are recorded separately from the Cash Book.

Each day the cash and cheques received are entered in the Bank Paying-in Book and are paid into the bank. The details of the cash received are entered in the Cash Book in the details column on the debit side. These details are added, and the total is carried to the bank column on the debit side. This amount should agree with the total shown in the Paying-in Book. The credit side of the Cash Book shows a bank column for the entry of the cheques drawn, and a details column for use if one cheque is drawn to cover two or more payments which have to be debited separately to the Ledger Accounts.

Bank Cash Book

Dr.

Date	Particulars	Folio	Discount Allowed £	Details £	Bank £
19.. July 1	Balance	b/d			370
" 2	R. Lloyd			57	
	B. Ward & Co.			10	
	Cash sales			14	81
3	Tanner & Sons		1	5	
	J. Thompson			19	
	Cash sales			21	45
" 4	Lawson & Co.		2	38	50
	Cash sales			12	
" 5	W. Jackson			67	
	W. Greenfield			11	78
" 6	Buxton & Co. Ltd.			37	
	Cash sales			15	52
			£3		£666
" 7	Balance	b/d			483

Cr.

Date	Particulars	Folio	Discount Received £	Details £	Bank £
19.. July 3	Brown & Co.		4		76
" 5	One quarter's rent				50
" 6	B. James		0·50		16
" 6	Sundries: Wages			36	
	Petty cash			5	41
	Balance	c/d			483
			£4·50		£666

There is no actual cash column as no cash is kept in the office. The petty cash is treated separately. It follows that there will be no cross entries of cash withdrawn from the bank for office use or for surplus cash paid into the bank.

The above points are illustrated on page 99.

EXERCISES 13

1. (*a*) What are the advantages to business people of the practice of allowing cash discount?

(*b*) Record the following transactions in the Cash Book. Balance the Cash Book as on 6th Feb., 19..

			£
Feb. 1.	Cash in hand		27
„ 1.	Cash at bank		110
„ 2.	Received from F. Johnson in cash £23, allowing him discount £2. Total..		25
„ 3.	Received from A. Bowman in cash..		2
„ 3.	Paid to R. Shipley, cash		3
„ 4.	Paid by cheque to L. Patterson his account of £20, less 2½% discount. Total		20
„ 4.	Received cheque from W. Winter and paid it into Bank		35
„ 4.	Paid in cash sundry expenses		3
„ 5.	Received payment in cash of A. Crowe's account £5, from which he deducted 5% discount. Total		5
„ 5.	Paid for postage stamps, cash		1
„ 6.	Sold goods for cash		12
„ 6.	Paid cheque to J. Williams, £30, having deducted discount £2 from his account. Total		32
„ 6.	Paid into bank		30

U.L.C.I.

2. On 1st July, 19.., G. Triptree commenced business as a furniture dealer with £400 in the bank. He paid into the bank a further sum of £300 borrowed at 5 per cent. interest from his father, T. Triptree.

Prepare a Cash Book with three columns recording the above and the following transactions. In writing up your Cash Book, show quite clearly the Ledger Account to which you would post each item.

July 1. Bought a motor van for £450, which was paid for by cheque.
„ 1. Drew cash from bank £30, bought for cash stationery and stamps, £5, and petrol and oil for motor van, £2.
„ 5. Cash sales, £39.
„ 5. Paid to W. Johnson & Sons by cheque the balance of their account, £89, less a discount of 5%.
„ 7. Bought by cheque 3 oak sideboards at £16 each.
„ 9. Paid in cash wages, £13.
„ 11. Received a cheque for £35 from S. Holmes, and accepted this in settlement of his account of £36. The cheque was paid into bank.
„ 12. Cash sales, £66.
„ 14. The bank returned S. Holmes' cheque marked R/D.
„ 14. Paid into bank, £50.
„ 16. Paid wages in cash, £13, and drew £10 in cash for personal expenses.

July 16. S. Slater, who owed £18, deducted £1 from the amount due and sent a cheque for the balance. Paid the cheque into bank, and wrote to Slater saying the deduction could not be allowed.

„ 16. Bought for cash job lot of dining-room chairs, £30.

Balance the Cash Book as on 16th July, 19.., and bring down the balance. No posting to the Ledger is required. *R.S.A.*

3. On 1st February, 19.., A. Ralph commenced business as a furniture dealer. He had £700 in the bank, stock of furniture worth £250, and his own fixtures and fittings were worth £72. He owed P. Gelling £31 and R. Lee £50.

Journalise these opening entries, and from the following transactions enter up a three-column Cash Book, Purchases Book, Sales Book, and Returns Book. Post all the items into the Ledger and draw out a Trial Balance, and prepare a Trading Account, Profit and Loss Account, and a Balance Sheet. The exercise should be folioed:—

Feb. 2. Sold on credit 6 dining-room chairs, value £5 each, to L. Peacock.
„ 3. Bought on credit from P. Gelling, 10 oak sideboards, value £9 each, less 10% trade discount.
„ 4. Drew cheque for office use, £8.
„ 5. Paid rent by cash, £3.
„ 6. Paid R. Lee the amount owing to him, less 5% cash discount.
„ 8. Sold on credit to L. Peacock, 20 oak tables, value £15 each.
„ 9. L. Peacock paid £28 and was allowed discount, £2.
„ 10. Drew cheque for private use, £30.
„ 11. Paid wages in cash, £6.
„ 12. Returned to P. Gelling, 4 oak sideboards, purchased on the 3rd inst., being faulty in construction.
„ 13. Paid trade expenses in cash, £1.
„ 15. Bought on credit from Austins, Ltd., 1 motor van, value £375.
„ 16. Paid into bank, £3.
„ 16. Sold for cash to R. Felton, 1 oak bookcase, value £22.

The stock on 16th February was £46. *U.E.I.*

4. The financial position of T. Burns, a furniture dealer, on 1st January, 19.., was as follows:—Cash in hand, £22; Cash at bank, £295; Fixtures and fittings, £280; Stock, £720; J. Johnson owed £50; and £110 was owing to F. Naylor.

Journalise these opening entries, and from the following transactions enter up the Cash Book (three columns), Purchases Book, Sales Book, and Returns Book. Post all the items into a Ledger, and draw out a Trial Balance, and prepare a Trading Account, Profit and Loss Account, and Balance Sheet. Balance off the Cash Book.

Jan. 2. J. Johnson paid by cheque the amount due from him, less 5% cash discount. Paid the cheque into the bank on the following day.
„ 3. Sold to L. Lister, 56 chairs at £4 each, 12 oak tables at £15 each, and 2 bedroom suites at £45 each. (15% trade discount was allowed on the total order.)
„ 5. Purchased from F. Naylor, 10 bookcases at £16 each, 10 suites of furniture at £46 each, and sundry job lots for £72. (15% trade discount was allowed on the total order.)
„ 6. Bought by cheque a new showcase, costing £50.
„ 7. Drew and cashed a cheque for £50 for office expenses, out of which the following payments were made:—Salaries £30, and rent £12.
„ 9. L. Lister returned as damaged 4 chairs sold to him on the 3rd instant.

Jan. 11. Remitted F. Naylor a cheque for £150, less 5% cash discount.
„ 12. Cash sales to date, £225 out of which £200 was paid into the bank.
Stock in hand on 14th January, £825. *U.E.I.*

5. R. Seymour carries on business as a retail hosier. On the 1st October, 19.., his assets were:—Shop fixtures and fittings, £1,250; Cash in hand, £72; Trade debtors, S. Silver, £54; Stock, £863. His liabilities were:—Loan from J. Robinson, £200; Trade creditor, H. Sorter, £74; Bank overdraft on Current Account, £19.

You are required to open the necessary accounts to record the above position in the books, and to post thereto through the proper subsidiary books the following transactions:—

Oct. 2. Purchased from H. Black, on credit, goods value £86.
„ 4. Borrowed a further £700 from J. Robinson.
„ 4. Paid H. Sorter by cheque £71 which, with discount receivable, cleared his account.
„ 6. Paid wages £35, and bought postage stamps £2 and stationery £1 from Cash.
„ 8. Received £20 cash on account from S. Silver.
„ 9. Purchased additional shop fittings for £450, and paid for them by cheque.
„ 19. Sold goods for cash, £28.
„ 20. Sold goods on credit to S. Silver, £31.
„ 24. Goods returned by S. Silver, valued at £12.
„ 24. Paid £50 of the cash in hand into the bank.

Balance the Ledger Accounts and Cash Book, bring down the balances and extract a Trial Balance as on 24th October, 19...

N.B.—No Trading Account, Profit and Loss Account, or Balance Sheet is to be prepared. *R.S.A.*

6. On 1st February, 19.., Albert Spence had the following assets and liabilities:—Cash in hand, £15; Cash at bank, £67; Sundry debtors—D. Dowty, £15, E. Evans, £72; Stock on hand, £250; Motor car, £75; Fixtures, £25. Liabilities:—Sundry creditors—W. Mix, £22, H. Harris, £5; M. Mason, £50, J. Johnson, £30; Capital Account, £412. During the month of February he transacted the following business:—

Feb. 2. Sold goods on credit to D. Dowty, £50.
Paid H. Harris by cash, £5.
„ 4. Bought goods on credit from W. Mix, £24.
„ 6. Received from D. Dowty, cash £14, and allowed him discount, £1.
„ 8. Paid cash into bank, £10.
Paid wages in cash, £11.
„ 9. Paid sundry expenses in cash, £2.
Drew for personal expenses by cheque, £15.
„ 11. Sold goods on credit to M. Jones, £40.
„ 13. Received cheque from E. Evans, £72, and paid same into bank.
„ 15. Paid M. Mason by cheque, £50.
„ 17. Bought goods on credit from J. Johnson, £30.
„ 19. Returned part of the goods supplied by J. Johnson on the 17th instant, and received credit note, £10.
Drew from the bank for office purposes, £20.
„ 21. Paid wages in cash, £11.
„ 24. Paid rent by cheque, £5.

Feb. 26.   Paid rates in cash, £4.

„   26.   Drew cheque for private purposes, £15.

Stock in hand at the end of the month, £238.

Enter the above transactions in the appropriate books, then extract a Trial Balance and prepare a set of accounts for the above, showing the profit or loss made during the period, and a Balance Sheet at the end of the month. *N.C.T.E.C.*

7. The following account is in the books of T. Jones:—

Dr.				K. Brown				Cr.
19..			£	19..				£
Jan. 15.	Returns ..	..	20	Jan. 1.	Balance ..	..		120
„ 20.	Contra account ..		95	„ 10.	Goods ..	..		340
„ 20.	Discount..	..	5					
Feb. 10.	Cash ..	..	323					
„ 10.	Discount..	..	17					
			£460					£460

Explain what is recorded by each entry in this account, from what subsidiary books the postings are made, and where the corresponding double entry would be found.   *R.S.A.*

CHAPTER 14

A WORKED EXAMPLE

This chapter concludes with the working of an exercise appropriate to this stage of the subject. The example should prove of value to the student in that it indicates the method of setting out the work for class use and for examinations.

For practice purposes the student is usually provided with two exercise books—one with Ledger ruling and the other with Journal ruling. In some cases a third book, ruled as a Cash Book, is available. Where two only are in use the Cash Book, subsidiary books, and Journal for an exercise are usually grouped together on a double page of the Journal exercise book. With the appropriate headings in bold writing it is possible for the student to consider each section of the page as a separate book. The upper halves of two facing Journal pages are suitable for the Cash Book, but if a three-column Cash Book is required, an additional cash column should be ruled on each side. The left-hand lower half-page is usually sufficient for the Purchase Day Book and Sales Day Book, leaving the right-hand lower half for the Returns Books and the Journal proper. The Trial Balance should, if possible, be included, but if space is insufficient the Trial Balances of all the exercises may, as some teachers prefer, be grouped together at the end of the Journal exercise book.

The student should arrange the Ledger Accounts in a definite order, and should abide by the arrangement for all exercises. In the worked example the real and nominal accounts are grouped together, and likewise the creditors' accounts and the debtors' accounts. The Trading Account, Profit and Loss Account, and Balance Sheet bring the exercise to its conclusion. In the example the full Journal entries are shown, but it may be pointed out that the journalising of the closing entries may not always be required in an examination test, and in actual practice the closing entries may be made direct between the Ledger Accounts. The student should, however, be conversant with the full use of the Journal.

In considering the example given overleaf, each transaction should be traced through the books of original entry to the Ledger Accounts. The student would find it profitable to work the example and then to compare his working with the printed key, any differences

104

being corrected and the reasons for the corrections being sought for and fully understood.

Example 17.—M. Redman's financial position on 1st December, 19.., was as follows:—Cash in hand, £5; cash at bank, £340; stock of bicycles and accessories, £480. He owed Smith's Cycle Company, £20; and T. Lawrence, £10; and was owed £40 by M. Lewis.

Journalise these items, and open Redman's books at 1st December. Enter the following transactions, extract a Trial Balance, and prepare Trading and Profit and Loss Accounts and a Balance Sheet as at 31st December.

Dec. 1. Arranged a loan from bankers for £2,800, which was credited to current account this day.

„ 2. Bought new premises—paid by cheque £3,000.

„ 2. Paid by cheque, £30, for fixtures and fittings.

„ 3. Paid expenses of removal to new premises by cheque, £18.

„ 3. Cashed cheque for office cash, £10, and paid cash for stationery, and printing of invoices, etc., with new address, £3.

„ 8. Cash sales to date, paid direct to bank, £60.

„ 10. Bought from Smith's Cycle Co., 6 "Speedwell" bicycles at £16 each, less 25% trade discount.

„ 12. Returned to Smith's Cycle Co., 1 "Speedwell" bicycle as faulty.

„ 16. Cash sales, paid to bank, £32.

„ 16. Sold to F. Logan, 10 "Rapid" bicycles at £16 each.

„ 17. Paid Smith's Cycle Co., their account by cheque, less 5% cash discount.

„ 18. Bought from T. Lawrence, 12 "Rapid" bicycles at £15 each, less 25% trade discount, and accessories and sundries, £120.

„ 20. Sold to M. Lewis, accessories, £45; bicycles £155.

„ 20. Bought typewriter for office from Roland Typewriter Company, £36.

„ 24. Cash sales to date £68, paid £40 direct to bank.

„ 24. Drew cash for private use, £30.

„ 28. M. Lewis paid his account by cheque, less 2½% cash discount.

„ 31. Repaid £100 of loan from bank.

„ 31. Bank charged interest on loan, £11.

„ 31. Stock on hand valued at £390.

Journal

19..			£	£
Dec. 1	Cash in hand	C.B.	5	
	Cash at bank	C.B.	340	
	Stock	3	480	
	M. Lewis .. .. .. Dr.	17	40	
	Smith's Cycle Co.	14		20
	T. Lawrence	15		10
	Capital, M. Redman	1		835
			£865	£865
	being assets and liabilities at this date.			
Dec. 20	Furniture and Fittings Account Dr.	5	36	
	Roland Typewriter Co.	16		36
	for typewriter purchased for office			

Note:—Closing Entries have been omitted from the Journal, as they are rarely entered in practice.

Purchases Day Book

19.. Dec. 10 „ 18	Smith's Cycle Co. .. .. T. Lawrence	14 15	£ 72 255
		6	£327

Purchases Returns Book

19.. Dec. 12	Smith's Cycle Co.: 1 "Speedwell" bicycle at £15 .. *less* 25% trade discount—faulty ..	14	£ 16 4	£ 12
		6		£12

Sales Day Book

19.. Dec. 16 „ 20	F. Logan.. .. .. M. Lewis	18 17	£ 160 200
		7	£360

	Trial Balance	*Dr.*	*Cr.*
19.. Dec. 31	Cash in hand	£ 10	£
	Cash at bank	261	
	Capital		835
	Drawings	30	
	Stock	480	
	Premises	3000	
	Furniture and fittings	66	
	Purchases	315	
	Sales		520
	General expenses	18	
	Stationery and printing	3	
	Loan Account		2700
	Interest	11	
	Discount received		4
	Discount allowed	6	
	T. Lawrence		265
	Roland Typewriter Co.		36
	F. Logan..	160	
		£4360	£4360

Cash Book

Dr.

Date	Particulars	Fo.	Discount	Cash	Bank
19..			£	£	£
Dec. 1	Balance	J.		5	340
" 1	Loan from bank	10			2800
" 3	Bank	✓		10	
" 8	Cash sales	7			60
" 16	"	7			32
" 24	"	7			40
" 28	M. Lewis	17	6	28	234
			£6	£43	£3506
			L13		
19..					
Jan. 1	Balances brought down	✓		10	261

Cr.

Date	Particulars	Fo.	Discount	Cash	Bank
19..			£	£	£
Dec. 2	Premises	4			3000
" 2	Fixtures and fittings	5			30
" 3	Removal expenses	8			18
" 3	Office cash	✓			10
" 3	Stationery and printing	9		3	
" 17	Smith's Cycle Co.	4	4		76
" 24	Drawings	2		30	
" 31	Bank, part loan repaid	10			100
" 31	Interest on loan	11			11
" 31	Balances carried down			10	261
			£4	£43	£3506
			L12		

Dr.   **Capital Account**   **Cr.**

19..			£	19..			£
Dec. 31	Drawings	J	30	Dec. 1	Balance ..	J.	835
„ 31	Balance ..	c/d	886	„ 31	Net Profit	J.	81
			£916				£916
				Jan. 1	Balance ..	b/d	886

2

Dr.   **Drawings**   **Cr.**

19..			£	19..			£
Dec. 24	Cash ..	C.B.	30	Dec. 31	Transfer to Capital A/c. ..	J.	30

3

Dr.   **Stock Account**   **Cr.**

19..			£	19..			£
Dec. 1	Balance ..	J.	480	Dec. 31	Transfer to Trading A/c. ..	J.	480
Jan. 1	Trading A/c. ..	J.	390				

4

Dr.   **Premises**   **Cr.**

19..			£	19..			£
Dec. 2	Cash ..	C.B.	3000				

5

Dr.   **Furniture, Fixtures, and Fittings**   **Cr.**

19..			£	19..			£
Dec. 2	Cash ..	C.B.	30	Dec. 31	Balance ..		66
„ 20	Typewriter Co. ..	J.	36				
			£66				£66
Jan. 1	Balance ..	b/d	66				

6

Dr.   **Purchases Account**   **Cr.**

19..			£	19..			£
Dec. 31	Sundries— by Pur- chase Day Book	P.B.	327	Dec. 31	Returns ..	R.B.	12
				„ 31	Transfer to Trading		
				327	A/c. ..	J.	315
			£327				£327

7

Dr.				Sales Account			Cr.
19..			£	19..			£
Dec. 31	Transfer to Trading A/c. ..	J.	520	Dec. 8 ,, ,, 24 ,, 31	Cash sales ,, ,, ,, ,, Sundries— by Sales Day Book	C.B. C.B. C.B. S.B.	60 32 68 360
			£520				£520

8

Dr.				General Expenses			Cr.
19..			£	19..			£
Dec. 3	Cash— removal expenses	C.B.	18	Dec. 31	Transfer to Profit & Loss A/c.	J.	18

9

Dr.				Stationery and Printing			Cr.
19..			£	19..			£
Dec. 3	Cash ..	C.B.	3	Dec. 31	Transfer to Profit & Loss A/c.	J.	3

10

Dr.				Bank Loan Account			Cr.
19..			£	19..			£
Dec. 31	Cash ..	C.B.	100	Dec. 1	Bank ..	C.B.	2800
,, 31	Balance ..	c/d	2700				
			£2800				£2800
				Jan. 1	Balance	b/d	2700

11

Dr.				Interest on Loan			Cr.
19..			£	19..			£
Dec. 31	Cash ..	C.B.	11	Dec. 31	Transfer to Profit & Loss A/c.	J.	11

12

Dr.			£			Discounts Received		Cr.	£
19..					19..				
Dec. 31	Transfer to Profit & Loss A/c.	J.	4		Dec. 31	Sundries ..	C.B.		4

13

Dr.			£			Discounts Allowed		Cr.	£
19..					19..				
Dec. 31	Sundries ..	C.B.	6			Transfer to Profit & Loss A/c.	J.		6

14

Dr.			£			Smith's Cycle Company		Cr.	£
19..					19..				
Dec. 12	Returns ..	PRB.	12		Dec. 1	Balance ..	J.		20
,, 17	Cash ..	C.B.	76		,, 10	Goods ..	P.B.		72
,, 17	Discount	C.B.	4						
			£92						£92

15

Dr.			£			T. Lawrence		Cr.	£
19..					19..				
Dec. 31	Balance ..	c/d	265		Dec. 1	Balance ..	J.		10
					,, 18	Goods ..	P.B.		255
			£265						£265
					Jan. 1	Balance ..	b/d		265

Dr.			£			Roland Typewriter Company		Cr.	£
19..					19..				
					Dec. 20	Furniture and fittings ..	J.		36

17

Dr.			£			M. Lewis		Cr.	£
19..					19..				
Dec. 1	Balance ..	J.	40		Dec. 28	Cash ..	C.B.		234
,, 20	Goods ..	S.B.	200		,, 28	Discount..	C.B.		6
			£240						£240

18
Dr.				F. Logan			*Cr.*
19..				£	19..		£
Dec. 16	Goods	..	S.B.	160			

Trading Account 19
Dr. for the month ending 31st December, 19.. *Cr.*

	£	£		£
Stock at start ..	480		Sales	520
Purchases ..	315			
	£795			
less Stock at close	390			
		405		
Gross Profit ..		115		
		£520		£520

Profit and Loss Account 20
Dr. for the month ending 31st December, 19.. *Cr.*

	£		£
General expenses ..	18	Gross Profit	115
Stationery	3	Discount received ..	4
Interest	11		
Discount allowed ..	6		
Net Profit to Capital A/c.	81		
	£119		£119

Balance Sheet
as at 31st December

LIABILITIES		£	£	ASSETS		£
Capital (1 Dec.) ..		835		Premises		3000
add Net Profit.. ..		81		Furniture and fittings ..		66
				Stock		390
		916		Debtors		160
Less drawings ..		30		Cash at bank		261
			886	Cash in hand		10
Bank loan			2700			
Creditors			301			
			£3887			£3887

CHAPTER 15 Dec. 6th.

THE COLUMNAR PETTY CASH BOOK
AND THE IMPREST SYSTEM

The growth of business may increase the pressure of work on the cashier so much that it may become necessary to relieve him of the duty of attending to the expenditure on small items that frequently occur in the ordinary routine of business. Minor expenses such as the cost of telegrams, parcel post, railways and omnibus fares for messengers, small purchases of stationery, and similar items of office expenditure, may be placed in the care of a clerk called the petty cashier. The petty cashier is given a cheque by the general cashier for a sum of money estimated to cover the normal expenditure of this nature during a week or a month. The general cashier posts the amount of the cheque to the credit column of the Bank Account in his Cash Book. The petty cashier enters the same sum on the debit side of the account he keeps in his Petty Cash Book. The Petty Cash Book thus contains a Ledger Account of petty expenses separated from the Ledger in a similar way that the main Cash Book is separated from the Ledger.

The expenditure of the petty cash is recorded on the credit side of the Petty Cash Account. Periodically, usually weekly or monthly, the debit aspect of these credit entries are posted to the respective expense accounts in the Ledger to complete the double entry. The Petty Cash Account is balanced at the same time, and the balance indicates the amount of cash the petty cashier should have in hand.

The Petty Cash Book contains, therefore, a cash account in simple form, but relating only to the petty expenses occurring in the office.

The Columnar Petty Cash Book

If certain items of expenditure on the credit side of the Petty Cash Book recur frequently many repetitive postings have to be made to the Ledger Expense Accounts. There may be, for example, a dozen instances during a week of the payment of messengers' fares. It would be an economy of labour to post the week's total for this item to the Travelling Expenses Account in the Ledger, as eleven

Petty Cash Book

Receipts	Cash Book Folio	Date	Particulars	Voucher No.	Total Payment	Postages and Telegrams	Cleaning	Stationery	Travelling Expenses	Sundries	Ledger	Ledger Folio
£					£	£	£	£	£	£	£	
10·00	24	19 . . Jan. 1	Cheque									
		,, 1	Postage stamps	1	2·50	2·50						
		,, 2	Travelling expenses—S. Smith, Hastings	2	2·10				2·10			
		,, 3	String and envelopes	3	0·50			0·50				
		,, 5	Clerks' teas	4	0·25					0·25		
		,, 5	Cleaners	5	1·00		1·00					
		,, 6	Telegrams		0·22½	0·22½						
			Letter scales		0·75						0·75	72
			Total		7·32½	2·72½	1·00	0·50	2·10	0·25	0·75	
			Balance, c/d		2·67½							
10·00					£10·00							
2·67½		Jan. 8	Balance, b/d									

entries would be saved.   To follow this out would require the credit side of the Petty Cash Book to be analysed to find the totals of like expenses.   A simple method is to make the analysis progressively as each item is entered.

On page 113 is a specimen page of a Petty Cash Book.   It shows on the debit side the entry of the petty cash received, and on the credit side the expenditure, the amount of each item being entered in the column headed "Totals."   These two columns provide the ordinary debit and credit columns of any Ledger Account. · There are, however, additional money columns on the credit side.   These are added to provide space for a continuous analysis of the entries as they are made, but these additional columns are for memorandum purposes only.   Each column carries its heading, and the headings correspond to the expense accounts in the Ledger.   As an entry is made in the credit column it is repeated in the appropriate analysis column.   The weekly, or monthly, totals of these analysis columns provide the amounts for posting to the expense accounts in the Ledger.   The Ledger folio is entered below each total for reference and as an indication that the posting has been made.   The ordinary debit and credit columns are balanced in the usual way, and the balance carried down to begin the new period.

The analysis columns are, of course, adaptable to the special needs of a business.   How many columns and what the particular headings should be is for experience to decide.   One column headed "Ledger" is useful for the items that are of infrequent occurrence, the appropriate Ledger Account being posted from that column.

The Imprest System

A common procedure is to hand to the petty cashier a cheque for the first sum sufficient to cover the usual petty cash expenditure for a week or a month.   On the Petty Cash Book being checked and posted the petty cashier is given a cheque to re-imburse him for the amount expended during the period.   He therefore starts the next period with the same sum as he started the last.   The procedure is followed week by week, or month by month, as the case may be. This is called the "Imprest" system of petty cash, and may be combined with the columnar method of recording the petty expenditure. In the specimen page (page 113) the starting balance, called the Imprest, is £10.   If during the week the sum of £7·32½ has been expended and at the end of the week the cashier refunds that amount, the balance brought down to begin the next period is again £10.   In these circumstances the Petty Cash Account would appear as below. The analysis columns have been omitted in this illustration as they would be the same as on page 113.

Petty Cash

Receipts	Cash Book Folio	Date	Particulars	Voucher No.	Total Payment
£ 10.00	24	19.. Jan. 1	Cheque		£
		,, 1	Postage stamps ..		2.50
		,, 2	Travelling expenses— ..		
			S. Smith, Hastings ..	1	2.10
		,, 3	String and envelopes ..	2	0.50
		,, 3	Clerks' teas	3	0.25
		,, 5	Cleaners	4	1.00
		,, 5	Telegrams		0.22½
		,, 6	Letter scales	5	0.75
			Total		7.32½
7.32½	26	,, 8	Cheque		
			Balance carried down ..		10.00
17.32½					17.32½
10.00		,, 8	Balance brought down ..		

An alternative method of treating petty cash is to regard the Petty Cash Book as a memorandum book only, and not as a Ledger Account or part of the double entry system. It would then be kept by the petty cashier to record his expenditure for information purposes and as a check on his expenditure. Under this method the Petty Cash Book for the example given above would show no change. What would occur is that the original sum of £10 for Petty Cash would be credited in the Cash Book as usual, but the debit entry would be in a Petty Cash Account in the General Ledger. The expenditure for the week as shown by the Petty Cash Book, would be credited to this account and debited to the respective expense accounts. Then the amount of the "imprest" to reimburse the petty cashier would be credited in the Cash Book and debited to the Petty Cash Account. This account is then closed and the balance carried down for the next weekly period.

In either case the balance of petty cash in hand should not be overlooked when a Trial Balance is extracted.

Vouchers

The petty cashier should be instructed that bills must be obtained for all payments and, if bills are not available, as in the case of travelling expenses, the recipient should sign a petty cash voucher or slip acknowledging receipt of the sum. The Petty Cash Book is usually checked against the vouchers, and the balance in hand inspected at the end of each week or month at the time of reimbursement of the amount expended.

EXERCISES 15

1. Write up a Petty Cash Book from the following particulars, and balance the book so that it will be ready for the cashier:—

Jan. 16. Cash in hand, £10.
„ 17. Parcel to Bradford, £0·08; stamps, £1; coke, £1·25.
„ 18. Bus fares, £0·06; repairs to typewriter, £0·90.
„ 19. Labels, £0·25; packing paper, £0·80.
„ 20. Goods by rail, £0·45; string, £0·07; window cleaning, £0·40.

N.C.T.E.C.

2. (*a*) What is the use of the Petty Cash Book?

(*b*) Enter the following in the Petty Cash Book, using separate columns for— (1) Postages and telegrams; (2) Carriage; (3) Stationery.

Balance the book as at 10th January.

		£
Jan. 4.	Balance in hand	15·00
„ 4.	Paid for postage stamps	1·50
„ 5.	Paid for stationery	3·50
„ 5.	Paid for carriage	0·52½
„ 6.	Paid for postage stamps	1·25
„ 7.	Paid for telegrams..	0·15
„ 7.	Paid for carriage	0·17½
„ 8.	Paid for stationery	1·50
„ 8.	Received from the chief cashier	8·60

U.L.C.I.

3. Rule a suitable Petty Cash Book with analysis columns for Postage and Telegrams, Stationery, Travelling Expenses, Carriage, and Sundry Office Expenses, and enter the following transactions:—

July 1. Petty cash balance in hand, £3.
        Received £3 cash to make Imprest up to £6.
„ 2. Paid 'bus fares, £0·04; telegrams, £0·32½; ink, £0·10.
„ 3. Paid parcel post charges, £0·70; railway fares, £0·75.
„ 4. Bought stamps, £0·50; paid window cleaner, £0·25.
„ 5. Paid telegrams, £0·15; office cleaner's wages, £2·00.
„ 6. Paid telegrams, £0·35; parcel post, £0·10; railway fares, £0·40.

Show the balance in hand on 6th July.

4. Explain shortly the working of the Imprest Petty Cash System. Give as an illustration a ruling (with three analysis columns), and enter therein the following items:—

			£
Jan.	1.	Balance in hand (float)	20·00
„	5.	Paid for postage stamps..	1·50
„	7.	„ „ telegrams	0·52½
„	10.	„ „ office tea, etc.	0·95
„	14.	„ „ sundry cash purchases of goods for re-sale	8·37½
„	20.	„ „ stationery	1·12
„	23.	„ „ parcel post	0·20
„	30.	„ „ subscription to trade periodical	2·10
„	31.	Received reimbursement for the month's expenditure, to restore the float.	*R.S.A.*

5. On 21st February, 19.., you are given a petty cash Imprest of £15 out of which to pay small expenses during the week. Write up a Petty Cash Book (no analysis columns required) showing (*a*) the Imprest received on 21st February, (*b*) four items of expenditure made during the week, amounting in all to £8·60, and (*c*) the amount added to the petty cash balance on 28th February, 19 .. Rule off and bring down the balance.   *R.S.A.*

6. Enter the following transactions in a Petty Cash Book, having analysis columns for Postages, Telegrams, Office Stationery, Travelling Expenses, Office Expenses.

Keep the book on the Imprest system, the amount of the Imprest being £5.

July 1.   Received from cashier for petty cash, £5.
„   1.   Paid taxi fares, £0·25; window cleaner, £0·30.
„   2.   Bought postage stamps, £0·75; string, £0·10.
„   3.   Paid parcel post, £0·10; telegram, £0·09.
„   4.   Bought envelopes, £0·50; nibs, £0·07.
„   5.   Paid 'bus fares £0·05; telegrams, £0·15.
„   6.   Bought ink, £0·10; typewriter erasers, £0·06; paid office cleaner, £2.

Balance the Book as on 6th July, carry down the balance, and continue.

July 8.   Received cheque from cashier to make up the Imprest.
„   8.   Bought shorthand notebooks, £0·05.
„   9.   Paid parcel post, £0·20; telegram, £0·12½.
„   10.   Paid railway fares, £0·60; telegrams, £0·30.
„   11.   Bought postage stamps, £0·75; paid 'bus fares, £0·05.
„   12.   Paid parcel post, £0·20; taxi fare, £0·25.
„   13.   Paid office cleaner, £1; 'bus fares, £0·05; telegram, £0·15.

Balance the Petty Cash Book as on 13th July, and carry down the balance.

7. Rule a Petty Cash Book with four analysis columns for Postages and Stationery, Travelling Expenses, Carriage, and Office Expenses, and enter up the following transactions. The book is kept on the Imprest system, the amount of the Imprest being £10.

Jan. 4.   Petty cash in hand, £1·50.
      Received cash to make up the Imprest.
      Bought stamps, £1·50.
.,   5.   Paid railway fares, £0·19, 'bus fares, £0·10; telegrams, £0·30.
      Bought shorthand notebooks for office, £0·50.

Jan. 6. Paid carriage on small parcels, £0·27½; railway fares, £0·25; bought envelopes, £0·62½

„   8. Paid for repairs to typewriter, £0·52½; paid carrier's account for December, £1·28.

„   8. Paid office cleaner, £1·20.

Balance the Petty Cash Book as on 9th January, 19.., and bring down the balance.   *R.S.A.*

CHAPTER 16

CHECKING THE BANK BALANCE. BANK RECONCILIATION STATEMENTS

Usually most, if not all, of a firm's cash is at the bank. The amount of cash there may be ascertained from two sources; either from the balance of the Bank Account in the Cash Book or from the Bank Statement. The one is the office record from the firm's point of view of dealings with the bank cash; the other is the bank's own record. These records should correspond, or if they do not, it should be a simple matter to account for the disagreement. The Statement is obtained from the bank at regular intervals for checking purposes to ensure that no error has crept into either the Cash Book or the Bank Statement, but it is not unusual for the Cash Book and Bank Statement balances to disagree. The disagreement arises from a difference in procedure. The Cash Book is entered up daily so that within a few hours of the posting of a cheque to pay an account or of the payment into the banking account of the day's receipts, the entries relating to these transactions have been made. The bank, however, is not aware that its customer's account is affected until a cheque is presented to it for payment, and amounts paid into bank may not immediately be credited to the customer's account in the bank's Ledger.

The balance in hand as shown by the Bank Statement may, therefore, at times, not agree with the balance as shown by the Cash Book for the following reasons:—

(1) Cheques drawn and entered in the Cash Book may not have been presented to the bank for payment.

(2) Cheques paid into the bank and entered to the debit of the Bank Account in the Cash Book have not been entered into the account in the bank's Ledger and, therefore, are not shown in the Bank Statement.

The following illustration should make these points clear.

Example 18.—At 31st December the balance at bank as shown by the Cash Book was £207, whereas the Bank Statement showed a balance of £217.

The items in the Bank Statement are usually called over against the Cash Book, and the items not ticked in the Cash Book are those which do not appear in the Bank Statement. The latter items appear in the Cash Book as below—

Cash Book
(Bank Columns Only)

19..		£	19..		£
Dec. 31	P. Johnson ..	10	Dec. 29	P. Jackson ..	15
			,, 30	P. Thompson..	5

Jackson's and Thompson's cheques, entered in the Cash Book as paid to them, have not yet been presented by them to the bank for payment. The bank, therefore, has at the moment £20 more on this account than is shown by the Cash Book.

Johnson's cheque was paid into the bank but had not yet been entered in the account in the banker's Ledger by the date to which the Bank Statement is made up. The bank balance as shown by the Bank Statement is therefore £10 less in respect of this item than the Cash Book shows.

Within a day or so the two cheques may be presented for payment, and the bank will be able to record in the Bank Statement the payments to Thompson and Jackson.

At any time it may be necessary to reconcile the Cash Book and Bank Statement balances. It is especially necessary at the close of a trading period and, as a record of the reasons for the apparent discrepancy between the balances, a statement showing the reasons is made in the Cash Book similar to the one below—

Reconciliation Statement
of Cash Book and Bank Statement Balances
31st December, 19..

		£
Bank Statement balance		217
Deduct Cheques not yet presented—		
P. Jackson £15		
P. Thompson £5		20
		197
Add Cheque not yet credited— ..		
P. Johnson £10		10
Cash Book balance		£207

Sometimes the difference between the balances is partly attributable to items appearing in the Bank Statement, such as bank charges for certain services, which have not been entered in the Cash Book. These points are discussed in the next chapter.

When there are items such as bank charges, receipt by the bank of dividends, and payments by the bank on standing orders, in the Bank Statement but not in the Cash Book they can be dealt with by adding back the bank charges and payments on standing orders to the balance as shown by the Bank Statement and deducting any dividends received by the bank and not yet entered in the Cash Book. It is, however, a better and more practical procedure to correct the Cash Book balance by entering these items in the Cash Book and ascertaining a corrected balance. A Bank Reconciliation Statement can then be made reconciling the corrected balance with the balance as shown on the Bank Statement. This is illustrated in the following example.

Example 19. On 31st December 19.. the balance at bank as shown by the Cash Book was £517, whereas the Bank Statement showed a credit balance of £567. Comparison of the Cash Book with the Bank Statement showed the following discrepancies.

	£
(i) Cheques drawn and not yet presented for payment ..	214
(ii) Cheques paid into bank on 31st December and not appearing in the Bank Statement	196
(iii) Items shown in the Bank Statement but not yet entered in the Cash Book:—	
Bank charges	4
Payment of insurance premium on 2nd December on bank standing order	26
Dividends collected by the bank	62

Enter the items shown under (iii) in the Cash Book to show a correct cash book balance and then prepare a Bank Reconciliation Statement.

Cash Book

			£					£
Dec. 31	Balance ..		517	Dec. 2	Insurance ..			26
	Dividends		62		Bank charges			4
					Balance ..	c/d		549
			£579					£579
„ 31	Balance ..	b/d	549					

Bank Reconciliation Statement
31st December 19. .

	£	£	£
Balance as Bank Statement	567		
add cheques paid in and not yet credited ..	196	763	
less cheques drawn and not yet presented for payment		214	549

EXERCISES 16

1. Draw up a Bank Reconciliation Statement from the following particulars:

	£
Cash at bank as shown by the Bank Statement on June 30th	293
Cheques drawn and entered in the Cash Book, but not yet presented for payment	54
Cheques paid into bank, but not entered in the Bank Statement	72
The debit balance of the Bank Account in the Cash Book was ..	311

2. From the following particulars draw up a Bank Reconciliation Statement:—

	£
Dec. 31. Bank Statement balance at bank	142
,, ,, Cash Book balance at bank	214
Cheques drawn and entered in the Cash Book, but not presented for payment..	32
Cheques received and paid into bank, but not yet entered in the Bank Statement	104

3. F. Smith's Cash Book showed a balance of cash at bank of £327·95 on December 31st. His Bank Statement showed an overdraft of £267·89 on that date. The difference arose as follows:—

A cheque for £32·94, drawn by F. Smith, had not been presented for payment; £616·40, received on December 31st, was not credited by the bank until January 1st; the bank had charged him £12·38 interest, which was not entered in the Cash Book.

Prepare the Reconciliation Statement. *R.S.A.*

4. On 30th June, 19. ., D. L's Cash Book showed a debit balance of £393·40 in the Bank Account. The Bank Statement of the same date showed a credit balance of £689·55.

On comparing the Cash Book with the Bank Statement the following differences were found.

(i) Cheques £76·45 had been paid into bank on 30th June but were not credited by the bank until the following day.

(ii) Cheques £284·35 had been drawn but not yet presented for payment.

(iii) Bank charges £5·50 appeared on the Bank Statement but not in the Cash Book.

(iv) A standing order £5 to Trade Protection Society, payable on 24th June had been paid by the bank but not entered in the Cash Book.

(v) Dividends £98·75 collected and credited by the bank did not appear in the Cash Book.

(*a*) Make additional entries in the Cash Book to show the balance which it should have shown on 30th June 1963.

Then

(*b*) Prepare a Bank Reconciliation Statement as on 30th June, 19...

A.E.B. G.C.E. "O" Level.

5. On 31st May, 19.., the debit balance in J. Carr & Sons Bank Account as shown in the Cash Book was £370·40. The Bank Statement at that date showed a credit balance of £409·50.

On checking the Bank Statement against the Cash Book the following differences were found:—

(*a*) Interest due on Westshire County Council Loan £36·75 had been collected by the bank during the month but not entered in the Cash Book.

(*b*) A standing order £12·85 payable each 20th May for fire insurance premiums had been paid by the bank but not entered in the Cash Book.

(*c*) Two cheques drawn on 30th May and entered in the Cash Book, one for £16·35 and one for £84·22 had not yet been presented for payment.

(*d*) On 31st May a cheque for £85·37 had been entered in the Cash Book and paid into bank after the Bank Statement had been collected from the bank.

Show your calculation of the balance that should appear in the Cash Book and then prepare a Bank Reconciliation Statement.

A.E.B. G.C.E. "O" Level.

CHAPTER 17 Dec 16th.

VARIOUS BANKING MATTERS

References to a banking account usually mean the tradesman's current account with a bank. The bank accepts the loan of money from its customer, but is liable to be called upon to repay all or part on demand. The cheque is the form that the demand takes, and the bank may be ordered by cheque to repay the owner or to pay a sum to a third person. Because of this liability for repayment on demand, banks do not as a rule allow interest on the balances on current accounts. If they do allow interest, then a charge is made for the services rendered in connection with the account. A customer may, however, have a balance at the bank larger than he is likely to need for use in the immediate future. To withdraw this temporary excess and to invest it in shares or other securities might be more profitable from an interest-bearing point of view, but the sum is not then immediately available should it be required. In such cases the customer may ask the bank to transfer a certain sum from the current account to a deposit account. The sum so placed "on deposit" cannot be withdrawn on demand but only after the expiration of an agreed length of notice. The bank is willing to grant interest for sums placed to deposit accounts, as it has the use of the customer's money for a definite period. The usual length of notice of withdrawal is 14 days, but the customer may agree to give longer notice, say, one month, in which case the bank may grant a slightly higher rate of interest.

Interest on deposit accounts varies from time to time, but is fixed by agreement between bankers at 2 per cent. below the Bank Rate, except when this is $2\frac{1}{2}$ per cent. or lower. The Bank Rate is the Bank of England's minimum rate of discount for first class bills of exchange.

The Bank Account in the Cash Book is the trader's current account at the bank. If he asks for a sum to be transferred from his current account to a deposit account an entry must be made in the Cash Book as his current account is affected, and a new account, the Deposit Account, must be opened in the Ledger to keep a record of the dealings with the amounts placed on deposit.

124

Example 20.—M. Redman's balance on current account at the bank at 1st January, 19.., is £800. He arranges for £500 to be placed on deposit.

Cash Book
(Bank columns only)

Dr.					Cr.

19.. Jan. 1	Balance ..	b/d	£ 800	19.. Jan. 1	Deposit Account ..	34	£ 500

In the Ledger the record will appear as follows:—

Deposit Account   34
(London Bank Limited)

Dr.							Cr.

19.. Jan. 1	Cash ..	C.B.	£ 500	19..			£

Example 21.—M. Redman gives notice of withdrawal of £500 on deposit to expire 1st July.

The entries for this will be the reverse of those shown above. Credit the Deposit Account in the Ledger, and debit the Bank Account in the Cash Book, as the bank will place that sum again in the current account where it will be available to be drawn on by cheque.

Interest on Deposit

Assuming that the deposit rate of interest is 2 per cent. per annum, and is payable half-yearly, Redman, in the above example, becomes entitled to £5 for interest on £500 for six months.

The bank pays this to Redman by crediting £5 to his account, thereby increasing his balance on current account by that amount. It will be noted by the bank in the Bank Statement, and that will be the first intimation to Redman of it.

Entries must be made in respect of it in Redman's books, so on finding the entry in the Bank Statement, it is entered to the debit of the Cash Book and credited to a new account, headed *Interest on Deposit Account* as a gain. It is not credited to the Deposit Account in the Ledger as that is a record only of the capital sum. The balance of the Interest on Deposit Account is transferred at the close of the trading period to the credit of Profit and Loss Account.

Interest on deposit being entered in the Bank Statement and not being shown in the Cash Book may be one of the reasons for non-agreement of the Bank Statement and Cash Book bank balances.

If so, it will be shown in the Reconciliation Statement, but it is seldom that the necessity arises, as the Cash Book is usually kept open until the amount of interest is known.

Bank Loans and Overdrafts

Traders sometimes require larger sums of money than they at the moment possess to finance business deals or to tide them over difficult periods of trading. They may, in such circumstances, have resort to their bankers and ask for the financial accommodation that they require. As the banker makes his profits largely from the interest on advances made to customers, he is usually willing to help, provided adequate security is given for repayment. Bankers' advances take the form of loans or overdrafts. A loan is the advance of a fixed sum to a customer for a definite period. The banker's procedure is to place the amount of the loan to the customer's current account and to open a Loan Account for the customer in the bank's Ledger. The customer's current account balance is thereby increased by the amount of the loan, and can be drawn upon by cheque. The trader will record the loan in his own books by debiting the Cash Book with the amount, and by crediting a "Loan from Banker's Account" in his Ledger; the entries on repayment being the reverse of these.

Interest is charged on the full amount of the loan whether all or only part is withdrawn from the current account. Such interest is a bank charge, and the bank recoups itself by entering the amount of the interest in the customer's account, thereby reducing the bank balance by that sum. The trader credits his Bank Account in the Cash Book with the interest, and debits the amount to an Interest on Loan Account or Bank Charges Account for transfer eventually to the Profit and Loss Account.

In other cases a trader may find it preferable to obtain permission to overdraw his account as a temporary expedient. A limit is fixed by the bank to the amount by which the account may be overdrawn.

Every business has certain weekly and monthly outgoings such as wages and salaries to meet. The income may come spasmodically though in total it is ample to cover all commitments. In such cases a standing permission to overdraw up to a certain limit is a definite advantage for which interest is willingly paid.

No special entries are required to record an overdraft—it happens as and when more is paid out by the bank than is to the customer's credit.

In the illustration below, there is on Jan. 1 a bank balance of £100. Payment by cheque of £300 to J. Jones immediately puts the trader in debt to the bank for £200. That is the overdraft. Note that the balance representing the overdraft appears on the opposite side of the account to which the normal bank balance appears. The overdraft is shown as a liability in the Balance Sheet, and there is no bank balance among the assets.

Cash Book

Dr.						(Bank columns only)				Cr.
19..				£	19..					£
Jan. 1	Balance	..	b/d	100	Jan. 3	J. Jones	..			300
,, 4	Balance over-									
	draft)	..	c/d	200						
				£300						£300
					,, 4	Balance	..	b/d		200

The trader having an overdraft at the time of balancing his books, starts the new period with a credit entry in the bank columns. Any cheques received and paid into the bank will automatically reduce the overdraft, and any further cheques paid out will increase it.

The bank charges interest on the varying balance only, deducting it as in the case of interest on loans. The trader makes the entries for the interest charged by a credit entry in his Cash Book, and a debit entry in the Bank Charges or Interest on Overdraft Account.

When a bank makes an advance by loan or overdraft it usually requires from its customer some form of security for repayment. The bank may be satisfied with the guarantee of a third person or the customer may assign a life assurance policy, or deposit with the bank share or stock certificates or debentures. In other cases the customer may deposit the title deeds to land or shipping documents of title to goods, such as Bills of Lading. Securities so deposited are termed collateral security for the overdraft or loan, but the bank takes no action to realise their value except in the event of the customer being in default.

Bank Charges

Banks make charges for certain services, some of which are referred to in later chapters. The bank usually pays itself by entering the charge against the customer's account, and shows the amount in the customer's Bank Statement. In addition, therefore, to the need to examine the Bank Statement periodically to check its accuracy, there is the need to ensure that all entries of this nature appearing in the Bank Statement are duly entered in the accounts. One simple charge which may be mentioned is that for cheque stamps. When a cheque book containing, say, 100 cheques is obtained from the bank, there will be an entry in the Bank Statement of £1 charged for the penny stamps on the cheques. This should be credited to the Bank Account, and debited to an appropriate expense account such as Bank Charges, or General Expenses.

Bankers' Credit Transfers

Instead of drawing individual cheques for each creditor a trader may supply his banker with a list of creditors to be paid together with the name and branch of the bank at which each creditor keeps his account. Credit Transfer Slips or Credit Transfer Schedules will be supplied by the banker for this purpose. The banker will then arrange to transfer the appropriate amounts to the banks named, to be credited to the account of the creditor and will inform the trader when this is done. The trader gives the bank one cheque to cover the total amount.

This system is a great convenience to traders who, instead of drawing and posting numerous cheques, simply supply the bank with a list of payments to be made. It is, of course, necessary for the trader to know the bank at which his creditor keeps his account, but it is becoming increasingly the custom to give this information on Invoices and Statements of Account to facilitate payment by this method. Credit Transfer Slips for the use of debtors may be incorporated as a detachable part of an invoice.

The banker makes a charge for his services which will be included in the bank charges appearing on the trader's Bank Statement. Banks are also willing to undertake this service for non-customers at a charge of £0·02½ per transfer. These transfers are made through the machinery of the Bankers' Clearing House, but if a transfer must be made very quickly, the banker is willing to arrange such a transfer direct to a creditor's account at a charge of £0·12½ per transfer.

When a trader adopts this method of payment the total amount transferred by the bank will appear as a single item on the Bank Statement. The trader may enter it also in his Cash Book as a single total, keeping a separate list of amounts paid to each creditor and post the relevant amounts from this list to the debit side of each creditor's account. Alternatively, the trader may enter in his Cash

Book the names of all creditors who have been paid, with the amounts paid to each creditor, in the "Details" column of his Cash Book and the total amount paid, corresponding to the amount on the Bank Statement, in the "Bank" column.

EXERCISES 17

1. M. F. Ford is in business trading in china and glassware. On 1st June his financial position was as follows:—

	£
Cash in hand	15
Bank overdraft	250
Stock	1400
Debtors—	
J. Austin	70
T. Rover	78
Creditors—	
K. Lanchester	90
M. Riley	80
Fixtures and fittings	200

extract. the Cash Book.

Open Ford's books to record his position and enter the following transactions:—

June 1. Sold glassware for cash, £40, and paid takings into bank.
„ 3. Paid in cash, wages, £10; sundry expenses, £2.
„ 5. Sold to W. Morris, china, £50.
„ 7. Bought from M. Riley, china and glass invoiced at £50, less 10% trade discount.
„ 8. J. Austin paid his account by cheque, deducting 5% cash discount.
„ 10. Cashed cheque for £25 and paid in cash, wages, £10.
„ 15. Sold for cash, £12, unwanted shop fittings.
„ 17. Paid K. Lanchester's account by cheque less 5% cash discount.
„ 19. Cash sales, paid into bank, £84.

Take out Trial Balance.

Prepare Trading and Profit and Loss Accounts and a Balance Sheet as at 19th June. Stock on hand at that date was valued at £1,325.

2. M. Gardiner's position on 14th June was as below:—

	£
Cash in hand	25
Cash at bank	1050
Stock	1500
Debtors—	
C. Smart	50
R. Sharp	40
Creditor—	
J. Cutler	70
Capital	2595

extract. the Cash.

Open M. Gardiner's books to record his position, and enter the following transactions:—

June 15. Obtained loan from bank of £3,000 at 6% per annum to assist in purchase of business premises.
„ 18. Purchased new premises, paying by cheque £3,800.
„ 20. Bought fittings on credit from Mint & Co., £150.

June 21. Paid cost of removal of stock, etc., to new premises by cheque, £20.
„ 30. Paid wages in cash, £10.
„ 30. Cash takings, paid to bank, £133.
„ 30. Bank charged interest on loan, £7.

Take out Trial Balance. Prepare Trading and Profit and Loss Accounts, and a Balance Sheet as at 30th June. Stock on hand at that date, £1,400.

3. From the following Trial Balance of A. Dealer, prepare Trading and Profit and Loss Accounts for the year ended 31st December, 19.., and Balance Sheet as at that date.

The stock on hand at 31st December was valued at £570.

Trial Balance. 31st December, 19..

	£	£
Purchases	5585	
Stock (1st January)	650	
Carriage on sales	40	
Discounts allowed	145	
Bank interest and charges	15	
Sales		7000
Returns outwards		138
Discounts received		162
Returns inwards	137	
Bank overdraft ..		344
Rent and rates ..	193	
Sundry debtors and creditors ..	680	366
A. Dealer—Capital		415
A. Dealer—Drawings ..	450	
Cash in hand	55	
Salaries ..	475	
	£8425	£8425

U.L.C.I.

4. State, very briefly, the object of preparing:—

(*a*) A Trial Balance.
(*b*) A Trading Account.
(*c*) A Profit and Loss Account.
(*d*) A Balance Sheet.

R.S.A.

5. The Balance Sheet of J. Abbots, a wireless dealer, was:—

Balance Sheet. December 31st, 19..

	£	£		£	£
Sundry Creditors—			Cash in hand	41	
J. Gibbs ..		78	Cash at bank	275	316
Loan from S. Roberts		200			
Capital, Jan. 1st ..	3400		*Sundry Debtors—*		
Add Profit for year ..	167	3567	R. Wright.. ..	19	
			T. Tomkins ..	27	46
			Stock		412
			Fixtures and fittings ..		121
			Premises	3000	
			Less Depreciation written off ..	50	2950
		£3845			£3845

His order book shows that during January 19.. he ordered and received delivery on credit of the following goods for re-sale:—

Jan. 3. From A. Robbins, 5 "Excel" loud-speakers at £4 each, less 10% trade discount.

„ 12. From B. Fearn & Co. Ltd., batteries, value £22.

„ 26. From Wireless Supplies Ltd., 2 radiogram sets at £48 each.

His other transactions during January were:—

Jan. 18. Sold for cash, £6, one of the loud-speakers received on 3rd January. Found one of the remaining four loud-speakers faulty, and returned it to Robbins.

„ 19. R. Wright paid by cheque the amount owing by him, less 5% cash discount, which was allowed.

„ 20. Paid by cheque to S. Roberts, a half-year's interest at 6% on the loan from him.

„ 28. Purchased new fixtures for use in shop and paid for them by cheque, £24.

„ 31. Received on account £14 by cheque from Tomkins. Paid sundry expenses in cash, £5.

You are required to open a set of books for Abbots, and record therein his position on 1st January, 19.., and his transactions for January, using proper subsidiary books to enter the transactions and posting from these to the Ledger. Balance the accounts, and draw up a Trial Balance on 31st January.

University of London General School Examination.

CHAPTER 18 *Dec. 14th.*

PROVISION FOR DEPRECIATION

The necessity for careful scrutiny of the items of the Balance Sheet in order that it may present a correct view of the financial position has already been emphasised. One of the essential points to note is the value at which the fixed assets appear. Premises, machinery, furniture, and fittings are all acquired for use in the course of business, and in the nature of things, wastage and wear occurs. Such deterioration leads to a fall in the monetary value of the asset, and should be taken into consideration when the statement of monetary values, that is, the Balance Sheet, is prepared.

Each asset must be considered separately as the nature of the assets and the use to which they are put vary considerably. The depreciation, as the fall in value is termed, is caused by the asset being put to use for productive purposes, and is part of the cost of production. An effort is therefore made to estimate the proportion of the monetary value of the asset that has been used up, both for the purpose of valuing the asset and to take it into account in arriving at the profits for the period. In general, the useful or "working" life of the asset is estimated, and the total fall in value is spread over such period. In every case the depreciation is made a charge against profits, and the asset is shown at the revised value in the Balance Sheet.

The question of depreciation is usually considered at the close of a trading period after the Trial Balance has been extracted and before the preparation of the Final Accounts. A credit entry is made in the asset account for the depreciation so that the balance of the account is the new figure at which the asset stands. The debit entry is made in a Depreciation Account, the balance of which is transferred to the Profit and Loss Account.

The main causes of depreciation are wear and tear in use, effluxion or passage of time, and obsolescence. Machinery and plant, loose tools, furniture and fittings, and delivery vans are examples of assets which lose value from wear and tear. Leases of premises become less valuable as the lease shortens, and patents and copyrights diminish in value as the date of expiration of the rights grows nearer, while machines become obsolete as new and more efficient machinery is invented and is brought into use.

Dr.			Office Furniture					Cr.
19.. Jan. 1	Cash ..	C.B.	£ 200	19.. Dec. 31	Depreciation Balance ..	c/d	£ 20 180
			£200				£200	
19.. Jan. 1	Balance ..	b/d	180					

Dr.			Depreciation Account				Cr.
19.. Dec. 31	Office Furniture ..		£ 20	19.. Dec. 31	Transfer to Profit and Loss A/c.		£ 20

To determine the depreciation the questions to be considered in most cases are:—

(*a*) The original cost of the asset.

(*b*) The probable period of time it will last in use.

(*c*) Its approximate value at the end of its "working life".

The difference between the original cost and the approximate value at the close of its useful life is the wastage in value of the asset that has to be apportioned over the period estimated to be its probable working life.

The Equal Instalment or Straight Line Method

Under this method of charging depreciation the total wastage is estimated and the loss in value is spread by *equal* instalments over the probable working life of the asset.

Example 22.—A machine, costing £1,000, is estimated to have a useful life of 10 years, and to be worth £100 at the end of that period. Depreciation is therefore £900, and is charged against profits by ten equal yearly instalments of £90.

The entries in the books would be—

Journal

19..				£	£
Dec. 31	Depreciation A/c .. .. .. Dr.			90	
	To Machinery Account				90
	being depreciation at £90 per annum.				

Dr.   **Machinery Account**   *Cr.*

19..			£	19..			£
Jan. 1	Balance ..	b/d	1000	Dec. 31	Deprecia-		
					tion A/c.	J.	90
					Balance ..	c/d	910
			£1000				£1000
Jan. 1	Balance ..	b/d	910				

Dr.   **Depreciation Account**   *Cr.*

19..			£	19..		£
Dec. 31	Machinery			Dec. 31	Transfer to	
	A/c. ..	J.	90		Manufac-	
					turing A/c.[1]	90

Some assets, such as patent rights, may have no value at the end of a term of years, and the value of the asset may be completely extinguished by charging against profits annual instalments of the original value as depreciation.

The Diminishing Balance Method

This method is probably more frequently used than the Straight Line Method.   The objection to the latter is that the depreciation is constant in amount whereas the expenses usually incurred for repairs and renewals, especially on plant and machinery, increases as a general rule with the age of the asset.   It follows that as time goes on the depreciation and repairs together make an increasing sum to be charged against revenue.   The Diminishing Balance Method makes the charge for depreciation lighter as the asset ages and repairs become more costly.

The method is to write off a fixed rate per cent. from the diminished annual debit balance of the Asset Account.

[1] See Chapter 19, page 142.

Example 23.—A machine cost £1,000, and stands on the books at that figure. Provide for depreciation at 20% per annum by the diminishing balance method, and show the Machinery Account for three successive years.

Journal

19.. Dec. 31	Depreciation Account .. .. **Dr.** To Machinery Account .. .. being depreciation at 20% per annum on diminishing value.	£ 200	£ 200

Dr.   **Machinery Account**   **Cr.**

Year 1 Jan. 1	Balance ..	b/d	£ 1000	Year 1 Dec. 31	Depreciation A/c. .. Balance ..	c/d	£ 200 800
			£1000				£1000
Year 2 Jan 1	Balance ..	b/d	800	Year 2 Dec. 31	Depreciation A/c. .. Balance ..	c/d	160 640
			£800				£800
Year 3 Jan 1	Balance ..	b/d	640	Year 3 Dec. 31	Depreciation A/c. .. Balance ..	c/d	128 512
			£640				£640
Year 4 Jan. 1	Balance ..	b/d	512				

The Depreciation Account is not shown. By this method the asset will be reduced to the probable value only if the percentage reduction is adequate. In the above example, 20 per cent. will reduce the value to approximately £107 at the end of ten years, and year by year the sums written off diminish.

In some instances additions are made during the year to the machinery or other asset, and the instructions are to provide for depreciation at a given rate. Whichever method of depreciation is adopted the depreciation should be provided for on the final value of the asset after the additions are made. If the instructions refer specifically to the depreciation on the additions during the year such instructions should, of course, be followed.

Periodical Re-valuation

With some assets, such as motor cars, loose tools, canteen crockery, re-valuation is the only satisfactory method of arriving at the depreciation. A valuation is made of the asset as at the Balance Sheet date, and any diminution in value as compared with the cost or former valuation is treated as depreciation.

Loose tools, patterns, and models are often made by a firm's own workmen and for particular jobs. The valuation of the stock of loose tools and patterns at the close of the trading period may show an increase over the value as at the commencement owing to the fact that a larger quantity has been made during the year. The cost of making has been included in the wages and materials, and the stock is continuously being used up and added to so that normal depreciation does not take place. For this reason, whether the value has increased or decreased, the usual practice is to debit the old value and credit the new value to the Trading or Manufacturing Account, which will bring the increase or decrease into account.

Example 24.—Two motor vans, standing on the books at 1st Jan. at £600, are re-valued at 31st December at £440. Show the Motor Vans Account for the year.

Journal

19..		£		£
Dec. 31	Depreciation Account .. .. Dr.	160		
	To Motor Vans Account			160
	being depreciation shown on re-valuation.			

Dr.				Motor Vans			Cr.
19..			£	19..			£
Jan. 1	Balance—Vans at valuation		600	Dec. 31	Depreciation A/c.		160
					Balance	c/d	440
			£600				£600
19..							
Jan. 1	Balance ..	b/d	440				

Though a firm may own several assets, all subject to depreciation, one Depreciation Account only is used to which all depreciation is debited.

The above methods are in common use, but brief reference may be made to the Sinking Fund Method and the Insurance Policy Method. In these cases the assets remain on the books at their original cost. Each year a fixed sum is debited to Profit and Loss Account, and a corresponding sum is paid out from cash. Under the Sinking Fund Method the cash is invested in gilt-edged securities. Under the Insurance Policy Method the cash is expended in meeting the premiums on an endowment insurance policy which is to mature at the expiration of the life of the asset. In both cases provision is made for replacement of the asset when it becomes necessary without affecting the working capital of the business.

A record is usually kept in a memorandum book of the assets, their original cost, the particular method of depreciation applied to each, and the action taken each year.

The asset is entered at its revised value in the Balance Sheet, the depreciation usually being shown as a deduction from the previous recorded value.

		£	£
Machinery and plant ..	.. ..	640	
less Depreciation ..	.. ..	128	512

An alternative treatment of depreciation which is now being employed by limited liability companies is to keep the value of the asset at cost price and show the accumulated depreciation in another account called the Provision for Depreciation Account.

Under this method Example 23 would be treated in the books as follows:—

Dr.		Machinery Account			Cr.
Year 1 Jan. 1	Cash	£ 1000	Year 1		£

Dr.		Provision for Depreciation on Machinery Account			Cr.
Year 1		£	Year 1 Dec. 31	Depreciation ..	£ 200
Year 2			Year 2 Dec. 31	„ ..	160
Year 3			Year 3 Dec. 31	„ ..	128

The Journal entries and Depreciation Account will be the same, but the Balance Sheet, which under the Companies Act, 1948, must in the case of a company, show the cost of the asset less the total depreciation written off, would appear in the third year as follows:—

Balance Sheet
as at 31st December, 19. .

£	£	Fixed Assets	£	£
		Machinery at cost ..	1000	
		less Provision for De-preciation ..	488	
				512

EXERCISES 18

1. Among the Assets Accounts of a manufacturing business are the following, with the balances as shown:—

		£
Dec. 31.	Plant and machinery	4000
,, 31.	Office furniture	400

Depreciation is to be provided for at the rate of 10% per annum on the plant and machinery, and at 5% per annum on the furniture.

Open the Ledger Accounts for the assets, and make the necessary entries for the depreciation.

Show how the assets should appear in the firm's Balance Sheet.

2. A firm bought a machine for £1,200. Its probable working life is estimated at 10 years, and its probable scrap value at the end of that time is estimated at £200. Depreciation is to be written off by equal instalments over the period of ten years. Show the Machinery Account for the first three years, including the provision for depreciation.

3. On what basis should "Fixed Assets" be valued for the purpose of the Balance Sheet of a trading business?

Illustrate your answer by showing how you would deal with a motor lorry bought for £450, which, it is expected, will have to be disposed of in 5 years' time, when it will probably realise £25.   *R.S.A.*

4. A business buys an electric lighting plant on 1st January, 19. ., for the sum of £2,550. The plant is estimated to last 10 years, and to have a scrap value at the end of that time of £250. Show how you would deal with this asset in the books of the business at the end of the first year.   *R.S.A.*

5. Explain what is meant by Depreciation and illustrate your answer by giving the account of a machine purchased on 1st January, 19. ., for £600 and estimated to be worth £150 at the end of a life of two years.   *R.S.A.*

6. An engineering firm has loose tools valued at 1st January at £1,425. At 31st December stock is taken of the loose tools, and their value is placed at £1,623. Show how you would deal with the matter in the firm's books and in the Balance Sheet.

7. The loose tools of an engineering firm were valued at the commencement of the year at £1,134. At 31st December, on stock being taken, the valuation of the loose tools stood at £921. Show how this matter should be dealt with in the firm's books, and the effect of the re-valuation on the Balance Sheet.

8. Motor lorries stand at £3,500, and loose tools at £941 on the books of a firm at the commencement of the trading period. At the close of the period, 31st December, re-valuation of the assets is made and discloses that the value at 31st December of the motor lorries is £3,150, and of the loose tools, £874.

Give the Journal entries and the Ledger Accounts to carry into the books the effect of this re-valuation.

9. (*a*) Enter the following transactions through their appropriate books.
(*b*) Post to Ledger.
(*c*) Take out Trial Balance.
(*d*) Prepare Trading and Profit and Loss Account and Balance Sheet.

The following Trial Balance was extracted from the books of K. Watts on 31st May, 19...

Trial Balance. 31st May, 19..

	Dr. £	Cr. £
Capital (1st July, 19..)		2000
Drawings	220	
Stock (1st July, 19..)	1345	
Freehold premises	1500	
Furniture and fittings	125	
Purchases	4624	
Sales		7012
Returns inwards	126	
Office expenses	480	
Carriage inwards	97	
Cash	33	
Bank	100	
Discounts allowed	74	
Discounts received		118
F. Haynes	69	
C. Peace		132
Salaries	469	
	£9262	£9262

During June Watts's transactions were as follows:—

Received from F. Haynes a cheque for the amount of his account, less 5% cash discount.
Sold goods, on credit, to G. Leach, £87.
Bought goods, and paid for by cheque, £63.
Bought goods on credit from F. Appleton, £44.
Received a credit note for £9 from F. Appleton for goods returned to him.
Paid by cheque Fire Insurance premium, £5.
Withdrew from bank £35 for office use.
Paid from cash: salaries, £30; office expenses, £12; and carriage on goods sold to G. Leach, £2.
Cash sales, £136, banked during month.
Cash sales, £14, not banked.
Drew cheque for £20 for private expenses.

Wrote off 10% of the furniture and fittings for depreciation.
Paid cheque, £100, on account to C. Peace.
The stock on 30th June, 19.., was valued at £1041.

N.B.—Unless otherwise stated, all moneys received were paid into Bank
same day.   *Oxford Local Examinations School Certificate.*

10. From the following list of balances draw up the Trial Balance of E. W.
Rowcroft as at 31st December, 19.., and then prepare Trading Account, Profit
and Loss Account, and Balance Sheet:—

	£
E. W. Rowcroft, Capital Account	3500
Purchases	4080
Heating and lighting	20
Drawings	82
Sales	7000
Returns outwards	70
Machinery and plant	1300
Discounts received	27
Land and buildings	1100
Returns inwards	116
Rent and rates	32
Fixtures and fittings	222
Repairs	118
Trade expenses	124
Motor vehicle	288
Sundry creditors	1029
Wages	1526
Commission received	90
Carriage outwards	39
Cash at bank	19
Sundry debtors	230
Carriage inwards	31
Stock, 1st July	2389

The stock on 31st December was valued at £1,275.

When preparing the Trading Account, Profit and Loss Account, and Balance
Sheet, you are required to depreciate the machinery and plant by 10% per
annum.   *U.E.I.*

11. From the following Trial Balance prepare a Trading Account, Profit and
Loss Account, and a Balance Sheet, as on 31st December, 19..:—

Trial Balance.—D. Gerrard

	Dr. £	Cr. £
Stock (1st January)	452	
Plant and machinery	560	
Furniture and fittings	280	
Sundry debtors	295	
Sundry creditors		442
Drawings	50	
Purchases	1675	
Sales		2587
Returns outwards		35
Returns inwards	73	
Manufacturing wages	381	
Carriage outwards	27	
Discount (balance)		58

	Dr. £	Cr. £
Bad debts (*debit P.* and *L. A/c.*)	89	
Insurance	54	
Trade expenses	13	
Rate and taxes	107	
Commission	36	
Cash at bank	196	
Cash in hand	34	
Capital (D. Gerrard)		1200
	£4322	£4322

10% depreciation to be written off plant and machinery, 7½% depreciation to be written off furniture and fittings. Stock on hand, 31st December, valued at £432. *U.E.I.*

CHAPTER 19 *Jan 25th.*

MANUFACTURING ACCOUNTS

Businesses may be divided broadly into two groups, trading and manufacturing; the one concerned in the distribution of goods bought in a finished condition, and the other with the making up of raw materials or partly finished goods into a more finished or completely finished state.

The Trading Account of a distributive business is prepared on simple lines, and contains on the debit side the opening stock of goods, the purchases made during the trading period, less any returns, and the cost of carriage inwards. On the credit side appear the net sales and the closing stock. Should the trader warehouse his goods, then the rent, lighting, heating, and other expenses of the warehouse are entered on the debit side of the Trading Account, together with wages and salaries of the warehouse staff, as the expenses incidental to warehousing are part of the cost of placing the goods in a condition ready for sale. These are the items that are directly affected by the turnover. All items in the Trial Balance referring to the selling and distribution expenses and the overhead charges of administration and distribution should be taken to the Profit and Loss Account.

In the case of a manufacturing business the account may be called the Manufacturing or Working Account, as it contains the items relating to the cost of manufacture. It is necessary for the manufacturer to ascertain the cost price of the goods produced, whereas the trader knows the cost price of the goods he deals in from his invoices. Accordingly, the Manufacturing Account will have, on the debit side, the value of the raw materials in stock at the start of the period, the cost of the raw materials purchased subsequently, the cost of carriage inwards, all the items of expense relative to the manufacturing process, such as factory rent, if any, coal, coke, heating, lighting, water and power, the wages of the factory workers, the salaries of the factory administrative staff and the charge for depreciation of machinery used in the manufacturing process. On the credit side will be the value at cost of the raw materials in hand at the close of the period.

As the process of manufacture is usually continuous, a certain amount of unfinished work will be on hand at the close of the financial year. The value of this "Work in Progress," as it is termed, must be taken into the Manufacturing Account. The valuation is made on the basis of the cost of the materials used, to which is added a sum representing the proportion of wages and factory charges appropriate to the job. In examination tests the work in progress at the opening of the financial year is shown in the Trial Balance. This item should be taken to the Manufacturing Account and appear on the debit side next to the stock of raw materials at start. The valuation of the work in progress at the close of the period is given as an instruction outside the Trial Balance, and should be credited to the Manufacturing Account after the stock of raw materials at close. It will also be necessary to show the item as an asset in the Balance Sheet.

If all the above items are included, the balance of the Manufacturing Account is the "Cost of Goods Manufactured during the trading period." The account, however, in this form, does not yield all the information that could be obtained from it. If certain of the items are grouped it is possible to ascertain the actual cost of the goods made, which would be a valuable piece of information for the trader both for the light it throws on the working for the current period and for purposes of comparison with preceding periods.

The "Cost of Goods Manufactured" is transferred to the Trading Account, taking the place of the item "Purchases" in the accounts of a trader.

Manufacturing Account
for the year ending 31st December, 19..

	£		£
Stocks at start:		Stocks at close:	
Raw materials ..	5000	Raw materials ..	4000
Partly manufactured		Partly manufactured	
goods	8000	goods	9000
Purchase of raw materi-		Balance carried down	
als	30000	(cost of manufac-	
Carriage on raw materi-		tured goods) ..	56500
als	300		
Manufacturing wages ..	20000		
Factory salaries	2000		
Factory lighting, heating,			
fuel	2500		
Carried forward	67800		69500

Manufacturing Account (*continued*)

	£		£
Brought forward	67800	*Brought forward*	69500
Factory rates, taxes, and insurance	700		
Depreciation of machinery	1000		
	£69500		£69500

Trading Account
for the year ending 31st December, 19..

	£	£		£
Stock of finished goods at start	5000		Sales (less Returns)	72000
Cost of goods manufactured (from Manufacturing A/c.)	56500			
	61500			
less Stock of finished goods at close	6000			
		55500		
Gross profit carried to Profit and Loss A/c.		16500		
		£72000		£72000

EXERCISES 19

1. Prepare Manufacturing and Trading Accounts for year ending 31st Dec. 19.., from the following balances:—

	£
Stock of raw materials, 1st Jan., 19..	2237
Raw material purchases	29314
Carriage on purchases	276
Stock of raw materials, 31st Dec., 19.. ..	3072
Manufacturing wages	21984
Manufacturing power	9431
Work in progress, 1st Jan., 19..	586
Work in progress, 31st Dec., 19..	317
Stock of finished goods, 1st Jan., 19..	5341
Sales	103127
Purchases of finished goods	873
Stock of finished goods, 31st Dec., 19.. ..	6095
Manufacturing expenses	892

Cambridge G.C.E. "O" Level.

2. From the following Trading Account of a manufacturer calculate in relation to the period covered by the account—

(1) The cost of the materials used; ✓

(2) The value at cost price of the goods manufactured;

(3) The percentage of gross profit on sales.

Do you think that the profit as stated below is adequate?

Trading Account for the Year Ended 31st December, 19..

Stock—	£	£		£	£
			Sales		50000
Finished goods ..	3500		Stock—		
Raw materials ..	1700		Finished goods ..	3000	
		5200	Raw materials ..	2000	
Purchases of raw					5000
materials.. ..		15000			
Wages		22500			
Factory power ..		1200			
Gross profit ..		11100			
		£55000			£55000

London Chamber of Commerce—Intermediate.

3. From the balances given below, prepare the Manufacturing and Profit and Loss Accounts of the Excelsis Manufacturing Company:—

	£
Raw materials purchased	24970
Travellers' salaries, expenses, and commission ..	3461
Transport costs—	
On goods sold	596
On raw materials purchased	82
Stock of raw materials and work in progress—	
1st June, 19....	5282
31st May in following year	4942
Returns inwards	117
Stock of finished goods—	
1st June, 19....	3565
31st May in following year	4116
Sales	51966
Factory wages	11861
Other factory expenses	3747
Office and administration expenses	2743

If it does not already appear in your answer as a separate figure, calculate the cost of goods manufactured.   *Oxford G.C.E. "O" Level.*

4. The following particulars are extracted from the Final Accounts of R. Ransford for the year ended 31st December, 19..:—

	£
Stock of raw materials (1st Jan., 19..)	2784
„ „ „ (31st Dec., 19..)	2321
Purchases „	9876
Sales of finished goods	24700
Stock „ (1st Jan., 19..) (valued at selling price)	3287
Stock of finished goods (31st Dec. 19..) (valued at selling price)	2945
Factory power	106
„ heat and light	34
„ rent and rates	840
„ wages	7850
Gross profit for year	5103
Net profit for year	1870
Capital	8500

From the above figures calculate (where necessary) and state:—

(a) The Turnover for the year.

(b) Cost of raw materials *used* during the year.

(c) Cost of Production of goods manufactured during the year.

(d) The percentage of Net Profit on Capital, correct to two places of decimals.

(e) Value (at selling price) of goods manufactured during the year.

London Chamber of Commerce—Intermediate.

5. (a) Name, and explain briefly the purpose of the various sections of the Revenue Accounts of a manufacturing company.

(b) From the following information prepare the necessary accounts to disclose the cost of goods manufactured and the gross profit for the six months ending 30th June, 19..:—

	1st Jan. 19..		30th June 19..
	£	£	£
Stock of raw materials	3421		3121
Stock of finished goods	5932		6360
Work in progress	1180		1420
Purchases of raw materials (net)		17843	
Sales (net)		98341	
Wages—Factory		33248	
Warehouse		7120	
Overhead expenses—Factory		4360	
Warehouse		2830	
Depreciation—Factory		2050	
Machinery		6241	
Warehouse		870	
Warehouse fittings		130	
Carriage inwards (raw materials)		261	

N.U.J.M.B.

6. C.D. is in business as a manufacturer of packing cases and at 31st December, 19.., the following balances were extracted from his books.

	£
Stocks at 1st January, 19..—	
Raw materials	400
Partly finished cases	450
Finished cases	300
Wages	4800
National Insurance	70
Purchases of materials	1400
Workshop expenses	210
Workshop insurance	90
Workshop power and lighting	330
Carriage on raw materials	70
Carriage on sales	480
Office expenses, salaries, and insurance	1120
Postage and telephone charges	85
Advertising	80
Sales of packing cases	11300
Stocks at 31st December, 19..—	
Raw materials	340
Partly finished cases	280
Finished cases	420

(a) Prepare Manufacturing, Trading, and Profit and Loss Accounts for the year ended 31st December, 19... The following must be brought into account: Depreciation at $12\frac{1}{2}\%$ on the plant and workshop tools valued at £8,000. Interest at 5% per annum on C.D.'s capital of £12,000.

C.D. is to be credited with a salary of £500.

(b) Express your reasoned opinion of the result of the year's trading.

A.E.B., G.C.E. "O" Level.

CHAPTER 20 ~~Jan't~~

RESERVES AND PROVISIONS

A matter for consideration in preparing the Final Accounts of a business is whether the whole of the trading profits disclosed are to be treated as available for distribution to the proprietors or, as an act of financial prudence, some portion of the profits should be retained in the business. To retain or to set aside profits is to create a reserve, and the purpose of such action may be general or specific.

Reserves for general purposes are voluntary appropriations of profit. The motive may be to strengthen the financial position of the business by increasing the working capital to the extent that profits are retained, or it may be, for example, to institute and maintain pension or provident funds for the benefit of employees. These reserves are dealt with further in Chapter 24 on the Final Accounts of a Company.

Reserves for Specific Purposes and Provisions

Where there is a definite charge against profits to meet known liabilities or to meet expenses already incurred, such as outstanding wages, rent, and travellers' commission, the reserve is said to be a specific one and is now known as a provision. Provisions, therefore, represent charges against profits for expenditure incurred and not yet paid, while reserves represent allocations or appropriations of profit for general or particular purposes.

Provisions may be made to meet certain contingencies which may arise, such as bad debts, but the actual amount of which is in doubt.

Bad Debts and Provisions for Doubtful Debts

A further step to ensure that the Balance Sheet presents a correct view of the financial position is to review the item "Sundry Debtors". Examination of the debtors' accounts included in this total may disclose that certain debts are actually bad debts which are irrecoverable, and that others are doubtful. To include these in the item "Sundry Debtors" in the Balance Sheet as if all were equally good debts would give a false value to the asset.

Bad debts must be written off the books either before or at the end of the trading period and, as they represent actual losses, they must be charged against profits in the Profit and Loss Account. A debtor may fail and, having no assets, the whole of his debt may be irrecoverable. Another debtor for, say, £40, may compound with his creditors and offer £0.37½ in the £. He would pay £15, and the remaining £25 would have to be written off as a bad debt. A debtor may be adjudicated bankrupt and his debts paid by instalments as and when his assets are realised. If his debt is £100, there may be a payment of £25, representing a dividend in the bankruptcy of £0·25 in the £. A second and equal instalment may be received, to be followed by a third and final instalment of £0·25 in the £. As it is known that no further payment will be received, the remainder must be written off as bad and irrecoverable.

The method of writing off the bad debts is to open a Bad Debts Account in the Ledger to which a debit entry is made for the balance outstanding and irrecoverable, a corresponding credit entry being made in the debtor's personal account. At the close of the trading period the balance of the Bad Debts Account is transferred to the Profit and Loss Account.

Example 25.—On 1st November, J. Watson, who owes £100 for goods supplied on March 10th, is declared bankrupt. Received cheque for £75, being first and final dividend at £0·75 in the £.

Received notice of the failure of B. Burton & Co., who owe £40 for goods supplied on June 20th. There being no assets, the whole of the debt is written off as bad.

Dr.				J. Watson			Cr.
19..			£	19..			£
Mar. 10	Goods ..	S.B.	100	Nov. 1	Cash ..	C.B.	75
				„ 1	Bad Debts A/c. ..	J.	25
			£100				£100

Dr.				B. Burton & Co.			Cr.
19..			£	19..			£
June 20	Goods ..	S.B.	40	Nov. 1	Bad Debts A/c. ..	J.	40

Journal

			£	£
Nov. 1	Bad Debts Account .. .. Dr. J. Watson .. .. being balance of account written off as bad.		25	25
	Bad Debts Account .. .. Dr. B. Burton & Co. .. .. being debt written off on their failure. No assets available.		40	40

Dr.   **Bad Debts Account**   Cr.

19..			£	19..		£
Nov. 1	J. Watson ..	J.	25	Dec. 31	Transfer to	
„ 1	B. Burton & Co... ..	J.	40		Profit and Loss A/c. ..	65
			£65			£65

Should payment be received subsequently for a debt written off as bad, cash is debited and a corresponding credit entry is made to Bad Debts Account. The payment is treated in the books as an unexpected gain.

Other debts may be doubtful, being considered so either from known facts about the debtor or from the debt being one of long standing. As doubt exists about some of the accounts it is prudent to adjust the item "Sundry Debtors" accordingly. A provision is made for doubtful debts which has the effect of reducing the profits available for distribution by the amount provided. The sum to be provided may be arrived at by a scrutiny of all the accounts to find the total of doubtful debts or a sum calculated as a percentage of the total debtors is set aside. Past experience is a safe guide to the percentage advisable as a provision, or an estimate may be made for the current year and revised in subsequent years in the light of experience.

The action taken is to debit the amount decided upon to the Profit and Loss Account, and to make a corresponding credit entry in a Provision for Doubtful Debts Account. On closing the books a credit balance remains on the latter account. As a provision it is a liability, but instead of its being shown on the left-hand side of the Balance Sheet, it is brought into relation with the asset Sundry Debtors, and shown as a deduction from it.

Example 26.—The Sundry Debtors amount to £5,000 at 31st December, and it is decided to create a provision for doubtful debts equal to 5% of this total.
Show the entries required.

Journal

19..		£	£
Dec. 31	Profit and Loss Account .. .. Dr.	250	
	Provision for Doubtful Debts Account being provision of 5% reserve on Sundry Debtors at this date.		250

Dr.		Provision for Doubtful Debts		*Cr.*
	£	19..		£
		Dec. 31	Profit and Loss A/c. .. J.	250

The debit entry is made to the Profit and Loss Account, and the item appears on the assets side of the Balance Sheet as below:—

	£	£
Sundry Debtors	5000	
less Provision for Doubtful Debts	250	4750

Actual bad debts which occur are written off to Bad Debts Account as shown earlier in this chapter. That is the common practice and is the simplest. As a provision exists they may, of course, be written off against it, the debit entry being to the Provision for Doubtful Debts Account instead of to a Bad Debts Account. It would then be necessary to restore the provision to its appropriate amount by charging a further sum, equal to the bad debts, against the Profit and Loss Account.

The student may observe a debit item for " Bad Debts " among the list of balances in a given Trial Balance. This refers to bad debts already written off, and is the balance of the Bad Debts Account as at the date of extraction of the Trial Balance. It should be debited to the Profit and Loss Account when this is prepared. Any instruction that is given with a Trial Balance to write off a sum for bad debts requires different treatment. This has not been passed through the books and therefore requires a two-fold entry as a deduction from the total of Sundry Debtors and a debit to the Profit and Loss Account. If a provision for doubtful debts has also to be made it should be calculated on the net figure for Sundry Debtors after deduction of the sum to be written off for bad debts.

To Increase the Provision

The provision carried forward to the next date of balancing may be insufficient as a provision on the Sundry Debtors on the books at that date. To carry on the above example, it may be found at the second date that the Sundry Debtors amount to £6,000. If 5 per cent. is considered adequate, the provision for the ensuing year should be £300, involving an increase of £50 on the existing provision. Such increase is provided for by a debit entry to Profit and Loss Account, and a credit entry to the Provision for Doubtful Debts.

Journal

19..		£	£
Dec. 31	Profit and Loss Account .. .. .. Dr.	50	
	Provision for Doubtful Debts Account.. ..		50
	being an increase to maintain Provision at 5% on Sundry Debtors.		

Dr.			**Provision for Doubtful Debts**			Cr.
		£	19..			£
			Jan. 1	Balance ..	b/d	250
			Dec. 31	Profit and Loss A/c. ..	J.	50

An instruction accompanying a Trial Balance to make a provision of a given sum or to maintain a provision at a certain percentage should not be acted upon until it is known from enquiry or observation whether or not a provision already exists. Any existing provision must be taken into account in calculating the new figure.

To Decrease the Provision

It may appear at the next balancing time that the existing provision is more than adequate owing to a fall in the total of Sundry Debtors. If the £6,000 in the above example had fallen to £4,000, and the provision is to be maintained at 5 per cent., £200 would be the new provision figure. As the existing provision is £300, £100 of that sum may be written back by a credit entry in the Profit and Loss Account, and a debit entry in the Provision Account as below:—

Journal

19..		£	£
Dec. 31	Provision for Doubtful Debts Account .. Dr.	100	
	Profit and Loss Account		100
	being excess written back to maintain Provision at 5% on Sundry Debtors.		

Dr.				Provision for Doubtful Debts				Cr.
19.. Dec. 31	Balance ..	c/d	£ 300	19.. Jan. 1 Dec. 31	Balance .. Profit and Loss A/c.	b/d J.	£ 250 50
			£300				£300
Dec. 31	Profit and Loss A/c.	J.	100	Jan. 1	Balance ..	b/d	300

Provision for Discounts

Another example of provision for contingencies, though of much less frequent occurrence in practice, is that for discounts likely to be taken by the debtors included in the total of Sundry Debtors. If the debtors take advantage of discount terms the sums received will be less than the full amount shown as an asset in the Balance Sheet. Of still less frequency is the making of a provision on Sundry Creditors for discounts. If provisions for discounts are required the procedure is similar to that described for bad debt provision. The sum provided is usually calculated at a percentage of the Sundry Debtors, but care must be taken that it is calculated on the net figure only after deduction of the provision for bad and doubtful debts, as such debts cannot be subject to discount.

Example 27.—Show the entries such as are necessary for a provision of $2\frac{1}{2}\%$ for discounts on Sundry Debtors which stand, at 31st December, at £4,000. A provision at 5% for bad and doubtful debts has also to be made.

Journal

19.. Dec. 31	Profit and Loss Account .. .. .. Dr. Provision for Discount on Debtors' Account.. being $2\frac{1}{2}\%$ provision for discounts.	£ 95	£ 95

Dr.			Provision for Discounts on Debtors			Cr.
19..		£	19.. Dec. 31	Profit and Loss A/c.		£ 95

The provision for discounts is calculated on £4,000 less 5 per cent. provision for bad debts, and it should be shown in the Balance Sheet as a deduction from the item Sundry Debtors in addition to the deductions for a provision for bad debts.

						£	£	£
SUNDRY DEBTORS	..	..	..	..	..		4000	
less Provision for Doubtful Debts		..	..	..	200		
Provision for Discounts	..	..	..	..	95	295	
								3705

A provision for discounts on creditors is created by converse entries. The sum is credited to Profit and Loss Account and is debited to a Reserve for Discounts on Creditors Account. The balance of the latter account remains open on the books and is taken to the Balance Sheet, to appear there as a deduction from the Sundry Creditors.

Contingent Liabilities

A firm may have certain contingent liabilities which are not included in the accounts. For example, a trader may have guaranteed payment of a cheque drawn by another party. If the drawer of the cheque fails to meet it when presented for payment the payee may have recourse to the trader for reimbursement. Until such contingency arises no actual liability exists, but as a reminder of the existence of the contingency a note of it is usually made for information at the foot of the Balance Sheet.

EXERCISES 20

1. At the close of the year the Sundry Debtors of a firm stand at a total of £5,000. It is considered that two of the debts, amounting to £450, are doubtful, and it is desired to create a provision to the extent of the doubtful debts.

Give the Journal entries to create the provision, and show the appropriate Ledger Accounts. Show also how the item "Sundry Debtors" should then appear in the firm's Balance Sheet.

2. The Trial Balance extracted from B. A. James & Co.'s books at 31st December shows the Sundry Debtors as at £2,750. It is decided to create a provision of 5% of the total debtors for doubtful debts.

Give the entries to effect this decision, and show how the item of Sundry Debtors should be set out in the firm's Balance Sheet.

3. Give the entries to carry into effect the decision to create a provision for doubtful debts of 5% of the total of Sundry Debtors which stand at £3,750 on 31st December. Show also the items of Sundry Debtors and the provision as they should appear in the Balance Sheet.

4. At 31st December the Sundry Debtors of the firm of Brown & Sons stand at £4,200. There is existing already a provision for doubtful debts of £150, but it is desired that the provision should amount to a sum equal to 5% of the present total of Sundry Debtors. Make the entries to carry this into effect.

5. It is decided to maintain the provision for doubtful debts on the books of B. Wilson & Co. at 5% of the Sundry Debtors. The present provision stands at £120, and at 31st December the Sundry Debtors amount to £3,100.

Give the Journal entries, and show the Ledger Accounts to carry out this decision.

6. The present provision for doubtful debts on the books of James Allen & Sons is £430. At 31st December the Sundry Debtors amount to £9,500. Give the entries required to increase the existing provision to £475, and show the item for Sundry Debtors as it should appear in the next Balance Sheet.

7. The existing provision for doubtful debts in the books of J. Scott stands at £360. The Sundry Debtors at 31st December amount to £6,000. Give the entries required to decrease the provision to £300.

8. The provision for doubtful debts of a company is to be maintained at 5% of the Sundry Debtors. The existing provision is £540. The Sundry Debtors amount to £8,200 at 31st December. Give the entries required to maintain the provision at 5% of the Sundry Debtors.

9. It was decided to reduce the provision for doubtful debts in the books of T. Layton from the present amount, £620, to £500. Show how this decision is carried into effect. At this date the Sundry Debtors stood at £10,020. Set down this item and the new provision as they should appear in the Balance Sheet.

10. The Sundry Debtors of W. Watson & Co. amount to £12,500. Provide for a provision for bad debts of 5%, and a provision for discounts on debtors of $2\frac{1}{2}$%, and show the item for Sundry Debtors as it should appear in the Balance Sheet.

11. In the books of Williams & Sons the Sundry Debtors stand at £8,000 at 31st December. It is proposed to create a Bad Debts Provision of 5%, and a Provision for Discounts on Debtors of $2\frac{1}{2}$%. Show the entries required to carry this into effect, and the items as they should appear in the Balance Sheet.

12. The existing provision for bad debts on the books of Thompson & Co. is £560. On 31st December the Sundry Debtors stood at £9,800. Give the entries required:—

(*a*) To reduce the bad debts provision to £490.

(*b*) To create a provision of $2\frac{1}{2}$% for discounts on debtors.

And show the items for Sundry Debtors and the provision as they should appear in the Balance Sheet.

13. Give the entries required to create a Provision for Discounts on Creditors of $2\frac{1}{2}$%, the Sundry Creditors standing at £5,000 on 31st December.

14. The Sundry Creditors of B. Hallett amount to £5,000, and his Sundry Debtors to £7,000 on 31st December. He decides to create—

(*a*) A provision of $2\frac{1}{2}$% for discounts on creditors.

(*b*) A provision of 5% on Sundry Debtors for bad debts.

(*c*) A provision of $2\frac{1}{2}$% for discounts on debtors.

Show the entries required to carry this decision into effect, and how the items should appear in his Balance Sheet.

15. On 1st January, Arthur Sharp, who owes you £77, is adjudicated bankrupt. On 8th February the first dividend of £0·10 in the £ is paid, and on 23rd March the second and final dividend of £0·05 in the £ is paid. Give the entries in your books which are necessary to record the above transactions and to close the account. Show the Ledger Account of Arthur Sharp in its final form. *N.C.T.E.C.*

16. John Baker carried on business as a manufacturer. On 30th June, 19... the following Trial Balance was extracted from his books:—

	Dr. £	Cr. £
Machinery and plant	576	
Office salaries and expenses	610	
Bad debts	180	
Returns inwards and outwards	350	337
Carriage on purchases	228	
Carriage on sales	200	
Depreciation	75	
Manufacturing wages..	1273	
Discounts allowed and received	95	170
Fixtures and fittings	209	
Sundry debtors and creditors	1627	1224
Drawings	420	
Purchase and sales	6727	10580
Cash in hand	67	
Cash at bank	354	
Rent and rates..	286	
Stock (1st July)	2234	
Capital (1st July)		3200
	£15511	£15511

You are required to prepare Trading and Profit and Loss Accounts for the year ended 30th June, and a Balance Sheet as on that date.   The stock on hand on 30th June, 19.., was valued at £1,896.   *R.S.A.*

17. The following Trial Balance was extracted from the books of J. Cooper, a trader, on 19th March, 19..:—

	Dr. £	Cr. £
Capital (1st April)		3000
Drawings..	330	
Freehold property	1200	
Furniture and fittings	150	
Stock (1st April)..	1436	
Sales		8041
Returns inwards	159	
Purchases..	6735	
Returns outwards		252
Office expenses	510	
Bad debts..	131	
Carriage outwards	159	
Carriage inwards..	145	
Salaries and commission	455	
Discount		15
F. Drake	74	
W. Wright	33	
H. Nelson		318
C. Blake		152
Cash	37	
Bank	224	
	£11778	£11778

Post the above balances direct to the appropriate accounts in the Ledger, then pass thereto, through the proper subsidiary books, the following transactions:—

Mar. 21. Received from F. Drake a cheque for the amount of his account. The cheque was paid into bank.

„ 22. Sold goods, on credit, to G. Cook, £94.

„ 23. Bought goods by cheque, £82.

„ 23. Received a final payment of £0·67 in the £ from W. Wright, the balance being irrecoverable. The cheque was paid into bank.

„ 24. Sold goods on credit to F. Drake, £154, and paid £5 out of cash for carriage on these goods.

„ 24. Paid salaries and commission in cash, £23.

„ 29. Paid H. Nelson £100 on account by cheque.

„ 30. Drew and cashed a cheque for £50, and paid in cash office expenses, £16, and private expenses, £30.

„ 30. Sent a Credit Note for £25 to F. Drake for goods returned.

„ 31. Cash sales, £36. (Not banked.)

„ 31. Write off 10% of the furniture and fittings for depreciation.

Extract a Trial Balance as on 31st March, and prepare Trading and Profit and Loss Accounts for the year ended 31st March, 19... Balance the Ledger and draw up a Balance Sheet as on that date. The stock on 31st March was valued at £1,075.

N.B.—The Trial Balance given above need not be reproduced. *R.S.A.*

18. From the following Trial Balance prepare a Trading Account, Profit and Loss Account, and a Balance Sheet, as on 30th June, 19..:—

Trial Balance. F. T. Layton

	Dr.	Cr.
	£	£
Capital A/c. (F. T. Layton)		830
Purchases	1200	
Sales		1750
Returns inwards	55	
Returns outwards		64
Plant and machinery	240	
Furniture and fittings	75	
Sundry debtors	137	
Sundry creditors		86
Wages	180	
Rent and rates	48	
Bad debts	36	
Discount		27
Stock (1st Jan.)..	500	
Insurance	16	
Commission		43
Trade expenses	22	
Cash in hand	17	
Cash at bank	274	
	£2800	£2800

7½% depreciation to be written off plant and machinery.
5% depreciation to be written off furniture and fittings.
Stock on hand, 30th June, valued at £630. *U.E.I.*

19. The following balances were extracted from the books of Walter Wilson, grocer and provision dealer, on the 31st December, 19..:—

Dr.	£	Cr.	£
Cash in hand	13	Sales	2565
Cash at bank	347	Returns outwards	14
Motor lorry	260	Discount	13
Fixtures and fittings	300	Creditors	603
Returns inwards	57	Capital Account	1844
Purchases	2128		
Stock, 1st Jan...	1220		
Bad debts	43		
Wages	312		
Discount	26		
Drawings Account	24		
Rent and rates..	67		
Sundry debtors	242		
	£5039		£5039

You are required to prepare the Final Accounts and a Balance Sheet as on the 31st December, 19... Before doing so, the following adjustments must be taken into account:—

Write 5% depreciation off fixtures and fittings, and 10% off the motor lorry. Make a provision of 2½% on debtors for doubtful debts. The value of the stock in hand at the end of the period was £1,380. *N.C.T.E.C.*

20. The following balances were extracted from the books of M. Robinson, ironmonger, on the 31st December, 19..:—

Dr.	£	Cr.	£
Motor van	280	Sales	2905
Shop fixtures	340	Returns outwards	24
Returns inwards	67	Discount	23
Purchases	2428	Sundry creditors	663
Stock in hand, 1st Jan. ..	1230	Capital Account	1859
Bad debts	53		
Wages	302		
Discount	6		
Drawings Account	48		
Rent and rates..	88		
Sundry debtors	262		
Cash in hand	20		
Cash in bank	350		
	£5474		£5474

You are required to prepare the Final Accounts and a Balance Sheet as on the 31st December, 19... Before doing so, the following adjustments must be taken into account:—(a) Write 5% depreciation off shop fixtures, and 15% off motor van; (b) make a provision of 2½% on sundry debtors for doubtful debts. The value of the stock in hand at the end of the period was £1,300. *N.C.T.E.C.*

CHAPTER 21

PROVISIONS AND ADJUSTMENTS

Almost invariably it is found at the close of the financial year that certain expenses or liabilities properly belonging to the period just ended have been incurred, but payment has not been made. Business comprises a continuous series of operations unaffected by the arbitrary dates of the accounting periods, and some overlapping may be expected.

Factory wages may be paid, for example, on Friday in each week. If 31st December falls on, say, Wednesday, part of the total wages for the week, for Saturday to Wednesday, should be charged in the accounts as an expense for the year ending 31st December. The payment, however, is made on 2nd January in the next period.

Similarly, rent, salaries, commission, interest, and other expenses may be outstanding. Each financial year should bear its own charges if the profits are to be stated fairly, and, to this end, it is necessary to bring into account all outstanding expenses and to apportion others so that each period bears its proper proportion. Accordingly a provision is made for each outstanding liability by charging against profits the appropriate amount, as shown in the following examples:—

Example 28.—The rent of the firm's premises is £500 per annum, payable quarterly in arrear. For the year under review the March, June, and September payments have been made. The final quarter's rent has accrued due, but remains unpaid at 31st December. Show the entries involved in bringing the accrued rent into account.

Dr.				Rent Account				Cr.
19..			£	19..				£
Apl. 2	Cash	C.B.	125	Dec. 31	Profit and			
July 5	,,	C.B.	125		Loss A/c.			500
Oct. 2	,,	C.B.	125					
Dec. 31	Provision for accrued rent *Balance*	c/d	125					
			£500					£500
				Jan. 1	*Balance* Provision for accrued rent	b/d		125

159

It will be observed that the two-fold entry for the rent outstanding is within the Rent Account itself. A debit entry is made for the sum accrued due and a corresponding credit entry is made in the Rent Account for the ensuing period. Sufficient space must be left to allow for the balancing and ruling off of the account.

By making this debit entry the balance of the Rent Account to be transferred to Profit and Loss Account is £125 more than it would otherwise have been. The effect is to charge against profits both the rent paid and the rent accrued. The credit entry in the Rent Account is an open balance representing the provision of profit to meet accrued rent, and when the Balance Sheet is prepared, it will be shown in it as a liability.

The effect of the payment eventually of the outstanding rent should be noted. The credit entry will be to Cash, and the debit entry to the Rent Account. The latter will counterbalance the credit entry for the provision, and the liability shown in the Balance Sheet is extinguished.

Example 29.—Factory wages paid during the year amounted to £61,200. Three days' wages, amounting to £600, had accrued due to 31st December. Show the entries as are necessary to bring this sum into account.

Dr.				Factory Wages Account			Cr.
			£	19..			£
19..				Dec. 31	Manufac-		
Jan. to					turing		
Dec.	Cash ..	C.B.	61200		A/c. ..		61800
Dec. 31	Provision						
	for 3						
	days						
	wages						
	accrued						
	due	c/d	600				
	Balance						
			£61800				£61800
					Balance		
				Jan. 1	Provision		
					for ac-		
					crued		
					wages	b/d	600

The provision for accrued wages, £600, will be shown on the liability side of the Balance Sheet.

The method of providing for accrued liabilities illustrated in the above two examples is applicable in all similar cases. A complete list of the various outstanding liabilities that may be met with in accounts cannot be given, but their treatment should present little difficulty to the student if the above examples are carefully studied.

Occasionally, in a test, unfamiliarity with the details of a particular kind of business may cause some difficulty, but usually a comparison of the adjustment to be made with the item in the Trial Balance to which it relates will help towards a solution. In the above examples the Ledger Account and the effect of the entries therein on the Profit and Loss Account and Balance Sheet have been shown. In many tests the Trial Balance, from which Trading and Profit and Loss Accounts and Balance Sheet are to be prepared, is accompanied by instructions to take certain adjustments into account, and many of such adjustments refer to outstanding liabilities. As no Ledger Accounts are required by the test, it is necessary to give the effect only of the appropriate Ledger entries on the Final Accounts. One aspect of the adjustment will be shown in the Trading Account or the Profit and Loss Account and the other aspect in the Balance Sheet. To take again the above example of outstanding rent. The rent actually paid, £375, would appear in the Trial Balance, in such circumstances, but the accrued but unpaid rent, £125, would be noted as an instruction to be taken into account. In preparing the Final Accounts from the Trial Balance the sum of £125 should be added to the £375 taken to the Profit and Loss Account, and should be included among the liabilities in the Balance Sheet. Similarly, in the above example of an adjustment for accrued wages, the sum of £600 should be added to the Wages, £61,200, taken to the Manufacturing Account, and should also be shown as a liability in the Balance Sheet.

It is imperative that the student should remember that items in the Trial Balance have been passed through the books, and that they will appear once only in the Trading or Profit and Loss Accounts or the Balance Sheet. Items given as adjustments or instructions outside the actual Trial Balance have not been passed through the books, and a two-fold entry affecting both the Balance Sheet and the Trading or Profit and Loss Account is required for them.

In practice such adjustments are made in the appropriate accounts before the Trading and Profit and Loss Accounts and Balance Sheet are prepared, but this is apt to be overlooked by students who become accustomed to the form in which examination tests are given.

Unexpired Values and Payments in Advance

Many items which have to be considered at the time of balancing are of a nature converse to the outstanding liabilities explained above. The periods covered by insurance premiums, rates, and other expenses do not always coincide with the accounting period, and part of the expenditure may be properly attributable to the next financial year. Payment, for example, in October, of £100 for rates for the half-year October to March when the financial year ends on 31st December, is to pay in advance the charge for rates for three months of the ensuing accounting period. If each year's accounts should be charged with the expenses of the year then charges such as the above should be apportioned. In the Rates Account, the above £100 will appear as a debit entry. On closing the books £50 only, representing the rates for October to December, is transferred to the debit of the Profit and Loss Account, that being the portion properly chargeable against the current year's profits. The balance of £50 is, at 31st December, the value of the unexpired portion of the rates payment and, as such, is shown in the Balance Sheet as a temporary asset.

Example 30.—The rates are paid in half-yearly instalments in advance for the period 1st April to 31st March; £100 on 30th April and £100 on 31st October. The financial year ends on 31st December. Show the Rates Account and the entries as are necessary to apportion the expenditure between the two accounting periods.

Dr.						Rates Account			Cr.
19..				£	19..				£
Apl. 30	Cash	..	C.B.	100	Dec. 31	Rates paid in advance ..	c/d		50
Oct. 31	Cash	..	C.B.	100	„ 31	Profit and Loss A/c.			150
				£200					£200
Jan. 1	Rates paid in advance		b/d	50					

Balance Sheet
as at 31st December, 19..
(Assets side only)

CURRENT ASSETS	£
Unexpired Rates	50

The procedure is to credit this year's account with the value of the unexpired portion, and to make the corresponding debit entry in the account for the ensuing period. Sufficient room must be left to permit the account to be balanced and ruled off. The new account opens with a debit balance which, in due course, will be transferred to the Profit and Loss Account for the next year. Meanwhile, it appears in the Balance Sheet as an asset representing the unexpired value in hand.

This method is applicable to all similar examples of payments in advance, and is also suitable for the treatment of items requiring the carrying forward of expenditure, either wholly or in part, to subsequent years.

Example 31.—A firm enters into an advertising contract for three years to obtain cheaper rates than a one-year contract would give. Payment of £1,200 is made on January 10th. At 31st December, on closing the books, it is decided to spread the advertising cost over the three years. Give the entries as are necessary to carry this decision into effect.

Dr.			Advertising Account				Cr.
19..			£	19..			£
Jan. 10	Cash ..	C.B.	1200	Dec. 31	Proportion of expense carried forward	c/d	800
				„ 31	Transfer to Profit & Loss A/c.		400
			£1200				£1200
19..							
Jan. 1	Proportion of expense brought forward	b/d	800				

As shown, one-third of the advertising cost is transferred to Profit and Loss Account. The remainder of the expenditure is held in suspense to be charged against the profits of the two succeeding years and, meanwhile, is shown in the Balance Sheet as a temporary asset representing advertising value in hand at that date.

As with outstanding liabilities, the forms which the adjustments of payments in advance and the apportionment of expenses may take depend upon the nature of the business and the particular circumstances under which the accounts are prepared. In whatever form they are expressed the treatment should follow the lines described above. If such adjustments are given as instructions to be observed

in the preparation of the Final Accounts from a given Trial Balance,
only the effect on the Final Accounts can be shown. As already
remarked, such items appearing outside the Trial Balance have not
been passed through the books, and the double entry effect must be
given. This will affect *both* the Balance Sheet *and* the Trading *or*
Profit and Loss Account. If the above examples had been given as
instructions, the actual expenditure on Rates, £200, and Advertising,
£1,200, would be shown as items in the Trial Balance, and the
adjusting entries would be made when the Profit and Loss Account
is prepared, and would be shown on the debit side.

Profit and Loss Account

Dr.   (Debit Side only)

	£	£
Rates	200	
less unexpired	50	150
Advertising	1200	
less amount carried forward	800	400

The sum shown in the effective debit cash column of the Profit
and Loss Account is the sum that would be transferred from the
Ledger Account for the expense item after the adjustment had been
made. The other entry for the adjustment is the amount brought
down in the respective accounts for the new period and, in the Final
Accounts, appears in the Balance Sheet on the assets side.

Whilst most adjustments deal with depreciation, reserves, outstanding liabilities, and payments in advance, other forms are
sometimes to be met, a few examples of which are mentioned below.

Apprentices' Premiums, for example, are sometimes the subject
of adjustment. The premium is paid down, but it is usual to spread
the sum over the period of the articles. The sum of £500 for five
years' apprenticeship would be taken into account £100 year by year.
The instructions may be to carry forward £400. The original
entries for the £500 were a debit entry to cash and a corresponding
credit entry to the Apprentices' Premiums Account. Without
adjustment, the £500 would be transferred to the credit of the Profit
and Loss Account. The adjusting item of £400 is, however, debited
to the Apprentices' Premiums Account, and is carried down to the
credit of the same account for the new period, leaving £100 only in
the old account to be transferred to Profit and Loss Account. The
credit balance on the new account will be taken to the Balance

Sheet as a liability under the heading "Unexpired Apprentices' Premiums." If the adjustment is asked for in the Final Accounts only, the net amount of £100 is credited to the Profit and Loss Account, and the sum of £400 is shown as a liability in the Balance Sheet.

Packing materials may appear as an expense item in the Trial Balance. If no stock on hand is stated the whole item is treated as an expense, and is debited to Profit and Loss Account. If the value of the packing materials on hand is given, this sum should be credited to the Packing Materials Account and debited to the same account for the new period. Only the used amount is then transferred to Profit and Loss Account, and the stock of packing materials on hand is shown as an asset in the Balance Sheet.

Similarly, the value of catalogues on hand may be given, and should be treated in the Catalogues Account in like manner to the packing materials. The cost only of the catalogues distributed is then charged against the profits of the current year, and the stock of catalogues on hand is shown as an asset in the Balance Sheet.

The factory wages may include payments for work done on, say, patterns for use in the firm. The amount of wages so expended should be deducted from the item for manufacturing wages and added to the value of the asset.

The owner of a business may take out goods from stock for his personal use. It is usual to debit the value at cost to the Proprietor's Drawings Account and to credit the Purchases Account. If it is the practice to make such withdrawals in kind a personal account should be opened in the owner's name.

Often the total expenditure on Rent, Rates, Insurance, and similar expenses is given, and the student is asked to apportion the sum in certain proportions between the factory and the office. If instructions are given of outstanding or prepaid items relative to this total they should be taken into account before the apportionment is made. The part attributable to the factory is debited to the Trading Account; the remainder, attributable to the office, is debited to the Profit and Loss Account.

As a final example, Goodwill (see p. 200) may appear as an asset, and the instructions may be to write down the value by a given sum. This amount should be credited to the Goodwill Account and debited to the Profit and Loss Appropriation Account, (see page 198) the effect being a reduction in the value of the asset in the Balance Sheet.

Other adjustments of special application to the accounts of a partnership firm or a limited company are referred to in the chapters treating of those accounts.

EXERCISES 21

1. The following items are taken from a Trial Balance extracted from B. Marchant's books on 31st December:—

	£
Insurance Account (debit balance)	60
Rates Account..	300

In each case three-quarters only of the expense is properly attributable to the year ending 31st December.

Show the Ledger Accounts for these items and the entries required to adjust the above amounts, taking into consideration that insurance, £15, and rates, £75, represent payments in advance. Show how such adjustments will affect the firm's Balance Sheet.

2. The Trial Balance extracted from the books of A. Macdonald at 31st December includes the following debit balances:—

	£
Rent Account	750
Rates	500
Wages	36000
Salaries..	4000
Interest on loan	100
Insurance	120
Advertising	2000

The following adjustments have to be made before the preparation of the Final Accounts:—

	£
Rent outstanding	250
Rates paid in advance	125
Wages accrued due	500
Salaries accrued due	45
Interest on loan unpaid	100 *c.L.*
Insurance paid in advance	30 *ASS*
Advertising cost to be carried forward ..	1000 *ASS.*

Show the Ledger Accounts as from which the Trial Balance was prepared, and make the necessary entries to effect the above adjustments.

3. The Trial Balance extracted on 31st December contains the following balances:—

	£
Rent Account	300
Wages Account	4800

At 31st December one quarter's rent, £100, remained owing, and three days' wages, £50, had accrued to the factory workers. Show the Ledger Accounts for rent and wages, enter the above balances, and show the adjusting entries to bring the outstanding items into account.

State how these outstanding items affect the firm's Balance Sheet.

4. William Robinson sub-lets the flat over his shop at an annual rent of £48 payable quarterly. During 19.. the tenant of the flat pays the rent due from him on 25th March, 24th June, and 29th September, but at 31st December has not paid the quarter's rent due. Show the Rent Account in William Robinson's books after the preparation of his Profit and Loss Account for the year ending 31st December, 19... *R.S.A.*

5. Set out the Journal entries necessary to deal with the following matters:—

(*a*) The writing off as bad debts of £55 due from A., £19 from B., and £27 from C.

(*b*) The allocation of £1,000 to General Reserve.

(*c*) The transfer to Furniture and Fittings of £45, the cost of a typewriter originally posted to Office Expenses.

(*d*) The bringing into account of three months' interest accrued on a loan of £500 at 5% per annum, due from D.

(*e*) The loss arising on the sale for £37 of a machine, the book value of which is £55. *R.S.A.*

6. A. Wholesaler carries on business in both home and export markets and requires his accounts to show the results separately. From the following Trial Balance prepare departmental Trading and Profit and Loss Accounts for the year ending 31st December, 19.., and Balance Sheet at that date:—

	£	£
A. Wholesaler, Capital Account		12382
,, Drawings Account	840	
Advertising (Home, £512; Export, £415)	927	
Carriage (Home)	261	
Cash in hand	70	
Freight, insurance, etc. (Export)	598	
Freehold premises	3500	
Lighting and heating (Home ½, Export ½)	70	
Office expenses (Home ½, Export ½)	654	
Office furniture and fittings	600	
Purchases (Home £24,710; Export £22,583)	47293	
Rates (Home ½, Export ½)	120	
Provision for bad debts		100
Sales (Home £28,027, Export £25,414)		53441
Salaries (Home, £726, Export £798)	1524	
Stocks at 1st Jan., 19.. (Home £2,962, Export £2,629)	5591	
Traveller's commission (Home)	520	
Sundry debtors	5325	
Sundry creditors		3756
Balance with bank	1786	
	£69679	£69679

When preparing the accounts the following must be taken into consideration:—

(1) The values of the stocks at 31st December, 19.., were Home £2,721 and Export £2,599.

(2) The traveller's commission due at 31st December, 19.., but not paid amounted to £40 (Home).

(3) An increase in the provision for bad debts of £173 is required (Home).

(4) The office furniture and fittings to be depreciated at the rate of 5% (Home ½, Export ½). *R.S.A.*

7. The following are the balances of the accounts appearing in the books of J. Munroe at December 31st, 19..:—

	Dr. £	Cr. £
Stock (January 1st, 19..)	672	
Rent of garage	140	
Repairs to motor delivery vans	89	
Cost of new motor delivery van	320	
Cost of printing catalogues	450	
Purchases and sales	5461	7943
Returns inwards and outwards	55	73
Sundry debtors and creditors	864	510
Cash in hand	226	
Cash at bank	180	
Drawings	240	
Capital		4650
Motor delivery vans	400	
Salaries	670	
Commission	105	
Sundry expenses	94	
Investment in Gold Bonds	800	
Premises	2200	
Bad debt written off recovered from Smith		15
Interest received on investment		28
Bad debts written off	112	
Lighting	97	
Rates	44	
	£13219	£13219

Stock on December 31st, 19.. was valued at £591, while there remained on hand at that date catalogues to the value of £46.

You are required to prepare Trading and Profit and Loss Accounts for the year and a Balance Sheet as at December 31st, 19.., and also to show the following Ledger Accounts as these would appear in the books of Munroe after preparation of the Final Accounts required: Stock Account, Purchases Account, Salaries Account, Cost of Printing Catalogues Account and Capital Account.

University of London General School Examination.

8. The figures of the following Trial Balance were extracted from the books of W. Walker, a wholesale provision merchant, on December 31st:—

	£	£
Capital		17874
Lease (to run 10 years from January 1st)	5000	
Advertising	127	
Motor vans	927	
Purchases	68485	
Postage	138	
Lighting and heating	91	
Wages	2837	
Rates and water	101	
Telephone	34	
Furniture and fittings	1104	
Sales		73498
Returns inwards and outwards	56	392

	£	£
Bad debts	26	
Insurance	192	
Debtors	4882	
Creditors		8405
Cash in hand	352	
Balance with bank	3792	
Stock at January 1st	12025	
	£100169	£100169

Prepare Trading and Profit and Loss Accounts for the year ending December 31st, 19.., and Balance Sheet at that date. In preparing the accounts, the following matters should be taken into consideration:—

(*a*) The stock at December 31st was valued at £10,787.

(*b*) An appropriate amount of depreciation should be written off the lease.

(*c*) 20% per annum on cost (£1,250) should be written off motor vans.

(*d*) £100 is to be reserved as a bonus to the staff.

(*e*) Make a provision of bad debts for £300.

(*f*) 10% per annum should be written off furniture and fittings.

Indicate in the accounts the rate of gross profit earned on the sales. *R.S.A.*

9. On 1st January, 19.., B. Jackson took over a shop at the rent of £300 a year, payable quarterly. He paid the landlord by cheque a quarter's rent on the following dates:—5th April, 4th July, 2nd October, and, for the final quarter of the year, on the following 4th January.

Show the entries in Jackson's Rent Account to the 31st December, in his Profit and Loss Account for the year ended 31st December, and in his Balance Sheet on 31st December.

CHAPTER 22 *Feb. 8th.*

PARTNERSHIPS

The ownership of a business may take one of several forms. Hitherto consideration has been given to one form of proprietorship only—that of the sole trader who is entitled to all the profits of his business, and is personally liable for the debts incurred. When two or more persons carry on a business in common with a view of profit, the relationship subsisting between them is termed a partnership, and the legal position of the partners to each other and to those with whom they have business dealings is governed by the Partnership Act, 1890. Under the Companies Act, 1948, no partnership or association consisting of more than ten persons may be formed for the purpose of carrying on a banking business, or of more than twenty to carry on any other kind of business, unless it is registered as a company.

The fact that the business is owned by two or more persons does not affect the trading records. Whether under the proprietorship of a sole trader or of partners the records of sale and purchases and the accounts of customers will be similar in all respects. The part of the bookkeeping record that is affected is the part showing the financial relationship of the business to the proprietors, namely the Capital Account. With two or more partners there must be two or more records of ownership, and the single Capital Account of the sole-trader will not suffice. If this point is borne in mind the new points to be discussed should present little difficulty.

Articles of Partnership

As there are two or more members in a partnership, the legal position of the partners to each other should be defined so that dispute may be prevented. Usually a Deed of Partnership or Partnership Agreement is drawn up containing the terms under which the partnership shall be carried on. The points usually covered by such agreements are as follows:—

1. The duration of the partnership.
2. The sum to be contributed by each partner to the capital of firm.

3. When, and in what ratio, the profits or losses are to be shared and profits may be drawn out.
4. The rate of interest, if any, to be allowed on capital.
5. Whether partnership salaries shall be paid and to whom.
6. The keeping of proper accounts.
7. How any dispute which may arise shall be settled.
8. The firm name under which the business shall be carried on.

The partners may determine for themselves all such matters affecting their relationship to each other, but in the absence of any agreement to the contrary certain rules laid down by Section 24 of the Partnership Act, 1890, apply. The chief of these are as follows:—

1. All the partners are entitled to share equally in the capital and profits of the business, and must share equally in its losses.
2. No partner is entitled to interest on his capital before the profits are ascertained.
3. No partner may receive a salary or remuneration for acting in the partnership business.
4. Advances by a partner beyond his capital are to bear interest at 5 per cent. per annum.
5. A new partner may be brought into the firm only with the consent of all the existing partners.
6. Every partner may take part in the management of the business.
7. In the event of any differences arising between the partners on matters of ordinary business the will of the majority shall prevail, but the consent of all the partners is necessary to any change in the nature of the business.
8. The books of the firm shall be at the principal place of business, and all partners have the right of free access to inspect or copy them.

The above rules are for guidance, in the absence of any agreement otherwise, in the relationship of partners with each other. As to their relationship with the outside public, the following extract from Section 5 of the Partnership Act, 1890, expresses the chief points:—

Every partner is an agent of the firm and his other partners for the purpose of the business of the partnership and the acts of every partner who does any act *for carrying on* in the usual way business of the kind carried on by the firm of which he is a member bind the firm and his partners unless the partner so acting has in fact no authority to act for the firm in the particular matter *and* the person with whom he is dealing either knows he has no authority or does not know or believe him to be a partner.

The name under which a partnership business is carried on is the "firm name," and the partners are collectively known as the "firm." Where the firm name does not consist of the true surnames or full names of all the partners the firm name must be registered under the Registration of Business Names Act, 1916, and the full names of all the proprietors disclosed. These full names must also appear in all trade catalogues, circulars, and business letters of the firm. The Act also applies to a sole trader carrying on business in a name not his own.

Liability of Partners

Every partner in a firm is liable for the debts of the firm incurred while he is a partner. In England a partner is liable jointly with all the other partners. If judgment is obtained against the firm as a joint liability of all the partners, each partner is liable for the full amount of the judgment. If, however, judgment is obtained only against some members of the firm without satisfaction, action cannot be taken against the remaining partners. In Scotland the partners are jointly and severally liable, and the firm is a separate legal entity and can sue and be sued.

Limited Partnerships Act, 1907

This Act provides that a "Limited Partnership" may be formed in which one member at least is a general partner, and one at least a limited partner. The limited partner invests capital in the partnership, but may not take any part in the management of the firm. He may, however, offer advice on the management to the other partners. He shares in the profits, but his liability for the debts and obligations of the firm is limited to the amount of capital he has put into the partnership. The management of the business is in the hands of the general partners whose liability is that of ordinary members of a partnership firm. Should a limited partner withdraw any part of his capital he is liable for the debts of the firm to the extent of the capital so withdrawn.

Limited Partnerships must be registered with the Registrar of Joint Stock Companies.

Sleeping or Dormant Partners

A "Sleeping or Dormant Partner" is one who takes no active part in the management of the business though he continues to share in the profits, and his capital remains in the firm. He is as fully liable for the debts and obligations of the firm as any active partner.

Partnership Accounts

The Capital Account in the books of a sole trader contains the record of the financial position between the business and the owner. It shows the capital invested in the business at the beginning of a trading period and, at the close of that trading period, the net profit or loss and any drawings made by the proprietor. Where there are two or more owners of the business, as in the case of a partnership, there must be two or more Capital Accounts; a separate one for each partner in which is recorded his contribution to the firm's capital.

Partners' Current Accounts

In the case of the sole trader the net profit is credited and his drawings debited to his Capital Account, so that his capital at the start of a new period varies from his capital at the opening of the previous period of trading by the excess of net profit over drawings. As, however, the capital contribution of each partner in a partnership business is usually fixed by agreement, the Capital Accounts are reserved for a record of the capital contributions only. An account for each partner, separate from his Capital Account, is opened to record his share in the net profit or loss, and any drawings he may make on account of profit. The separate account is called the partner's Current (or Drawings) Account. The Current Account and the Capital Account together would correspond with the Capital Account of the sole trader.

> **Example 32.**—M. Redman and J. Butcher are in partnership under the firm name of Redman and Butcher. Each has contributed £1,500 as capital and is entitled to half share of profits. The partnership agreement provides that Redman may draw £200 and Butcher £250 half-yearly on account of profits. The profits for the year to 31st December amounted to £1,100.
>
> Show the Capital Accounts and Current Accounts of the partners.

The trading record in the partnership books will differ in no way from the record required had the business been under the proprietorship of a sole trader.

The net profit will appear as usual as the balance of the Profit and Loss Account. The profit, however, is shared between the partners in the agreed proportions, and is placed to the credit of their Current Accounts, the Capital Accounts remaining unaffected.

The Cash Book contra entries for the drawings are not shown below as these are simple credit entries.

Dr.				M. Redman's Capital Account			Cr.
19..			£	19.. Jan. 1	Cash ..	C.B.	£ 1500

Dr.				J. Butcher's Capital Account			Cr.
19..			£	19.. Jan. 1	Cash ..	C.B.	£ 1500

Dr.				M. Redman's Current Account			Cr.
19.. June 30 Dec. 31	Cash .. „ ..	C.B. C.B.	£ 200 200	19.. Dec. 31	½ share of profit ..		£ 550

Dr.				J. Butcher's Current Account			Cr.
19.. June 30 Dec. 31	Cash .. „ ..	C.B. C.B.	£ 250 250	19.. Dec. 31	½ share of profit ..		£ 550

The credit balances of the Current Accounts represent undrawn profit, and as such are a liability of the firm to the respective partners.

Occasionally it may be found that a debit balance is shown on a Current Account, indicating that the partner is in debt to the firm to that extent. The balance on a Current Account, whether debit or credit, is carried forward to the next accounting period.

Profit and Loss Account

Partnership Profit and Loss Accounts vary slightly in form from those of sole traders. They are prepared in two sections—the first part shows the ordinary gross profit brought down from the Trading Account and the expenses to be charged against it, giving, on balance, the net trading profit or loss for the period. The net profit or loss is then carried down to a second section—sometimes called the Appropriation Section—in which the division of the balance between the partners is shown.

This sub-division of the Profit and Loss Account enables the net result of the year's trading to be seen at a glance and to be available for comparison with the corresponding information of preceding years.

The second section of the Profit and Loss Account for the above example would appear as below:—

Profit and Loss Account
(Appropriation Section only)

Dr.		£		Cr.
19.. Dec. 31	M. Redman, ½ share of profit ..	550	19.. Dec. 31 Balance (net trading profit) brought down	£ 1100
	J. Butcher, ½ share of profit ..	550		
		£1100		£1100

The corresponding credit entries for the half-shares of the profit are made in the partners' respective Current Accounts as shown above.

The Balance Sheet

A further slight variation in form is the setting out of the partners' accounts in the firm's Balance Sheet. This makes the Balance Sheet more informative, as it discloses the financial position of the firm and, at the same time, the financial position of each partner in relation to the firm.

The Balance Sheet for the above example would contain the following details in addition to the ordinary assets and liabilities.

Balance Sheet
as at 31st December, 19..
(Left hand side only shown)

		£	£
CAPITAL—			
M. Redman		1500	
J. Butcher		1500	
			3000
CURRENT ACCOUNTS—			
M. Redman			
Share of profits		550	
less Drawings		400	
			150
J. Butcher			
Share of profits		550	
less Drawings		500	
			50

Though a partner may draw periodically only the sums permitted by the Partnership Agreement, yet the results of the year's working may, at the close of the year, disclose that the profits were less than the total drawings on account of profit. Unless the partner's Current Account was sufficiently in credit at the beginning of the trading period to cover this deficiency, the partner will be in debt to the firm to the amount of the debit balance on his Current Account. Such debts are carried forward in partnership accounts, and are not placed against the partner's capital in the Ledger Accounts, but, in the Balance Sheet, the debit balance of a partner's Current Account is best shown as a deduction from his capital.

EXERCISES 22

1. D. P. Graves and E. Coffin enter into partnership, profit and losses to be shared in proportion to their capitals which are respectively £5,000 and £3,000. Graves drew £600 and Coffin £500 during the year on account of profits. The net trading profit for the year amounted to £2,000. Show the partners' Capital Accounts and Current Accounts as at 31st December.

2. J. Groom and T. B. Bride entered into partnership with capitals respectively of £2,000 and £1,000. Profits and losses are to be shared in proportion to their capitals. The net trading profit for the year ending 31st December amounted to £1,800. During the year Groom drew £400 and Bride £300 on account of profits.

Show the partners' Capital Accounts and Current Accounts as at 31st December and, also, how these particulars should appear in the firm's Balance Sheet.

3. M. J. Childs and T. Carr are in partnership, sharing profits and losses equally. Their respective capitals are £2,000 and £1,200. Childs drew £40 a month and Carr £30 a month on account of profits. At 31st December the net trading profit for the year amounted to £2,200. Show the Capital Account and Current Account for each partner as at 31st December.

4. G. Reader and A. Storey are in partnership sharing profits and losses as to two-thirds and one-third respectively. On 1st January, 19.., the total capital of the firm was £5,000, held by the partners in equal shares, and on 1st July each partner paid into the business Bank Account £500 as additional capital. During the year each partner drew from the business £80 at the end of each quarter. On 31st December the credit balance of the Profit and Loss Account was £840. Show the Ledger Accounts of the partners as they would appear after the books had been balanced on 31st December, 19...   *R.S.A.*

5. Palmer and Pye are partners in a garage business. They share profits and losses: Palmer 3/5ths; Pye 2/5ths.

Prepare their Trading and Profit and Loss Accounts for the year ended 31st December, 19.., with a Balance Sheet as at that date, from the following Trial Balance.

The stock at 31st December, 19.., was valued at £2,621.

Trial Balance
31st December, 19..

	£	£
Fixed Capital Accounts:—		
Palmer		3300
Pye		2200

	£	£
Current Accounts, 1st January, 19..:—		
Palmer		182
Pye	230	
Drawings during year:		
Palmer	1582	
Pye	912	
Freehold property	1500	
Stock, 1st January, 19..	1939	
Sundry debtors	1413	
Sundry creditors		1324
Sale of motor cars		6430
Sale of petrol, oils, etc.		2948
Charges for repairs to cars		989
Plant and machinery	750	
Vans and breakdown lorry	925	
Advertising	75	
Wages: Works	2100	
Office	412	
Electric power (Works)	427	
Electricity (Office)	48	
Purchases	4307	
Office expenses	156	
Insurances	89	
Cash at bank	508	
	£17373	£17373

R.S.A.

6. D. Sinclair and B. Clark are partners sharing profits and losses, three-fifths and two-fifths respectively.

On 31st March, 19.., the balances in their books were as follows:—

	£
Sinclair, Capital Account	6883
,, Drawings Account	1800
Clark, Capital Account (Dr. Balance)	230
,, Drawing Account	1200
Plant and machinery	2600
Furniture and fixtures	180
Stock, 1st April	3742
Creditors	3814
Debtors	5190
Cash in hand	122
Cash at bank	977
Provision for bad debts	85
Rent and rates	230
Purchases, less returns	5043
Insurance	34
Manufacturing wages	3900
Carriage inwards	168
Discounts allowed	387
,, received	82
Salaries	720
Sundry manufacturing expenses	870
Sundry expenses (other than manufacturing) ..	116
Sales, less returns	16645

Draw up a ~~Trial Balance~~ as at 31st March, 19. .; then prepare Trading and Profit and Loss Accounts and Balance Sheet, noting that—

(*a*) Stock at balancing date was valued £3,084. ✓

(*b*) On 30th March, 19. ., goods valued at £125 were returned by a customer and were taken into stock, but no record of this return was made in the books until 1st April.

(*c*) Depreciation should be written off as follows:—Furniture and fixtures, 5%; Plant and machinery, 7½%.

(*d*) £72 of book debts should be written off as bad, and the Provision for Bad Debts raised to £100.

(Journal entries are not required.)   *U.E.I.* (modified)

Twice

e. Wages accrued £10. ✓

f. Rates prepaid £36 ✓

g) Insurance " 20. ✓

h. Salaries in arrears £40 ✓

i) Rent in advance £54 ✓

CHAPTER 23

PARTNERSHIP ACCOUNTS

The terms of a Partnership Agreement may be such that further accounts than those already discussed are required to record the financial relationship of the partners.

Partners' Salaries

It may happen that there are certain inequalities between the partners. One may give more time to the firm's business, another may have exceptional skill or experience. A junior partner may have brought little capital and be entitled to a small share only of the profits, yet he may devote considerable skill and attention to his business. In such cases the reward for this difference may take the form of a fixed salary.

A partnership salary is a charge against profits prior to division between the partners, and may be dealt with in one of two ways, namely—

(a) Paid direct to the partner in cash at stated intervals.

(b) Placed to the partner's credit at the close of the financial year.

In either case a new account, Partnership Salaries Account, is required. The balance of this is transferred to the second section of the Profit and Loss Account at the close of the trading period.

If the salary is paid in cash, *credit* Cash Book; *debit* Partnership Salaries Account at the time of payment.

If the salary is to be credited to the partner, *credit* the partner's Current Account; *debit* Partnership Salaries Account.

Interest on Capital

The capital introduced by the partners is an important factor in the success of an undertaking, especially if the nature of the business requires considerable quantities of fixed assets, such as plant and machinery, or considerable capital resources to finance business deals. Where there are equal contributions of capital in such cases, equal sharing of profits is a satisfactory proposal for equally hardworking partners. But some agreements bind the partners to a

179

ratio of profit distribution different from the ratio of capital contribution. A and B may, for example, contribute £4,000 and £2,000 respectively as capital, but agree to share profits equally. Any benefit to the firm from A's larger capital comes equally to A and B in the sharing of profits.

A method of rewarding A for the larger capital introduced is to give a first share from the profits to both A and B based on their respective capitals, and then to share the remainder of the profit in the agreed proportions.

This prior appropriation of profit is calculated at about the income that would be derived if the partners' capital were invested outside the firm. It cannot be made unless the Partnership Agreement provides for it, as shown in Chapter 22, and, because of its purpose and the basis of its computation, it is referred to as allowing interest on capital.

No immediate payment out of cash is involved. Interest on capital is a book entry only, the placing of a first share of the profit, calculated at a percentage on the respective capitals, to the credit of each partner, to be followed by the crediting of the remainder in the agreed proportions. For example, A and B are in partnership, sharing profits equally,

$$A's capital = £4,000$$
$$B's capital = £2,000$$
$$Profits = £1,500.$$

Without allowing interest on capital each will be credited with £750 as half share of profits.

Allowing, first, interest on capital at 5 per cent. per annum absorbs £300 of the profits, leaving £1,200 for division equally between A and B.

	A £	B £
Interest on capital	200	100
Share of remainder	600	600
Total	£800	£700

The benefit accruing to A under this method is the reward to him for the use of his greater capital.

The prior allocation of profit under interest on capital is, roughly, the return that might be expected from the capital if invested in securities. The remainder of the profit may therefore be regarded as the reward for the labour and skill exercised in the business by the partners. If this amount is negligible it might be necessary to consider whether the partnership should be continued.

The method of recording the interest on capital in the accounts is to debit the interest to a new account headed "Interest on Capital Account," the corresponding credit being made in the partners' respective Current Accounts at the close of the trading period. The Interest on Capital Account is closed by transferring the balance to the debit of the second section of the Profit and Loss Account. The balance of the second section is then the profit available for division in the ordinary way.

New accounts, namely, the Partnership Salaries Account and the Interest on Capital Account, have been suggested, but in the case of small partnerships the entries may be made direct to the debit of the Profit and Loss Account, thus avoiding the opening of new accounts for one or two entries only which are immediately transferred to the Profit and Loss Account.

Interest on Drawings

Reasons somewhat similar to those for charging interest on capital are advanced for charging interest on drawings. If A draws £250 each quarter on account of profits, and B draws nothing until the end of the financial year, A has had the use of money which, had it not been drawn, would probably have been of use to the business and to the profit of both A and B. An advantage is given to A which B does not enjoy. If, however, the Partnership Agreement provides that interest shall be charged on drawings, the partners pay for the use of money drawn in anticipation of profits. They pay the firm and the firm's profits are increased to that extent. The partners who do not draw, or draw smaller sums, are compensated by the proportion of the interest that is included in their share of profits. The interest is charged by adjustments in the partnership accounts, not by direct payment of cash by the partner to the firm. The amount to the credit of a partner shown in his Current Account is diminished by the debiting to that account of the interest, and the firm is given a credit entry in a new account called Interest on Drawings Account. At the close of the trading period the balance of the Interest on Drawings Account is transferred to the credit of the second section of the Profit and Loss Account.

The interest, usually at five per cent. per annum, is calculated for the period from the date of the drawing to the date of the closing of the books for the financial year.

To facilitate the calculations and the entries it is usual to have two additional columns on the debit side of the partners' Current Accounts, one for the number of days and the other for the amount of interest. The total of the interest column is carried to the ordinary debit column of the Current Account at the close of the financial year, and the credit entry of the amount is made in the Interest on Drawings Account.

The following example illustrates the entries required for partners' salaries, interest on capital, and interest on drawings.

Example 33.—J. Moore and B. Burgess began to trade in partnership on 1st January, 19.., under the firm name of Moore & Co., Moore contributing £3,000 and Burgess £1,000 in cash. They agree as follows:—

To share profits equally. To allow interest on capital at 6% per annum. To charge interest on drawings at 6% per annum. That prior to division of profits Burgess shall be credited with £400 as partnership salary. That Moore may draw £400 on 1st July and Burgess £200 on 1st April, 1st July, and 1st October in each year on account of profits.

The net trading profit for the year to 31st December, 19.., amounted to £2,500. Show the accounts rendered necessary by these provisions.

Dr.				J. Moore. Capital Account				Cr.
19..			£	19..				£
				Jan. 1	Cash	..	C.B.	3000

Dr.				B. Burgess. Capital Account				Cr.
19..			£	19..				£
				Jan. 1	Cash	..	C.B.	1000

Dr.			Interest on Capital			Cr.
19.. Dec. 31 „ 31	J. Moore .. B. Burgess	£ 180 60	19.. Dec. 31	Transfer to Profit and Loss A/c.		£ 240
		£240				£240

Dr.			Interest on Drawings			Cr.
19..		£	19..			£
Dec. 31	Transfer to Profit and Loss A/c.	30	Dec. 31 ,, 31	J. Moore .. B. Burgess ..		12 18
		£30				30

Dr.			Partner's Salary Account			Cr.
19..		£	19..			£
Dec. 31	B. Burgess	400	Dec. 31	Transfer to Profit and Loss A/c.		400

Profit and Loss Appropriation Account

Dr. For the Year ended 31st December 19.. Cr.

	£			£
Interest on capital ..	240	Trading profit ..	b/d	2500
Partner's salary ..	400	Interest on drawings		30
Share of profits:—				
J. Moore	945			
B. Burgess ..	945			
	£2530			£2530

Cash Book

Dr. (Showing only appropriate items, Bank Columns) Cr.

		BANK				BANK
		£				£
19..			19..			
Jan. 1	Capital—		Apl. 1	B. Burgess ..		200
	J. Moore	3000	July 1	B. Burgess ..		200
	B. Burgess	1000	,, 1	J. Moore ..		400
			Oct. 1	B. Burgess ..		200

J. Moore. Current Account

Dr.			MONTHS	INTEREST	DRAWINGS			Cr.
				£	£	19..		£
19.. July 1	Cash		6	12	400	Dec. 31	Interest on capital	180
Dec. 31	Interest				12	,, 31	½ share of profits	945
,, 31	Balance c/d				713			£1125
					£1125	Jan. 1	Balance b/d	713

B. Burgess. Current Account

Dr.			MONTHS	INTEREST	DRAWINGS, ETC.			Cr.
				£	£	19..		£
19.. Apl. 1	Cash		9	9	200	Dec. 31	Interest on capital	60
July 1	Cash		6	6	200	,, 31	Salary	400
Oct. 1	Cash		3	3	200	,, 31	½ share of profits	945
Dec. 31	Interest			18	18			£1405
,, 31	Balance c/d				787	Jan. 1	Balance b/d	787
					£1405			

Balance Sheet
as at 31st December, 19..
(Left hand side and required items only are shown)

	£	£	£
CAPITAL—			
J. Moore		3000	
B. Burgess		1000	
			4000
CURRENT ACCOUNTS—			
J. Moore			
Share of profits	945		
Interest on capital	180	1125	
less Drawings	400		
Interest on drawings	12	412	
			713
B. Burgess			
Share of profits	945		
Interest on capital	60		
Salary	400		
		1405	
less Drawings	600		
Interest on drawings	18	618	
			787

Had Burgess been permitted to draw the salary of £400 in cash during the year the debit entry for it would have been made in the Partners' Salary Account as shown above, but the credit entry would have been made in the Cash Book. No entry in that case would have appeared in the Partner's Current Account.

Partners' Advances and Sundry Adjustments

If the partnership firm is in need of more working capital or requires money temporarily to help over a difficult financial period, a partner may give assistance by making a loan to the firm. There is an advantage to the partner in assisting by way of a loan rather than by an addition to his capital, as partners' loans have priority of repayment over capital in the event of dissolution. A separate Loan Account is kept in respect of each advance. The interest on the loan is debited periodically to the Interest on Loan Account for eventual transfer to the Profit and Loss Appropriation Account. The credit entry for the interest is made to the Partner's Current Account unless it is paid in cash—in which case the Cash Book is credited.

In the preparation of the Trading and Profit and Loss Accounts and Balance Sheet of a partnership, the usual adjustments have to be made to take into account outstanding liabilities, payments in advance, allowances for depreciation and for bad and doubtful debts. These are necessary for sound accounting whatever form the business ownership takes. Some adjustments may be required, in addition, arising from the type of ownership. These include the taking into account of the interest on partners' capital, interest on drawings, and any partnership salary outstanding. The treatment of these items in the accounts has already been discussed, but often the items are given as instructions with a Trial Balance from which Final Accounts are to be prepared. As the Ledger Accounts are not required in such a test, only the effect on the Final Accounts has to be shown. Such adjustments are, of course, normally entered in the appropriate Ledger Accounts but, as the test is concerned only with the Final Accounts, it is necessary to show in them the two-fold effect of each adjustment.

For interest on capital the appropriate sum should be debited to the second section of the Profit and Loss Account, and added to the balance of the Partner's Current Account in the Balance Sheet.

The interest on drawings is credited to the appropriation or second section of the Profit and Loss Account, and shown in the Balance Sheet as a deduction from the balance of the Partner's Current Account.

The partnership salary for which credit is to be given to the partner is entered to the debit of the second section of the Profit and Loss Account, and the sum is added to the Partner's Current Account balance in the Balance Sheet.

In each of these cases one entry of the two-fold aspect is entered in the Balance Sheet. It does not follow that the Balance Sheet is treated as a Ledger Account. The Balance Sheet item has been adjusted to show the figure at which it would stand if the item had been extracted from the Ledger after the proper Ledger entries for the adjustments had been made. As, however, in this kind of test the Ledger Accounts are neither given nor required, it is necessary to arrive at the Balance Sheet figure without reference to them.

EXERCISES 23

1. Robinson and Jones are in partnership, sharing profits and losses equally, Their fixed capitals are: Robinson, £1,500, Jones, £1,400. Jones is entitled to a salary of £400 per annum which is to be credited to him at the close of the year. During the year Robinson drew £300 on account of profits. The net profit at 31st December, prior to these adjustments, amounted to £2,100.

Show the final section of the Profit and Loss Account, the partners' Capital Accounts and Current Accounts, and the appropriate entries in the Balance Sheet.

2. Brown and Tomlinson are in partnership, sharing profits and losses in equal proportion. Brown's capital is £10,000, and Tomlinson's capital is £4,000.

The partners are entitled to 5% interest on capital, and are to be charged interest on drawings at 5% per annum.

Brown drew £200 on 1st March and 1st August.

Tomlinson drew £200 on 1st April, 1st July, and 1st October.

Prior to any of the above adjustments the profits for the year to 31st December were £6,000.

Give the accounts to record the above information, and the partners' accounts as they would appear in the Balance Sheet.

3. Toogood and Waring are equal partners whose capitals are £2,000 and £1,500 respectively. They are entitled to interest on capital at 5%, and are to be charged interest on drawings at 5% per annum.

Waring drew £100 on 1st March, 1st June, 1st September, and 1st December.

The profits prior to these adjustments amounted at 31st December to £2,130.

Show the accounts required to record this information, including the partners' Capital and Current Accounts, and show the details that should be given in the firm's Balance Sheet.

4. Record the following facts in the personal accounts of A. and B. Moore, two partners, who share profits and losses in the ratio of 5 to 3; and allow interest on capital at the rate of 4 per cent. per annum. No interest is to be allowed on Current Accounts or charged on drawings. B. Moore is to be credited with a salary of £300 for the year.

			A. Moore	*B. Moore*
			£	£
Jan.	1.	Capital Accounts	4000	3000
June 30.		Additional capital brought in and banked	1000	—
Jan.	1.	Current Accounts	72 (*Dr.*)	100 (*Cr.*)
„	1–Dec. 31.	Drawings	650	650

The partnership's total divisible profit for the year, after charging the salary, was £1,188. *R.S.A.*

5. Dickson is a partner in a business and is entitled to an eighth of the net profits of the firm. From the following particulars write up the Capital and Current Accounts of Dickson for the year to 31st December, 19.., as they would appear in the Ledger of the partnership.

			£
19..			
Jan.	1.	Balance on Dickson's Capital Account (*Cr.*)	1000
„	1.	„ „ „ Current „ „	300
July	1.	Additional cash capital brought in by Dickson	600
Dec. 31.		Dickson's drawings for year	520
„	31.	Interest charged on Dickson's drawings..	13
„	31.	Interest allowed on Dickson's capital	65
„	31.	Interest allowed on Dickson's Current Account	15
„	31.	Net profits for year (after adjustment of partners' interest) divisible between the partners	6400
„	31.	Amount transferred from Dickson's Current Account to his Capital Account	400

R.S.A.

6. The Partnership Agreement between A, B, and C contains the following provisions:—

(a) The partners' *fixed* capitals shall be—A, £10,000; B, £8,000; C, £6,000.

(b) A and B are each to receive a salary of £600 a year.

(c) Interest on capital is to be calculated at 5% per annum.

(d) A, B, and C are to share profits and losses in the ratio 3; 2; 1.

(e) No interest to be charged on Drawings or Current Accounts.

On January 1st, 19.., the balances on Current Accounts were—A, Cr. £500; B, Cr. £200; C, Cr. £350.

During the year the drawings were—A, £1,200; B, £1,000; and C, £500. The Profit and Loss Account for the year showed a profit of £4,500 before charging interest on capital and partners' salaries.

Show the Capital and Current Accounts of A, B, and C, as at 31st December, after the division of the profit. *U.E.I.*

7. X, Y, Z are in partnership. They share profits: X two-fifths, Y two-fifths, and Z one-fifth. The partnership provides that interest at 4% per annum shall be paid on the credit balance of each partner's Capital Account at the beginning of each financial year, that no interest is to be charged on drawings, and that Z is to receive a salary of £750 per annum and 2% commission on the balance of trading profit after charging his salary but before charging interest on capital.

The balances of the Capital Accounts at 1st January, 19.., are: X, credit £4,000; Y, credit £3,000; Z, credit £1,000.

The balances of the Current Accounts at 1st January, 19.., are: X, credit £250; Y, debit £50; Z, debit £100.

Drawings during the year amount to: X, £1,300; Y, £925; Z, £1,200.

The trading profit for the year ended 31st December, 19.., was £3,650.

Prepare:—

(a) An account showing the division of the trading profit in accordance with the terms of the partnership agreement.

(b) The Capital and Current Accounts of each of the partners for the year.
College of Preceptors—Senior.

8. Copping and Watts were equal partners in a business, and a Trial Balance taken from their books on 31st December, 19.., was as under:—

Trial Balance. 31st December, 19..

	£	£
Copping, Capital		1000
Watts, Capital		500
Sales, net		8673
Purchases, net	7328	
Freehold premises..	2500	
Copping, Drawings Account	250	
Watts, Drawings Account	400	
General expenses	462	
Bad debts	50	
Discount	136	29
Creditors		2874
Debtors	3118	
Cash	86	
Bank		4071
Stock, 1st January	2317	
Repairs to premises	150	
Fixtures and fittings	350	
	£17147	£17147

Prepare a Trading Account and Profit and Loss Account for the year ending 31st December, and a Balance Sheet as at that date, making the necessary allowances for the following:—

Watts is entitled to a salary of £250 per annum, which has not been paid.

Fixtures and fittings to be depreciated at the rate of 10%. Allow interest on capital at the rate of 5% per annum. Insurance premium prepaid, £36, included in general expenses. Stock on hand, 31st December, valued at £2,885.

U.L.C.I.

9. A. Carrick and G. Furgus are trading in partnership, and the following list of balances appeared in the books of the firm on 31st March, 19..:—

	£
Fixtures and fittings	400
Machinery	5000
A. Carrick—Capital Account	20000
G. Furgus—Capital Account	2250
A. Carrick—Drawings Account	1200
G. Furgus—Drawings Account	600
Rent received	150
Telephone charges	177
Bank balance (in hand)	1645
Discount allowed	461
Factory wages	13397
Freehold premises	9000
Sales	53944
Factory power	1592
Salaries	2479
Sundry creditors	4392
Sundry expenses	849
Purchases	34118
Stock at 31st March, (previous year)	3763
Sundry debtors	5649
Bad debts	158
Discount received	121
Cash in hand	369

GROSS P. 22,608

Net P. 2,564

You are required to prepare:—

(*a*) ~~The Trial Balance at 31st March, 19...~~

(*b*) The Trading and Profit and Loss Account for the year ending 31st March, 19.., and Balance Sheet as on that date, taking into consideration the following:—

1. The Stock at 31st March, 19.., was valued at £6,545.
2. Provide for further bad debts, £102.
3. Depreciate machinery by 10% of cost (£10,000).
4. Depreciate fixtures and fittings by 12½% of cost (£800).
5. A. Carrick is entitled to three-quarters and G. Furgus one-quarter of the profits or losses.

R.S.A.

10. L. and M. are in partnership sharing profits and losses equally. Before profits or losses are shared each partner is entitled to 5% per annum interest of capital, after which M. is entitled so far as profits are available to a bonus of £500 per annum. Final Accounts are made up half yearly.

Approp'ation Acc. Balance Sh.

From the following details extracted from the books at 30th June 19.. you are required to prepare the Profit and Loss Appropriation Account for the half year ended 30th June 19.. and a Balance Sheet as on that date.

	£
Capital Accounts (1st January 19..):—	
L. £4,000; M. £6,000	10000
Current Accounts (Cr. balances at 1st January 19..):—	
L. £25; M. £30	55
Cash in hand and at bank	2335
Stock	2705
Sundry debtors	1980
Provision for bad debts	100
Sundry creditors:—Trade	2510
Expense	104
Advertising brought forward (debit balance)	800
Furniture and equipment	475
Freehold premises	8000
Mortgage on freehold premises	3500
Credit balance of Profit and Loss Account (before providing	
for interest on capital and M.'s bonus)..	3126
Partners' drawings for the half year:—	
L. £1,250; M. £1,850	3100

A.E.B., G.C.E. "O" Level.

11. F. Winter and G. Frost are in partnership trading as "Utensils Supply Company". The partners have fixed capital contributions: Winter, £6,500, and Frost, £5,500. Each partner is allowed interest on capital at 6% per annum and profits and losses are shared equally. Winter has made a loan to the firm of £2,500 at 7% per annum interest which is credited to his Current Account at the end of each year. At the 30th September, 19.., one year's interest was still due on this loan.

The Net Trading Profit (before allowing for any sums due to partners) for the year ended 30th September, 19.., was £4,369.

In addition the following balances were extracted from the books at 30th September, 19..:

	£
Current Accounts:—	
Credit balances at start of year:—Winter	40
Frost	30
Drawings for year of account:—Winter	2300
Frost	2000
Sundry creditors	2570
Sundry debtors	5490
Provision for bad debts	170
Goodwill	2000
Stock-in-trade	5980
Furniture and equipment	740
Cash in hand and balance at bank	3169

(a) Prepare the Appropriation Account of the partnership for the year ended 30th September, 19.., and a Balance Sheet at that date.

(b) If there had been no agreement between the partners with regard to interest on capital and loans and the division of profits:
   (i) Would partners be entitled to interest on capital and, if so, at what rate?
   (ii) Would Winter be entitled to any interest on loan and, if so, at what rate?
   (iii) How would profits and losses be shared?

A.E.B., G.C.E. "O" Level.

CHAPTER 24 *Jan. 25th.*

GENERAL PRINCIPLES: THE LEDGER, TRIAL BALANCE, AND FINAL ACCOUNTS

The student who has worked carefully through the preceding chapters should have, at this stage, a good grasp of the principles of double-entry bookkeeping. The chapters have dealt with the basic principle of the two-fold aspect of all transactions and with the recording of the two aspects in the accounts. They have included reference to the principle of classification which underlies the Ledger Accounts and makes them of informative value to the proprietor of the business, and the student should now be able to gather for himself the information the accounts contain. To be able to make the correct entries is a valuable acquisition, but to be able to understand quickly and clearly the meaning of the entries in an account and the financial situation disclosed is of still greater value, and the student should not be satisfied with the lesser attainment.

Another point the student should now appreciate is the development of the books in which the record is made to adjust the methods to the pressure of business requirements. For a simple system of accounts the Ledger is sufficient. The growth in the number of transactions to be recorded and the consequent pressure on the bookkeepers has led to the separation of Ledger Accounts and the introduction of other books to ease the volume of work required on the Ledger. It will have been observed that the basic principles of double entry have been maintained, yet the system is elastic enough in form to permit its adaptation to meet special conditions arising from the growth of business. Full appreciation of the adaptive nature of the system should prepare the student for further developments to meet the needs of the different types of business units and the different demands made upon the bookkeeping system.

The earlier chapters show the separation of the cash accounts from the Ledger, and the benefits derived from a separate Cash Book. Later, the subsidiary books are introduced to provide a means of recording details from which summary totals may be posted to the Ledger. For the purpose of ascertaining the gross profit, for example, for a trading period it is necessary to know,

191

among other things, the total sales for the period. It is sufficient for this purpose to know the total only and not the details of which the total is composed. This being so, it is unnecessary to overload the Sales Account in the Ledger. Periodical totals are enough, and the details, as they are wanted for other purposes, can be recorded separately. The separate record, however, halves the written record of sales, and at the same time provides a classified record readily available for reference, and one that permits of division of duties among the staff. This method of grouping details into special books, and the using of totals only for the Ledger entries, is capable of indefinite extension as need arises, and renders the system adaptable without abrogation of basic principles.

Later chapters deal with the further developments of the separation of the Ledger into parts. The growth of large-scale business involves the maintenance of large clerical staffs, and the work has to be subdivided to be properly carried on. Recognising that customers and suppliers are seldom identical in person, an easy division is possible—one Ledger for the accounts of customers, and another for the accounts of firms from whom purchases are made. The former, known as the Sales, or Sold, Ledger, contains the debtors' accounts, and the latter, the Purchase Ledger, or Bought Ledger, contains the creditors' accounts. A third Ledger, called the General Ledger—sometimes the Nominal Ledger—contains the real and nominal accounts relating to the assets and liabilities and the gains and expenses of the business. In sole trading and partnership concerns a fourth Ledger, known as the Private Ledger, may be used to contain the Capital Account, the Drawings Account, and the Trading and Profit and Loss Accounts and Balance Sheets for each period. It is also kept for the Final Accounts of limited companies.

Further growth may demand further subdivision of these Ledgers, so that in some businesses the Sold Ledgers and the Bought Ledgers are divided into sections. One firm may find that to have separate Ledgers for Town, Country, and Foreign Accounts answers best. Another may prefer to make an alphabetical division on customers' names, as A-K, L-R, S-Z, or departmentally, according to the nature of the business, as for example, China Dept., Glass Dept., Hardware Dept.

Increasing use is being made of Loose Leaf Ledgers and Card Ledgers in substitution for the ordinary bound books. A Loose Leaf Ledger consists of an expanding binder into which is inserted separate sheets printed in Ledger ruling. Card Ledgers consist of similarly printed cards which are kept in trays or drawers arranged in cabinets. The advantage of these forms over the ordinary bound book is that the "dead" accounts may be removed and kept separately. The binder or drawer then contains only the "live" accounts, and sheets or cards can be added as new accounts are wanted. This avoids the work of opening a new Ledger as the old bound Ledger is filled. Further, as the sheets or cards are loose the accounts may be arranged alphabetically, rendering a separate index unnecessary. In times of pressure, as for example, when the monthly statements of account have to be prepared, loose leaf or card systems make for expeditious work, as they may be used by a large number of clerks each taking a number of accounts. Time is saved in ordinary posting, since the accounts are continuous. As one leaf or card is filled a new one is added next to it. In the bound Ledger an estimate has to be made of the space to be allotted to an account, and if this proves insufficient, the account is continued in another place.

The disadvantage of the Loose Leaf and Card Ledgers has been that leaves or cards may be wilfully destroyed or substituted or fresh cards inserted for fraudulent purposes, but it has been largely overcome by the introduction of safety locking devices and by instituting control of the issue of blank leaves or cards.

All these variations in form have their uses. They are introduced to meet the needs of particular types of businesses, and in every case the purpose is to facilitate the recording in order that it may keep pace with the volume of the business. The principles of bookkeeping remain constant—it is only the material form of the recording medium that is changed to meet new conditions.

The Trial Balance

The Trial Balance is a list of all the debit and credit balances extracted from the Ledger Accounts, including the cash and bank balances from the Cash Book. Its use as a means of checking the arithmetical accuracy of the postings to the Ledger has already been referred to. A further use is as a list of Ledger balances from which to prepare the Trading and Profit and Loss Accounts and the Balance Sheet. It is important, therefore, that the Trial Balance should be accurately drawn up, and that any error disclosed should be traced and rectified.

Examination tests often take the form of a Trial Balance from which the Final Accounts are to be prepared. In some cases a list only of the Ledger balances is given, and it is necessary to draft from it the Trial Balance in its normal form, separating the debit and credit balances. If the capital is not shown in the list it is to be found by ascertaining the difference between the total of the debit and the total of the credit balances. Frequent practice in drawing up Final Accounts from given Trial Balances is apt to cause one to forget the existence of the Ledger Accounts from which the Trial Balance is prepared. It should be borne in mind that the Trading and Profit and Loss Accounts are part of the double entry system, and that the items contained in them must have their corresponding contra entries somewhere in the Ledger Accounts if the double entry for the trading period is to be complete. In other words, in the preparation of the Final Accounts from a given Trial Balance, one aspect only of each of the items is used, it being assumed that it is known that the other aspect must be entered in its appropriate Ledger Account if the double entry record is to be complete.

When preparing the Final Accounts from the Trial Balance the first step is the drafting of the Trading Account to find the gross profit, and the next is the preparation of the Profit and Loss Account. After these accounts have been prepared the items remaining in the Trial Balance are those which are necessary for the compilation of the Balance Sheet.

Certain difficulties may arise in the drafting of Final Accounts as the items present many variations according to the nature of the business. It is possible, however, to agree upon a few broad rules for guidance.

The Trading Account

The first purpose of the Trading Account is to discover the gross profit for the trading period under review, not so much for the amount in itself as for the usefulness of knowing the ratio the gross profit bears to turnover, and the value of the ratio for comparison with similar information from preceding business years.

The percentage of gross profit on turnover should be fairly constant from year to year. Fluctuations in the percentage indicate a need for enquiry into causes. The stock valuation may be at fault, or pilfering may cause loss and consequently a low figure for stock on hand. Over-stocking of goods followed by sales to clear at prices near or below cost may be another reason, or, on the other hand, the buying may be at fault.

As the value of the gross profit figure lies in its usefulness for purposes of comparison, it is essential that the basis of its calculation should be consistent. To this end the component items of the Trading Account should not vary from year to year, but should remain constant. What those component items are necessarily varies from business to business, but a general rule to apply to all businesses is to include in the Trading Account only those items which vary directly with the turnover.

The business man will therefore not only call for a Trading Account showing the gross profit for the period under review, he will also require the percentage of gross profit on turnover to be shown and to make these more intelligible, figures and percentages for previous trading periods. A simple example is given herewith—

Comparative Trading Accounts

	1966 £	1967 £	1968 £
Stock at commencement	2000	3000	2050
Purchase (less returns)	7000	5000	6900
Wages	900	850	900
	9900	8850	9850
Less Stock at close..	3000	2050	3050
Cost of Goods Sold	6900	6800	6800
Sales (or Turnover)	13800	13000	13900
Gross profit..	6900	6200	7100
Percentage G/P on Turnover	50%	47·7%	51·1%

A study of the above figures will prove of great value; a comparison of the percentages in conjunction with the turnover figures and the cost of goods sold would be the most obvious things to look at first. Of course, comparative profit and loss figures could be added as well as may other percentages found to assist comparison, *e.g.* percentage of gross profit on cost; of net profit on capital; of total expenses on turnover, etc.

Stock in Relation to Trading

Too many students regard stock as a bookkeeping figure instead of as a quantity of physical material waiting to be sold. When goods are bought they are entered in the Purchases Account at cost price; when they are sold these same goods appear in the Sales Account at selling price. While waiting to be sold the goods are said to be "in stock," and at the end of the trading period, if they are still unsold, they are valued at cost and entered in the Stock

Account. So goods will appear in three different accounts and students should be quite sure that they understand the relationship between them, especially as all three accounts have transfers to Trading Account. The following example should help.

> **Example 34.**—A trader had in stock 100 articles valued at £0·15 each on 1st Jan. During the month he bought 600 more of these articles at the same price but returned 20 as useless. He sold 650 articles during the month for £0·25 each. Customers returned 40 as not suitable. His Trading Account for the month would appear as follows:—

Trading Account
for the month ended 31st January

	Articles	Price £	£		Articles	Price £	£
Stock ..	100	0·15	15	Sales ..	650	0·25	162·5
Purchases ..	600 —	0·15	90	*Less* Returns	40	0·25	10·0
	700		105		610		152·5
Less Returns	20 —	0·15	3	Stock ..	70	0·15	10·5
	680		102		680		
Gross profit c/d ..			61				
			£163				£163·0

In the information given, no mention is made of the closing stock, but it is evident that this must be the number of articles in hand at the end of the trading period and valued at cost price, viz. 70 articles at £0·15 each.

Rate of Turnover

The gross profit of any business will naturally be affected by the rate, or velocity, of turnover; that is, the number of times in a trading period that any particular line of goods is bought and sold. Obviously, the more rapid this rate of turnover is, whether the gross profit on the article be large or small, the greater must be the total gross profit.

The rate of turnover is computed by finding the average of stocks in the trading period in question and dividing it into the cost of goods sold, or alternatively, the turnover less the gross profit.

Consider the figures in the Trading Account below:—

	£			£
Stock, 1st Jan. ..	1000	Sales		12000
Purchases	8000	Stock, 31st Jan. ..		1500
Gross profit ..	4500			
	£13500			£13500

The *cost of goods sold* is £1000 + £8000 — £1500 = £7500.

The *average stock* is $\dfrac{£1000 + £1500}{2}$ = £1250.

The *rate of turnover of stock* is $\dfrac{£7500}{£1250}$ = 6 times per month.

By finding the rate of turnover on particular lines of goods in this way, it is possible to discard unprofitable lines (that is those on which the rate of turnover is considered too low) and to step up the sales of profitable lines (those on which the rate of turnover is high or at least adequate).

In the event of stock being destroyed by fire it is possible to work out the estimated loss so long as the percentage gross profit on turnover is known. Consider the following:—

Example 35.—The premises of S. James were damaged by fire on 5th November and all his stock was destroyed with the exception of £200 worth which was salvaged. His stock on 1st January last was £6,000. Purchases to 5th November were £13,800, and sales £18,000. James was accustomed to making 20% gross profit on turnover.

Trading Account of S. James
for the period ended 5th November, 19..

	£		£	£
Stock, 1st Jan.	6000	Sales		18000
Purchases	13800	Stock salvaged ..	200	
Gross profit (estimated 20% on turnover)	3600	,, (estimated lost in fire)	5200	
				5400
	£23400			£23400

A study of the above Trading Account will show that by putting in an estimated gross profit it becomes possible to total the debit side. The amount by which the debit side now exceeds the credit side, viz. £5,200 must be the estimated value of the stock destroyed.

Before proceeding to some observations on the Profit and Loss Account it is as well to remind students at this point that a frequent examination question concerns the effect of errors found in the books on the gross profit. It is of the utmost importance for a student to be able to trace errors through to the Trading and Profit and Loss Account and practice should be had in answering the following type of question:—

The Returns Inwards Journal was over-cast by £10. Say what effect, if any, this would have on the gross profit for the period.

Profit and Loss Account

The gross profit as shown by the Trading Account is carried to the Profit and Loss Account, and against it are set all the charges incurred in the course of the business other than those which have already been taken to the Trading Account. Any gains other than those arising from the sale of goods included in the Trading Account are added to the gross profit. The difference is the net profit or loss, as the case may be, for the trading period. This is of importance as it represents the amount available for distribution to the proprietors of the business, and because of this, it is also of importance that in the process of arriving at the net profit every form of expense should be taken into account. Certain adjustments may have to be made in the expenses in order that the true net profit may be shown. For example, account must be taken of any shrinkage in value of the assets and of any outstanding expense properly attributable to the year under review. These and similar adjustments are considered more fully hereafter.

No particular form of Profit and Loss Account is in general use, but it makes for orderly presentation of the facts if like items are grouped together. Broadly speaking, the expense items may be placed in one of the following groups: Administration Expenses, such as office salaries, directors' fees, office rent, and the general overhead charges for rates, lighting, etc.; Selling Expenses, such as advertising, travellers' salaries and commission; Distribution Expenses, such as carriage outwards (carriage inwards is charged in the Trading Account), cartage and freight, charges in regard to delivery vans.

The disposal of the net profit varies according to the nature of the ownership of the business. It may be posted to the Capital Account of the sole trader, or, as in the case of a partnership business, carried down to a second section for the purpose of recording its distribution among the partners. In company accounts the net profit is carried to an Appropriation Account in which the actual appropriation of the profit is shown.

The Balance Sheet

The purpose of a Balance Sheet is to present a true and correct view of the financial position of the business at a given date. It is prepared from the balances of the accounts that remain open on the books after the preparation of the Trading and Profit and Loss Accounts. Such balances are assets or liabilities, or are regarded temporarily as such for Balance Sheet purposes. The Balance Sheet is not a Ledger Account. It is a statement only in a particular form, and may best be defined as a classified list of the debit and credit balances remaining on the books after the preparation of the Trading and Profit and Loss Accounts.

If the Balance Sheet is to present a correct view of the financial position, it is essential that its component items should be examined with the greatest care to ensure that each appears at its true value. Much will depend upon the work done to ensure that all outstanding debts and all shrinkage in value of the assets have been provided for. Provision for depreciation was dealt with in Chapter 18 where it was explained that normal wear and tear in use of plant and machinery, furniture and fittings, for example, must cause some loss of value, and that to ignore such wastage would give a false value for the asset in the Balance Sheet. Such valuations are necessarily reasonable estimates only of the value of the assets to the business as a going concern. It is impossible to make an actual test unless the business is wound up, and assets converted into cash and the liabilities paid off. Then, and then only, could it be said whether the valuations were fair estimates, and the Balance Sheet a true picture of the financial position. Failing such a test, the only action possible is to ensure that there is no overstatement of value, and that all precautions are taken to make the Balance Sheet a reasonable and honest statement.

Comparison of a series of Balance Sheets may help in assessing correctly the position as disclosed by the last Balance Sheet of the series. An interested party may then form some idea of the periodical treatment of the assets and whether sufficient allowance has been made for wastage in value. Further, some insight is possible on the trading position of the firm. The fact that the assets exceed the liabilities, other than capital, shows that the concern is solvent and could pay its debts in full. The soundness or otherwise of the trading position is also indicated. The current liabilities should be less than the current assets, such as cash, stock, sundry debtors, and investments, *i.e.* there should be sufficient working capital. If not, the firm is overtrading and disaster may follow on the contracting of debts without sufficient means of payment.   It does not follow that there should be cash of an amount equivalent to the total trade creditors.   Trade debts have not all to be paid at one time, and meanwhile trade continues and stock is converted into cash.   The flow is continuous and may be ample to meet needs as they arise, but debts should not be created of a nature and to an extent that pressure for payment may jeopardise the continuance of the business through lack of ability to meet the demand.

An item that sometimes appears in Balance Sheets is Goodwill, and the fact that it is placed among the assets of the business some-times causes difficulties for students.   Goodwill as an accounting item usually arises from the purchase of a business as a going concern.   The assets of a business may be worth, say, £4,000 on valuation.   The purchaser may pay £5,000, that is, £4,000 for the stock, fittings, and other assets, and £1,000 for the Goodwill.   He believes that the custom, reputation, and other similar advantages attaching to the business will accrue to him on his taking over, and that this prospect is worth £1,000 over and above the value of the assets.   If he founded a new concern it would take time to create similar advantages, and during that time he could not expect his profits to be so great.   The purchase of the Goodwill is capital expenditure on something of value, and for this reason it is placed among the assets, although it is not of a concrete nature.   The Balance Sheet of the above purchaser, if drawn up on the day of purchase, would contain the following items:—

		£			£
Capital ..	.. ..	5000	Goodwill..	.. ..	1000
			Stock, fittings, and other assets ..	.. ..	4000

There will be a Goodwill Account in the Ledger to which the £1,000 will be debited.

The custom from which the Goodwill arises may be attracted by the personal service of the proprietor, or from that and the site of the premises.   Trade is better, in some cases, on one side of a road than on the other, and, for some shops, proximity to a railway station or a marketing centre is an advantage.   The advantage, however, may not prove permanent, and it may be prudent to write down the value of the Goodwill.   In cases where there is no definite evidence of decline in value, it is often the practice to lower the figure at which the Goodwill stands to avoid possible overstatement of value.

There is no statutory compulsion regarding the form of a Balance Sheet except that in the case of limited companies certain information must be disclosed. It is customary in England to summarise the credit balances on the left-hand side, and the debit balances on the right-hand side, of the Balance Sheet, and that the purpose of the statement may be fully served, it is advisable to give full information on all essential points, as, for example, the rate or amount of depreciation and the method of valuation of the assets. The component items should be presented in an orderly manner and in a sequence that should be adhered to year by year. In many commercial concerns the form adopted is to arrange the assets in the order of their realisability or ease of conversion into cash, starting with the least easily convertible asset and ending with the cash balance itself. Somewhat similarly, the liabilities are arranged in the reverse order to that in which they must be met, starting with the proprietor's capital.

The fixed assets are grouped together, followed or preceded by the current assets. Unrealisable assets or "fictitious assets" also appear in the Balance Sheets of some concerns. Such are the preliminary expenses[1] on the formation of a company, the items for unexpired values of insurance, advertising, etc., and the debit balance, if it occurs, of a company's Profit and Loss Account.

In these days the headings liabilities and assets are usually omitted altogether from a Balance Sheet. In their place appear sub-headings to groups of items, as for example sub-headings Capital, Loans, and Current Liabilities on the left-hand side of the Balance Sheet and sub-headings such as those already referred to, namely Fixed Assets and Current Assets on the right-hand side of the Balance Sheet.

To reveal, at a glance, the total of fixed assets, the total of current assets, the working capital, the net book value of the assets and the amount of capital employed a balance sheet may, as explained in Chapter 11, be set out as on page 202.

The capital employed consists of funds contributed by the proprietor of the business and funds (long term loans) borrowed from other sources and is equal to the net book value of the assets employed in operating the business.

---

[1] These are more fully explained on p. 338.

Balance Sheet
as at 31st December, 19. .

	£			£	£	£	£
Capital	9300	FIXED ASSETS					
Loan (long term)	4000	Machinery			10000		
		less depreciation			4000		
						6000	
		Furniture and fittings..			1000		
		less depreciation			300		
						700	
							6700
		CURRENT ASSETS					
		Stock			5500		
		Sundry debtors			3600		
		Cash in hand and balance at bank			1750		
						10850	
		LESS CURRENT LIABILITIES					
		Creditors:—					
		Trade			4150		
		Expense			100		
						4250	
		Working capital..					6600
		Net book value of					
Capital employed	£13300	assets					£13300

EXERCISES 24

1. A. Reynolds commenced business as a dealer in machinery and spare parts with the following assets and liabilities:—

	£
Stock on hand	8320
Debtor—The Pulman Sawmills Ltd.	5350
Creditor—Torquay Machinery Co.	2525
Premises	1500
Balance at bank	1762
Cash in hand	158

Open a set of books for the business as at July 1, 19. ., and record the following transactions:—

July 7. Received from the Pulman Sawmills Ltd. a cheque for the balance of the company's account, less 1¼% cash discount.

„ 20. Sold on credit, to the Wood & Lumber Co., machinery to the value of £2,500.

„ 31. Paid by cash, wages, £41.

Aug. 5. Purchased from the Torquay Machinery Co., machinery to the value of £1,750.

„ 19. Sold machinery, on credit, to the Pulman Sawmills Ltd., for £3,575.

„ 31. Paid by cash, wages, £41.

Sept. 11. Paid by cheque, to the Torquay Machinery Co., the sum of £1,262 on account.
„ 30. Paid by cash, wages, £41.
„ 30. Cash takings paid into bank, £420.

Prepare Trial Balance and Trading and Profit and Loss Accounts for the three months ending September 30th.

The stock on hand at September 30th was valued at £5,125.

Balance the Ledger Accounts at September 30th, and record the following transactions:—

Oct. 5. Purchased adjoining premises for the purpose of extending showrooms and stores, and paid by cheque, £3,500.
„ 30. Sold machinery on credit, to the Export Co. for £2,205.
Nov. 17. Paid, by cheque, the balance of the Torquay Machinery Co.'s account.
Dec. 2. Cashed a cheque for £200 and handed proceeds to the petty cashier.
„ 31. Paid, by cash, wages, £75.
„ 31. Cashed a cheque for private use, £100.

Prepare Trial Balance and Trading and Profit and Loss Accounts for the three months ending December 31st, 19.., and Balance Sheet at that date.

The stock on hand at December 31st was valued at £3486   *R.S.A.*

2. The Trial Balance given below was extracted from the books of G. Britton on December 31, 19... You are required to—

(1) Open Ledger Accounts showing the balances.

(2) Prepare Trading and Profit and Loss Accounts for the year ended December 31, 19.., closing off the proper Ledger Accounts.

Note—(*a*) The Stock on December 31 was valued at £1410. (*b*) Two-thirds of wages is to be charged to Trading Account, and one-third to Profit and Loss Account.

(3) Bring down the remaining balances of Ledger Accounts and prepare a Balance Sheet as on December 31, 19...

Trial Balance. December 31, 19..

	Dr. £	Cr. £
Capital (fixed) January 1		3000
Drawings during year	364	
Creditors (W. Miles & Co.)		428
Debtors (Lightwood Bros.)	878	
Stock (January 1)	1234	
Investment 3½% War Loan	400	
Plant and machinery	960	
Purchases	3702	
Sales		5724
Carriage on purchases	58	
Returns inwards	72	
Rent and rates	208	
Travellers' salaries	326	
Discounts on sales	115	
Wages	849	
Interest on investment		14
	£9166	£9166

R.S A

3. Explain in as detailed a way as you can the reasons why a business would use the following books:—

(i) Sales Day Book.
(ii) Cash Book.
(iii) Returns Outwards Book. *Purchases*

4. From the following information prepare the account of S. Fane as it would appear in the Ledger of G. Mason.

(i) Fane owed Mason £20 on 1st Feb.
(ii) Mason sold goods to Fane, £126 on 12th Feb.
(iii) Fane returned goods, £14, to Mason on 17th Feb.
(iv) Fane bought goods from Mason, £49 on 20th Feb.
(v) Fane sent Mason a cheque for £150 on account, 25th Feb.
(vi) Balance off the account and bring down the balance as at 28th Feb.
(vii) Mason received notification of the bankruptcy of Fane and a cheque for a first and final dividend of £0·5 in the £. Rule off and close the account.

5. Define—(a) Fixed Asset.
(b) Current Asset.
(c) Working Capital.
(d) Current Liability.

6· Explain why stock-taking is carried out periodically. What are the bases for valuing stock?

7. (a) State how each of the following errors would affect the gross profit of a business. (b) The gross profit before discovery of the errors was £3,000. Give the correct gross profit.

(i) The Sales Returns Book was over-added by £20.
(ii) An invoice for goods bought totalling £60 was omitted from the books.
(iii) The closing stock was under-valued by £649.
(iv) Carriage on purchases had been entered as £189 instead of £198.

(c) If the turnover was £6,000, state what difference the above errors would make to the percentage of gross profit on turnover.

8. The following is the Balance Sheet of V. Williams as at 29th February, 19...

Balance Sheet

	£	£			£	£
Capital	5100			Goodwill		1000
Add Net Profit	900			Freehold premises		4000
		6000		Sundry debtors	1500	
Loan from S. Roberts		3000		*Less* Provision for		
Sundry creditors		1970		bad debts	100	
						1400
				Stock		2800
				Bank		1700
				Cash		70·
		£10970				£10970

(i) State the total of the Fixed Assets. *4000*
(ii) State the total of Current Assets. *5970*
(iii) What is the figure of Working Capital? *4000.*

(iv) If Goodwill were written off, what would be the effect on the Balance Sheet?

(v) If a Provision for Salaries due £200 had to be made, what would be the effect on the Balance Sheet?

(vi) If goods bought on credit for £300 had been omitted, what would be the effect of the correction of this error on the Balance Sheet?

(vii) Was Williams solvent or insolvent? Give your reasons.

(viii) State the effect on the Balance Sheet of making the provision for bad debts 5% of the sundry debtors.

(ix) Re-write the Balance Sheet as it would appear after all necessary adjustments had been made and put the assets under appropriate headings.

9. From the following details draw up a Balance Sheet in such a way as to show *within the Balance Sheet:*—

(i) The total of Fixed Assets.
(ii) The total of Current Assets.
(iii) The total of Current Liabilities.
(iv) The Working Capital.
(v) The net Book Value of the assets.
(vi) The Capital employed.

	Dr. £	Cr. £
Capital (1 Jan., 19..)		8000
Net profit for year to 31st December, 19 ..		3450
Drawings	3000	
Machinery at cost	7000	
Provision for depreciation on machinery		2500
Furniture and fittings	250	
Stock	4750	
Trade debtors	3800	
Provision for bad debts		182
	£	
Sundry creditors: Trade	3240	
Expense ..	88	
		3328
Loan (20 years) from X.L. Loan Co. ..		1000
Bank overdraft		340
	£18800	£18800

10. J.K. started business on 1st January, 19.. with £2,000. He borrowed a further £1,000 from his uncle on a long-term basis. He paid both amounts into a business bank account.

During the ensuing six months J.K.:—

(i) Purchases furniture and fittings £450 and a motor van £860 and paid both amounts by cheque.

(ii) Purchased stock-in-trade on credit for £6,150.

(iii) Sold goods (cost price £4,140) on credit for £5,240.

(iv) Paid business expenses by cheque £320.

(v) Received from trade debtors and paid into bank £3,310.

(vi) Paid trade creditors by cheques, £3,490.

On 30th June, 19.., J.K. depreciated the motor van by £70 and the furniture and fittings by £30. On that date £20 was still owing for business expenses.

(*a*) Calculate as at 30th June, 19. . :—
   (i) The bank balance.
   (ii) The value, at cost price, of the stock-in-trade.
   (iii) The total of trade debtors.
   (iv) The total of trade creditors.

(*b*) Prepare a Trading and Profit and Loss Account for the half year ended 30th June 19. . and a Balance Sheet as at that date.

Note—The Balance Sheet is to be prepared in such a way as to show *within the Balance Sheet* the totals of fixed assets, current assets and current liabilities; the amount of working capital, the net book value of the assets, and the capital employed.

CHAPTER 25 *Feb. 22ⁿᵈ.*

INCOMPLETE RECORDS

This term is applied, in general, to any system of bookkeeping that does not adhere strictly to the principles of double entry. The term "Single Entry Bookkeeping" is sometimes used to denote such incomplete records.

A trader may deem it sufficient for his purposes if he has a Cash Book and a Customers' Ledger containing his customers' accounts. He records all his cash dealings in his Cash Book, and posts the sums received from customers to their respective accounts in the Ledger, but otherwise he makes no attempt to complete the two-fold aspect of his transactions. His Ledger, therefore, contains no record of his expenses, of his capital, or of the value of any business assets. He relies, probably, on the invoices as a record of his purchases, and the only entry in his books for these is the cash payment as and when he pays his creditors.

This is typical of the nature of incomplete records, but as a variation from it a trader may keep a Sales Book, and may post the entries to his Customers' Ledger Accounts, but refrains from posting the total sales in any form to the Ledger. Some traders may go further and keep a Purchase Day Book and accounts for creditors in the Ledger but, even so, the record is still one of the personal aspects only of the business transactions with the exception of some of the Cash Book entries.

It is obvious that a record of this kind lacks the fullness and informative value of the double entry system, and that it has positive disadvantages. No Trial Balance, for example, can be extracted to test the arithmetical accuracy of the entries, and the gross and net profit cannot be ascertained without recourse to other sources of information. Further, in the absence of records of any assets and, if such assets exist, of any record of allowance for depreciation or other loss of value, it is difficult to present a Balance Sheet of reasonable accuracy.

Statement of Affairs under Incomplete Records

To ascertain the trading results with these records it is necessary to know the capital at the start of the trading period and also the

capital at the close of the period under review.   As a trader's capital
on any given date is represented by the excess of value of his assets
over his liabilities, it follows that in order to ascertain his capital it
is necessary, where proper books of account are not kept, to prepare
a statement of the trader's assets and liabilities.   Such a statement
is known as a Statement of Affairs and is in appearance like an
ordinary Balance Sheet.   It follows, also, that unless the capital at
the commencement of the trading period is known, it is necessary
to prepare two Statements of Affairs—one as at the beginning of the
trading period, and the other as at the close of the period.

The steps to be taken to prepare a Statement of Affairs are—

(*a*) Value the stock on hand.

(*b*) Check the cash in hand and at bank.

(*c*) Ascertain the total of the debtors and trade creditors.

(*d*) Ascertain and evaluate any other assets.

(*e*) Ascertain the liabilities, if any, which exist in addition to the
trade creditors.

(*f*) Take into account all outstanding expenses and payments
made in advance.

This information having been obtained, the Statement of Affairs
is formulated by placing the assets on the credit side and the liabilities
on the debit side.   The difference between the two sides represents
the capital, or deficiency, and by inserting the amount of this difference on the appropriate side the two sides are made equal in total
and the Statement is closed.

By way of simple illustration of the principle involved in the
foregoing paragraphs, let it be assumed that a trader's capital on a
given date is £1,000, that it is known that a year earlier it was £900,
and that during the year he drew from the business a weekly allowance making, say, £410 for the period.   His profit for the year is
arrived at as follows:—

Statement of Profit

			£
Capital on 1st January, 19..	..	..	900
Capital on 31st December, 19..	..	..	1000
Net *increases* of capital	..	..	100
add Drawings during the year	..	..	410
Profit for the year ..	..	..	£510

If his capital position had been the reverse, that is, his capital had been £1,000 at 1st January and £900 at 31st December, his profit would have been £310, arrived at as follows:—

			£
Capital on 1st January, 19..	..	..	1000
Capital on 31st December, 19..	..	..	900
Net *decrease* of capital	..	..	100
add Drawings during the year	..	..	410
Profit for the year ..	..	..	£310

While in the above simplified illustration the only adjustment required is in respect of personal cash drawings, various other adjustments may be necessary in practice, such as adjustment for additional capital brought into the business—whether it is brought in in cash or in the form of assets purchased for the business from private funds, adjustment for withdrawals of capital, or, for further example, cost of fire damage not recovered from the Insurance Company. In short, all transactions not reflected in the Statement of Affairs from which the capital figure is derived and which are not strictly relevant trading expenses must be taken into account.

Provided the principle underlying the foregoing simple illustration is grasped no difficulty should arise in following the examples given below.

Example 36.—R. Benson prepared the following Statement of Affairs as at 1st January, 19..:—

Statement of Affairs
1st January, 19..

LIABILITIES		£	ASSETS		£
Sundry creditors	.. ..	5200	Freehold premises ..	..	2800
Capital Account	.. ..	2800	Fittings ..	.. ..	300
			Stock ..	.. ..	1800
			Sundry debtors	.. ..	2500
			Cash	.. ..	600
		£8000			£8000

His liabilities and assets at 31st December of that year were valued as follows:—
Sundry creditors, £4,900; premises, £2,800; fittings, £400; stock, £1,950; sundry debtors, £2,700; and cash, £320.

The fittings include £150 of new fittings purchased during the year and paid for by R. Benson from his private account.

210

Practical Bookkeeping and Accounts

Drawings during the year amounted to £400.
Find his profit or loss on the year's working.

The solution is as below:—

Statement of Affairs
31st December, 19..

LIABILITIES	£	ASSETS	£
Sundry creditors	4900	Premises	2800
Capital—excess of assets over		Fittings	400
liabilities at this date ..	3270	Stock..	1950
		Sundry debtors	2700
		Cash	320
	£8170		£8170

Statement of Profit

	£
Capital, 31st December, 19..	3270
Add Drawings	400
	3670
Deduct Capital introduced	150
	3520
Deduct Capital as at 1st January	2800
Net profit for the year	£720

Partnership Profits from Incomplete Records

The preparation of a Statement of Profit must not be assumed to be a process restricted to a sole trader. It may be necessary in the case of a partnership, and the only addition entailed to adapt the system to partnership records is to elaborate the Statement of Profit to give effect to the relationship existing between the partners. Let it be assumed by way of further illustration that, in Example 36 above, R. Benson had brought his son, S. Benson, into the business on 1st January, 19..., on the following terms:—

(a) R. Benson to credit £800 of his capital to his son, leaving a sum of £2,000 to his own credit as at 1st January.

(b) Each partner to be credited with 5 per cent. per annum interest on capital.

(c) R. Benson to draw £20 and S. Benson to draw £5 a calendar month on account of profits.

(d) S. Benson to draw a further sum of £25 each quarter as salary.

(e) The profits remaining, after provision for interest on capital and for S. Benson's salary, to be divided between father and son in the proportion of ⅔ to R. Benson and ⅓ to S. Benson.

The Statement of Profit would then have been as follows:—

Statement of Profit

	£	£
Surplus of assets over liabilities at 31st December, 19..		3270
(Details in Example 41.)		
add Drawings—R. Benson	240	
S. Benson	60	
Salary—S. Benson	100	
	400	
less Capital introduced by R. Benson	150	250
		3520
Capital on 1st January, 19..:—		
R. Benson	2000	
S. Benson	800	2800
Profit for the year..		£720

Division of Profit—

	R. Benson £	S. Benson £	Total £
Interest at 5% p.a.	100	40	140
Salary	—	100	100
Balance of profit in ratio 2 : 1	320	160	480
	£420	£300	£720

Statement of Affairs at 31st December, 19..

LIABILITIES	£	£	ASSETS	£
Sundry creditors ..		4900	Premises	2800
Capital Accounts—			Fittings	400
R. Benson			Stock	1950
As at 1st Jan. ..	2000		Sundry debtors	2700
add Capital addition ..	150		Cash	320
Interest	100			
Profit	320			
	£2570			
less Drawings	240	2330		
S. Benson				
As at 1st Jan. ..	800			
add Salary	100			
Interest	40			
Profit	160			
	£1100			
less Drawings and salary	160	940		
		£8170		£8170

Comparison of the above Statements with Example 36 will reveal that the total profit at £720 is the same in both cases, and that in the former case the capital in the business was shown as R. Benson's at £3,270, whereas, in the latter case, the capital has been apportioned between the two partners but remains in total the same, thus, R. Benson's capital is £2,330, S. Benson's capital £940—total partnership capital, £3,270.

Conversion to Double Entry

It has been shown that with due care in the compilation of the basic figures it is possible to prepare as accurate a survey of the trader's business for any given period from incomplete records as by double entry. While this may be so, there is no comparison between the two methods in regard to the amount of detail available for showing how the results have been arrived at. The method from incomplete records cannot inform the trader of the ratio of his gross profit to turnover or of the relative proportions of the various overheads which represent the difference between his gross and net profit. This is the point where incomplete records fail in practice, and if the practical question of cost is not insurmountable the obvious remedy is to convert the records to double entry form. If Benson decides that his books are, in future, to be kept on double entry principles, the new set of books will be opened by recording all the items contained in the closing Statement of Affairs. The items should be journalised as opening entries and posted from the Journal to the respective Ledger Accounts, including the cash balance to the Cash Book. Proper subsidiary books will have to be brought into use and instructions should be issued that all transactions must be recorded strictly on double entry principles.

Unfortunately, however, it is not always possible in practice for a trader to bear the extra cost of a bookkeeper competent to keep a complete set of books on double-entry principles. In such cases it is necessary to use such information as can be made available for the preparation of detailed accounts on double entry lines. If the trader already keeps, or agrees to keep in future, a Customers' Ledger, a Creditors' Ledger, and a Cash Book, the work involved in preparing proper accounts is governed solely by the number and variety of the trader's transactions during the period under review. All the necessary information will have been recorded, and it will be necessary only to collate it in the desired manner. It must be emphasised, however, that whilst the lack of personal Ledgers only increases the amount of work necessary to prepare detailed accounts, the keeping of a Cash Book and the accurate recording in it of *all* receipts and payments—with sufficient narration to enable them to be identified, is vital. Great care must be taken to see that where disbursements are made out of cash takings—only the net cash on hand being banked or otherwise disposed of—such cash takings are entered gross on the receipts side of the Cash Book, the cash disbursements being entered on the payments side of the Cash Book. To the extent to which this fundamental rule is broken to that extent are the Final Accounts rendered inaccurate. The turnover or total sales, the gross profit ratio to turnover, and the expenses totals and their ratio to turnover will be correspondingly inaccurate.

If the trader is convinced of the importance of a correct record of the cash transactions and agrees to keep such a record, he may be assured of a Profit and Loss Account comparable in accuracy to that prepared from a standard set of books kept on double-entry principles.

As an example, let it be assumed that Benson, in the above example, on taking his son into partnership, kept incomplete records, but that he agreed to keep a detailed Cash Book on the above lines. To prepare his Profit and Loss Account the first step is to classify all the entries in the Cash Book. The simplest method is to use multi-column analysis paper and to head the columns according to the information required for the Profit and Loss Account with an additional column for items affecting the Balance Sheet. The following is an example of the summary of the cash transactions taken from the analysis paper and consisting of the totals under each of the appropriate headings in the columns—

	£
Balance shown in Cash Book, 1st January ..	600
Cash sales	3000
Cash from sundry debtors	21300
	£24900

	£
Cash paid to creditors	20050
Wages and commission	2750
Rent, rates, and taxes	810
Fuel and light	250
Insurance and telephone	120
Carriage and packing	200
Partners' drawings	400
Balance shown in Cash Book, 31st December..	320
	£24900

It is obvious that the foregoing summary contains most of the usual items appearing in the Trial Balance of a set of books kept by double entry. The following items, as at 31st December, are still required:—

Sundry debtors.
Sundry creditors.
Stock.
Cost of fittings purchased by R. Benson privately.
Sales on credit.
Purchases on credit.

Benson can supply the first four items, and the summary of the Cash Book provides the details from which the last two items may be obtained by the compilation of a Sundry Debtors Summary Account for the sales, and a Sundry Creditors Summary Account for the purchases.

When completed, these accounts would appear as below:—

Sundry Debtors Summary Account

	£		£
Sundry debtors, 1st Jan. ..	2500	Receipts from sundry debtors	21300
Sales on credit	21500	Sundry debtors, 31st Dec.	2700
	£24000		£24000

Sundry Creditors Summary Account

	£		£
Cash payments to creditors	20050	Sundry creditors, 1st Jan.	5200
Sundry creditors, 31st Dec...	4900	*Purchases on credit* ..	19750
	£24950		£24950

All the items in these accounts are known with the exception of the sales and purchases figures respectively. In each case these are ascertained by simple arithmetic as the difference between the two sides.

It is now possible to prepare a complete Trial Balance, Profit and Loss Account, and Balance Sheet. The Balance Sheet will be identical with the Statement of Affairs of the partnership shown on page 211. The Trial Balance and Profit and Loss Account will appear as below.

Trial Balance. 31st December, 19..

	Dr. £	Cr. £
Cash sales		3000
Credit sales		21500
Credit purchases	19750	
Stock on hand, 1st January	1800	
Fittings, 1st January	300	
Fittings purchased by R. Benson	150	
R. Benson for fittings		150
Depreciation credited to Fittings Account		50
Profit and Loss Account (Depreciation)	50	
Freehold premises	2800	
Capital Accounts, 1st January—		
R. Benson		2000
S. Benson		800
Wages and commission	2750	
Rent, rates, and taxes	810	
Fuel and light	250	
Insurance and telephone	120	
Carriage and packing	200	
Drawings—R. Benson	240	
S. Benson	160	
Cash in bank, 31st December	320	
Sundry creditors		4900
Sundry debtors	2700	
	£32400	£32400

Note.—The Stock at 31st December is given as £1,950. The fittings were valued at £300 at 1st January, to which new purchases, £150, are added. At 31st December the fittings were re-valued at £400—hence the depreciation (£50) shown above.

Profit and Loss Account

for year ended 31st December, 19..

	£		£
Stock on 1st Jan.	1800	Cash sales	3000
Purchases	19750	Credit sales..	21500
Gross profit carried down		Stock, 31st December ..	1950
(20% of turnover).. ..	4900		
	£26450		£26450

	£		£
Wages and commission ..	2750	Gross profit brought down	4900
Rent, rates, and taxes ..	810		
Fuel and light	250		
Insurance and telephone ..	120		
Carriage and packing ..	200		
Depreciation on fittings ..	50		
Net profit carried down ..	720		
	£4900		£4900

		£		£
Interest on capital—			Net profit brought down ..	720
R. Benson		100		
S. Benson		40		
Salary—S. Benson		100		
Balance of profit—				
R. Benson (⅔)		320		
S. Benson (⅓)		160		
		£720		£720

It will be observed that the net profit is identical, at £720, with the figure arrived at on page 211.

From the Profit and Loss Account figures it is now possible to inform the trader that his average gross profit on turnover is 20 per cent., calculated as follows:—

		£
Stock, 1st January ..	..	1800
add Purchases	..	19750
		21550
less Stock, 31st Dec. ..	..	1950
Cost of sales.. ..	..	£19600
Actual sales	..	24500
Cost of sales.. ..	..	19600
Gross profit	..	£4900 = 20% of £24,500 turnover.

It is possible also to calculate the percentages of the various expenses to turnover and by comparison with the percentages of similar businesses to ascertain whether or not this particular business may be managed more efficiently or whether efforts should be made to increase turnover or gross profit to obtain a greater net profit for distribution.

In conclusion it may be remarked that the above example has referred to an extreme case in which only a Cash Book is kept. In practice the available information may be contained in books ranging from a Cash Book only to a case where all the books of original entry are kept, but no one in the business may possess the requisite knowledge to post the appropriate periodical totals to the proper impersonal accounts in the General or Private Ledger. In all cases before commencing the preparation of a detailed Profit and Loss Account from incomplete records, full information should be obtained as to the extent and dependability of the existing record, as otherwise much unnecessary analysis work may be undertaken. Students should pay particular attention to this aspect of examination questions.

EXERCISES 25

1.—The following "Statements of Affairs" have been drawn up to give the financial position, as on 31st March, 1969, and 31st March, 1970, respectively, of A. Brown, who keeps his books on a single entry basis:—

Statement of Affairs

31st March, 1969

				£					£
Capital ..	..	..	..	6192	Fixtures	..	..	..	250
Creditors	..	..	..	742	Stock..	..	..	..	2305
					Debtors	..	..	..	4176
					Cash ..	..	..	..	203
				£6934					£6934

Statement of Affairs
31st March, 1970

				£					£
Capital ..	..	..	..	5933	Fixtures	..	..	..	230
Creditors	..	..	..	817	Stock	..	..	..	2562
					Debtors	..	..	..	3777
					Cash ..	..	..	..	181
				£6750					£6750

Brown has transferred £100 a month regularly from his business banking account to his private banking account by way of drawings, and he has taken £25 worth of stock for his private use. The alteration in the value of the fixtures represents an amount written off by way of depreciation.

Calculate Brown's trading profit for the year. *R.S.A.*

2. (*a*) Define Single Entry, and state briefly the disadvantages of this system.

(*b*) A manufacturer, Philip Morgan, kept his books on what is known as the Single Entry system. The position of the business at the 31st December, 19.. revealed the following:—

						£
Freehold premises	..	..	..	..	..	1000
Plant and machinery		..	..	..	..	600
Stock in trade	..	..	..	..	..	1300
Sundry debtors	..	..	..	..	..	1750
Cash at bank	..	..	..	..	..	300
Sundry creditors	..	..	..	..	..	1875

At the 1st January, 19.., his capital was £5,500.

During the year his drawings amounted to £500, and the sale of his private motor car realised £200, which he paid into the business bank account.

You are required to prepare the Statement of Affairs showing the financial position of Philip Morgan as at the 31st December, 19.., compile his Capital Account at that date, and ascertain his profit or loss for the year. *R.S.A.*

3.

				£					£
		Balance Sheet							
Creditors	..	..	..	721	Freehold premises ..		..	..	1560
Capital ..	..	..	..	3150	Machinery and plant			..	420
					Stock	..	..	..	876
					Debtors	..	..	..	982
					Cash ..	..	..	..	33
				£3871					£3871

The above is a copy of Samuel Wood's Balance Sheet as on the 31st December, a year ago. The only books kept are a Cash Book and a Ledger. The following is a summary of his receipts and payments for the year ended 31st December, 19..:—

Receipts			£	Payments			£
Cash on account of credit sales			4276	Creditors for goods purchased			3954
Cash sales	..	..	1863	Wages	..	..	743
Capital paid in	..	..	200	General expenses	..	..	627
				Additions to machinery		..	160
				Drawings	..	..	536
			£6339				£6020

On 31st December, 19.., the amount due to creditors was £816, and the debtors and stock amounted to £918 and £854 respectively. You are required to prepare Trading and Profit and Loss Accounts for the year ended 31st December, 19.., and a Balance Sheet as on that date, after making adjustments in respect of the following:—

(a) Depreciation of 10% is to be written off the machinery and plant, including additions during the year.

(b) £150 is to be provided for doubtful debts.

(c) The sum of £38 for goods supplied to the proprietor was included in the debtor's balances at 31st December, 19... *R.S.A.*

4. A. N. Ironmonger's Statement of Affairs at 1st January, 19.., was as follows:—

			£	£				£	£
Capital ..	..	..		5776	Premises	..	..		1000
Creditors—					Fixtures and fittings ..				285
Trade	..	..	1372		Stock ..	..	..		2740
Expense	..	..	100		Debtors	..	..		2218
				1472					
					Cash—				
					In hand	..	..	30	
					At bank	..	..	975	
									1005
				£7248					£7248

Ironmonger's records are incomplete but you ascertain the following position at December 31st, 19...

Debtors .. .. £2485 (including bad debts £115)

```
Creditors:—              £
  Trade    ..    ..    1588
  Expense ..    ..     121
```
and Ironmonger informs you that he estimates his stock at £2,800 and values his fixtures at £250.

An analysis of his Bank Pay-In Book and Bank Statement reveals the following:—

```
                                                    £
Bank lodgments—
  Cash sales      ..    ..    ..    ..    ..    2029   + 250.
  Received from credit customers    ..    ..    9805
  Interest from private investments   ..    ..    105
Bank drawn—
  For goods       ..    ..    ..    ..    ..    6490   + 120.
  Business expenses    ..    ..    ..    ..    2515
  Self     ..    ..    ..    ..    ..    ..    1400
  Income Tax    ..    ..    ..    ..    ..     370
```

Ironmonger also informs you that approximately £250 of the cash takings had been retained and not banked to cover petty items which included £120 for purchases. £20 of this sum was in hand at December 31st, 19...

You are required to prepare Trading and Profit and Loss Account for the year ended December 31st, 19.., and the Statement of Affairs at that date.
London Chamber of Commerce Intermediate

5. W. Fairfax does not keep proper books of account. The following information is available for the year ended 30th June, 19..:

	1st July previous year £	30th June 19.. £
Stock-in-trade	1841	1762
Cash in hand and at bank	647	498
Trade debtors	470	350
Trade creditors	1074	998
Fixtures and fittings	400	360
Motor van	370	765

Note:—During the year Fairfax had sold the old motor van and purchased a new one for £850 which was valued at £765 at the end of the year of account.

(a) Find the profit or loss made by Fairfax for the year ended 30th June, 19.., taking into account the following:—
  (i) An account for light and heat, £11, is due.
  (ii) Rates, £58, had been paid for the period 1st April, 19.., to 30th September, 19...
  (iii) A provision of £35 is to be made for bad debts.
  (iv) During the year Fairfax had withdrawn £100 from the business each month.

(b) Calculate the amount of Fairfax's working capital at 30th June, 19...
A.E.B., G.C.E. "O" Level.

6. L. Hunter does not keep proper books of account. The following information is available for the year ended 31st December, 19..

	1st Jan. 19.. £	31st Dec. 19.. £
Stock-in-trade	1368	1294

			£	£
Trade debtors	..	.. ..	428	386
Amounts prepaid	..	.. ..	23	29
Bank overdraft	..	.. ..	210	—
Cash in hand and balance at bank	..		—	147
Motor vans	..	.. ..	520	416
Furniture and fittings		.. ..	340	323
Trade creditors	..	.. ..	989	1037
Expense creditors	..	.. ..	17	14

(a) Prepare a statement to show the profit or loss made by Hunter for the year ended 31st December, 19.., taking account of the following:

    (i) £38 of the trade debtors at 31st December, 19.., were considered to be bad debts and in addition it was decided to make a provision of £39 for doubtful debts.

    (ii) During the year 19.. Hunter had withdrawn £90 each month from the business.

    (iii) During the year Hunter had won a football pool and paid £200 of the proceeds into the business bank account.

(b) With the information given above and the following additional information calculate Hunter's gross profit for the year ended 31st December, 19...

                                      £

Receipts from trade debtors for the year 8122

Payments to trade creditors for the year 6262

University of London, G.C.E. "O" Level.

CHAPTER 26

INCOME AND EXPENDITURE ACCOUNTS OF
NON-TRADING INSTITUTIONS

The purpose of trading concerns is primarily to make a profit whereas the purpose of non-trading institutions is to render a service. It follows that the Trading and Profit and Loss Accounts required by the former would serve no purpose in the accounts of non-trading bodies, but as hospitals, social and athletic clubs, benevolent and similar institutions are maintained by subscriptions from members or the public, an annual financial statement is desirable. Under Section 148 of the Companies Act, 1948, it is compulsory for a company registered under the Act as not trading for profit, to lay an Income and Expenditure Account before the company in general meeting.

For small clubs or associations a Receipts and Payments Account may be suitable. Such an account is prepared by analysing the entries in the Club Cash Book and presenting the receipts and payments in summarised form as below. The use of a tabular Cash Book facilitates the preparation of the account.

DAFFODIL BADMINTON CLUB

Receipts and Payments Account

Dr.   for the year ended 30th April, 19. .   Cr.

RECEIPTS	£	PAYMENTS	£
Balance brought forward ..	8	Wages	55
Subscriptions	93	Rent	25
Profit on refreshments ..	20	Hire of equipment	20
		Postage	2
		Printing	4
		Affiliation fees	3
		Balance in hand	12
	£121		£121

The Receipts and Payments Account is simply a cash account. If there are amounts owing or amounts prepaid it would not show these. It may also include items of capital expenditure and takes no account of depreciation of fixed assets.

221

To ascertain whether there is a surplus of income over expenditure or a deficiency for the period of account it is necessary to draw up an Income and Expenditure Account. This would, like the Profit and Loss Account of a trading concern show the actual revenue expenditure for the period taking account of expenses outstanding and prepaid and bringing into account such items as depreciation of fixed assets. The income for the period, appearing on the credit side of the account, would take into account items *e.g.* subscriptions, still due and exclude those paid in advance by adding the amounts due to and deducting those paid in advance from the amount actually received. Items of capital expenditure would not be included as these would be represented by fixed assets in the Balance Sheet.

An Income and Expenditure Account is similar in form to the Profit and Loss Account of a trading concern. The revenue appears on the credit side and the expenditure on the debit side, and when all outstanding income and expenditure is brought into account, the balance represents a surplus or deficiency for the period. This is added to, or deducted from, the opening capital or surplus, if any, shown in the Balance Sheet.

Example 37.—The following Receipts and Payments Account for the Crocus Badminton Club for the year to 30th April, 19. . was issued to the members by the secretary.

CROCUS BADMINTON CLUB

Receipts and Payments Account

for the year ended 30th April, 19. .

RECEIPTS	£	PAYMENTS	£
Balance, 1st May, 19..	12	Wages	100
Entrance fees	2	Stationery	20
Subscriptions	166	Printing, postage and misc.	
Locker rents	4	charges	15
		New equipment	10
		Loss on refreshments	6
		Balance carried down	33
	£184		£184
Balance brought down	33		

A footnote showed that subscriptions, £10, were in arrear and unpaid, and that locker rents, £1, were due but not paid. No reference was made to the fact that the club owned its premises, valued at £500; that £2 was owing for printing charges, and that the club's equipment was worth £125.

In the above example, the first step is to eliminate the expenditure on new equipment (£10), and to bring in the locker rents and subscriptions outstanding and the unpaid printing bill. The next step is to ascertain the amount of the Capital Fund at the beginning of the period. This consisted of cash, £12; premises, £500; and equipment, £125—a total of £637.

CROCUS BADMINTON CLUB

Income and Expenditure Account

Dr.   for the year ended 30th April, 19. .   Cr.

	£		£
Wages	100	Subscriptions	176
Printing and postage	17	Locker rents	5
Stationery	20	Entrance fees	2
Loss on refreshments	6		
Balance carried to capital	40		
	£183		£183

Balance Sheet

as at 30th April, 19. .

		£			£	
CAPITAL[1]			Club premises		500	
At 1st May	£637		Equipment	£125		
			Additions during year	£10		
Add					135	
Surplus from Income and Expenditure Account	£40		Debtors		11	
		677	Cash in hand		33	
Sundry creditors (Printing)		2				
		£679			£679	

[1] The term "Accumulated Fund" is often used to denote the capital of a non-trading institution.

EXERCISES 26

1. From the following Receipts and Payments Account and the given particulars, prepare an Income and Expenditure Account and, if necessary, a Balance Sheet.

LONGTOWN SPORTS CLUB

Receipts and Payments Account

to 31st December

RECEIPTS	£	PAYMENTS	£
Balance from last year	31	Wages	104
Entrance fees	6	Printing, postage and	
Subscriptions and donations	210	stationery	28

	£		£
Competition fees	10	Purchase of new equipment	32
Profit on refreshments ..	42	Prizes	16
		Sundry expenses	12
		Rent of grounds	60
		Balance carried down ..	47
	£299		£299
Balance brought down ..	47		

The Secretary stated that the club *now* possessed equipment of a total cost of £87, that subscriptions in arrear amounted to £17, and that a printing bill of £4 was unpaid.

2. The following Receipts and Payments Account is submitted for the period ending 31st December, 19...

THE LONDONERS' CLUB

Receipts and Payments Account

RECEIPTS	£	PAYMENTS	£
Balance from last year ..	27	Payment for new lockers ..	32
Entrance fees	16	Wages	150
Subscriptions:—		Printing and postage ..	36
Current year	220	Stationery	3
In advance	24	Sundries	8
Profit on refreshments ..	53	Lighting and fuel	19
Locker rents	12	Taxes and insurance ..	54
Interest on deposit	2	Balance carried down ..	52
	£354		£354
Balance brought down ..	52		

Of the subscriptions due for the current year, £21 are in arrear. Locker rents in arrear, £2. Printing bill unpaid, £2. Stationery account unpaid, £3. There is a sum of £200 on deposit at bank and the club house and equipment is valued at £1,125.

From the above particulars prepare an Income and Expenditure Account and a Balance Sheet as at 31st December.

3. The assets and liabilities of the Firs Social Club on 1st January, 19.. were: Cash in hand and balance at bank, £268; liquor stocks, £210; subscriptions outstanding for previous year, £20; insurance prepaid, £3; furniture and equipment, £430; creditors for liquor supplies, £150.

From the following summary of receipts and payments and the notes appended prepare the Income and Expenditure Account of the club for the year ended 31st December, 19.. and a Balance Sheet as on that date.

RECEIPTS	£	PAYMENTS	£
Subscriptions	845	Creditors for liquor ..	1415
Sales of liquor..	1840	New furniture	60
Sale of old furniture	15	Dance and social expenses..	269
Dances and socials	347	Rent and rates	645
		Wages	520
		Light and heat	106
		Insurance	8
		Postages and stationery ..	18

Notes.

 (i) The subscriptions received included £15 relating to the previous year of account. The remainder of the subscriptions for that year were written off as a bad debt.

 (ii) On 31st December, 19.., £45 subscriptions were outstanding for the current year of account.

 (iii) The old furniture sold during the year of account had a book value of £9 at the date of sale.

 (iv) The payment for insurance is a yearly premium paid on 1st July in each year.

 (v) Depreciation £25 is to be written off furniture and equipment.

 (vi) Liquor stocks on 31st December, 19.., were valued at £180.

 (vii) On 31st December, 19.., there were outstanding amounts due to creditors for liquor £175 and for light and heat £27.

A.E.B., G.C.E. "O" Level.

4. The following information is supplied to you by the treasurer of the O.K. Social Club. From these details you are required to prepare an Income and Expenditure Account for the year ended 30th September, 19.., and a Statement of the club's financial position on that date.

 (*a*) The total membership of the club is 120, all of whom had paid their annual subscription of £2·5 except 10 members who are in arrears for one year's subscription.

 (*b*) During the year ended 30th September 19.. the treasurer had paid the following expenses: Rent of club premises £200; light and heat, £55; cleaning £26; sundry expenses £24. At the end of the year the treasurer had an outstanding account for electricity, £8.

 (*c*) Socials held during the year brought gross proceeds, £50. Expenses in connection with the socials amounted to £20.

 (*d*) Purchases of refreshments during the year amounted to £60 and sales of refreshments £80. There was a stock of refreshments in hand at 30th September, 19.., valued at £10 compared with £15 at the beginning of the year of account.

 (*e*) On the 30th September, 19.., cash in hand and at bank was £73 and the value of furniture and fittings was estimated at £190.

 (*f*) The capital of the club at the beginning of the year of account was £258.

A.E.B., G.C.E. "O" Level.

CHAPTER 27 _(8th March)_

THE PURCHASE OF A BUSINESS

The purchase of a business as a going concern is of fairly frequent occurrence, as there is the attraction of existing Goodwill and the trend of future trade may be estimated more easily for an established concern than for a newly started business that has to make its entry into the market. Such businesses may, of course, be owned by sole traders or partnerships or registered companies, and the purchase may be made by one of these forms of business ownership. For the most part the method of recording the purchase of the business in the books of the purchaser is the same whether the purchaser is a sole trader, a partnership firm, or a company. The difference will be in the Capital Accounts and, probably, in the case of a company as a purchaser, in the form the purchase consideration may take, as it may be wholly or partly in shares.

The purchase price is usually based on the particulars disclosed in the final Balance Sheet of the vendor. The assets may be subject to independent valuation, and the agreement will include some reference to the limitation of the liabilities, if any, taken over. Each sale stands by itself as the terms vary considerably. One purchaser may take over only the assets; another may take over all the assets and liabilities. Sometimes the cash balance is taken over and in other cases it is retained by the vendor. A further provision in the agreement may refer to the Goodwill of the business and the price to be paid for it. There may also be a clause restraining the vendor from starting a similar business within a certain radius of the present concern. On the sale of Goodwill the vendor is prevented from canvassing former customers, but unless he binds himself to the contrary, he is not prevented from starting a similar business and dealing with former customers if they come to him unsolicited.

Purchase of Business Account

The following example will illustrate the entries that are necessary to record the purchase of a business in the purchaser's books and to open the accounts. The illustration is of a purchase by a partnership firm. The differences in the record when a limited liability company makes a similar purchase and pays partly in shares are discussed in a later chapter.

226

goodwill.

Example 38.—B. Rose and P. Thorn enter into partnership to take over from 1st January, 19.., as a going concern, the business carried on by R. Briar. They are to share profits and losses equally. The following is the final Balance Sheet of R. Briar.

Balance Sheet

	£		£
Capital—R. Briar	20000	Freehold premises ..	9000
Sundry creditors	4500	Plant and machinery ..	6000
		Furniture and fittings ..	800
		Stock	5000
		Debtors	3300
		Cash	400
	£24500		£24500

The purchase price was £24,000, and was paid by cheques by Rose and Thorn direct to Briar in equal shares. R. Briar retained the cash balance. All other assets and the liabilities were taken over by the partners. Each partner contributed a further sum of £1,000 in cash to the firm's capital.

Make the necessary Journal entries, and show the firm's Cash Book and opening Balance Sheet.

Temporary accounts called the Business Purchase Account and the Vendor's Account are opened, and the following is the sequence of entries to record the purchase:—

1. *Debit* the Business Purchase Account ⎫ with the agreed pur-
   Credit the Vendor's Account   ⎭ chase price.

2. *Debit* the assets, including Goodwill, if any, to their respective accounts.
   Credit the total value of assets taken over in one amount to the Business Purchase Account.

3. *Debit* the total value of liabilities taken over in one amount to the Business Purchase Account.
   Credit the liabilities to their particular accounts.

4. *Debit* Vendor's Account   ⎫ with the purchase price
   Credit Partners' Capital Account ⎭ when paid.

Usually the vendor is paid by the purchasing firm itself, in which case Cash Book is credited with the purchase price.

The cash balance, if any, taken over should be debited to Cash.

The posting of these entries will bring all the assets and liabilities into the firm's books, and will close the Business Purchase Account and the Vendor's Account.

These steps are evident in the working of the above example:—

Journal

19..			£	£
Jan. 1	Business Purchase Account .. Dr. To R. Briar (Vendor) .. .. .. being purchase price as agreed.		24000	24000
„ 1	Freehold premises.. .. .. Dr. Plant and machinery .. .. .. Furniture and fittings .. .. .. Stock .. .. Debtors .. .. To Business Purchase Account .. being assets acquired from R. Briar.		9000 6000 800 5000 3300	24100
„ 1	Business Purchase Account .. Dr. Sundry creditors .. .. being liabilities taken over from R. Briar.		4500	4500
„ 1	R. Briar (Vendor).. .. .. Dr. B. Rose—Capital Account .. .. P. Thorn.—Capital Account .. .. being purchase price paid direct to vendor.		24000	12000 12000
„ 1	Goodwill .. .. Dr. Business Purchase Account .. .. being value of Goodwill acquired.		4400	4400

Balance Sheet
as at 1st January, 19..

CAPITAL—	£	£	FIXED ASSETS	£	£
B. Rose	13000		Goodwill	4400	
T. Thorn	13000		Freehold premises	9000	
		26000	Plant and machinery	6000	
CURRENT LIABILITIES—			Furniture and fittings	800	
Sundry creditors ..	4500				20200
		4500	CURRENT ASSETS—		
			Stock	5000	
			Sundry debtors ..	3300	
			Cash	2000	
					10300
		£30500			£30500

Dr.		Cash Book				Cr.
19..		£	19..			£
Jan. 1	B. Rose— Capital ..	1000				
„ 1	P. Thorn— Capital ..	1000				

The Ledger Accounts are not shown as they are not required by the example. Their preparation from the Journal entries above would show clearly the use of the Business Purchase Account as a means of transferring the assets and liabilities, and would show, further, the position of the accounts on the opening of the firm's books.

The balance of the Business Purchase Account after the entry of the purchase price and the liabilities and assets taken over, is the value of the Goodwill acquired. Should the purchase price be less than the nominal value of the assets—less liabilities, then the credit balance of the Business Purchase Account should be treated as a Capital Reserve against which, should the need arise, the value of the assets might be written down.

EXERCISES 27

1. R. B. Graham agrees to purchase R. Foreman's business as at 1st January on the basis of the Balance Sheet shown below. Graham agrees to take over all the assets and liabilities with the exception of the cash balances, and to pay Foreman the sum of £4,500 as the purchase price.

R. Foreman's Balance Sheet
31st December, 19..

LIABILITIES	£	ASSETS	£
Capital ..	4450	Premises	1500
Creditors	950	Fittings and fixtures	160
Bills payable ..	462	Stock	2180
		Debtors	830
		Bills receivable	720
		Cash at bank	452
		Cash in hand	20
	£5862		£5862

Graham paid the purchase price by cheque on 1st January. Record the purchase in Graham's books, and show his Balance Sheet as at 1st January.

2. A, a sole trader owning an established business, took B into partnership on 1st January, 19.., at which date the Goodwill of the business was agreed to be worth £6,000. A's capital (exclusive of Goodwill) was £10,000 and B brought in £3,000 as his capital. Interest on Capital Accounts was to be allowed at 5%, and A and B were to divide the remaining profit in the ratio of 2 to 1.

The profit for the year, before charging interest, was £2,600. Calculate the division of this sum between A and B on the alternative assumptions that (1) Goodwill was ignored on B's entering the business. (2) Goodwill was taken into account at its correct value. *R.S.A.*

3. R. Jacobs and B. Mosley enter into partnership to purchase and take over as from 1st January the business carried on by B. Macintosh. They are to share profits and losses equally, and the purchase is to be on the basis of the last Balance Sheet as shown below.

B. Macintosh's Balance Sheet

31st December, 19..

LIABILITIES	£	ASSETS	£
Capital	10000	Freehold premises	4800
Sundry creditors	2640	Machinery and plant ..	2750
		Furniture and fittings ..	100
		Sundry debtors	1920
		Stock..	2800
		Cash at bank	270
	£12640		£12640

Jacobs and Mosley each contributed £6,000 in cash as capital, and the sums were paid into a banking account opened in the firm's name. The purchase price was agreed at £11,000, and a cheque for that amount was paid over to Macintosh. All the assets and liabilities were taken over with the exception of the cash balance. The purchase price includes a sum for Goodwill, and a Goodwill Account is to be raised in the firm's books. Record the purchase in the partnership books, and show the firm's opening Balance Sheet.

4. T. B. Jones and A. M. Wilmot entered into partnership as equal partners to acquire the business carried on by J. B. Duncan as from 1st January, 19.. The purchase is to be made on the basis of the following Balance Sheet:—

J. B. Duncan's Balance Sheet

31st December, 19..

LIABILITIES	£	ASSETS	£
Capital	9500	Freehold premises	4000
Sundry creditors	2165	Machinery and plant ..	2200
		Furniture and fittings ..	350
		Sundry debtors	1840
		Stock	2900
		Cash at bank	375
	£11665		£11665

The purchase price is agreed at £10,500, and Jones and Wilmot pay this sum in equal shares by cheques direct to Duncan. A firm's banking account is opened, into which Jones and Wilmot pay £750 each. All the assets and liabilities are taken over with the exception of the cash balance.

The partners decide to re-value the assets for the purposes of the partnership, and the following reductions were made:—

The stock was reduced to £2,750; furniture and fittings to £200; and the machinery and plant to £1,800.

These reductions are to be considered as an appreciation of the value of the Goodwill included in the purchase price.

Record the purchase and the adjustments in the partnership books, and give the firm's opening Balance Sheet.

5. George Wright and Henry Dobson enter into partnership, upon equal terms, to acquire the business carried on by Amos Atkinson. The business was taken over as at 1st January, 19.., on the basis of the last certified Balance Sheet which was as follows:—

Amos Atkinson's Balance Sheet
31st December, 19..

LIABILITIES	£	ASSETS	£
Capital Account—		Freehold premises	14200
Amos Atkinson	26000	Plant and machinery ..	8100
Sundry creditors	3400	Furniture and fittings ..	600
Reserve for bad debts ..	300	Stock in trade	4100
		Sundry debtors	2700
	£29700		£29700

The purchase price was agreed at £28,000, and was paid in equal shares by Wright and Dobson direct to Atkinson. A Bank Account was opened in the name of the firm, into which each partner paid the sum of £1,000. For the purpose of the partnership the assets were revalued, and the following reductions in value were made:—

Plant and machinery, £500; Stock, £450; and Furniture and fittings, £200.

A Goodwill Account is to be raised in the partnership books for the difference between the total purchase price paid and the amended valuation.

You are required to make the Journal entries necessary to record the above transactions in the books of Messrs. Wright and Dobson, and prepare Balance Sheet as at the commencement of the new partnership.   *R.S.A.*

CHAPTER 28

CONTROL ACCOUNTS

When a large number of Sales Ledgers and Purchases Ledgers are in use it is necessary to devise a system whereby the accuracy of the personal accounts *in each ledger* may be checked. This is done by constructing a *Control Account* for each Sales or Purchases Ledger, *e.g.* Sales Ledger No. 4 Control Account.

 This account is constructed entirely apart from the system of double entry and is no part of that system. It is simply a means of checking the accuracy of the entries.

Constructing Control Accounts
Sales Ledger Control Accounts

The Sales Ledgers contain the accounts of debtors. An analysis of the items in such accounts would show that they are of the following kinds.

(i) Opening debit balances brought down from the previous period.

(ii) Debit entries for goods sold to customers (sales).

(iii) Credit entries for cash received from debtors.

(iv) Credit entries for allowances made and discounts allowed.

(v) Credit entries for bad debts.

1. If there are, say, 200 accounts in Sales Ledger No. 1, then the Sales Ledger No. 1 Control Account would open with the total of all the debit balances in that Ledger checked as correct from the previous period of trading.

2. The total of individual sales items to the personal accounts in Sales Ledger No. 1 for the month can be ascertained from Sales Book No. 1 or other subsidiary records.

3. By incorporating analysis columns in the Cash Book, debit side, corresponding to each Sales Ledger the total of cash received from debtors and posted to the credit side of debtors accounts in Sales Ledger No. 1 can be ascertained.

4. Analysis of the discount column of the Cash Book will give the total of discounts posted to the credit side of the debtors' accounts in each Sales Ledger including Sales Ledger No. 1.

5. Totals of amounts credited to the accounts in Sales Ledger No. 1 can be ascertained by analysis of the Sales Returns Books or appropriate subsidiary records.

6. Bad debts and any other extraneous items affecting the accounts of debtors in Sales Ledger No. 1 will have been journalised and by analysing the Journal entries the total of such items either debited or credited to the accounts in any Sales Ledger can be ascertained.

We can now construct an account *in total* of all the individual items which have been entered in the debtors' accounts contained in any particular Sales Ledger during a particular period, usually one month.

Dr.			£	19..		£
19..				June 30	Cash ..	55000
June 1	Balance,			,, 30	Discounts	1000
	total			,, 30	Bad debts	200
	debtors			,, 30	Returns	
	at this				inwards	300
	date ..		12000	,, 30	Balance	
,, 30	Sales ..		75000		carried	
					down ..	30500
			£87000			£87000
July 1	Balance					
	brought					
	down ..		30500			

Sales Ledger Control Account — Cr.

Purchases Ledger Control Account

In the same way as above the totals of the individual items posted to creditors' accounts in a particular Purchases Ledger can be ascertained: the total of creditors' opening balances from the previous month's Trial Balance or Control Account, the total of purchases from the relevant Purchases Book or other record, the total of cash paid and discounts received from the analysis of the credit side of the Cash Book, the total of returns and allowances from the Purchases Returns Book and any other items from an analysis of the Journal.

When complete a Purchases Ledger Control Account might appear as on page 236.

These Control Accounts are prepared by a senior clerk working independently of the Ledger clerks. It is clear that the final balance of the Control Account for a particular Sales or Purchases Ledger

Sales Book

DATE	PARTICULARS	LEDGER FOLIOS	TOTAL	SALES LEDGER			DEPT. A	DEPT. B	DEPT. C
				A—K	L—R	S—Z			
			£	£	£	£	£	£	£

Cash Book
(Debit side)

Dr.

DATE	PARTICULARS	FOLIO	DISCOUNT	DETAILS	BANK	SALES LEDGER			GENERAL LEDGER
						A—K	L—R	S—Z	
			£	£	£	£	£	£	£

Cash Book (Credit side) — Cr.

Date	Particulars	Folio	Discount	Details	Bank	Bought Ledger A—M	Bought Ledger N—Z	General Ledger
			£	£	£	£	£	£

should agree with the total of the balances in the individual accounts in that Ledger. The clerk in charge of each Ledger will extract and total the balances on the accounts in his Ledger at the end of each month. This total should agree with the balance on the Control Account for that Ledger constructed independently by another clerk. If it disagrees then any discrepancy must be investigated and rectified in the same way as with a Trial Balance. Unlike a Trial Balance, however, it is possible, by using Control Accounts to isolate an error to a particular Ledger.

When all the Sales and Purchases Ledgers have been agreed with their respective Control Accounts then the total balances on all the Sales Ledger Control Accounts will give the total of sundry debtors at the end of any particular month and the total of balances on the Purchases Ledger Control Accounts the total of sundry creditors.

When comparatively few Sales and Purchases Ledgers are in use the Cash Book and subsidiary records may be adapted to facilitate analysis of entries for the construction of Control Accounts. Rulings of subsidiary books are illustrated here and on page 234. Where columns become too numerous then a separate Sales Book corresponding to each Sales Ledger may be used. Special analysis sheets may be used for the analysis of cash, discount, and journalised transactions.

One of the great advantages of mechanised accounts is the economy in time and labour. Machines accumulate the amount of individual postings as they are made. These totals are posted by machine to a Control Account so that the total balances in any Sales Ledger may be ascertained day by day. This is more fully explained in the chapter on mechanised accounts.

Dr.			Bought Ledger Control Account		*Cr.*
19..		£	19..		£
June 30	Cash ..	35000	June 1	Balance,	
,, 30	Discounts	700		being total	
,, 30	Returns			creditors at	
	and al-			this date	10000
	lowances	140	June 30	Purchases	40000
,, 30	Balance				
	carried				
	down	14160			
		£50000			£50000
			July 1	Balance	
				brought	
				down ..	14160

EXERCISES 28

1. What is the purpose of Sales Ledger and Purchases Ledger Control Accounts? How are they constructed and from what sources are the entries in them derived?

2. Complete the Bought Ledger and Sales Ledger Control Accounts, from the following details:—

19..							£
Jan. 1.	Debit balances in Sales Ledger	..	..	..	..	..	3694
,, 1.	Credit balances in Sales Ledger	..	..	..	..	..	149
,, 1.	Debit balances in Bought Ledger		..	..	..	..	58
,, 1.	Credit balances in Bought Ledger		..	..	..	..	983
,, 31.	Sales ..	..	..	..	..	..	8523
,, 31.	Purchases ..	..	..	..	..	..	2938
,, 31.	Cash received from customers	..	..	..	..	6954
,, 31.	Discount received ..	..	..	..	..	..	56
,, 31.	Discount allowed ..	..	..	..	..	..	80
,, 31.	Sales returns..	..	..	..	..	..	193
,, 31.	Purchases returns ..	..	..	..	..	..	100
,, 31.	Sales Ledger debits transferred to Bought Ledger		..	..	50
,, 31.	Customers' balances transferred to Bad Debts Account		..	25
,, 31.	Cash paid to creditors	..	..	..	..	..	2659
,, 31.	Credit balances in Sales Ledger	..	..	..	..	49
,, 31.	Debit balances in Bought Ledger..		..	..	..	83

R.S.A.

cash sales – nothing to do with it. creditors.

Provision for bad debts do not go in.

3. From the following particulars, relating to a particular Sales Ledger construct a Sales Ledger Control Account for the month of May, 19...

	£
Total debtors' balances in Sales Ledger at 1st May, agreeing with balance of Sales Ledger Control Account at 30th April	4607
Sales for month	5291
Returns and allowances for month	342
Cash received from debtors during the month	3996
Discounts allowed to debtors during the month	197
Bad debts during the month	47

4. From the following particulars relating to a particular Purchases Ledger construct a Purchases Ledger Control Account for the month of May, 19...

	£
Total of creditors' balances in Purchases Ledger at 1st May, agreeing with balance of Purchases Ledger Control Account at 30th April	8409
Purchases for month	7308
Returns and allowances for month	243
Cash paid to creditors during the month	6504
Discounts received during the month	292

5. F. Kay both sells goods to R. Tyler and buys goods from him. He keeps one account for Tyler in his Sales Ledger and another in his Purchases Ledger.

On 31st May, 19.., the debit balance on Tyler's account in the Sales Ledger was £137. This was transferred to Tyler's account in the Purchases Ledger which had a credit balance of £207. Make a Journal entry to show this transfer.

Where would the entries for this transfer appear in the Control Accounts for (i) the Sales Ledger and (ii) the Purchases Ledger?

6. Johnson & Son keep a Sales Ledger. At the end of each month a Sales Ledger Control (or Adjustment) Account is prepared.

(*a*) From the following particulars construct the Control (or Adjustment) Account for the month of October, 19..:—

19..		£
Oct. 1.	Debit balance	10461
	Credit balance	81
„ 31.	Sales for month	12484
	Sales returns for month	140
	Cash received from debtors during month	11058
	Discounts allowed to debtors during month	582
	Transfers of debit balances in the Sales Ledger to debit of Purchases Ledger during month	104
	Credit balances in Sales Ledger at end of month	131

(*b*) The debit balance on the Control Account did not agree with the total of debit balances in the Sales Ledger. On investigation the following errors were discovered:

(i) A total in the Sales Book had been carried forward as £2,749 instead of £2,479.

(ii) A discount allowed £6 to F. Ames had been entered in the Cash Book but not posted to Ames' account.

(iii) The total of the discount allowed column in the Cash Book for October had been undercast by £10.

(iv) A sale to J. Bragg had been entered correctly in the Sales Book as £195 but had been posted to Bragg's account as £95.

(v) A credit note for £21 sent to W. Carr had been entered in the Sales Returns Book and posted to Carr's account as £12.

State what corrections you would make in:—
1. The Sales Ledger, and
2. the Sales Ledger Control Account
to rectify the above errors.

A.E.B., G.C.E. "O" Level.

CHAPTER 29

MECHANISED ACCOUNTING

Students will appreciate that when there are many thousands of transactions, hand written methods of bookkeeping, as described in previous chapters, entail a great deal of labour and the services of large numbers of clerks and skilled bookkeepers. Sales are usually the most numerous of all transactions and the writing up of Sales Books, Sales Ledgers, and customers' Statements of Account may involve many hours of work on the part of many clerks.

Hand written methods involve the ever present possibility of error. Errors may be made in writing up the Sales Books, posting to the Sales Ledgers, and in making out Statements of Account at the end of each month. Moreover, there are peak periods of work, particularly at the end of each month when Statements are sent to customers and the books proved by means of a Trial Balance. If the Trial Balance does not agree, by reason of errors, then hours of search may be entailed before such errors are located.

Control Accounts, as described in Chapter 28, may help a great deal in locating such errors, but it would be a great advantage to have a system in which, at the time of making the records, Sales Book, Ledger Account, and Statement of Account are written up simultaneously and a system of control which would prove the postings correct after each run of work. This would save a great deal of labour, not only in writing up the records, but also by ensuring that all postings are correct from day to day.

This is made possible by the adoption of a simple system of mechanised accounts which will give the advantages of accuracy, improved records, speed, economy, and up-to-date information.

Accounting machines, when first used, were based on a combination of typewriter and adding machine, but these were superseded by machines based solely on adding machines. Such is the simple machine whose operation is described in this chapter. More sophisticated methods, using electronic devices and computers, are now in use, but these must be left to a later stage of study.

The operation of a simple accounting machine now described is based on information kindly supplied by the British Olivetti Company

DAY BOOK

LEDGER

NAME **PEARSON & CO LTD**

ADDRESS **82, HIGH STREET, LONDON S.W.25**

ACCOUNT No. **3273**

SHEET No. **1**

DATE	PARTICULARS	DEBIT	CREDIT	BALANCE	PROOF CODE
21 JUN 71	AK/1702 DETAILS	1 2 1.7 8.		1 2 1.7 8.	2 4 3.5 6
23 JUN 71	AK/1943 DETAILS	5 6.9 8.		1 7 8.7 6.	3 5 7.5 2.
24 JUN 71	AK/2196 DETAILS	5 3.5 5.½			
24 JUN 71	AK/2197 DETAILS	4 5.6 3.½		2 7 7.9 3.	5 5 5.8 6.
27 JUN 71	AK/2275 DETAILS	3 2.9 0.		3 1 0.8 3.	6 2 1.6 6.
10 JUL 71	AL/1068 DETAILS	2 7.7 5.		3 3 8.5 8.	6 7 7.1 6.
13 JUL 71	56/CASH		2 7 9.7 5.		
13 JUL 71	56/DISC		3 1.0 8.	2 7.7 5.	5 5.5 0
18 JUL 71	AL1914 DETAILS	8 1.6 3.		1 0 9.3 8.	2 1 6.7 6
19 JUL 71	AL/1943 DETAILS	4 3.5 3.		1 5 2.9 1.	3 0 5.8 2
22 JUL 71	AL/2173 DETAILS	2 1.9 0.		1 7 4.8 1.	3 4 9.6 5
30 JUL 71	AL/2532 DETAILS	3 2.9 6.		2 0 7.7 7.	4 1 5.5 4

SPECIMEN STATEMENT

olivetti
BRITISH OLIVETTI LIMITED
Marketing Division
30 Berkeley Square London W1
TELEPHONE 01-629 8807

PEARSON & CO LTD

82, HIGH STREET,
LONDON S.W.25.

3273

DATE	REFERENCE	DEBITS	CREDITS	BALANCE
	BALANCE FORWARD ▶			3 1 0.8 3.
10 JUL 71	AL/1068 DETAILS	2 7.7 5.		3 3 8.5 8.
13 JUL 71	56/CASH		2 7 9.7 5.	
13 JUL 71	56/DISC		3 1.0 8.	2 7.7 5.
18 JUL 71	AL1914 DETAILS	8 1.6 3.		1 0 9.3 8.
19 JUL 71	AL/1943 DETAILS	4 3.5 3.		1 5 2.9 1.
22 JUL 71	AL/2173 DETAILS	2 1.9 0.		1 7 4.8 1.
30 JUL 71	AL/2532 DETAILS	3 2.9 6.		2 0 7.7 7.

THE LAST AMOUNT IN THIS
COLUMN IS THE SUM DUE

this is a specimen from an Olivetti **Audit** Mechanised Accounting **System**

1,0 6 0,7 5

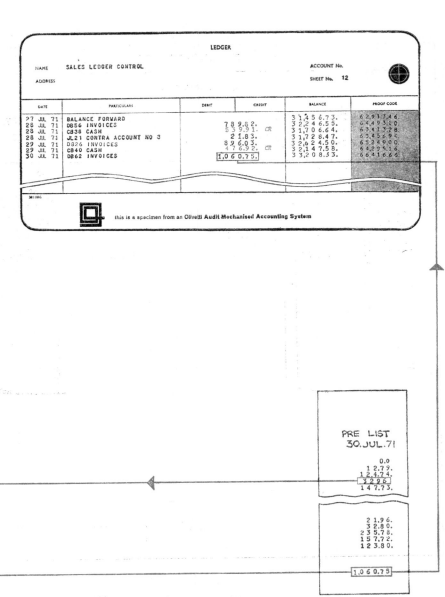

(Reproduced by courtesy of British Olivetti Company Ltd)

B   Purchase Ledger

PURCHASES DAY BOOK

LEDGER CARD

NAME Pearson & Co. Ltd.,

ADDRESS 82, High Street,
London, S.W.25.

ACCOUNT No. 3273

SHEET No 10

DATE	REFERENCE	POSTING CODE	DEBIT	CREDIT	BALANCE		PROOF CODE
-1 NOV 71							
13 NOV 71	2 0,4 2	1.			8 4 1.5 3.	CR	2,5 2 4.5 9.
17 NOV 71	2 0,5 6	1.		4 7.6 3.	8 8 9.1 6.	CR	2,6 6 7.4 3.
18 NOV 71	2 0,6 8	1.		2 5.8 7.	9 1 5.0 3.	CR	2,7 4 5.0 9.
19 NOV 71	4,5 0	6.		6.0 0.	9 2 1.0 3.	CR	2,7 6 3.0 9.
19 NOV 71	4,5 0	6.	8 4 1.5 3.		7 9.5 0.	CR	2 3 8.5 0.
21 NOV 71	2 1,8 3	1.		2 5.0 0.	1 0 4.5 0.	CR	3 1 3.5 0.
26 NOV 71	2 1,9 2	1.		1 7.6 3.	1 2 2.1 3.	CR	3 6 6.3 9.

7 2 5.2 7

LEDGER CARD

NAME   Purchase Ledger Control

ADDRESS

ACCOUNT No.

SHEET No. 2

DATE	REFERENCE	POSTING CODE	DEBIT	CREDIT	BALANCE	PROOF CODE
14 NOV 71					1,1 9 2.6 3. CR	3,5 7 7.8 9. CR
15 NOV 71				2 5 6.5 4.	1,4 4 9.1 7. CR	4,3 4 7.6 1. CR
16 NOV 71				9 8 4.7 2.	2,4 3 3.8 9. CR	7,3 0 1.6 7. CR
16 NOV 71			1,4 3 8.5 0.		9 9 5.3 9. CR	2,9 8 6.1 7. CR
17 NOV 71				9 7 4.6 6.	1,9 7 0.0 5. CR	5,9 1 0.1 5. CR
18 NOV 71				3 4 1.7 0.	2,3 1 1.7 5. CR	6,9 3 5.2 5. CR
19 NOV 71			2 5 6.6 2.		2,0 5 5.1 3. CR	6,1 6 5.3 9. CR
21 NOV 71				2 2 5.0 0.	2,2 8 0.1 3. CR	6,8 1 0.3 9. CR
26 NOV 71				7 2 5.2 7.	3,0 0 5.4 0. CR	9,0 1 6.2 0. CR

PRE-LIST
26th Nov'71.

3 2 0.8 0.
1 1 2.6 6.
2 9.7 0.
6 2.2 0.
2 2.0 0.
2 1.5 3.
4 3.6 4.
2 2.5 2.
7 2.5 9.
1 7.6 3.

7 2 5.2 7.

Ltd., and it is treated in its application to sales and purchases records.

The sources of information for compiling sales records will be copy invoices of goods sold to customers, copy receipts or bank paying-in slips for remittances received from debtors, copy credit notes sent to customers for returns and allowances, and Journal vouchers for miscellaneous items such as bad debts.

The Ledger Accounts will take the form of cards ruled in three columns as shown on page 3. These cards may be kept in drawers in alphabetical order or in numerical order when the customers' accounts are numbered. This facilitates the selection of cards for any particular run of postings. A run of postings may consist, for example, of posting copy invoices, copy credit notes or remittances from debtors. Whatever the run may be, the material, *e.g.* copy invoices, is sorted into ledger order, listed and totalled on an adding machine for agreement purposes. This is known as a "pre-list" and its total should agree with the total of postings as shown by the accounting machine at the end of the run of postings.

The Ledger cards are then selected and arranged in the same order as the material to be posted. For ease of operation when posting to Ledger cards, the cards and relevant documents, *e.g.* copy invoices, each card accompanied by its relevant invoice, may be arranged in a tray from which card and relevant document are withdrawn together.

Accounting machines are so constructed that they add or subtract automatically and may, or may not supply narrative detail on documents. In the specimen of Sales Ledger postings on pages 239*a* and 239*b*, the entries are collated with narrative, but in the illustration of Purchases Ledger postings (pages 239*c* and 239*d*) these are omitted.

The machines also incorporate devices to ensure the accuracy of the postings. To do this it is necessary first to introduce the old balance into the machine. This is known as "picking up" the old balance. It is necessary to prove the accuracy of this "pick up". In some machines when the posting has been made the "pick up" balance is repeated and if there has been an error in the "pick up" the machine locks. There is always the possibility of the operator making the same error in both "pick ups". To avoid this more advanced types of machine are capable of giving an automatic proof of the entry of the correct "pick up" of the old balance. This operates in the following manner. On completion of a line entry after recording the up-to-date balance the machine automatically produces a non-accounting figure that is mathematically related to the account balance and is printed in a special column on the card known as "proof code". When a new entry is to be made to an account *both* the account balance *and* the "proof code" are picked up, i.e. *two different figures*. The machine will then decide if the balance has been picked up correctly. If this has not been done the machine will not operate. A proof code column appears in the Inset at the end. The only possibility of error now remaining is in the actual posting. This can be checked at the end of the posting run by comparing the automatic total of entries accumulated by the machine with the pre-list, *i.e.* the predetermined total of postings made by adding machine. This may be done visually, but some machines are made in such a way as to make this comparison by entering the pre-list total into the machine at the end of the run of postings. The machine will then automically compare this total with the total of accumulated postings and make this total entry in the Sales Ledger Control Account.

In making Sales Ledger entries a pre-list is made and the Ledger cards are selected and arranged. A Sales Day Book sheet with carbon jacket is inserted into the rear feed of the accounting machine and the machine is cleared ready for posting. The clearing operation is printed on to the Day Book so that in the event of non-agreement of totals after posting the error is known to be confined to the batch of postings just completed.

A Ledger card and statement are then inserted with carbons (see Inset at the end). For each Ledger card the old balance is picked up and is automatically rejected if incorrect. The postings are made from the copy invoices, copy credit notes, or whatever media is being posted. The new balance is calculated and printed by the machine. It is, of course, the insertion of the old balance and then the amount of the transaction that enables the machine to add (in the case of debit postings) or subtract (in the case of credit postings) and thus calculate and print the new balance on both Ledger card and statement. Where the system of proving the "pick up" of the previous balance by printing it again is in use this is then done to prove the accuracy of the "pick up".

At the end of the posting run the pre-list total is fed into the machine and automatically compared with the accumulated total of postings. If the system adopted is one in which the pre-list total is visually compared with the total accumulated by the machine this is done. If the total is incorrect the machine, in the first case becomes inoperable or alternatively, it is seen visually that the totals are not the same. In either case the necessary correction must be made.

When the total is proved correct the Control Account card is inserted, the balance picked up and proved, and the agreed total of postings made on the Control Account card. The student will readily see that, unlike hand written methods, the accuracy of the posting is proved after each run of postings and the Sales Ledger Control Account will show at a glance the total of trade debtors to date.

In the case of Purchases Ledgers the procedure of posting invoices received (credits), credit notes received, Cash Book summaries of accounts paid (debits) will be basically the same as for the Sales Ledgers except that Statements will be omitted. The Purchases Ledger Control Account will then show, at the end of each run of postings, the total of trade creditors. This is illustrated in the Inset at the end of the book.

Accounting machines may be used for Cash Book postings and analysis, the making up of Pay Rolls, Stock Sheets, and Stock Control Records.

EXERCISES 29

1. Give a brief explanation of the posting of Sales Ledger Accounts by means of a simple accounting machine.

2. What advantages does the use of an accounting machine have as compared to hand written methods of bookkeeping?

3. How would the use of an accounting machine economise in clerical labour?

4. How is the accuracy of posting ensured when using an accounting machine and what advantages ensue?

5. Why is the use of Control Accounts enhanced by the use of an accounting machine?

APPENDIX I

ADDITIONAL EXERCISES

1. The following transactions took place between D.E., a wholesaler, and R.V., a retailer, during January, 19...

Jan. 1. Balance due to D.E. £100.
  ,, 4. Goods sold to R.V. £180 less 33⅓% trade discount.
  ,, 11. Part of the above goods invoiced at £60 gross were returned by R.V.
  ,, 20. Goods sold to R.V. £120 less 33⅓% trade discount.
  ,, 27. R.V. sent a cheque to D.E. in settlement of the amount due from him less 2½% discount.

Show the account of R.V. as it should appear in the books of D.E. at 31st January, 19...   *A.E.B., G.C.E. "O" Level.*

2. D.A., a wholesale dealer in electrical goods, has two departments: (*a*) Radio and television, (*b*) Electrical sundries. During the period 7th to 13th January, 19.., he had the following credit transactions.

Jan. 7. Purchased 6 television sets, No. 216, from E.M. & Co. Ltd., at £80 each, less trade discount of 25%.
  ,, 9. Sold 4 of the above sets, No. 216, to R.B. at £80 each, less trade discount of 10%.
  ,, 10. Purchased from R.M. & Co. Ltd., 1 dozen electric irons at £3 each, less trade discount of 25%, 6 electric sweepers, No. 105, at £33 each, less trade discount of 33⅓%.
  ,, 11. R.B. returned 2 of the television sets, No. 216, sold to him on 9th, as defective. Sent him a credit note. Returned the above 2 television sets, No. 216, to E.M. & Co. Ltd.

Record the above transactions in columnar books of original entry and post to the Ledger.   *A.E.B., G.C.E. "O" Level.*

3. After the closing of his books for the year ended 31st December, 19.., the Capital Account of S.T. was as follows:—

S.T. Capital Account

19..			£	19..		£
Mar. 31.	Drawings .. C.B.		250	Jan. 1.	Balance b/d. ..	1600
June 30.	,, .. ,,		250	Dec. 31.	Interest on Capital	80
Sept. 30.	,, .. ,,		250		Balance c/d. ..	70
Dec. 31.	,, .. ,,		250			
	Profit and Loss A/c.		750			
			£1750			£1750

19..
Dec. 31. To Balance b/d. .. 70
Explain the meaning of the entries in this account.
         A.E.B., G.C.E. "O" Level.

4. The following are *some* of the balances of E. Ellenborough, wholesale grocer, on 1st April, 19...

Cash at bank, £258; cash in office, £55.
E. Eldon—a creditor, £25; M. Mansfield—a debtor, £36.

243

Office furniture and equipment, £380.

Open the accounts in Ellenborough's books to show these balances; then enter the following in the appropriate subsidiary books and post to the Ledger.

All cheques received are paid direct to the bank.

19..

April 1.   Received cheques—
     (*a*) From M. Mansfield in settlement of his account less 5% cash discount;
     (*b*) For sale of some of the office equipment (valued in books at £80), £95.

„ 2.   Bought on credit from E. Eldon—
     Canned goods invoiced at £160 less 25% trade discount;
     Packeted goods, £180, less 33⅓% trade discount.

„ 3.   Returned to E. Eldon one-quarter of the packeted goods bought on 2nd April.

„ 4.   M. Mansfield's cheque banked on 1st April returned marked "Refer to drawer".

„ 6.   Paid to E. Eldon by cheque the amount owing to him less 5% cash discount.

Balance the Cash Book.   *W.J.E.C., G.C.E. "O" Level.*

5. Give brief answers to any *three* of the following:—
    (*a*) Why does capital usually appear on the liabilities side of the Balance Sheet?
    (*b*) Why is net profit entered on the debit side of the Profit and Loss Account?
    (*c*) Why is the balance of cash at bank referred to by the trader as his "credit balance" at the bank?
    (*d*) Purchases are entered in the Ledger in any case. Why are they also entered in a subsidiary book?
    (*e*) When Final Accounts are being compiled the stock at the end of the trading period is entered in the Trading Account. Where is the offsetting double entry found?
     W.J.E.C., G.C.E. "O" Level (Commercial Subjects).

6.   **M. Butler's Ledger**
Dr.   **B. Mitchell's Account**   *Cr.*
19..   £ 19..   £
(*a*) May 1. Balance .. .. 60 (*b*) May 2. Bank 57
(*d*) „ 6. Goods .. .. 28 (*c*) „ 2. Discount 3
                                 (*e*) „ 9. Returns 7

Examine the above account carefully and
   (i) briefly interpret each of the items (*a*)-(*e*);
  (ii) state in which of M. Butler's books each of the items (*b*)-(*e*) was entered before being posted to the Ledger;
 (iii) state the account in M. Butler's Ledger where each of the items (*b*)-(*e*) has its double entry;
 (iv) state the conclusions you draw from the account as a whole.
     W.J.E.C., G.C.E. "O" Level (Commercial Subjects).

7. From what sources would you expect a wholesaler to obtain the information for writing up (*a*) the Sales Day Book, (*b*) the Returns Inwards Book, (*c*) the Purchases Day Book?   *A.E.B., G.C.E. "O" Level.*

8. Although the Trial Balance of A.B. agreed, the audit of his books of account revealed the following errors.

£15 paid for advertising charges had been debited to the personal account of the advertising contractor.

£60 paid for the purchase of an additional typewriter had been debited to the Purchases Account.

State (*a*) why these errors were not revealed by the Trial Balance, (*b*) the effect of their *correction* on the balance of the net profit at the end of the trading period.   *A.E.B., G.C.E. "O" Level.*

9. During the audit of the books of a business the following errors were discovered:—

(*a*) An amount of £20 for the sale of a typewriter used in the business had been credited to Sales Account.

(*b*) An amount of £16 paid for carriage on purchases had been debited to Carriage on Sales Account.

(*c*) A sale of goods £49 to J. Brown had been debited to the account of G. Brown.

You are required—

(i) to give the Journal entries necessary to correct the errors.

(ii) to state the effect of the corrections on the gross profit, the net profit, and on any items in the Balance Sheet.   *College of Preceptors—Senior.*

10. (*a*) It is sometimes said that "Petty Cash should be kept on the imprest system". What do you understand by this, and what advantage has this system to offer?

(*b*) Draft a Petty Cash Book with separate analysis columns for Purchases, Fares, and Sundry Expenses, and enter in it the following:—

		£
19..		
Feb. 1.	Balance in hand	10·00
	Payments—	
Feb. 2.	Office teas	0·15½
	Fares	0·08½
„ 3.	Cash purchases	2·22½
	Fares	0·13½
„ 4.	Office cleaner's wages and materials ..	2·08
„ 6.	Office teas	0·18
	Fares	0·24
	Cash purchases	1·37½

Balance the Petty Cash Book on 6th February and enter as drawn from the bank the sum needed to restore the imprest to £10.   *R.S.A.—Elementary.*

11. Trot, a retailer, finds himself in need of additional capital in order to pay for an expansion in his business, and arranges for a loan from the Downshire Bank to be drawn as required. You are asked to record the following in Trot's Ledger—

		£
Jan. 1.	Received loan from bank	500
„ 10.	„ „ „ „	750
„ 31.	„ „ „ „	250
Mar. 1.	Repaid on account of loan	325
„ 16.	„ „ „ „	125
„ 31.	Paid interest	18

Balance the Loan Account on 31st March, 19...

Note.—Cash Book and Journal entries are *not* required.

R.S.A.—Elementary.

12. Included among the bookkeeping records of a firm of wholesalers is a "Journal Proper". What types of entry would you expect to find in this book?

At the close of the firm's financial year on 31st December, 19.., their stock in trade was valued at £1,290: give the journal entry to record this.

R.S.A.—Elementary.

13. On 1st March, 19.., J. Wilkes, a dealer in perambulators and toy cycles, had the following stock—

					£
20 Grade A perambulators valued at cost		..	..	15 each
30 Grade B perambulators	,,	,,	..	..	12 ,,
50 Toy cycles	,,	,,	..	5 ,,

During the month his sales and purchases were:—

	SALES	PURCHASES
Grade A perambulators ..	10 at £20 each	12 at £16 each
Grade B ,, ..	6 at £15 each	—
Toy cycles ,, ...	20 at £8 each	10 at £5 each

(a) Calculate the value of Wilkes's closing stock, showing the method and details of your valuation.

(b) Show by means of a Trading Account the gross profit or loss for the month.

(c) Express the gross profit earned as a percentage of total sales.

R.S.A.—Elementary.

14. The following Trial Balance was extracted by a not too competent book-keeper at 31st March, 19...

You are asked to redraw it *to the extent that it is wrong*—the *whole* Trial Balance is *not* required to be redrawn.

	£	£
Capital—		
1st April (previous year)		5000
Additional capital introduced during year (the		
proceeds of a private investment)	1000	
Interest received thereon to date of sale ..	25	
Loan got from bank during year	1500	
Premises	3500	
Fixtures	500	
Sales		25000
Purchases	17500	
Returns inwards	300	
Returns outwards		900
Office and administration charges	3700	
Selling and distribution charges..		4500
Discount received..	100	
Debtors	5000	
Creditors		3250
Proceeds sale of old fixtures	20	
Rents received from sublet of part of premises	75	
Cash in hand	20	
Bank overdraft	1750	
Stock 1st April (previous year)	3600	
	£38590	£38650

15. (*a*) You are asked to interpret the following account for the benefit of someone who knows nothing whatsoever about bookkeeping or the technical "jargon" associated with it.

John Smith & Co.

19..			£	19..			£
Jan. 1.	Balance b/d	.. ..	1000	Jan. 6.	C/N		100
„ 22.	Goods..	.. ..	500	„ 15.	Contra Account		300
				„ 15.	Cash		588
				„ 15.	Discount ..		12
				„ 31.	Balance c/d ..		500
			£1500				£1500
Feb. 1.	Balance b/d	.. ..	500				

(*b*) Indicate the source from which the various entries in the above account would be derived.

(*c*) In which Ledger would you expect to find the account?

London Chamber of Commerce—Elementary.

16. Show by means of Journal entries how to deal with the following:—

(*a*) Credit note £10 sent to a customer, L. Adams, as an allowance on damaged goods.

(*b*) Wages £76 paid to the firm's workmen for erecting new plant and machinery.

(*c*) A decision to reduce the value of stock by £150.

(*d*) Goods taken by proprietor of the business for his own use £25.

(*e*) Paid cheque to XL Garage Ltd. for motor van maintenance, £4.

(*f*) A payment, £26, made to B. Smith had been posted to the account of D. Smith. *London Chamber of Commerce—Elementary.*

17. The following account appeared in J. Lawson's Debtors' Ledger.

A. Saville

19..				£	19..				£
Jan. 1	Balance	..	b/d	160	Jan. 8	Cash	..	CB4	156
„ 11	Goods	..	SB1	95		Discount	..	CB4	4
„ 27	Goods	..	SB3	81	„ 15	Returns	..	RIB	21

State—

(*a*) The meaning of each of the items in this account.

(*b*) The subsidiary book from which each item is posted.

(*c*) The documents used in connection with each transaction.

London Chamber of Commerce—Elementary.

18. From the following details find CD's capital and show his Balance Sheet at 31st December, 19..:—

Trade creditors, £1,977; expense creditors, £129; debtors, £2,845; stock, £3,848; amounts prepaid, £57; plant and machinery, £4,100; furniture and fittings, £680; freehold premises, £10,000; cash in hand, £40; bank overdraft, £2,600.

From the completed Balance Sheet answer the following questions:—

(*a*) State the items which are current assets and give the total of such assets.

(*b*) State the items which are fixed assets and give the total of such assets.

(*c*) State the items which you consider to be current liabilities and give the total of such liabilities.

(*d*) How would you find the working capital and what is its amount?
(*e*) What is meant by "Freehold" premises?

London Chamber of Commerce—Elementary.

19. (*a*) Why is capital considered to be a liability of a business firm?
(*b*) What is meant by saying a firm is insolvent and how would this fact be apparent from its Balance Sheet?

London Chamber of Commerce—Elementary.

20.   **Ledger of E. Huish**
Dr.   **T. Smith's Account**   *Cr.*

19..			£	19..			£
(*c*) May	5.	Returns ..	.. 30	(*a*) May	1.	Balance	.. 180
(*d*) „	5.	Bank ..	.. 361	(*b*) „	2.	Goods ..	.. 230
(*e*) „	5.	Discount	.. 19	(*g*) „	15.	Bank ..	.. 152
(*f*) „	12.	Goods ..	.. 160	(*h*) „	15.	Discount	.. 8

Indicate in respect of each of the eight items (*a*) (*h*):—

(i) its meaning;
(ii) the subsidiary book in which it was first entered;
(iii) the Ledger Account in which the offsetting double entry is to be found.
What deductions do you make in respect of the account as a whole?

W.J.E.C., G.C.E. "O" Level.

21. A. Gwynn's business is divided into two departments, A and B, and on 31st May, 19.., the following balances were extracted from the books.

	A	B
	£ *thousands*	
Stock at beginning of year	4·5	5·4
Sales	13·5	22·6
Purchases	11·5	15·6
Returns inwards	0·3	0·6
Returns outwards..	1·4	2·2
Stock at 31st May, 19..	4·7	5·6

(*a*) Prepare, on the columnar system, Trading Account for the year ended 31st May, 19...
(*b*) Express the gross profit as a percentage of turnover in respect of each department and of the business as a whole.

W.J.E.C., G.C.E. "O" Level.

22. Indicate—*briefly* giving your reasons in each case—which of the following represent capital receipts, capital expenditure, revenue income, revenue expenditure:—

(*a*) Bank overdraft interest;
(*b*) purchase of typewriters for re-sale by the Office Supplies Company;
(*c*) purchase of typewriter for office use by the H.T.C. Social Club;
(*d*) sale of a delivery van by the Office Supplies Company;
(*e*) receipt of commission by a firm of brokers.

W.J.E.C., G.C.E. "O" Level (Commercial Subjects).

23. Indicate—*briefly* giving your reasons in each case—which of the following represents capital receipts, capital expenditure, revenue income, revenue expenditure, in respect of the H.T.C. Social Club:—

(*a*) purchase of new piano;
(*b*) annual subscriptions received from members;
(*c*) interest on bank deposit;

Additional Exercises 249

(d) purchase of office stationery;
(e) sale of Club's old office typewriter.
W.J.E.C., G.C.E. "O" Level (Commercial Subjects).

24. On 1st January, 19.., B. Forecast, a retailer, had stock valued at £3,750. In planning for the next six months he estimated that his gross sales would amount to £20,500 and that he would have sales returns of £500. He was anxious to have at 30th June, 19.., stock valued at not more than £3,500. Assuming that this trader's average ratio of gross profit to turnover is 25%, calculate, in account form, the amount to which he should limit his purchases during the period.
R.S.A.—Elementary.

25. You are required to set out or correct the following by way of Journal entries:—

(a) The bringing into account of the stock at 31st December (the financial year end) valued at £1,200.
(b) The transference at 31st December, 19.. (the financial year end), of the following balances to the appropriate section of the Revenue Account—

	£
Sales	30000
Purchases	20000
Stock, 1st January, 19..	1500
Office and administration charges	3200
Selling and distribution charges	4500

(c) The purchase of a machine for production purposes from Engineering Suppliers Ltd., passed through Purchases Account .. £1750
(d) The bringing into account of interest for six months on an overdue account owing by A. D. Faulter £5
(e) The necessary adjustment in respect of goods returned by A. B. Emit of a *gross* invoice value of £60 and recorded at that amount. The goods were subject to a trade discount of $33\frac{1}{3}$%.
London Chamber of Commerce—Elementary.

26. The following is the Balance Sheet of B. Jones at 1st April, 19...

	£	£		£
Capital		5000	Premises	2000
Creditors—			Fixtures	75
Trade	2500		Motor vehicles	675
Accrued rent	180		Stock	3200
Bank	1500		Debtors	3180
		4180	Cash on hand	50
		£9180		£9180

His transactions for the month of April can be summarised as follows:—

	£
(a) Received from customers (all banked)	2800
(b) Discount allowed to customers	62
(c) Goods returned by customers (cost value £30)	48
(d) Goods sold on a credit basis (cost value £1,640)	2460
(e) Paid to suppliers by cheque	2700
(f) Discount allowed by suppliers	40
(g) Returns to suppliers	100
(h) Goods bought on a credit basis	3000
(i) Paid rent accrued at 1st April, 19.., by cheque	180

£

(*j*) Borrowed from A. Chance by cheque lodged in bank .. 2000
(*k*) Proceeds of motor vehicle (book value £280) banked.. .. 200
(*l*) Cost of new vehicle paid by cheque 900
(*m*) Paid by cash—
 Office and administration charges 200
 Selling and distribution charges 250
 Cash purchases 75
 Proprietor for self 50
(*n*) Received in cash—
 For cash sales (cost value £120) 180
 ex Bank for till purposes 400

You are required to produce a Balance Sheet at 30th April, 19.., *without going to the trouble of writing up any Ledger Accounts.*

It is suggested that cash ruling might conveniently be used for this purpose and the transition from the Balance Sheet at 1st April, 19.., to that at 30th April, 19.., shown as follows—

Balance Sheet

LIABILITIES				ASSETS	
At		At	At		At
1st April, 19..	+	− 30th April, 19..	1st April, 19..	+	− 30th April, 19..

London Chamber of Commerce—Elementary.

27. F. W. Pickles & Sons are manufacturers of sauces and pickles.

From the following information relating to the year ended 31st December, 19.., select the items which you consider should be charged to the Trading and Profit and Loss Accounts of the firm and draw up the accounts in proper form.

N.B.—A Balance Sheet is *not* required.

£

Stocks of raw materials 1st January, 19..	3100
Stocks of raw materials 31st December, 19..	2870
Purchases of raw materials	69100
Stocks of jars and bottles 1st January, 19..	980
Stocks of jars and bottles 31st December, 19..	1060
Purchases of jars and bottles	9250
Stock of packing cases and crates for despatch of finished goods 1st January, 19..	270
Cost of making new packing cases and crates during the year..	1840
Stock of packing cases and crates 31st December, 19..	210
Factory wages	75100
Office wages and salaries	6800
Delivery vanmen's wages	4900
Salesmen's salaries, expenses, and commission	10950
Advertising	6500
Factory power	1850
Light and heat (Factory $\frac{5}{6}$, Office $\frac{1}{6}$)	780
Rates (Factory $\frac{5}{6}$, Office $\frac{1}{6}$)	822
Delivery van expenses	2100
Insurance (Factory $\frac{5}{6}$, Office $\frac{1}{6}$)	420
Depreciation of machinery	1615
Depreciation of office equipment	75
Drawings	18000
Office and administrative expenses	950
Purchases of new machinery	3500
Repairs to premises	340

	£
Extension of premises	2500
Sales	215000
Stocks of finished goods 1st January, 19..	4780
Stocks of finished goods 31st December, 19..	5220

Notes—

Factory wages due at 31st December, 19.., and not paid	1200
Insurance prepaid at 31st December, 19..	102

College of Preceptors—Senior.

28. From the information given below prepare the account of T. Matthew as it would appear in the Ledger of O. Paul (furniture dealer) for the month of April, 19...

April 1. Balance due to Matthew, £120.

„ 6. Purchased from Matthew 6 dozen chairs at £2 each, *less* 25% trade discount.

„ 8. Returned to Matthew 6 damaged chairs and received credit note therefor.

Paid carriage on returned chairs (chargeable to Matthew) £2.

„ 15. Sold to Matthew an old board-room table for £15.

„ 20. Paid to Matthew the balance due on 1st April, *less* 5% cash discount.

„ 30. Purchased from Matthew a job lot of furniture for £20.

Balance the account on 30th April, 19...

(a) Has it a debit or credit balance?

(b) Is O. Paul due to receive or pay the amount? *R.S.A.—Elementary.*

29. (a) What do you understand by Capital Expenditure and Revenue Expenditure? Why is this distinction important in bookkeeping?

(b) Steven and James, retailers, have spent £250 for complete redecoration of their premises. Steven says this is Capital Expenditure but James says it is Revenue Expenditure. State with your reasons which of them you consider to be right.

(c) What difference will it make to the profits for the year if Steven's rather than James's view is adopted, but one-fifth of the cost is written off? *R.S.A.—Elementary.*

30. The following information is taken from the books of the X.Y.Z. Company.

	YEAR 1	YEAR 2 (following year 1)
	£	£
Turnover	11000	12000
Gross profit as a percentage of turnover	41	43
Net profit as a percentage of turnover ..	16	15

State, with reasons, the conclusions you draw from this information. *W.J.E.C., G.C.E. "O" Level (Commercial Subjects).*

31. The following balances were extracted from the books of M.N., a retailer, for two completed years of trading.

	YEAR 1	YEAR 2
	£	£
Stock at 1st January	4000	5000
„ 31st December	5000	3000
Purchases	20000	21000
Salaries	4000	4800
National Insurance..	120	130
Rent and rates	1200	1500

	£	£
Heating and lighting	400	625
Advertising	75	80
Sundry expenses	200	325
Depreciation of fittings ..	50	50
Cost of delivery of sales	220	350
Insurances	120	120
Sales	28500	34400

(*a*) Prepare accounts showing the gross and net profit in each year. Provide for interest at 5% per annum on M.N.'s capital, which for the year ended 31st December in Year 1, was £35,000, and for the year ended 31st December in Year 2, £36,000.

(*b*) State, with reasons for your opinion, which of the two years has yielded the better result. *A.E.B., G.C.E. "O" Level.*

32. (*a*) What is a Balance Sheet?

(*b*) How does it differ from—
   (i) A Trial Balance?
   (ii) A Trading and Profit and Loss Account?

(*c*) From the following list of balances prepare a Balance Sheet at 31st March, 19.., in good style bringing out totals for the following—

   Fixed Assets.
   Current Assets.
   Fixed Liabilities.
   Current Liabilities.

The list is complete save for the balance on the Capital Account.

	£
Premises	2500
Loan from A. Goodman	2000
Bank overdraft	2350
Plant	5000
Fixtures	750
Accrued charges	150
Accounts payable	3350
Accounts receivable	4500
Sundry prepayments..	120
Six months' interest accrued on Goodman's loan, payable 31st March, 19..	50
Petty cash imprest	30
Stock and work in progress	3000

(*d*) Assuming that the proprietor had paid in additional capital during the year of £1,500, had had drawings as follows:—

	£
Cash	450
Goods	150

and that the profit for the year ended 31st March, 19.., was £1,100, write up the proprietor's Capital Account for the year ended 31st March, 19.., bringing out the balance at the beginning of the year.

London Chamber of Commerce—Elementary.

33. On 31st December, 19.., A. Bass's Statement of Account (from the bank) showed a balance in his favour of £650. On comparing the Statement with his Cash Book he found that the following entries in the Cash Book had not yet been entered on the Statement:—

Cheques paid in 31st December, £125

Cheques drawn up to 31st December, £275

and the following entries on the Statement had not yet been entered in his Cash Book:—

Bank charges for the half year £26.

Payment direct to the bank by one of his debtors £116.

Draw up a bank Reconciliation Statement so as to show the bank balance according to his Cash Book on 31st December, 19...

W.J.E.C., G.C.E. "O" Level (Commercial Subjects).

34. The following Trial Balance was extracted from Peter Pliney's books *after* the Trading and Profit and Loss Account had been prepared—

Trial Balance. 31st December, 19..

	£	£
Profit and Loss Account (Net profit for year to date)		1800
Cash in hand	10	
Cash at bank	500	
Bank Deposit Account	320	
Trade debtors and creditors	1600	925
Bad debts provision		185
Plant and machinery (see note)	740	
Insurance unexpired	25	
Stock in trade	1200	
Peter Pliney: Capital Account		1500
,, ,, Drawings Account	500	
Rent accrued		160
Delivery van (see note)	450	
Loan Account: D. Garrick		400
Cibber Garages—balance due for van		375
	£5345	£5345

Notes.—(1) Plant and machinery has been depreciated by £120 during the year and stood in the books at £860 on 1st January, 19.., this being its cost less depreciation to date;

(2) The delivery van cost £500 during 19.. and £50 had been written off for depreciation.

From the above information prepare Peter Pliney's Balance Sheet as on 31st December, 19...

R.S.A.—Elementary.

35. Joan Peters is in business as a wholesale draper. It is her practice to maintain a bad and doubtful debts provision equal in amount to 5% of the debts outstanding at the end of each financial year.

From the following information prepare the Bad Debts Account for the year 19.. (including the provision for bad and doubtful debts)—

		£
Total Debtors on 31st December in previous year		3220
,, ,, ,, ,, ,, 19..		4340
Debts written off as irrecoverable—		
On 30th June, 19..—A. Luke		15
N. Abel		120
30th November—B. John..		97
K. Simon		49

On 1st November, 19.., a first and final dividend of 2s. in the £ was received in respect of the debt due from Abel (previously written off on 30th June, 19..) and on 18th December, £20 in respect of a debt due from O. Adam (written off in a previous year).

Balance the account as on 31st December, 19.., and show the amount chargeable against the Profit and Loss Account for the year. *R.S.A.—Elementary.*

36. (i) Distinguish between (*a*) a Receipts and Payments Account, (*b*) an Income and Expenditure Account, and (*c*) a Profit and Loss Account.

(ii) Prepare the Income and Expenditure Account for the Western Vale Hockey Club for 19.. from the following information:—

	£
Subscriptions for the year	250
Receipts for hire of pitch	25
Club dances (net income)	18
Rent paid	60
Secretarial expenses	30
Wages (groundsman)	104
Paid for repairs to club house	40
Lighting and other club house expenses	56

On 31st December, 19.., £15 was due to the club for the hire of the pitch and £26 was unpaid for repairs to the club house.   *R.S.A.—Elementary.*

37. Jack Store owns a group of shops to which goods are charged at selling prices (*i.e.* the prices at which they are expected to be sold) so as to secure a check on the shop stocks held at any time, the theory being that to the extent that the goods sent to the shops have not been sold, goods of that invoice value ought to be on hand.

(*a*) From the following details relative to his Argyle Street shop you are required to bring out—in statement or account form—what the actual physical stock at 30th April, 19.., ought to be.

	£
Shop stock, 1st April, 19.., at invoice values	3500
Shop stock, 30th April, 19.., at invoice values	?
Goods charged to shop during April	10000
Goods returned by shop to suppliers at invoice value ..	200
Goods returned to shop by credit customers	60
Shop cash sales	9000
Shop credit sales (gross)	1160

(*b*) On the basis that the actual stock at 30th April, 19.., was also the theoretical stock and that the invoice value of the goods is such that a profit of 25% on cost price is earned and that the shop expenses for April were £1,000, calculate—

(i) the shop gross profit;
(ii) the shop net profit for the month.
London Chamber of Commerce—Elementary.

38. A and B enter into partnership on 1st March, 19... A contributes £2,000 cash and B £1,200 cash and a motor van valued at £650. The cash is paid into a Bank Account, which is also credited with an additional £2,000 borrowed from the bank.

Premises are rented and £500 paid as rent in advance.

The following items were purchased and paid by cheque: Furniture and fittings, £400; machinery, £1,500; stock in trade, £2,000.

Items purchased on credit were: Machinery £500; stock in trade £900

Cash £50 is withdrawn from the bank to be used as petty cash.

Draw up A and B's Balance Sheet on the opening of business.
College of Preceptors—Senior.

39. B. Graham and P. Thornton enter into partnership to take over from 1st January, 19.., the business carried on by O. Jessop. They are to share profits and losses equally. The following is the final Balance Sheet of O. Jessop:—

Balance Sheet

LIABILITIES	£	ASSETS	£
Capital—O. Jessop	20000	Freehold premises.. ..	9000
Sundry creditors	4500	Plant and machinery ..	6000
		Furniture and fittings ..	800
		Stock	5000
		Debtors	3300
		Cash	400
	£24500		£24500

The purchase price was £24,000, and was paid by cheques by Graham and Thornton direct to Jessop in equal shares. O. Jessop retained the cash balance. All other assets and the liabilities were taken over by the partners. Each partner contributed a further sum of £1,000 in cash to the firm's capital.

Make the necessary Journal entries, and show the firm's Cash Book and opening Balance Sheet. *Cambridge Local Examinations, G.C.E. "O" Level.*

40. R and T are in partnership, sharing profits and losses equally. On 1st January, 19.., the following balances appeared in the partners' personal accounts:

Capital Accounts: R—£4,000; T—£3,000.
Current Accounts—credit balances: R—£17; T—£10.

From the above and the details which follow, show the Balance Sheet of the partnership at 31st December, 19...

Net profit for the year was £3,750 after providing for interest on capital R—£200, T—£150 and interest on drawings R—£33; T—£39.

	£
Partners' drawings for the year:—	
R	2000
T	2000
Sundry creditors	1980
Sundry debtors	2980
Provision for bad and doubtful debts	150
Stock	2760
Amounts pre-paid	40
Furniture and fixtures	470
Machinery and equipment, at cost	2600
Depreciation fund for machinery and equipment ..	1250
Cash at bank..	1535
Petty cash	50

Set out the Balance Sheet to show clearly the amount of current assets and the amount of fixed assets. *College of Preceptors—Senior.*

41. The following balances were extracted from the books of M and N respectively at 31st December, 19...

	M	N
	£	£
Freehold premises..	2000	1750
Machinery and tools	1500	1400
Delivery vans		350
Stock of materials..	500	400

	M £	N £
Stock of finished goods	800	600
Cash at bank	600	
Cash in hand	40	25
Bank overdraft		575
Sundry creditors	1380	965
Rates and insurance prepaid	40	
Provision for bad debts		40
Sundry debtors	900	480

M and N agreed to combine and trade as partners from 1st January, 19.., on the following terms:

(a) N was to pay off the amount of his bank overdraft out of his private funds.

(b) Profits and losses were to be shared in proportion to the amount of capital brought in by each partner.

Draft the opening Balance Sheet of the new firm at 1st January, 19.., and state the ratio in which the profits and losses are to be shared.

A.E.B., G.C.E. "O" Level.

42. A and B are in partnership as wholesalers, sharing profits and losses equally, and at the 31st December, 19.., the following balances were open in their books after the compilation of the Trading and Profit and Loss Account for the year which ended on that date.

		£
Capital Accounts	A (Cr.)	10000
	B (Cr.)	10000
Current Accounts	A (Cr.)	600
	B (Cr.)	400
Sundry creditors	.. ..	7000
Sundry debtors	.. ..	8000
Bank overdraft	.. ..	2650
Loan from C.D. (secured by mortgage of warehouse)	..	5000
Freehold warehouse (at cost)	.. ..	10000
Fixtures and fittings at cost less depreciation	.. ..	2000
Delivery vans at cost less depreciation	.. .. ..	4000
Office furniture at cost less depreciation	.. .. ..	250
Stock on hand..	.. ..	11000
Cash in hand ..	.. ..	80
Item prepaid (rates)	.. ..	70
Provision for items outstanding: Salaries ..	.. ..	300
	Interest on loan	..	50

Profit and Loss A/c. Dr. Balance at 31st December, 19.. 600
You are required:—

(a) to transfer the Balance of the Profit and Loss Account to the partners' Current Accounts in equal shares;

(b) to prepare the Balance Sheet of the firm at the 31st December, 19..;

(c) to state what you consider to be the net value of the current assets of the firm at that date.

A.E.B., G.C.E. "O" Level.

43. A. Anson and B. Benson are in partnership, sharing profits and losses equally. On 31st March, 19.., their Trial Balance is:—

	Dr. £	Cr. £
Capital: A. Anson		7000
B. Benson		4000
Drawings: A. Anson	340	
Cash	56	
Bank Current Account	134	
Bank Deposit Account	600	
Interest on bank deposit..		10
Debtors and creditors	2500	1855
Stock, 1st October, in year of account	2400	
Purchases and sales	14080	19437
Returns	177	352
Carriage inwards	182	
Carriage outwards	432	
Commission		152
Leasehold premises (cost £10,000)	8000	
Furniture and fittings	860	
Salaries and wages	2260	
Discounts	334	276
General expenses	727	
	£33082	£33082

Prepare Trading and Profit and Loss Accounts for the half-year ended 31st March, 19.., and a Balance Sheet as at that date, taking the following into consideration:—

(a) Value of stock, 31st March, 19.., £3,240;

(b) Leasehold premises are to be written down at the rate of 10% per annum on the orignal cost;

(c) Bank Deposit interest on £600 accrued for 3 months at 4% per annum not yet entered in books;

(d) Provision for bad debts: 5% of debtors;

(e) For managing the business B. Benson is to be credited with £800 salary for the half-year before distribution of profit or loss;

(f) Interest at the rate of 5% per annum on the partners' capitals is to be allowed. *W.J.E.C., G.C.E. "O" Level.*

44. The following balances appear in the books of J. & R. Brown on 31st May, 19.., after the Trading and Profit and Loss Accounts for the half-year ending that day have been prepared.

	Dr. £	Cr. £
Cash in hand	45	
Bank Current Account		266
Debtors and creditors	2894	3543
Stock	4684	
Freehold premises at cost	6000	
Furniture and fittings	1350	
Loan from W. Brown		154u
Rent owing by tenant	65	
Commission owing to traveller		40
Investment in War Loan valued at cost ..	850	
Profit and Loss Account balance		1800

	Dr. £	Cr. £
Capital: J. Brown		6000
R. Brown		3000
Current Accounts: J. Brown	392	
R. Brown		91
	£16280	£16280

The partners share profits and losses in proportion to the balances shown in the Capital Accounts, these shares being transferred to the Current Accounts.

Before the Balance Sheet as at 31st May, 19.., is drawn up, it is decided to give effect to the following:—

(a) sell War Loan for £910; cheque for that amount is received and banked that day;

(b) accepting expert advice, to write up the value of the freehold premises from £6,000 to £9,000;

(c) loan from W. Brown is reduced to £1,000 by giving him cheque for £540;

(d) transfer shares of balance of Profit and Loss Account for the half-year to partners' accounts.

Draw up the Balance Sheet, assuming the necessary entries in the books to give effect to the above adjustments have been made.

W.J.E.C., G.C.E. "O" Level (Commercial Subjects).

45. **Balance Sheet of B. Barclay & C. Courage**
1st June, 19..

LIABILITIES	£	ASSETS	£
Capital: B. Barclay	8500	Premises	5600
C. Courage ..	8500	Plant	4200
Creditors	2045	Furniture, etc.	1200
		Stock	6050
		Debtors	1260
		Cash	735
	£19045		£19045

The partners share profits and losses equally.

On 1st June, 19.., they—

(a) re-valued premises at £7,000;

(b) received payment £360 from debtors;

(c) pay creditors £245;

(d) sell one-fifth of the stock for £1,350 cash;

(e) write off £160 debts as bad.

Re-write the Balance Sheet at the end of the day.

W.J.E.C., G.C.E. "O" Level (Commercial Subjects).

46. Distinguish between:—

(a) Capital and Revenue Expenditure. Give *two* examples of each;

(b) Capital and Working Capital

W.J.E.C., G.C.E. "O" Level (Commercial Subjects).

47. Arthur and George Makin are in partnership as engineers. Their business, which is expanding, owns its factory and distributes its products by its own motor lorries.

(a) Give one example each of capital expenditure, revenue income and revenue expenditure that you might expect to find in the above firm.

(b) How would you deal with the examples chosen in the Final Accounts of the partnership? *R.S.A.—Elementary.*

48. E. Flint and S. Stone are manufacturers, sharing profits and losses: Flint two-thirds and Stone one-third. The following is the Trial Balance of the firm as on 31st December, 19...

	Dr. £	Cr. £
Stock (1st January, 19..)	5002	
Purchases and sales	8236	14300
Returns inwards and outwards	306	160
Wages	2575	
Discount allowed and received	85	120
Insurance	175	
Heating and lighting	384	
Salaries	724	
Carriage outwards	271	
Trade expenses	72	
Loan interest..	100	
Cash in hand..	55	
Bank	370	
Debtors and creditors	2248	1955
Loan		2000
Machinery (1st January, 19..)	3000	
Machinery additions	500	
Land and buildings	3200	
Goodwill	300	
Capital Accounts: E. Flint		5700
S. Stone		4300
Current Accounts: E. Flint		400
S. Stone	100	
Drawings: E. Flint	832	
S. Stone	400	
	£28935	£28935

(a) The stock at 31st December, 19.., was valued at £4,700.

(b) £125 was owing in respect of wages.

(c) The balance of machinery at 1st January, 19.., is to be depreciated by 10% and the additions by 5%.

You are required to prepare the firm's Trading and Profit and Loss Accounts for the year ending 31st December, 19.., and a Balance Sheet as on that date. *R.S.A.—Elementary.*

49. S.J. started business on 1st January, 19.., with a balance at the bank of £2,000, of which he had borrowed £500 from R.T. At the end of the year some of the records kept by S.J. were lost but at 31st December, 19.., a valuation showed the following assets and liabilities.

					£
Fittings	..	..	..	..	600
Van ..	..	..	..	..	450
Stock in trade		..	..	..	850
Sundry debtors		..	..	..	270
Cash at bank		..	..	..	600
Sundry creditors	..	..	..	..	620

The loan from R.T. was outstanding and interest at 5% per annum was to be charged on this loan. During the year S.J. had drawn £8 per week in anticipation of profits.

From the above information draw up a statement showing the profit or loss for the year ended 31st December, 19.., and a Balance Sheet at that date.

A.E.B., G.C.E. "O" Level.

50. R. C. Workman has a small business and does not keep proper accounts. At the end of the year 19.. he submits the following statement to show his profit or loss for the year.

You are required to draw up the accounts in proper form to show his true profit or loss for the year.

Statement of Trading

	£	£		£	£
Stock on 1st January ..	1215		Sales	21300	
Less Stock on 31st De-			*Less* Purchases ..	10300	
cember	1140				11000
		75	Goods returned to		
Carriage on goods bought		125	suppliers		210
Carriage on goods sold ..		215	Discount allowed ..		465
Light and heat		95			
Rent and rates		525			
Office expenses		150			
Office salaries		1600			
Workmen's wages ..		6140			
Depreciation		210			
Sales returns		650			
Drawings		950			
New office furniture ..		220			
Profit		720			
		£11675			£11675

Note.—There is an outstanding electricity bill for the September-December quarter, £17. *College of Preceptors—Senior.*

51. The Furzdown School has a Social Fund for school journeys and visits and for social functions.

From the following details prepare the Receipts and Payments Account of this fund for the year 19...

Use a total column and columns for (*a*) school journeys, (*b*) social functions.

	£
Balance at bank at 1st January, 19..	160
Amounts paid in for journey to Paris..	500
Amounts paid in for summer camp	130
Fares and passport expenses to Paris	180
Amount paid in France for coach trips	45
Amount paid in France for food and accommodation ..	275

	£
Rail fares to summer camp	57
Expenses of Parents' Open Day	18
Sales of refreshments on Open Day	13
Sales of tickets for school play..	25
Printing of tickets for school play	4
Hire of costumes for school play	15
Cost of food and accommodation at summer camp.. ..	127
Earnings from harvest work at summer camp	65
Hire of equipment for summer camp	10
Decorations for Christmas party	3
Refreshments for Christmas party	12
Prizes for Christmas party	5
Sale of tickets for Christmas party	17
Contribution by pupils to Social Fund	35

College of Preceptors—Senior.

52. The following is the Trial Balance of the Carefree Social Club on 31st December, 19...

	Dr.	Cr.
	£	£
Capital at 1st January, 19..		568
Office and club room equipment	210	
Sports equipment	135	
Subscriptions received for year of account		490
Subscriptions outstanding for previous year	7	
Receipts from club room games		157
Maintenance of club room games, and sports equipment ..	21	
Rent and rates	132	
Postages	67	
Insurance	12	
Wages	196	
Sundry expenses	64	
Printing and stationery	67	
Cash in hand and at bank	304	
	£1215	£1215

You are requested to prepare an Income and Expenditure Account for the year ended 31st December, 19.., and a Balance Sheet at that date, taking into consideration the following:—

(a) Sports equipment to be depreciated at 20% per annum and office and club room equipment at 10% per annum.

(b) The outstanding subscriptions for previous year to be written off as a bad debt.

(c) Subscriptions due for year of account and not yet paid, £6.

London Chamber of Commerce—Elementary.

53. A. Flower started up business as a provision merchant on 1st April, 19.., taking over the business of B. Rice, whose Statement of Affairs at 31st March, 19.., was as follows:—

	£	£				£
Capital—B. Rice	..	2280	Fixtures			750
Creditors—			Stock			2000
Trade Accounts	.. 720		Prepayments (Insurance)		..	20
Expense	 50		Bank			280
	—	770				
		£3050				£3050

All the assets were taken over save the bank balance and Flower also assumed responsibility for the creditors. The purchase price was £2,500 which was the first withdrawal from a Bank Account which Flower opened up in the sum of £4,000.

The only records which Flower kept were of cash sales which amounted to £16,500 at the end of the first year of trading. There were no credit sales.

The following facts are ascertained:—

(*a*) All the expenses of the business have been met by cheque and an analysis of the Bank Statements for the year showed the following payments:—

	£
Purchases	12750
Wages	2200
Rent and rates	520
Advertising	280
Other expenses	576

(*b*) At the end of the first year of trading:—

(i) The sum standing to his credit with the bank was £1,300.
(ii) The value of the stock was £3,000.
(iii) Liabilities outstanding were as follows:—

	£
Trade creditors for goods supplied ..	1500
Advertising	50
Other expenses	35

(iv) Amounts paid in advance were:—

	£
Rates	20
Other expenses (Insurance)	15

(*c*) Goods had been taken for private consumption of an estimated cost value of £150 during the year.

(*d*) Private drawings were met out of cash receipts, the balance being banked.

(*e*) Private income of £200 had been paid into the Bank Account during the year.

On the basis of the foregoing information you are required to prepare—

(1) Trading and Profit and Loss Accounts for the first year of trading.
(2) Balance Sheet as at the end of the year.

London Chamber of Commerce—Intermediate.

54. X, Y, and Z entered into partnership on 1st July, 19.., without any agreement as to profit sharing save that X guaranteed that Z's share of profit, after bringing interest into account, would not be less than £850 per annum.

The initial capital provided was as follows:—

X £5,000.
Y £3,000.
Z £1,000 increased on the following 1st January, to £1,500.

In addition to the above capital X and Y made temporary loans to the partnership as follows:—

X £2,000 advanced 1st October, 19.., and repaid 1st April, following.

Y £4,000 advanced 1st September, 19.., and repaid 1st December, 19...

The profit for the following year ended 30th June, before providing for any interest, was £2,200.

You are required to show the Profit and Loss Appropriation Account for the year. *London Chamber of Commerce—Intermediate.*

55. The following details relate to the manufacturing and selling activities of a business for the year ended 31st March, 19..:—

	£	£
Stocks, 1st April, in year of account—		
Raw materials		2000
Finished goods		5000
Purchases (raw materials)		50200
Carriage inwards (raw materials)		1495
Returns outwards (raw materials)		3100
Sales (finished goods)		76000
Returns inwards		1000
Wages (productive)		10970
Work in progress, 1st April, in year of account, made up of—		
Raw materials	650	
Wages	150	
Carriage	20	
		820
Stocks, 31st March, 19..:—		
Raw materials		2200
Finished goods		7000
Work in progress, 31st March, 19.., made up of:—		
Raw materials	550	
Wages	120	
Carriage	15	
		685

You are required to set out the foregoing in such a form as to bring out:—

(a) the material cost ⎱ of the production for

(b) the labour cost ⎰ the year.

(c) the prime cost (*i.e.* material plus labour cost)

(d) the cost of the goods sold

(e) the gross profit. *London Chamber of Commerce—Intermediate.*

56. R.L. is a small builder and contractor who does not keep proper books of account.

From the following particulars you are required to prepare Trading and Profit and Loss Accounts for the year ended 31st December, 19.., and a Balance Sheet at that date.

The Balance Sheet at the end of the previous year was as follows:—

	£		£
Trade creditors	325	Cash in hand	40
Capital	3850	Cash at bank	560
		Rates and insurance prepaid	15
		Debtors	490
		Stock..	270
		Tools and equipment	300
		Premises	2500
	£4175		£4175

Bank Statements for the year showed— £
Credits: Customers' remittances paid in 3610
Debits: Paid to creditors 1335
  Withdrawn for office cash 680
  Withdrawn for private use 800
  Rates and insurances 76
  Telephone 52
Cash payments were—..
  Wages 416
  Lighting and heating 18
  Van expenses.. 205
  Sundry expenses 42
At 31st December, 19.., the following valuations were made—
  Stock 210
  Debtors 380
  Unexpired rates and insurance 16
  Tools and equipment 270
  Premises 2500
and there were the following liabilities:—
  Trade creditors 290

Notes.—Candidates must show below their accounts how they arrive at the amount of sales and purchases.

London Chamber of Commerce—Intermediate.

57. (*a*) State how each of the following errors would affect the net profit of a firm for the year ended 31st December, 19..:—
  (i) Stock at 1st January, 19.., overvalued by £100.
  (ii) Stock at 31st December, 19.., undervalued by £150.
  (iii) Discounts received £210, debited to Profit and Loss Account.
  (iv) Proprietor's drawings £1,000 charged to Profit and Loss Account.
  (v) Interest on loan from bank £113, omitted from the accounts.
  (vi) Omission from Purchases Book of a purchase of £65.

(*b*) What information is conveyed to you by each of the following in the books of a sole trader after balancing for Final Accounts.
  (i) A debit balance on Packing Materials Account.
  (ii) A debit balance on Rates Account.
  (iii) A debit balance on Capital Account.
  (iv) A credit balance on Bank Account as it appears in the Cash Book.
  (v) A credit balance on Wages Account.

London Chamber of Commerce—Intermediate.

58. On 31st December, 19.., the Trial Balance of J. Smith included the following balances:—

			£	£
Stock (1st January, 19..) ..	..	Dept. A	7686	
,, ,, ..	..	,, B	4485	
Purchases and sales ..	..	Dept. A	6312	15736
,, ,, ..	..	,, B	7688	11702
Inter-departmental transfers of goods.		Dept. A	200	
,,	,,	,, B		200
Returns inwards ..	..	Dept. A	400	
,, ,, ..	..	,, B	200	
Rent, rates, and taxes ..	..	..	840	
General expenses ..	..	..	1504	
Salaries ..	..	..	1200	
Carriage inwards ..	..	..	728	
Wages (productive) ..	..	Dept. A	1660	
,, ,, ..	..	,, B	900	

Stocks on 31st December, 19.., were:—Dept. A £2,734, Dept. B, £3,063.

From such of the above items as you think should be included prepare, in columnar form, a Departmental Trading Account for the year ended 31st December, 19...

You should also enter any charges not already shown separately, in such proportions to the nearest £ as you consider proper, stating below your accounts the basis on which you have made the apportionment.

London Chamber of Commerce—Intermediate.

59. The following balances appeared in the books of a business at 1st January, 19...

	£
Cash balance	262
Bank balance (credit)	1117
Debtors' Ledger Control Account	2037
Creditors' Ledger Control Account	1812

During the month of January, 19.., the following transactions took place:—

			£
Jan.	2.	Received cheque from A. Debtor (discount allowed £1).. ..	10
„	3.	Paid petty cash by cheque	17
„	7.	Received cheque from C. Debtor (discount allowed £6) ..	114
„	7.	Paid cheques to bank	124
„	9.	Received cheque from C. Debtor	292
„	9.	Paid L. Creditor by cheque	450
„	17.	Received cheque from D. Debtor	213
„	20.	Paid M. Creditor by cheque (discount received £11)	222
„	30.	Paid wages for month by cheque	412
„	30.	Paid petty cash expenses	27

The Credit Sales for the month were £612 (less Returns and Allowances £12) and the Purchases £497.

Write up the Cash Book for the month and compute the amounts of trade debtors and creditors at 31st January.

Cambridge G.C.E. "O" Level.

60. From the following details you are required to write up the Sales Ledger and Purchases Ledger Control Accounts for the month of January.

	£
Debtors at January 1st, 19..	9753
Creditors at January 1st, 19..	3456
Credit sales for month	19506
Credit purchases for month	6912
Returns outward for month	115
Returns inward for month	97
Cash got from customers	18912
Customers cheques dishonoured	100
Cash paid to suppliers	5814
Discount allowed	178
Discount received	117
Interest charged to customers on overdue accounts ..	5
Bad debts written off	76
Accounts settled by "contra"	345
Dr. Balances in Purchases Ledger at January 31st, 19.. ..	28
Cr. Balances in Sales Ledger at January 31st, 19.. ..	49

London Chamber of Commerce—Intermediate.

APPENDIX 2

ROYAL SOCIETY OF ARTS

SINGLE-SUBJECT EXAMINATIONS

BOOKKEEPING (PRINCIPLES OF ACCOUNTS)

STAGE I (Elementary)

[TWO HOURS ALLOWED]

All questions in Section A and TWO *questions in Section B are to be attempted.*

PAPER I

SECTION A

ALL *questions are to be attempted.*

1. D. Rain, a trader, keeps a full set of books of original entry in which the first record of each of his transactions is made before it is posted to the Ledger. Also, he banks all his business receipts daily and meets all but small items of cash expenditure by cheque.

You are required to name the book of original entry in which the first record would be made of the following transactions:—

(i) Rain sends to D. Mist, one of his customers, an invoice for goods supplied on credit.

(ii) Rain sells on credit to A. Shower an old filing cabinet which is no longer required in the office.

(iii) Rain receives an invoice from Space and Co. for goods supplied by them to him.

(iv) Rain sends to A. Cirrus a credit note for goods invoiced and dispatched to Cirrus in excess of the quantity ordered.

(v) Rain pays the window cleaner £0·5 in cash.

(vi) Rain's bank notifies him that a cheque he had paid in last week has been dishonoured by non-payment.

(vii) Space and Co. agree to reduce their price for the goods invoiced to Rain in transaction (iii), and send to Rain the necessary document making this adjustment.

2. Show, by Journal entries, how the following should be dealt with in the books of C. Cakebread, a baker:—

(1) The correction, on 1st June, of the error made in charging to the repairs account £18 spent on advertising.

(2) On 7th June Cakebread accepted a cupboard, as valued at £8, from A. Joiner in settlement of his debt.

(3) Cakebread was notified, on 10th June, that £1 cash discount which he had deducted when paying an amount due to D. Sharp was not allowable.

(4) On 20th June Cakebread bought a new oven from Steel & Co., on credit, for £180.

3. The following is the Trial Balance of a manufacturer taken out at the close of business on 31st March, 1968:—

	£	£
Capital		26898
Drawings	1295	
Freehold land and buildings	9570	
Debtors and creditors	7045	1075
Purchases and sales	53050	95105
Discounts allowed and received	110	320
Returns inwards and outwards	65	150
Factory wages	28270	
Light, heat, and power	500	
Factory expenses	818	
Bad debts	35	
Carriage outwards	325	
Carriage inwards	60	
Plant, furniture and equipment, less depreciation	11150	
Depreciation (for current year)	1680	
Office salaries and expenses	2355	
Provision for bad debts		120
Rates	335	
Stock	5520	
Balance at bank	1485	
	£123668	£123668

You are required to draw up the Trading and Profit and Loss Account of the business for the year ended 31st March, 1968, taking into account the following additional information:—

(a) Stock in hand on 31st March, 1968, was valued at £4,010.

(b) Four-fifths of the expenses for light, heat, and power is to be charged to the factory.

(c) There is an amount of £32 owing for factory expenses.

(d) It is decided to write off as an additional bad debt a balance of £45 due by a debtor and to adjust the Provision for Bad Debts Account to 2% of remaining balance of the sundry debtors.

(*Note:*—You are *not* required to draw up the Balance Sheet.)

4. From the following list of balances you are required to prepare the Profit and Loss Appropriation Account of the partnership of Lester & Payne for the year ended 31st December, 1967, and their Balance Sheet as at that date.

	£
Profit and Loss Account (net profit)	4012
Cash in hand	35
Cash at bank	630
Trade debtors	938
Trade creditors	416
Provision for bad debts	70
Insurance prepaid	25
Rent owing	40
Furniture, fittings, and equipment (cost £2,200)	1880
Stock	2840
Motor van	490
Loan (Lester)	600
Capital Accounts (1st January):—	
Lester	2000
Payne	1500

						£
Drawing Accounts:—						
Lester	..	..	..	..	..	1210
Payne	..	..	..	..	..	920
Current Accounts (Cr.): (1st January):-						
Lester	..	..	..	..	..	208
Payne	..	..	..	..	..	122

Note:

(1) The motor van had been purchased for £600 on 1st January, 1967.

(2) Lester's loan—made for the purchase of the van—is for five years and bears interest at 6% per annum, and this has not been provided for.

(3) Payne is entitled to be credited with a partnership salary of £600.

(4) The partners share profits and losses in the proportions: Lester three-quarters; Payne one-quarter.

SECTION B

TWO, *and only* TWO, *of the questions in this Section are to be attempted.*

5. (*a*) In as few words as you can, give a clear definition of a credit balance.

(*b*) State, briefly, why it is wrong to head the Trading and Profit and Loss Account of a business "For the Period ended 31st December, 1967".

(*c*) Give the term which should be used in the Final Accounts of a club for the amount which a trading business would call its net profit.

6. Four clerks—Smith, Jenks, Albright, and Sharp—are responsible for keeping the books of four different businesses. During May, 19.., each of them made one undiscovered mistake in his books, as follows:—

(1) When posting from the cash book, Smith posted correctly to the Ledger Account a cheque for £47 received from Hawkins, but overlooked the posting of £3 discount allowed to Hawkins which had been correctly entered in the discount column of the cash book.

(2) Jenks, when adding the sales returns book, made the total £10 less than it should have been.

(3) Albright, when posting from the cash book a cheque for £4, correctly entered there as received from Drake, had posted it to the debit of Drake's account.

(4) Sharp wrongly entered in the purchases book as £5 an invoice received from Grenville for £50.

State, in each case, what difference would appear in the Trial Balance at the end of the month in consequence of the error, giving (*a*) the amount of the difference and (*b*) the side which would be in excess.

7. On 1st January, 1968, B. Bright appears in your books as a debtor for £30. He becomes bankrupt and on 1st June, 1968, you receive a cheque in respect of a first and final dividend of £0·6 in the £. Show B. Bright's account as it should then appear in your Ledger.

PAPER II

SECTION A

ALL *questions are to be attempted.*

1. The Bullhead Engineering Company have offices in four cities, viz. London No. 1; Birmingham No. 2; Newcastle No. 3; Glasgow No. 4.

All accounts are kept in the London Office, where sales are recorded in a book with a column for each branch, and a total sales column.

Enter the following sales in the Sales Day Book. (The figure by each item indicates the office concerned.) Total the columns.

			£
June 4.	1	J. Brown & Sons, Ealing	57
	4	Clyde Builders Ltd., Glasgow	37
„ 5.	2	Former Eng. Co. Ltd, Stratford-on-Avon ..	93
	1	L. Edwards, Southampton	29
	2	Metal Products Ltd., Walsall	38
„ 6.	1	R. Keating, Southwark	34
	3	East York Construction Co. Ltd, York. ..	83
„ 7.	4	Modern Plant Supplies, Dumfries ..	28
	1	J. Homer Ltd., Richmond	29
	2	Gilchrist & Wright Ltd, Wolverhampton ..	47

2. From the following information prepare a Cash Account and an "Income and Expenditure Account" for the year ended 31st March, 1968, of the Brownridge Town Band.

1967   £
April 1. The band treasurer held £29 in the band account.
 „ 3. The council paid a grant of £50.
Oct. 3. The council paid a further grant of £50.

Paid engagements during the year were as follows: £

May 28.	Brownbank Park	. 10
June 3.	Tolverton Park	25
„ 10.	St John's Church Fete	5
„ 24.	Brownbank Park	10
July 1.	Little Barr Park	20
„ 8.	Brownbank Flower Show	30
„ 29.	Little Barr Horse Show	20
Sept. 1.	Tolverton Labour Club	5
„ 15.	Brownbank Conservative Club	25

All cash was received on the day of the engagement.

Payments made during the year were as follows: £

May 28.	Two guest instrumentalists	1 each
June 30.	Payment for performing rights	2
July 8.	One guest instrumentalist	1
Oct. 23.	Music	2
1968		
Feb. 20.	Music	2

During the year the band entered for one contest. This was held on 11th March, 1968, at Nottingham. In connection with this event the following payments were made:— £

Feb. 17.	Entrance fee	2
„ 21.	Hire of rehearsal room	2
Mar. 11.	Hire of coach	15

A charge of £0·25 per head for friends on the coach brought in £2.
The band won the second prize which included £7 in cash.
On 31st March, 1968, the following accounts were due and unpaid:—

		£
Repairs to tenor trombone		2
Two new uniforms		24

3. Priest & Vicar are in partnership sharing profits and losses in the ratio of 2 to 1. They have agreed to keep their drawings in that ratio. At the end of their second year, they have attempted to draw up a Balance Sheet, and produced the following:—

Balance Sheet for first two years starting 1st June, 1966.

Capital invested:	£	£					£
Priest	5000		Premises ..	..	..		4000
Vicar	2000		Motors ..	..	..		3000
		7000	Fixtures ..	..	..		500
Profit for the first two years		480)	Stock ..	..	..		2300
			Debtors ..	..	..		2150
Creditors		1700	Bank ..	..	..		820
Depreciation:			Cash ..	..	..		50
Motor vehicles	350		Drawings	..	..		1500
Fixtures	120						
		470					
Provision for bad debts ..		350					
		£14320					£14320

Set out the Balance Sheet in acceptable form, with fixed Capital Accounts and Current Accounts for each partner.

4. R. Durcan keeps a Petty Cash Book with three analysis columns: Postages, cleaning, and sundries. The imprest amount is £10.

On 29th June, 1968, the petty cashier reaches the bottom of a page, and carries forward the following totals:—

					£
Postages ..	..	..	..	..	4·138
Cleaning ..	..	..	..	..	1·225
Sundries ..	..	..	..	..	0·938

The following payments were made on the last two days of the month:—

					£
June 29.	Postages	..	..	..	0.133
„ 30.	Window cleaner	..	..	0·225
	Bus fare	..	..	..	0·075
	Postages	..	..	..	0·15

Write up the Petty Cash Book as it would appear for the last two days of the month, obtain a refund, balance, and post to Ledger Accounts.

Two, *and only* TWO, *of the questions in this section are to be attempted.*

5. From the following particulars write up P. Mugleston's electricity account for the year ending 31st December, 1967. Show the amount transferred to the Profit and Loss Account.

						£
Jan.	1.	Electricity used since last reading				20
Feb.	8.	Paid Electricity Board Cash	..			38
May	13.	„	„	„	..	36
Aug.	11.	„	„	„	..	27
Nov.	12.	„	„	„	..	31

On 31st December, P. Mugleston read his meter and found he had used 1,680 units since his meter was last read for the account in November. He is charged 3d. per unit.

6. Westcliffe Transport Company Ltd, has a fleet of old lorries written down to £2,000 book value. On 1st August, 19.., the management decided to purchase a new fleet. The following agreement was made with the Nuffend Road Vehicles Ltd.

1. The old lorries were to be taken in part exchange for £3,500.
2. New lorries were purchased on credit for £20,000.
The transaction took place on 5th August, 1968. Draft the entries required in the Journal, and show the Motor Vehicles Account as it would appear in the ledger.

7. You have been shown the Profit and Loss Account set out below. Give *two* other pieces of information you would require before forming any opinion about the state of the business.

Profit and Loss Account

	£			£
Sundry office expenses	428	Gross profit ..	..	3420
Salaries	2000			
Bad debts	792			
Net profit	200			
	£3420			£3420

PAPER III

Section A

All questions are to be attempted.

Part A

1. Driver, Porter, and Guard are three customers of Chair & Sleeper, Wholesale Hardware Merchants.

From the information given below, write up the accounts of Driver, Porter, and Guard as they would appear in the Sales Ledger kept by Chair & Sleeper.

		£
February 1, 1969. Debit balances—Driver	.. ..	100
Porter..	.. ..	70
Guard	.. ..	10

Sales during the month:—

February	3, 1969.	Driver	..	..	..	..	..	70
„	5, 1969.	Guard	..	..	..	..	..	45
„	7, 1969.	Driver	..	..	..	..	..	20
„	14, 1969.	Porter	..	..	..	..	..	80
„	21, 1969.	Porter	..	..	..	..	..	70
„	28, 1969.	Guard	..	..	..	..	..	40

Returns during the month:—

February	15, 1969.	Driver	..	..	..	..	..	20
„	21, 1969.	Porter	..	..	..	..	..	10

On 12th February, 1969, a letter was received from Guard, pointing out that the total of the invoice dated 5th February should have been £40. He was sent a credit note on the following day.

The balances due on 1st February, 1969, were settled by all three customers on the following dates:—

Driver	February	7, 1969.
Porter	„	11, 1969.
Guard	„	12, 1969.

The three customers were entitled to deduct 2½% cash discount.

2. W. Davis is the proprietor of a small cafe. His sales are strictly cash, and he banks all takings every night. All purchases are paid for by cheque on delivery. He lives on the premises with his family.

A statement of affairs on 1st January, 1968, showed his position to be as follows:—

		£				£
Capital	.. ..	4670	Premises	..	..	3000
			Furniture	..	..	1000
			Stock	..	..	150
			Bank	..	..	500
			Cash	..	..	20
		£4670				£4670

A study of his Cash Book provides the following information:—

	£
Takings during year ended 31st December, 1968 ..	10000
Purchases „	7400
Personal expenses „	1500
Light and heat „	200
Cleaning „	30
Wages „	500
New furniture bought during year	200
Cash in hand (31st December, 1968)	30
Bank balance („)	660

You are asked to prepare a statement showing W. Davis his profit or loss for the year ended 31st December, 1968, and a Balance Sheet on that date. The following are to be taken into consideration:—

    (*a*) Valuation of stock on 31st December, 1968—£150.

    (*b*) £100 of the light and heat was allocated to his private accommodation.

3. William Williams Ltd, has Machinery & Plant written down to £250 in their books. On 1st March, 1969, the company decided to re-equip the factory with modern plant. The following transactions took place:—

1969		£
March 3.	Sold old machinery for scrap. Cash	300
„ 3.	Purchased new machinery on credit from Machinery & Plant Ltd	7000
„ 7.	Of the wages paid on this date, £300 was estimated as the amount due to the company's own staff for fixing and wiring new machines.	
„ 10.	Paid Machinery & Plant Ltd. on account	3000

Show by means of Journal entries how the above would be recorded in the books of William Williams Ltd.

4. The following figures were supplied to you by the treasurer of the Forsyth Tennis Club. They refer to the year ended 31st December, 1968.

1968		£
January 1.	Balance in bank and in hand	300
	Rates due and unpaid	10
	Subscriptions owing to the club ..	5

Receipts and payments for the year ended 31st December, 1968, were as follows:—

			£
Subscriptions (including £5 arrears)	..	..	350
Tournament (entrance fees received)	..	..	70
Tournament (cost of prizes) ..	..	..	40
Postage and stationery ..	..	..	10
Light and heat (Club House)	..	..	30
Rates (including arrears for 1968, £10)	..	..	60

	£
Cost of new roller, bought for cash	40
Repairs to netting	10
Club House decorations (expected to last five years)	50
Wages of part-time groundsman	250

On 31st December, 1968, subscriptions £15 due for the year 1968 had not been paid, but were certain to be received.

The rates paid included £10 for the first quarter of 1969.

The Club's furniture and fittings is depreciated by £20 every year.

You are asked to prepare the Forsyth Tennis Club's Receipts and Payments Account and Income and Expenditure Account for the year ended 31st December, 1968.

A BALANCE SHEET IS NOT REQUIRED.

PART B

Only TWO *of the following questions are to be attempted.*

5. From the following information write up the Sales Day Book of Samson & Co., Ltd, for the day, Tuesday, 11th March, 1969. Samson & Co. Ltd keep their Sales Day Book in such a manner that it is possible to see both the daily total, and monthly total of sales.

Total brought forward from Monday, 10th March, 1969   £1,700
Robert Home—invoice No. 141D—£120 less 20%.
William Davey—invoice No. 142D—£70 less 10%.
C. Gilchrist & Co. Ltd—invoice No. 143D—£120 less 20%.
J. Woodward Ltd—invoice No. 144D—£50 less 20%.
L. McWorthy—invoice No. 145D—£70 net.

6. The Unworthy Wholesaling Co. Ltd, pays its wages on the system of keeping a week in hand. On 1st January, 1968, the company held £7,000 in hand. During the year they paid £360,000 in wages and held £6,500 on 31st December, 1968.

Of the wages paid, it was calculated that £12,000 should be charged to warehouse maintenance.

Write up the Wages Account for the year ended 31st December, 19.., and show the amount transferred to the Trading Account.

7. On 28th February, 19.., F. Underwood's Bank Cash Book showed the following:—

				£
Discount allowed	B/F	Total	..	94·7
Discount received	B/F	Total	..	78·667
Main Bank Columns	B/F Debit	Total	..	1170·712
	B/F Credit	Total	..	1317·6

A comparison with his bank statement showed the following items which had not been entered in the cash book:—

						£
A standing order for insurance	..	..	..	5
Bank charges ..	..	..	..	..	..	2·5
A credit transfer from A. Brown. (This payment
was in settlement of an account for £80) ..	..	78

You are required to re-open F. Underwood's Bank Cash Book, and bring it up to date.

What should be the balance shown on the Bank Statement?

THE LONDON CHAMBER OF COMMERCE

(INCORPORATED)

ELEMENTARY BOOKKEEPING

INSTRUCTIONS TO CANDIDATES

(a) *All questions should be attempted.*

(b) *Marks may be lost by lack of neatness.*

PAPER I

1. Paul Pickering is a sole trader whose year end is on the 30th September in each year. On 30th September, 1968, he finds that he is so busy that he is unable to count and value his stock-in-trade. In fact he is not able to do this until the close of business on 4th October, 1968, when he values his stock-in-trade (at cost price) at £2,927.

During the period 1st-4th October, 1968, he purchases goods costing £198 of which goods costing £22 were not delivered to him until 5th October, 1968.

His sales—for the period 1st-4th October, 1968—all of which were delivered out of stock before the close of business on 4th October, 1968—amounted to £265. His gross profit is 20% of selling price.

From the above you are required to draw up a statement showing the true stock-in-trade total (valued at cost price) as it was on 30th September, 1968. Calculations must be shown.

(20 marks)

2. Alfred Adams keeps his Petty Cash on the Imprest System—the imprest amount being £25. On 1st September, 1968, the balance of Petty Cash in hand is £2·3 and on that date the Petty Cashier is given sufficient cash to restore his balance to the imprest amount.

During September the following amounts were paid out of Petty Cash:—

Sept.	3.	Wages—£2·4.
,,	5.	Postage stamps—£2·25.
,,	8.	Envelopes bought—£1·675.
,,	12.	Paid £2 to D. Dyson—a creditor.
,,	15.	Telegrams—cost £1·135.
,,	17.	Wages—£2·325.
,,	21.	Stationery purchased—£2·885.
,,	27.	Paid £4·25 to J. Jackson—a creditor.
,,	29.	Postage stamps—£3.

From the above you are required to draw up the Petty Cash Book of Adams for the month of September, 1968, balance the book, carry down the balance and, on 1st October, 1968, show a receipt of cash sufficient to restore the balance to the imprest amount.

(20 marks)

274

3. At the close of business on 30th September, 1968, Robert Rogers, a sole trader, extracts a Trial Balance from his books of account. The Trial Balance does not agree but Rogers enters the difference in a Suspense Account and then prepares his Trading and Profit and Loss Accounts for the year ending 30th September, 1968. The Net Profit as shown in this Profit and Loss Account amounts to £1,497.

During October, 1968, the following errors are discovered, some of which account for the entire difference in the Trial Balance.

1. The Purchases Day Book was undercast £40.

2. A bad debt of £27 had been debited to Bad Debts Account but the double entry had not been completed.

3. The Sales Returns total (in the Sales Returns Book) amounted to £116 but this total had been posted on the *wrong* side of the Sales Account in the Ledger.

4. During the year £22 had been spent on wages of workmen engaged in the installation of office fixtures. The amount had been debited to Wages Account.

(*a*) From the above you are required to state the extent to which the Trial Balance differed on account of each error. Your answer should be in the form of the following table:—

ERROR	EXCESS DEBIT OR UNDERSTATED CREDIT	EXCESS CREDIT OR UNDERSTATED DEBIT
1.		
2.		
3.		
4.		

(*b*) You are also required to draw up a statement to show the correct Net Profit.

(25 marks)

4. Norman North and William West are in partnership, sharing profits and losses on the basis of two-thirds and one-third respectively. The following Trial Balance was extracted from their books at the close of business on 30th September, 1968.

	Dr.	Cr.
Capital Accounts—North		3080
West		1750
Purchases and sales	3450	5760
Stock—1st October, 1967	820	
Wages and salaries	1440	
Debtors and creditors	990	810
Drawings—North	760	
West	470	
Discounts	210	130
Rent and rates	280	
General expenses	240	
Bank	2030	
Delivery vans	600	
Cash	60	
Office furniture	180	
	£11530	£11530

From the above, and from the notes given below, you are required to prepare the Trading and Profit and Loss Accounts of the partnership for the year ending 30th September, 1968, together with a Balance Sheet as on that date.

(a) Stock at 30th September, 1968, £1,510.
(b) Rates prepaid at 30th September, 1968, £20.
(c) Wages and salaries accrued due at 30th September, 1968, £30.
(d) Create a provision for bad and doubtful debts, £50.
(e) Ignore depreciation.

(35 marks)

PART TWO

CHAPTER 30

BILLS OF EXCHANGE. BILLS PAYABLE

The granting of a period of credit in business transactions implies that the seller of goods under such conditions must wait for payment, and that the purchaser takes possession of the goods but postpones payment. The advantage lies with the purchaser for he may sell the goods in the ordinary course of business and receive cash, including a profit, before the expiration of the credit period. The seller knows that cash against goods is an impossible demand in every case if he wishes to sell his goods, yet it is to his own interest to shorten or extinguish the credit period.

One way open to the seller by which he may allow the purchaser to defer payment for a period and yet at the same time obtain cash for his own use, is to arrange for the transaction to be settled by a Bill of Exchange.

Consider the following transactions:—

Jan. 1.   M. Redman bought bicycles value £100 from T. Lawrence's Cycle Works on three months' credit.

If this takes the ordinary course, Redman will pay the account at the end of March, meanwhile having the use of £100 worth of Lawrence's goods. Lawrence will have his own expenses to meet, but he cannot expect Redman to pay his account before the expiration of the agreed credit period.

It may be arranged, however, between buyer and seller that, for their mutual advantage, a Bill of Exchange shall be used to finance the transaction.

A Bill of Exchange is defined in the Bills of Exchange Act, 1882, as:—

"An unconditional order in writing, addressed by one person to another, signed by the person giving it, requiring the person to whom it is addressed to pay on demand, or at a fixed or determinable future time, a sum certain in money to, or to the order of, a specified person or to bearer."

This is the legal definition. How it applies in practice will be gathered from the procedure followed for the above and subsequent examples.

A Bill of Exchange in the form that would be used in the above transaction is shown below:—

£100	1st January, 19...
Stamp duty paid	Three months after date pay to my order the sum of One hundred pounds value received. *T. Lawrence.* To M. Redman, Exchange Street, London, S.W.4.

Reference to its wording will show that it is addressed by Lawrence to Redman, is signed by Lawrence, and orders Redman to pay him at a determinable future time—three months from 1st January—a fixed sum of money.

The person who draws up and signs the bill is known as the *drawer*. The person on whom the bill is drawn is the *drawee*. The person to whom the drawee is ordered to pay is known as the *payee*.

In the example, Lawrence is both the drawer and payee, and Redman is the drawee.

On it being agreed to use a Bill of Exchange, Lawrence draws up the bill. He forwards it to Redman for his "acceptance," which means that Redman accepts the liability under the terms of the bill, indicating his acceptance by signing his name across the face of it. His signature alone is sufficient to bind him, but the word "accepted" is usually added.

Redman may "domicile" the bill by adding to his signature the place of payment. This is usually the name and address of the drawee's bankers. In the event of the place of payment not being mentioned, the bill is payable at the acceptor's usual place of business.

Redman then returns the acceptance, as the accepted bill is called, to Lawrence.   What Lawrence may do with the bill is discussed in the next chapter.   To him, as he is to receive the money, the bill is a Bill Receivable.   To Redman, who has to pay the money in due course, it is a Bill Payable.

Days of Grace

The acceptor, by accepting the bill, engages that he will pay it according to the tenor of his acceptance.   In this example, the date of maturity is three months from 1st January, the date of the bill. Bills may be payable on demand or, as in this case, at some future date, and, except for bills payable on demand, three extra days beyond the date mentioned are allowed for payment.   The legal date for payment of Redman's acceptance is, therefore, April 4th, and no right of action in the event of non-payment accrues until after the last of the three days of grace.

The day for payment may happen to fall on a Sunday, Christmas Day, or Good Friday.   The bill is then payable on the preceding business day.   Should it fall due for payment on a Bank Holiday, other than Christmas Day, or Good Friday, it is payable on the succeeding business day.

Stamp Duties

A fixed stamp duty is payable on all Bills of Exchange.

Bills Payable

The example given at the beginning of this chapter is now repeated.

Example 39.—On Jan. 1st M. Redman bought bicycles value £100 from T. Lawrence's Cycle Works, and gave his acceptance for three months for that amount.

The entry to be made in Redman's books for the purchase follows the normal course.   It will first be entered in the Purchase Day Book, and posted thereform to the credit of Lawrence's account in the Ledger.

The new point is that Redman accepts a Bill of Exchange, and forwards it to Lawrence.   For Redman it is a Bill Payable.   He is liable on the bill, and in three months' time it will be presented for payment either to him personally, or, if he has so arranged, through his bankers.   Lawrence receives the bill in the first place but, as will be discussed later, he may dispose of it without Redman's knowledge, and Redman has no means of knowing who will be presenting the bill for payment or to whom, pending presentment, he is liable.

For the Bill Payable Redman's book-keeper will *debit* Lawrence's Account as he received the bill, and will *credit* Bills Payable Account to record the giving of the bill, as shown below:—

Dr.   **T. Lawrence**   81 *Cr.*

19..			£	19..				£
Jan. 1	Bills Payable	40	100	Jan. 1	Goods .. *(Contra entry is in Purchases A/c.)*	P.B.		100

Dr.   **Bills Payable**   40 *Cr.*

		£	19..			£
			Jan. 1	T. Lawrence..	81	100

So far as Lawrence's Account is concerned it is now closed. In place of the debt due to Lawrence which appeared on that account is a debt due to an unknown holder of the bill, and this is shown in the Bills Payable Account.

Had no bill been given, and it had happened that a Balance Sheet was being prepared, the debt of £100 due to Lawrence would have been included under the item "Sundry Creditors" on the liabilities side of the Balance Sheet. Now there is a change in the nature of the liabilities, as Lawrence's Account is closed and cannot be included among the creditors, and a new form of liability, "Bills Payable," appears in the Balance Sheet.

Payment on Presentation

Redman will arrange with his bankers to pay the bill on presentation. He must, of course, see that his banking account is sufficiently in funds to meet it. The bill will be taken by the bank on presentation, and it will reach Redman in due course with his paid cheques, when he may cancel or destroy it.

The entries that are necessary in Redman's books to record the payment on April 4th are—

(i) A *Credit* to Bank Account in the Cash Book, as the money is paid away.

(ii) A *Debit* to Bills Payable Account, as the bill is received back.

The accounts will now appear as below:—

Dr.				T. Lawrence			Cr. 18
19.. Jan. 1	Bills Payable	40	£ 100	19.. Jan. 1	Goods .. (*Contra entry is in Purchases A/c.*)	P.B.	£ 100

Dr.				Bills Payable			Cr. 40
19.. Apl. 4	Cash ..	C.B.	£ 100	19.. Jan. 1	T. Lawrence ..	81	£ 100

Dr.				Cash Book			Cr.
			Bank £	19.. Apl. 4	Bills Payable .. (T. Lawrence)	40	Bank £ 100

Ultimately, therefore, the Bills Payable Account is closed and a credit entry is in the Bank Account. The financial position and the accounts are now as they would have been had a cheque been sent direct to Lawrence. The use of a bill has involved the opening of the Bills Payable Account, and the creation, temporarily, of a new liability called Bills Payable in place of the original creditor.

EXERCISES 30

1. Give the entries to record the following transactions in B. W. Payne's accounts:—

Sept. 1. Bought goods to the value of £500 on credit from J. Smith & Sons.

„ 2. Accepted a Bill for three months for £500 drawn by J. Smith & Sons.

Dec. 5. Bankers paid the Bill on presentation.

2. On 5th April T. Williams bought goods, £600, from R. B. Robinson, and gave him his acceptance for two months for that amount. Williams arranged with his bankers to meet the Bill, and it was duly paid on presentation. Show how T. Williams should record these transactions in his books.

3. J. W. Firth bought goods, £340, from McIntosh & Sons on 12th June who drew on him at three months for the amount. Firth accepted the Bill and arranged with his bankers to meet the Bill on presentation. Record in Firth's books the purchase, the giving of the acceptance, and the payment of the Bill at maturity.

4. From the following particulars draw up a Bill of Exchange in the usual form:—

Drawer: Yourself.
Drawee: B. Worthington, 12 Lane Rd., London.
Payee: W. Baxter.
Date: 10th December, 19...
Amount: £221·50.
Term: Three months.

Show on the Bill the appropriate amount of stamp duty and state the due date.

5. The following Trial Balance was extracted from the books of G. Roberts as on June 30th, 19... You are required to prepare therefrom Trading and Profit and Loss Accounts for the year ended June 30th, and a Balance Sheet as on that date.

Trial Balance. June 30th, 19..

	Dr. £	Cr. £
Cash at bank: Current Account	198	
„ „ Deposit Account	1000	
Warehouse salaries and expenses	1462	
Freehold property..	4876	
Capital Account ..		8000
Office salaries	758	
Discount received..		76
Purchases and sales	6481	10527
Stock at the beginning of the year	2106	
Office expenses	236	
Bills payable		500
Sundry creditors ..		2274
Sundry debtors ..	3786	
Bank deposit interest		23
Rates and taxes ..	497	
	£21400	£21400

The stock at the end of the year was valued at £1,968.   _R.S.A._

6. The following Trial Balance was extracted from the books of James Marsden as on the 31st December, 19..:—

	Dr. £	Cr. £
Cash in hand	31	
Cash at bank	623	
Land and buildings ..	1980	
Fixtures and fittings..	824	
Motor lorry ..	265	
Stock in hand, Jan. 1st	1127	
Sundry debtors	732	
Purchases	3964	
Discount	137	
Interest	45	
Wages	488	
Drawings	156	
Bad debts	28	
Rates and taxes	62	
Gas and electricity ..	47	

	Dr.	Cr.
	£	£
Sundry expenses	205	
Mortgage on buildings		960
Sundry creditors		641
Sales		5642
Returns outwards		76
Discount		158
Bills payable		280
Capital Account		2957
	£10714	£10714

You are required to prepare the Final Accounts and a Balance Sheet as on the 31st December, 19... Before doing so the following information and adjustments must be taken into account:—

Make a provision of 5% on sundry debtors for doubtful debts.

Write 5% depreciation off fixtures and fittings, and depreciate the motor lorry by 10%.

The value of the stock in hand on December 31st was £872.   *N.C.T.E.C.*

7. The following Trial Balance was extracted from the books of Ernest Midgeley as on the 31st December, 19..:—

Dr.	£	Cr.	£
Cash in hand	20	Provision for doubtful debts	30
Cash at bank	627	Sundry creditors	641
Land and buildings	1080	Sales	6942
Fixtures and fittings	820	Returns outwards	76
Motor vehicle	365	Discount	149
Stock in hand, Jan. 1st ..	1127	Bills payable	258
Sundry debtors	832	Capital Account	3261
Purchases	4964		
Returns inwards	40		
Discount	137		
Interest	80		
Wages	490		
Drawings A/c.	420		
Bad debts	30		
Rates and taxes..	60		
Gas and electricity	53		
Sundry expenses	212		
	£11357		£11357

You are required to prepare the Final Accounts and a Balance Sheet as on the 31st December. Before doing so the following information and adjustments must be taken into account:—

Write 5% depreciation off fixtures and fittings, and depreciate the motor vehicle by 10%.

Make the provision for doubtful debts up to 5% on sundry debtors.

The value of the stock in hand on 31st December was £680.   *N.C.T.E.C.*

CHAPTER 31

BILLS OF EXCHANGE. BILLS RECEIVABLE

The person who is to receive the money on a Bill of Exchange regards it as a Bill Receivable. The transaction discussed in the preceding chapter may, therefore, be viewed from another standpoint, that of the holder of the bill. From his point of view the transaction would appear as follows:—

Example 40.—On Jan. 1st, T. Lawrence sold to M. Redman bicycles valued £100, and received from him his acceptance for three months for that amount.

The sale of goods would be recorded in Lawrence's books in the usual manner. For the Bill of Exchange it is necessary to record the receipt of it and from whom it was received; *credit* the giver—in this example M. Redman, and *debit* Bills Receivable Account.

56

Dr.				M. Redman				*Cr.*
19.. Jan. 1	Goods (*Contra entry is in Sales Account*)	S.B.	£ 100	19.. Jan. 1	Bills Receivable	74	£ 100	

74

Dr.				Bills Receivable			*Cr.*
19.. Jan. 1	M. Redman	56	£ 100	19..			£

The effect of these entries is to close M. Redman's Account, and in the place of the debt due from him to show a new asset, a Bill Receivable for £100. In a Balance Sheet prepared at this point, the Bill Receivable, being a debit balance of the Bills Receivable Account, would appear under that heading among the current assets.

Now Lawrence has a choice of methods of dealing with the bill in his possession. He may retain it until the due date, April 4th, and then present it through his bankers for payment. Alternative methods are discussed later. If he decides to do this, and the bill is met at maturity, his bankers will credit his account with the

284

amount received. The bill will have been given up by him, and that Redman now has possession of the bill is *prima facie* evidence that he has paid it. No other receipt is necessary. The entries to record the giving up of the bill and the receipt of the cash are—

(i) *Credit* Bills Receivable Account, and

(ii) *Debit* Bank Account in the Cash Book.

The whole transaction will appear in Lawrence's books as below:—

56

Dr.				M. Redman			Cr.
19.. Jan. 1	Goods (*Contra entry in Sales A/c.*	S.B.	£ 100	19.. Jan. 1	Bills Receivable	74	£ 100

74

Dr.				Bills Receivable			Cr.
19.. Jan. 1	M. Redman	56	£ 100	19.. Apl. 4	Cash ..	C.B.	£ 100

		Cash Book				
Dr.		(Bank Columns only)				Cr.
19.. Apl. 4	Bills Receivable (Redman)	74	£ 100	19..		£

In practice bills are paid into the bank for collection soon after receipt, the bank holding them in safe custody and presenting them for payment at due date. The above entries in the Bills Account and the Cash Book are made on the bill being duly honoured at maturity. On being requested the bank will notify its customer immediately a bill is honoured.

Dishonoured Bills

Should payment be refused or cannot be obtained for any reason, the bill is said to be dishonoured on presentation. If the bill has been paid into the bank for collection and it is dishonoured, the bank will notify its customer and it will be necessary to revive the personal debt of the acceptor, as the bill is valueless as an asset, though it is valuable as legal evidence against the acceptor. Further, the bank may have thought it necessary to have further evidence of dishonour, and may have taken steps for it to be re-presented by a

Notary Public whose charges they will have paid. The Notary Public affixes to the bill a printed slip bearing his name, the reason for the dishonour, and a note of his charges. This expense being caused by the acceptor, it is recoverable from him and, until recovered, must be recorded as an additional debt due from him.

On dishonour—

(i) *Credit* Bills Receivable Account with the amount of the bill.

(ii) *Credit* Bank Account in the Cash Book with the amount of the bank charges.

(iii) *Debit* the personal account of the acceptor with the amount of the bill and the bank charges.

In the above example the dishonour would make Redman's Account appear as below:—

Dr.			M. Redman				*Cr.*
19..			£	19..			£
Jan. 1	Goods ..	S.B.	100	Jan. 1	Bill Receivable	74	100
Apl. 5	Bill Receivable A/c. .. (Dishonoured Bill)		74	100			
„ 5	Bank Charges	C.B.	0 25				

Sometimes a trader may pay his bills into the bank for collection two or three days prior to the due date, and he may then credit Bills Receivable Account and debit his Bank Account on the assumption that the bill will be met. Should dishonour occur he would have to make a credit entry in his Bank Account to cancel the debit entry— the corresponding debit entry being made in the acceptor's account for the amount of the bill and the charges.

Discounting Bills of Exchange

The holder of the bill may decide to discount it with his bankers, and not to retain it until maturity. This will place him in funds at once, and is one of the advantages afforded by the use of a Bill of Exchange to finance a business deal. Banks are prepared to discount bills for customers provided that the standing of the person liable on a bill offers reasonable prospect of payment at due date, or that the bank's customer is of good standing so that in the event of dishonour his account may be debited without risk of loss. The bank charges for the service, as it will not be re-imbursed until the bill is met. The amount of the charge depends upon the financial standing of the acceptor and upon the current rates for discounting, and is calculated at a percentage on the face value for the period of the bill. If the discount rate is 4 per cent. per annum, the charge on the above bill for £100 for three months would be £1, if discounted immediately after receipt from the acceptor.

The discount charge should not be confused with cash discount or trade discount. On discounting—

(i) *Credit* Bills Receivable Account, as the bill will be handed over to the bank.

(ii) *Debit* Bank Account in the Cash Book with the full value of the bill.

The bank credits its customer with the full amount of the bill discounted, but makes a contra entry of the discount charge. The holder, therefore, receives somewhat less than the face value but considers that the lesser sum is worth as much to him now as the full value would be in three months' time.

Later, examination of the Bank Statement will disclose the amount of the discount charges. For these charges—

(i) *Credit* Bank Account in the Cash Book.

(ii) *Debit* Discount on Bills Account, for eventual transfer to the debit of Profit and Loss Account.

74

Dr.				**Bills Receivable**				*Cr.*	
19..			£	19..				£	
Jan. 1	M. Redman		100	Jan. 3	Bank ..	..	C.B.	100	

Dr.				**Cash Book**				*Cr.*	
19..			BANK	19..				BANK	
			£					£	
Jan. 3	Bill Receivable discounted .. (M. Redman)	74	100	Jan. 6	Discount charge on B.R. .. (Redman)		82	1	

82

Dr.				**Discount on Bills**				*Cr.*	
19..			£					£	
Jan. 6	Bank (Redman's Bill)	C.B.	1						

In the event of the dishonour of a discounted bill the bank has the legal right to look to its customer for re-imbursement, and the trader will *credit* his Bank Account in the Cash Book with the amount of the bill and the bank charges for presenting, and *debit* the acceptor's account with these sums to revive the debt and to record the additional debt for the charges. The bank's original charge for discounting cannot be placed to the acceptor's account, since that charge was for the personal convenience of the holder.

The following entries illustrate the example given above on the assumption that the bill was discounted and was dishonoured on presentation:—

56

Dr.			M. Redman					Cr.
19.. Jan. 1	Goods	S.B.	£ 100	19.. Jan. 1	Bill Receivable..	74		£ 100
Apl. 5	Dishonoured Bill	C.B.	100					
	Bank Charges	C.B.	0 25					

74

Dr.			Bills Receivable					Cr.
19.. Jan. 1	M. Redman ..	56	£ 100	19.. Jan. 3	Bank	C.B.		£ 100

Dr.	Cash Book (Bank Columns only)							Cr.
19.. Jan. 3	Bill Receivable discounted (Redman)	74	£ 100	19.. Jan. 6	Discount on B/R (Redman)	82		£ 1
				Apl. 5	Redman Dishonoured Bill	56		100
				,, 5	Redman Bank Charges on dishonoured Bill	56		0 25

82

Dr.			Discount on Bills Account					Cr.
19.. Jan. 6	Bank (Redman's Bill)	C.B.	£ 1	19..				£

Contingent Liabilities

Bills under discount are not actual liabilities, but they remain as contingent liabilities until payment at maturity precludes any possibility of dishonour. Discounted bills do not appear in the Balance

Sheet, but it is important to draw attention to the fact that there are bills under discount at the date of the Balance Sheet, and that a contingent liability exists in respect of them by making a note at the foot for information only, *e.g.* "Contingent Liabilities, Bills under Discount, £———."

The Transfer of a Bill

Another method of dealing with a Bill of Exchange is to transfer it to another person who then acquires all the rights to it. A trader may arrange to do this to settle one of his own debts. To record the transfer a credit entry is made to Bills Receivable Account, and a debit entry to the account of the person to whom the bill is transferred.

Indorsement

A Bill of Exchange that is made payable to order requires the signature of the holder before being passed on, whether such transfer is to a bank for discounting or to another person. Such signature is an indorsement, and is usually made on the back of the bill. A bill may continue to be indorsed over, or transferred, until it is discharged by payment or otherwise, or until restrictively indorsed, such as "Pay —— only." Every indorser becomes liable as a party to the bill in the event of dishonour.

Renewing a Bill of Exchange

The acceptor of a bill may not be in a position to honour the bill on presentation, and it may be mutually arranged that he accepts a fresh bill in place of the existing one. This will extend the credit period by the tenor of the new bill, but interest is usually added in the new bill as compensation for the delayed payment.

In the books of the holder the exchange of the old bill for the new bill will involve the cancellation of the old bill by crediting Bills Receivable Account and debiting the personal account of the acceptor. The new bill will be recorded in the usual manner, being credited to the acceptor's account and debited to Bills Receivable Account. If these entries include a sum for interest, further entries will be required, namely, a debit entry to the acceptor's account for the interest, and a credit entry in the Interest Account for eventual transfer to Profit and **Loss** Account.

Assuming that Redman, in the above Example 40, renews his bill, the accounts would appear as below. Note the three transactions, the withdrawal of the bill, the charging of the interest, and the giving of the new bill.

Dr.					M. Redman			Cr. 56
19.. Jan. 1	Goods	S.B.	£ 100	19.. Jan. 1	Bill Receivable	74	£ 100
Apl. 1 „ 1	Bill withdrawn Interest	74 96	100 2	Apl. 1	Bill Receivable (new Bill)	74	102

								74
Dr.					Bills Receivable			Cr.
19.. Jan. 1 Apl. 1	M. Redman .. M. Redman (new Bill)	56 56	£ 100 102	19.. Apl. 1	M. Redman .. (Bill withdrawn)	56	£ 100

								96
Dr.					Interest Account			Cr.
			£	19.. Apl. 1	M. Redman ..	56	£ 2

Converse entries would be made in the books of the acceptor.

Retiring a Bill of Exchange

To take up a bill and to pay it before it is due is called retiring a bill. The holder may be willing to give up the bill and to allow a rebate on the full amount. In his books, he will credit Bills Receivable Account with the full value, and debit Cash for the cash received, and debit Interest Account or Discount on Bills Account for the rebate given. The acceptor, in his books, would credit the rebate to the Interest or Discount Account and the Cash payment to the Cash Book, debiting both items to the Bills Payable Account.

Inland and Foreign Bills

An inland Bill of Exchange is one that is both drawn and payable in Great Britain and Northern Ireland; all other bills are foreign bills. Bills drawn in the Irish Free State continue to be stamped as Inland bills.

Promissory Notes

A Promissory Note is defined by the Bills of Exchange Act, 1882, as follows:

An unconditional promise in writing made by one person to another, signed by the maker, engaging to pay on demand, or at a fixed or determinable future time, a certain sum in money to or to the order of a specified person, or to bearer.

Promissory Notes are used chiefly in loan transactions. They are promises to pay made out by the debtor, and therefore do not require acceptance. There are two parties only to a promissory note—the maker, who writes out the note, and the payee to whom the note is made payable. Stamp duty is the same for notes as for Bills of Exchange, except that notes payable on demand must bear the *ad valorem* duty.

No special form of wording is prescribed by the Act for either Bills of Exchange or Promissory Notes. The specimen bill above is worded according to the usual practice, and a promissory note usually takes the following form:—

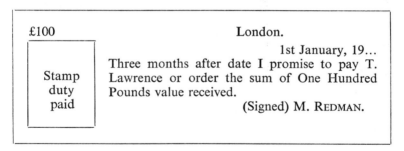

£100	London.
	1st January, 19...
	Three months after date I promise to pay T.
Stamp	Lawrence or order the sum of One Hundred
duty	Pounds value received.
paid	(Signed) M. Redman.

The entries in the books of account are similar for Promissory Notes as for Bills of Exchange.

The Use of Bills of Exchange

Bills of Exchange are less widely used than formerly as a means of settling debts, but they offer certain advantages to a trader. He has an acknowledgment of the debt due to him, and his debtor cannot dispute the amount. He possesses legal evidence of the debt, and the bill fixes the date for payment. Further, the trader may, if he so wishes, discount the bill and obtain the use of cash before the expiration of the period of the bill. From the debtor's point of

Bills Payable Book

Bill No.	Date	Debit to:—	Ledger Folio	Amount	Drawer	Payee	Where Payable	Date of Bill	Term	Due Date	How Disposed Of
1	Jan. 1	T. Lawrence	81	£ 100	T. Lawrence	T. Lawrence	London Bank, E.C.	19.. Jan. 1	3 Mos.	19.. Apl. 4	Paid Apl. 4

Bills Receivable Book

Bill No.	Date	Credit to:—	Ledger Folio	Amount	Drawer	Acceptor	Where Payable	Date of Bill	Term	Due Date	How Disposed Of
1	Apl. 2	B. Brown	96	£ 200	Self	B. Brown	London and Counties Bank	19.. Apl. 1	2 Mos.	19.. June 4	Discounted Apl. 4

view, by accepting a bill he avoids immediate payment for goods that he might not be able otherwise to obtain, and has a definite period within which he may dispose of the goods and place himself in funds to meet the bill. If, however, his credit is good and he is able to obtain as long a credit period as he needs, there is no direct advantage to him in the use of a Bill of Exchange. Probably he would accept a bill only at the request of his supplier.

Bill Books

If bill transactions are not numerous, the original entries may be made in the Journal, to be posted therefrom to the appropriate Ledger Accounts. As the bills become numerous it will be advantageous to introduce special Bill Books for the original entries, and to discontinue the use of the Journal for this purpose. The Bill Books provide a means of keeping an adequate record of the particulars of the bills for reference, and at the same time permit periodical postings of the totals to be made to the Bill Accounts to avoid frequent use of the Ledger for the posting of individual entries. The Bill Books are subsidiary books, and, like the other subsidiary books discussed in earlier chapters, make for better organisation and efficiency in the work of the counting house.

Specimen rulings of Bill Books are given on page 292. The first few columns give the information for the bookkeeping record, the remainder are memoranda columns for particulars of the bills and the manner of their disposal.

EXERCISES 31

1. On 1st September P. Beaumont sold goods to the amount of £350 to R. Sinclair who accepted that day a Bill of Exchange at two months for the sum due.

Beaumont paid the bill into his bank for collection, and the bill was met at the due date.

Record these transactions as in Beaumont's books.

2. Record the following transactions in R. Rosendale's books:—
Feb. 10. Sold goods to J. B. Whittaker, £250.
 „ 10. Drew on Whittaker at three months for £250. Received from Whittaker the bill duly accepted.
May 13. Bank notified that Whittaker had paid the bill on presentation.

3. S. J. Hull sold goods to T. Yorke on 1st March to the amount of £500, and received from Yorke his acceptance for three months for the amount due. On 2nd March Hull discounted the bill with his bankers whose discounting charges were £3.75.

Make the entries to record these transactions in S. J. Hull's books.

4. Record the following transactions of R. J. Westrop in his books:—
Feb. 1. Sold goods, £400, to L. Newton.
 „ 1. Received from Newton his acceptance for two months for £400.
 „ 4. Discounted Newton's bill at bankers who charged £2 for discounting.

5. Record the following transactions in B. Johnson's books:—
Mar. 1. He sold to L. T. Smith, goods, £600.
 „ 1. Received from L. T. Smith his acceptance for £600 at three months.
 „ 4. Discounted Smith's bill with bankers.
      Discounting charges, £4.
June 5. Bank returned Smith's bill as dishonoured on presentation.

6. On 1st May B. Leslie received from L. Herbert his acceptance for two months for £500 for goods supplied on that date. He at once discounted the bill with his bankers who charged £2. On due date his bankers notified him that Herbert had dishonoured his bill on presentation.

Record the sale, the receipt of the bill, the discounting, and the dishonour in B. Leslie's books.

7. On 1st October, 19.., Thomas Drake purchased goods from William Harris to the amount of £200. On 11th October, a Bill of Exchange was drawn for this amount at two months and accepted, but when presented in due course it was dishonoured. On 15th December Drake accepted a further bill at two months, plus 5% interest from the latter date, and this was met at the proper time. You are required to show the entries in the books of William Harris in connection with the above.   *N.C.T.E.C.*

8. On 1st January, 19.., the following balances appeared in the books of Oxford, Ltd.:—

Debtors	£	Creditors	£
Hull, Ltd.	250	Bristol & Sons, Ltd. ..	300
Exeter & Co.	400	Cardiff Bros.	100

Open the accounts to record the above in the books of Oxford, Ltd, and record the following transactions in the Journal and Ledger and Cash Book:— 19..

Jan. 2.   Accepted a bill drawn by Bristol & Sons, Ltd, for the balance due at one month.

  ,,   9.   Received bill for two months from Exeter & Co. for £400 duly accepted.

  ,,   16.   Hull, Ltd forwarded draft duly accepted at two months for balance due.

  ,,   23.   Accepted Cardiff & Co.'s bill for three months for £100.

Feb. 5.   Bill due to Bristol & Sons, Ltd, duly honoured.

  ,,   9.   Discounted Exeter & Co.'s draft at 6% per annum.

Mar. 19.   Proceeds of Hull, Ltd's, bill collected by bankers and credited in account.   *R.S.A.*

9. R. Kingston had the following assets and liabilities on 1st June, 19..:—Cash in hand, £16; Cash at bank, £175; Plant and machinery, £85; Stock, £700; S. Jameson owed him £73, and £79 was owing to B. Luckworth.

Open the books of R. Kingston as on 1st June, 19.., and record the following transactions:—

June 2.   Sold goods to R. Freeman, £74.

  ,,   3.   Paid wages in cash, £19.

  ,,   3.   Paid £5 into the bank.

  ,,   4.   Cash sales, £206.

  ,,   5.   Sold goods to S. Jameson, £79.

  ,,   7.   R. Freeman proves insolvent and pays £0·50 in the £ in settlement of the amount owing.

  ,,   10.   Drew cheque for private use, £30.

  ,,   12.   Bought goods for cash, £21.

  ,,   14.   S. Jameson sends his acceptance at 14 days for the amount due.

  ,,   15.   Discounted S. Jameson's acceptance at bank, discounting charges being £0·50.

  ,,   16.   Cash sales, £227.

  ,,   17.   Bought goods from B. Luckworth, £33.

  ,,   18.   Paid into bank, £230.

  ,,   19.   Bought by cheque, office furniture, £21.

  ,,   20.   Paid B. Luckworth cheque £77, being allowed discount £2.

  ,,   21.   Sold goods to S. Jameson, £76.

  ,,   22.   Bought stationery for cash, £15.

  ,,   22.   Paid rent in cash, £15.

  ,,   23.   Bought on credit from R. Austin, plant and machinery, £58.

  ,,   24.   Paid wages in cash, £83.

June 25. Returned to B. Luckworth, goods, £7.
„ 30. Received a debit note from S. Jameson, £6.
„ 30. Bank returned S. Jameson's bill dishonoured.

You are required to extract a Trial Balance as at 30th June, and also a Trading Account, Profit and Loss Account, and Balance Sheet as at that date. When preparing the Final Accounts, the following items are to be brought into account:—

    (1) Stock, 30th June, 19.., is £23.
    (2) £15 is owing for wages.
    (3) Plant and machinery is to be depreciated by £4.
    (4) £3 is to be allowed for interest on capital.
    (5) Value of unused stationery, £12.   *U.E.I*

10. At 1st November, 19.., my assets and liabilities were as follows:—

	£
Premises	1500
Plant and machinery	525
Motor car	273
Cash at bank	362
Bills Receivable	185
Stock on hand	225
I owed A. B. for goods	136
C. D. owed me for goods	88

The transactions of my business during November were as follows:—

Nov. 3. C. D. paid his account, less £8 discount.
„ 6. Bought goods from E. F., £50.
„ 8. One Bill Receivable matured and was honoured, £70.
„ 9. The other Bill Receivable was discounted. The bank charges were £3.
„ 15. Bought new machinery for cash, £33.
„ 18. Paid A.B.'s account, less £5 discount.
„ 20. Sold goods to C.D., £202.
„ 25. Paid rates in advance, £12.
„ 28. Paid wages and expenses, £25.
„ 30. Stock of goods valued at £155.

All payments are made by cheque, and all amounts received are paid immediately into the bank.

    (*a*) Open the books as on 1st November, 19.., by means of Journal entries.

    (*b*) Do not use the Journal for the transactions during November, but post direct to the Ledger.

    (*c*) All the appropriate Ledger Accounts must be opened. Direct entries to the Profit and Loss Accounts are not permitted.

    (*d*) Prepare a Trial Balance, close the Ledger Accounts, and draw up the Profit and Loss Account and Balance Sheet.

    (*e*) Candidates must attempt both the Profit and Loss Account and the Balance Sheet.

11. (*a*) Enter the following transactions through their appropriate books.
(*b*) Post to Ledger.
(*c*) Take out Trial Balance.
(*d*) Prepare Profit and Loss Account and Balance Sheet.

A. ARMITAGE
Balance Sheet.   30 June, 19..

LIABILITIES AND CAPITAL	£	£	ASSETS	£	£
Sundry Creditors—			Cash in hand	12	
H. Hall	83		Cash at bank	58	70
M. Marks	137	220	Bill Receivable due 30 Sept.		150
Capital A/c.		1110	Stock of goods		785
			Sundry Debtors—		
			B. Bowen ..	65	
			C. Charles	80	145
			Fixtures and fittings ..		180
		£1330			**£1330**

During July 19.., Armitage's transactions were as follows:—
Armitage paid into bank £390 as additional capital.
Received cheque for £62 from B. Bowen in settlement of his account.
Paid to H. Hall a cheque for the amount of his account.
Sold goods, on credit, to B. Bowen, £116.
Purchased motor van by cheque, £540.
Paid by cheque, tax and insurance on motor van, £40.
Purchased goods, on credit, from H. Hall, £75.
Drew and cashed cheque £38 for office cash.
Paid from cash salaries, £25, office expenses, £5, and private expenses, £15.
Discounted Bill Receivable, due 30th Sept., at bank, discount charged being £1·75.
Paid rent for month, £6.
Write off 10% depreciation from fixtures and fittings.
Cash sales during month, £165, which was banked.
The stock on hand at 31st July, 19.., was valued at £810.
N.B.—All cheques received were paid into bank same day.

12. On 1st June, 19.., after trading for eleven months, B. Somers, a Wholesale Ironmonger, had the following balances on his books:—

		£
Capital Account	.. ..	2500
Drawings Account	.. ..	275
Stock Account	.. ..	3345
Purchases Account	.. ..	9000
Sales Account ..	.. ..	11000
Furniture and fittings..	.. .. ..	600
Bank overdraft	.. ..	50
J. Fish (Debtor)	.. ..	140
R. Stagg (Debtor)	.. ..	60
B. Blunt (Creditor)	.. ..	342
Bills Receivable	.. ..	230
Sundry expenses	.. ..	242

At the end of each year 10% of the value of the furniture and fittings is to be written off for depreciation.

After these deductions, £50 of the remaining net profit is to be set aside to meet possible future bad debts.

The remaining net profit, if any, is to be credited to the proprietor's Capital Account.

All the accounts are then to be closed, and the balances carried forward as on 1st July.

The transactions which took place during the month of June were as follows:

June   3.   Bill Receivable £130, paid into bank for collection.

,,   6.   Cheque for £36, received from B. Judge on May 31st and paid into bank on that day, returned dishonoured.

,,   8.   Purchased from the Trustee in Bankruptcy, the whole of the stock of Williams & Co. for £1,200, payment to be made by two equal acceptances due 8th July and 8th August. The transaction was duly completed and the drafts accepted.

,,   15.   Cash sales to date paid into bank, £400.

,,   17.   Wrote off B. Judge's Account as a bad debt.

,,   19.   Received cheque from R. Stagg in settlement of his account, less 5% discount.

,,   20.   Paid B. Blunt cheque for £325 in settlement of his account.

,,   21.   Received J. Fish's Acceptance for £140.

,,   24.   Discounted with bank all Bills Receivable in hand, the bank charging £3 for discounting.

,,   30.   Drew cheque for sundry expenses, £12.

All payments were made by cheque and all amounts received were at once paid into the Bank.

Enter *direct into the Ledger* the opening balances and the transactions. Take out a Trial Balance. Make the adjustments required. Then prepare Trading and Profit and Loss Account for the twelve months ended June 30th, 19.., and Balance Sheet at that date. *No subsidiary books whatever are to be used.*

The stock at June 30th was valued at £3,912.   *Joint Matriculation Board.*

CHAPTER 32

CONSIGNMENT ACCOUNTS AND JOINT VENTURES

Much of the trade between different parts of the country and between different countries is carried on by the intervention of agents who sell goods on behalf of their principals. In this way the manufacturer or merchant exporting the goods avoids the expenses of a local branch, and has the benefit of the agent's knowledge of local conditions and likely markets. The goods are forwarded for sale on commission. The agent deducts from the gross proceeds his expenses and commission, and remits the net proceeds to his principal. Goods so dispatched are called consignments. The principal, who forwards the goods, is known as the consignor, and the receiver as the consignee. From the consignor's point of view a consignment is a Consignment Outwards; from the consignee's it is a Consignment Inwards.

A consignment outwards is not a sale to the agent. The goods are held by the agent for sale, and if he cannot sell them he may return them to the consignor. There is a change only in the location of the goods. It is necessary to bring the transaction into account when the sale takes place, but meanwhile the consignment must be treated separately from the ordinary trading transactions of the business.

The agent is usually remunerated by an agreed commission calculated as a percentage on the gross proceeds of sale. Should he guarantee the consignor against loss from bad debts he is paid an additional commission, called a *del credere* commission.

The consignor usually sends to the agent a *pro forma* invoice, giving a description of the goods consigned, the weight, quantity, shipping marks, and other relevant details, and sometimes including the price as an indication of the minimum selling price the consignor expects to be realised. The invoice does not charge the consignee with the value; it is sent to him for information and guidance only.

The agent informs his principal of his dealings with the consignment by rendering an *Account Sales*, which is a statement containing particulars of the consignment, the gross proceeds of sale, the agent's expenses and commission, and the net proceeds due to the

298

consignor. The transactions relative to the consignment are completed when the consignor receives the net proceeds from the consignee.

> **Example 41.**—Butcher & Co., of London, consigned ten cases of fancy goods to their agents, Lawson & Brown, of Bombay, on 20th August, paying freight, insurance, etc., £40.
>
> The goods were valued at cost, £1,000, and were shown on the *pro forma* invoice at £1,350. An Account Sales was received from the consignees on 10th October showing the gross proceeds of sale, £1,500; landing and dock charges and duty paid, £50; and commission at 5% + 1% *del credere*.
>
> A banker's draft on London for the net proceeds was forwarded by the consignees with the Account Sales.
>
> Show the entries for the consignment in the books of the consignors.

The first step is to record the consignment of the goods to Lawson & Brown. The entries cannot be made in the Sales Account as this is not a sale, and, until they are sold, the goods remain the legal property of the consignor. For the same reason Lawson & Brown cannot be debited personally with the value of the goods consigned. They are not debtors until the goods are sold. Two special accounts are opened instead: one, the "Goods Consigned Outwards Account" to record that the goods have left the warehouse on consignment, and the other, the "Consignment to Lawson & Brown Account," to record that Lawson & Brown have received the goods, but on consignment only. The former account is credited, and the latter account is debited with the goods consigned at *cost* price, as until the sale takes place the entries are a record only of stock transferred from the warehouse to another place.

Journal

19..		£	£
Aug. 20	Consignment to Lawson & Brown Account Dr.	1000	
	To Goods Consigned Outwards Account being 10 cases of fancy goods consigned to Lawson & Brown, Bombay.		1000

The purpose of the "Consignment to Lawson & Brown Account" is to show the dealings with the consignment, the expenses incurred, and the eventual profit or loss on the venture. The shipping and other charges paid by the consignor are debited to this account (and credited to Cash), and no other entries are made until the Account Sales is received from the consignee.

The Account Sales shows the gross proceeds of sale, the expenses paid, the commission deducted, and the net proceeds due to the consignor. When the goods are sold and the proceeds collected, the consignees become debtors for the net proceeds, but if they are acting *del credere* they are liable to the consignor as soon as the goods are sold.

ACCOUNT SALES of 10 cases of Fancy Goods *ex* SS. *Lamina* sold by Lawson & Brown of Bombay for the account of Messrs. Butcher & Co., London.

		£	£
	10 Cases of Fancy Goods at £150		1500
B. Co.			
1–10	Deduct charges and expenses—		
	Landing, dock charges, and duty..	50	
	Commission, 5%	75	
	Del Credere, 1%	15	140
	Sight Draft herewith for		£1360
	Bombay, (*Sgd.*) LAWSON & BROWN		
	18 *Sept.*, 19..		

The sum representing the net proceeds is credited to the Consignment to Lawson & Brown Account, and is debited to the personal account of Lawson & Brown as a debt due from them. An alternative method to the same effect is to credit the Consignment to Lawson & Brown Account with the gross proceeds, and to debit the account with the expenses and commission shown in the Account Sales. The contra entries are made in Lawson & Brown's personal account by debiting the gross proceeds and crediting the expenses and commission.

Lawson & Brown's personal account is closed by a credit entry when they remit the proceeds, the debit entry being made to Cash.

The balance of the Goods Consigned Outwards Account is transferred to the Trading Account at the close of the year. It is preferable to show this balance, on taking it to the Trading Account, as a deduction from the total purchases and not as a credit entry. If shown as a credit entry it should be stated separately from the total sales, as the latter includes the gross profit, whereas the consignment figure is at cost. To include it with the sales figure would render that ineffective for purposes of comparison with previous sales figures and for the calculation of the percentage of gross profit on turnover.

The balance of the Consignment to Lawson & Brown Account, which represents the profit on the venture, is transferred to Profit and Loss Account.

The following Ledger Accounts illustrate the record required:—

Dr.   **Goods Consigned Outwards Account**   *Cr.*

19..			£	19..			£
Dec. 31	Transfer to Trading A/c.		1000	Aug. 20	Consignment to Lawson & Brown	J.	1000

Dr.   **Consignment to Lawson & Brown, Bombay**   *Cr.*

19..			£	19..		£
Aug. 20	Goods Consigned A/c.	J.	1000	Oct. 10	Consignees' Account: Gross Proceeds	1500
,, 20	Cash: Freight and Insurance ..		40			
Oct. 10	Consignees' Account— Landing and other expenses ..		50			
	Commission, 5% ..		75			
	Del credere, 1% ..		15			
	Profit and Loss A/c.		320			
			£1500			£1500

Dr.   **Lawson & Brown's Account**   *Cr.*

19..			£	19..		£
Oct. 10	Consignment Account, Gross Proceeds		1500	Oct. 10	Consignment Account:— Landing and other expenses ..	50
					Commission, 5% ..	75
					Del credere. 1¼% ..	15
					Cash ..	1360
			£1500			£1500

Remitting by Bill

The consignees may remit by Bill of Exchange, in which case the consignees' account is credited and Bills Receivable Account is debited with the amount of the bill. The Bills Receivable Account is credited, and Cash is debited when the bill is paid. The consignors are, of course, at liberty to discount the bill and should they so decide, the usual entries on discounting will be required.

Documentary Bill

The consignor may arrange to draw on the consignee at the time of shipment. In that case the bill is drawn for about three-quarters of the value of the goods consigned, and for a period after sight that will give the consignee time to sell the goods before the bill has to be met. The consignor attaches the shipping documents to the bill and sells the bill outright, subject to recourse, to his bankers, who then proceed to obtain the consignee's acceptance against the handing over of the shipping documents. The documentary bill, as this is termed, is credited to the consignee's personal account as part payment by him, and is debited to Bills Receivable Account. On selling the bill the consignor credits Bills Receivable Account with the cash and the discount charge, and debits the cash to the Cash Book and the discount charge to the Consignment Account. The balance due from the consignee will be treated as in the above example when the Account Sales is received and the amount is known.

Goods on Consignment and the Balance Sheet

Should the Final Accounts and Balance Sheet have to be prepared before the goods are sold, it will be necessary to take the consignment into account. Reverting to the above example, the Consignment to Lawson & Brown Account would be balanced and closed, and the balance carried down to the debit side for the next trading period. This balance would be shown in the Balance Sheet, among the assets, as Stock on Consignment.

If part only of the goods have been sold when the Balance Sheet has to be prepared, the value of the unsold portion must be ascertained in order that it may be shown in the Balance Sheet as unsold stock on consignment. As the consignors' expenses and some part of the consignees' expenses probably relate to the whole consignment, it will be necessary to apportion these between the sold and the unsold parts of the consignment, and to include the appropriate proportion of the expenses in the valuation figure of the unsold portion.

When this value has been ascertained it is credited to the Consignment to Agent Account, and is carried down as the opening debit balance of the Consignment to Agent Account for the new financial period.

The apportionment spreads the expenses over the whole of the stock on consignment and enables the correct profit on the sold portion to be ascertained. After the value of the unsold portion and its proportion of expenses have been credited, the balance of the Consignment to Agent Account represents the profit or loss on the sold portion, and is carried to the Profit and Loss Account in the ordinary way.

Assuming, as an example, that Lawson & Brown sold only half the above consignment and forwarded an Account Sales conveying this information, and that the expenses should be related equally to the sold and unsold portions, the Consignment Account would appear at balancing time as shown on p. 304.

The sum of £545 would appear in the Consignors' Balance Sheet as an asset under the heading "Stock on Consignment".

Should consignments form a considerable proportion of a firm's business it is the practice to keep special books comprising a Consignment Ledger and Cash Book. A special Profits on Consignments Account may also be used to summarise the profits, the balance of which is transferred to the Profit and Loss Account at the close of the financial year.

Consignments Inwards

The trader receiving the goods on consignment for sale on behalf of the consignor is dealing with a Consignment Inwards. The consignee is not a debtor for their value so that he makes no entry in his financial books on their arrival. He will find it necessary to keep an adequate record of the kind of goods and the quantities in an appropriate memorandum book—usually called a Consignment Inwards Stock Book—but apart from this his only concern is to record the expenses he has incurred, the sales, his commission, and his financial relationship with the consignor. A personal account for the consignor is the only additional account a Consignment Inwards involves.

Dr.   **Consignment to Lawson & Brown, Bombay**   Cr.

19..			£	19..		£
Aug. 20	Goods Consigned A/c. Cash: Freight and Insurance ..	J.	1000 40	Oct. 10	Consignees' A/c. Gross proceeds of half consignment	750
Oct. 10	Consignees' Account—Landing and other Expenses Commission, 5%.. *Del credere*, 1% ..		50 37 50 7 50	,, 31	Unsold Stock on Consignment at cost (£500) and half consignees' and consignors' expenses (£20 + £25) carried down ..	
,, 31	Profit and Loss A/c. (Profit on half consignment)		160			545
			£1295			£1295
Nov. 1	Balance brought down (unsold stock on consignment and proportion of expenses)		545			

The above Example 41, taken from Lawson & Brown's point of view, will serve as an example of a Consignment Inwards. Lawson & Brown will open in their books a personal account for Butcher & Co., the consignors. The entries may be summarised as follows:—

EXPENSES   *Debit* Consignors' Account.
                 Credit Cash.

SALES   *Debit* the customers' personal accounts, or Cash, if sold for cash.
                 Credit Consignors' Account.

COMMISSION   *Debit* Consignors' Account.
                 Credit Commission Account for eventual transfer to Profit and Loss Account.

REMITTANCES   *Debit* Consignors' Account.
                 Credit Cash or Bills Payable Account as the case may be.

After the expenses, sales, and commission have been entered in the Consignors' Account, the balance represents the sum due to the consignors.   When the sum remitted is entered the account is closed.

The Consignors' Account for the above example would appear in the books of the consignees as below:—

Dr.		Butcher & Co.'s Account			Cr.
19..		£	19..		£
Sept. 15	Cash, Landing and other expenses ..	50	Oct.	Sundry Debtors (Proceeds of Consignment) ..	1500
	Commission Account ..	90			
	Cash (Banker's draft to settle)	1360			
		£1500			£1500

Goods on Approval

The dispatch of goods to a customer on approval cannot be treated as an ordinary sale until the customer signifies his acceptance of them.   Pending such acceptance the property in the goods remains vested in the sender.   It is usual to keep a special Goods on Sale or Return Journal in which the goods sent out on sale or return are recorded, and from which the sales as they take place are posted to the Ledger Accounts.   The ruling of such a Journal might be as below:—

Goods on Sale or Return Journal

Date	Particulars	Dispatched		Returned		Sales		Remarks
		Date	Amount	Date	Amount	Sales Ledger Folio	Amount	
			£		£		£	

When a sale takes place an entry is made in the appropriate sales column in the Journal, and is posted therefrom to the personal account of the customer. The periodical totals of the sales column are posted to the credit of the Sales Account. The goods still with customers on approval must be taken into account at the close of a trading period, being taken into stock at cost or market price, whichever is the lower.

Goods on approval should not be confused with consignments. In the latter case the goods are sent to an agent for sale on behalf of the consignor. In the former, the customer is given an option to purchase or return the goods, which he is expected to exercise within a reasonable or specified time.

Joint Ventures

A joint venture is a partnership of a limited kind, formed to carry out a particular trading operation, undertaking, or speculation, and is confined to that particular purpose. The trading operation may be on a scale to warrant the opening of a separate set of books to record the transaction. In such a case the record will follow the lines of the ordinary partnership accounts. In other cases each of the adventurers takes a part in the conduct of the business and records in his own books the transactions he carries out on behalf of the joint enterprise.

Each adventurer opens in his own books a Joint Venture Account. This is treated as a personal account; all payments and charges in respect of the venture are debited to the account, and all receipts and other credit items are credited to it. On completion of the venture, each adventurer sends a copy of his own account to his co-adventurer.

The separate accounts are combined into a single Joint Venture Account, which is of the nature of a Profit and Loss Account for the venture. It will show the profit for division between the adventurers or the loss to be borne by them. Each adventurer debits his own venture account with his share of the profit, or credits his account with his proportion of the loss, as the case may be. The contra entry is made in his Profit and Loss Account.

The balance of each adventurer's account after the entry of the profit or loss is the amount due from him or due to him. With the entry of the adjusting payments the separate accounts are closed.

Example 42.—Jackson and Dawson enter into a joint transaction to purchase and sell a quantity of salvaged goods, and agree to share expenses and profits equally. Jackson acquires the goods, paying £5,000 by cheque. Dawson gives a cheque for £2,500 to Jackson as his proportion of the outlay. Dawson pays for advertising, £250. Jackson pays warehousing charges, £100; cartage expenses, £20; and sundry minor expenses, £6. Jackson is allowed £50 for office expenses. Dawson sells three-quarters of the goods for £5,200 in cash. Jackson sells the remainder for £1,600, taking a Bill at three months which he discounts at once. The discount charge, £16, is an expense of the venture. Prepare the Joint Venture Account and the appropriate Ledger Accounts as in Jackson's and Dawson's books.

Combined Account—a memorandum account only.

Joint Venture in Salvaged Goods

	£			£
Purchase of goods	5000		Proceeds of sales	6800
Warehouse charges	100			
Cartage expenses..	20			
Sundry expenses ..	6			
Discount charges..	16			
Office allowance ..	50			
Advertising	250			
Profit, Jackson ..	679			
Dawson ..	679			
	£6800			£6800

In Jackson's Books.

Dr.   **Joint Venture with Dawson**   *Cr.*

	£			£
Cash purchase of goods	5000		Cash received from Dawson	2500
Cash, warehouse charges ..	100		B/R for proceeds of sale	1600
Cash, cartage expenses	20		*Cash from Dawson*	1771
Cash, sundry expenses	6			
Discount charges on bill	16			
Office allowance	50			
Share of Profit to Profit and Loss Account ..	679			
	£5871			£5871

In Dawson's Books.

Dr.		Joint Venture with Jackson		Cr.
	£			£
Cash to Jackson	2500	Cash—proceeds of		
Cash, advertising	250	sale		5200
Share of Profit to				
Profit and Loss				
Account ..	679			
Cash to Jackson..	1771			
	£5200			£5200

The contra entries in Jackson's and Dawson's Cash Book are not shown. The items in italics are known only after the preparation of the Joint Account.

EXERCISES 32

1. On 1st April, 19... The Export Co. consigned 72 cases of cutlery to A. Dennis & Co. of Kingston, Jamaica, and forwarded a *pro forma* invoice at the cost price of £427. On the same day, the consignors paid freight charges £2 and insurance £1 per case.

On 1st August, 19.., the following was received by the consignor together with the bill as stated:—

ACCOUNT SALES of part consignment of 72 cases received from The Export Co. per S.S. "Empire" by Dennis & Co. up to 30th June, 19..:—

		£	£
72 cases at £9 per case..	.. .. ..		648
Less—			
Landing Charges, etc.	.. .. ..	36·2	
Commission due to us	.. .. ..	32·8	
			69
Sight draft herewith for	.. .. ..		£579

Dennis & Co.

Record these transactions in the books of The Export Co., showing the profit on the consignment.   *R.S.A.*

2. On Nov. 1st, 19.., Horrocks & Co. Ltd., of Manchester, shipped per the S.S. Lancaster "on consignment" to Alva & Co., Buenos Aires, 5 bales of piece goods which were invoiced to them *pro forma* as follows:—5 bales of 20 pieces each (80 yd. in each piece) printed goods at £0·15 per yd. The following expenses were paid by the consignors:—
Packing charges, £4·5; Shipping charges and freight, £12·5; Marine insurance, £10. Under date Jan. 26, Messrs. Alva submitted an A/S showing the consignment to have realised £1,860 gross, and showing the following deductions for expenses:—Customs duty, £15·8; Landing charges, £4; Fire insurance, £8; Warehousing, £6·1; and their own commission of 5% on gross sales. A demand draft on the Anglo-South American Bank was enclosed. Show the whole of the entries which are necessary, and close off the accounts in the books of the consignors only.   *N.C.T.E.C.*

3. Watson & Co., of London, consigned to Stevenson Bros., of Cape Town, for sale, goods which cost £1,240, but were invoiced *pro forma* at £1,500. Watson & Co. paid freight, £83, and insurance, £21. In due course, Stevenson Bros. sent an Account Sales showing that part of the goods had been sold for £1,210, and that their charges were £98 *plus* a commission of 4% on the gross proceeds. They also sent to Watson & Co. a sight draft for the amount due.

Show the Account Sales and the necessary accounts in Watson & Co.'s Ledger, noting that the unsold goods were valued at £573.   *U.E.I.*

4. On 1st January, 19.., A. N. Exporter forwarded a consignment of 200 cases of tropical helmets to A. Trader, his agent in West Africa, together with a *pro forma* invoice for £360. On the following day, the consignor paid the freight charges amounting to £55 and insurance charges £9. On 15th March, 19.., an Account Sales was received from the agent showing that 150 cases had been sold for £380, and that landing and storage charges on the consignment amounting to £28 had been paid by the agent. The agent's commission of 5% of the gross sales was deducted and the balance due was remitted by sight draft.

Record these transactions in the books of the consignor showing the profit or loss on the consignment.   *R.S.A.*

5. On 1st January, 19.., A. Exporter & Co. forwarded a consignment of 100 steel filing cabinets to J. Dyke, his agent in South Africa, and also sent a *pro forma* invoice showing the price at £7·50 each. On 7th January, 19.., the firm paid freight and insurance charges on the consignment amounting to £65.

On 30th June, 19.., an account sales was received from the agent showing that 50 cabinets had been sold at £10 each and that various landing and storage charges had been paid by him on the whole of the consignment amounting to £85. The agent also deducted his commission of 5% of the gross sales, forwarded a draft for the net proceeds of the sales, and intimated that the balance would be sold shortly at the same price. Record these transactions in the books of the consignor, showing the profit or loss at the 30th June, 19...   *R.S.A.*

6. C. Cave received goods from R. Medfield, Karachi, invoiced at £400. Cave made the following payments on 1st April:—Dock charges, £5, Carriage £10; Duty, £20. Cave sold the goods for cash, £550, on 14th April. His commission is agreed at 2½% on the gross proceeds. Cave remitted to Medfield the amount due to him on 16th April. Show the entries to record these transactions in Cave's books.

7. C. Nelson and S. Bennett join in the purchase of a cargo of flour, and agree to share the expenses and profits in equal proportions.

Nelson agrees to arrange the purchase, and Bennett undertakes the sale of the flour. The cost of the cargo was £9,600, and Bennett at once paid £4,800 to Nelson for his share.

Nelson incurred the following expenses:—Unloading, £185; Cartage, £103; Warehousing, £211.

Bennett sold the flour for cash for £12,500, his expenses amounting to £56, and he remitted to Nelson cheque for the amount due to him.

Show the necessary accounts in Bennett's Ledger.   *U.E.I.*

8. A. Blake entered into a joint venture with M. Day. A. Blake agreed to manage the joint venture, and on 1st March M. Day remitted a cheque value £700 to A. Blake to assist in financing the venture. Profits and losses are to be divided two-thirds to A. Blake and one-third to M. Day.

On 4th June A. Blake bought goods value £1,130, and incurred the following expenses: carriage, £21, and insurance, £9. By agreement, he is allowed to charge a commission of £10. The goods were sold for £1,590 on 11th June.

You are required to show the joint account. *U.E.I.*

9. Adams and Bell were art dealers who agreed to purchase certain pictures on joint account, the arrangement being that the party effecting the sale was to be allowed a commission of 5% on the amount realised, the remaining profit being divided equally.

On 25th June, 19.., Adams bought three pictures for £1,600, and Bell purchased two others for £1,350. Expenses of £35 were incurred, of which Adams paid £25 and Bell £10.

On 17th July Adams sold one of the pictures for £600 and on 25th July forwarded another picture to Bell, the cost of carriage and insurance (paid by Adams) being £7. Bell sold this picture on 5th August for £720, and on the same day sent Adams a cheque for the amount realised, less 5%. The pictures purchased by Bell were sold by him on 10th and 29th July for £850 and £780 respectively.

At 30th September the remaining picture was still unsold, and it was arranged that Adams should take this over for £400. On 5th October the amount due from one party to the other was settled by cheque.

Prepare a general statement showing the result of the venture and write up the joint account as it would appear in the books of Adams. *R.S.A.*

10. A and B enter into a venture to purchase a cargo of timber from Kotka. The expenses, profits or losses, are to be shared equally. It is arranged that A should make the purchase, and B undertake the selling. A purchased a parcel valued at £4,800, and B at once paid half this amount to A. The following expenses were incurred by A:—freight, £160; unloading, £70; cartage, £93. Sundry expenses incurred by B: £30. The timber was sold by B for £6,500, payable by bill at three months, which he immediately discounted at the rate of 5% p.a. You are required to prepare accounts as they would appear in A and B's Ledgers when the venture was completed. *N.C.T.E.C.*

CHAPTER 33

PARTNERSHIP ACCOUNTS: THE ADMISSION
OF NEW PARTNERS

The growth of a business may make urgent the need for additional supervision or additional capital, and the decision may be to take in a new partner to supply the need. Whether the existing business is owned by a sole trader or a partnership firm, the admission of a partner brings a new firm into being, and it is essential to agree upon the terms of his admission and the conditions of the new partnership.

Take the example in Chapter 22 in which Redman and Butcher are shown as trading in partnership, each with a capital of £1,500, and sharing profits equally. They may decide to admit Robinson to partnership, who is to contribute £1,000 as capital, and is to have $\frac{1}{5}$ share of the profits of the new firm; Redman and Butcher to share equally the remaining profits.

If that is all, the entries in the firm's books are simple, requiring only a credit entry for £1,000 in Robinson's Capital Account, and a corresponding debit entry for the sum in the firm's Cash Book. But the matter is seldom so simple as that. The new partner is being admitted to an existing business, and he will benefit from the connections and reputation already established. The old partners, on their part, forgo these advantages to the extent that the new partner shares in them. In short, Goodwill attaches to the business created by the old firm, and will continue for the new firm of which Robinson is a member. Not only will Robinson derive present benefit in the form of profits, but should any event happen, such as the dissolution of the partnership, and the Goodwill be realised by sale, he has the right to share in its value. It is therefore customary for the new partner to pay for the privilege of admission to an existing business. Such payment, called a Premium, is made to the old members and may be regarded as compensation to them for the share in the Goodwill that will accrue to the new partner at their expense.

The premium must not be confused with the capital the new partner may introduce, which is credited to his own account, whilst the premium is for the benefit of the partners of the old firm. It is normally anticipated that the cash or other assets brought in by the new partner and credited to his Capital Account will produce additional profits by its use. If cash is brought in, the corresponding entry to the credit of the new partner's Capital Account is a debit to the Bank Account through the Cash Book. If the new capital is in kind, such as book debts, stock, and other assets, an appropriate Journal entry is made from which the agreed values are posted to the debit of the respective asset accounts, and the total value to the credit of the new partner's Capital Account.

The premium, however, may be treated in one of several ways, and in none of these is the new partner's Capital Account affected.

Example 43.—On Jan. 1st Redman and Butcher, trading in partnership, each with a capital of £1,500 and sharing profits equally, decide to admit Robinson as a partner on the condition that he brings in £1,000 as capital and pays them a premium of £1,000. The profits in future are to be shared as follows: Redman, $\frac{2}{5}$; Butcher, $\frac{2}{5}$; Robinson, $\frac{1}{5}$.

Method 1. The premium is to be paid by Robinson direct to Redman and Butcher.

In this case no entries are made in the firm's books. The premium is shared between Redman and Butcher in the proportion in which they shared profits, so that Robinson hands direct to each of them a cheque for £500 as a private transaction between him and the old partners.

Method 2. The £1,000 premium is to be paid by Robinson into the firm, but it is to be paid out to Redman and Butcher in the proportions in which they are entitled to share it. This method differs from Method 1 only in that an entry is made of the premium in the firm's books. It may be the wish of the partners to have the transaction on record.

Dr.			£	19..			£
19..				Jan. 2	Redman:—		
Jan. 1	Robinson:—				$\frac{1}{2}$ Robinson's		
	Capital ..	10	1000		Premium ..		500
	Premium..	9	1000		Butcher:—		
					$\frac{1}{2}$ Robinson's		
					Premium ..		500

Cash Book (*Cr.* 20)

9

Dr.				Robinson.	Premium Account		Cr.
19..			£	19..			£
Jan. 1	Current Ac-counts:—			Jan. 1	Cash ..	C.B. 20	1000
	Redman	J.	500				
	Butcher	J.	500				
			£1000				£1000

10

Dr.				Robinson.	Capital Account		Cr.
19..			£	19..			£
				Jan. 1	Cash ..	C.B. 20	1000

11

Dr.				Redman.	Current Account		Cr.
19..			£	19..			£
Jan. 2	Cash:— Premium withdrawn	C.B. 20	500	Jan. 1	½ Premium from Robin-son.. ..	J.	500

12

Dr.				Butcher.	Current Account		Cr.
19..			£	19..			£
Jan. 2	Cash:— Premium withdrawn	C.B. 20	500	Jan. 1	½ Premium from Robinson ..	J.	500

Method 3. The premium is to be paid by Robinson into the firm, and is to remain in the business. The premium is the property of Redman and Butcher. As they agree that it shall be left in the business and not withdrawn by them, the effect is to increase their capital contributions by the amount of the premium. This is recorded in their respective Capital Accounts. If interest is allowed on capital they will receive interest on these sums in addition to the interest on their original capital.

20

Dr.   Cash Book   Cr.

19.. Jan. 1	Robinson:— Capital	10	£ 1000	19..			£
	Premium:— Redman, £500	13					
	Butcher, £500	14	1000				

10

Dr.   Robinson. Capital Account   Cr.

19..			£	19.. Jan. 1	Cash	C.B. 20	£ 1000

13

Redman. Capital Account

19..			£	19.. Jan. 1	Balance Cash, ½ Robinson's Premium..	b/d C.B. 20	£ 1500 500

14

Dr.   Butcher. Capital Account   Cr.

19..			£	19.. Jan. 1	Balance Cash, ½ Robinson's Premium..	b/d C.B. 20	£ 1500 500

Whichever of these methods is decided upon for the treatment of the premium, the old partners have been compensated in cash for the share in the Goodwill and for the proportion of future profits they surrender to the new partner.   It has not been necessary to raise a Goodwill Account in the firm's books.

Cases may arise, however, where the new partner may be unable or may find it inconvenient to pay the premium in cash, and some other method must be devised to compensate the old partners for what they forgo on admitting the new partner.   As no value either in cash or other form passes between the old partners and the newcomer the method of compensation becomes a series of book-keeping entries to increase the old partners' claims on the new firm.

As a set-off against the bookkeeping entries of these additional claims an increase is made in the total value of the assets. A value is placed upon the Goodwill of the business, and is included among the assets of the new firm—a Goodwill Account being opened to record it.

Example 44.—On Jan. 1st Redman and Butcher, trading in partnership, each with a capital of £1,500 and sharing profits equally, decide to admit Robinson as a partner on condition that he brings in £1,000 as capital and pays them a premium of £1,000. Profits to be shared in the new firm: Redman ⅖; Butcher ⅖; Robinson ⅕.

Robinson finds it inconvenient to pay the premium in cash. It is agreed that in lieu of the cash premium a Goodwill Account of £5,000 shall be created, and that a similar sum shall be credited to Redman and Butcher in the same proportion in which they shared profits.

The £1,000 as capital will be debited on receipt to the firm's Cash Book, and credited to Robinson's Capital Account. A Goodwill Account will be opened, and the following entries made in the Journal and posted therefrom to the Goodwill Account and to the old partners Capital Accounts:—

Journal

19.. Jan. 1	Goodwill Account.. .. .. **Dr.** Redman's Capital Account .. .. Butcher's „ „ .. .. being the apportionment of the Goodwill valuation as agreed on admission of Robinson to partnership.	17 13 14	£ 5000	£ 2500 2500

17

Dr.			**Goodwill Account**			*Cr.*
19.. Jan. 1	Sundries ..	J.	£ 5000			£

13

Dr.			**Redman. Capital Account**			*Cr.*
		£	19.. Jan. 1 „ 1	Balance .. Goodwill A/c.	b/d J.	£ 1500 2500

14

Dr.			**Butcher. Capital Account**			*Cr.*
		£	19.. Jan. 1	Balance .. Goodwill A/c.	b/d J.	£ 1500 2500

By this method the old partners have an additional capital claim as creditors of the new firm, and will be further compensated by the larger sum which will accrue to them annually as interest on their increased capitals.

The amount at the debit of the Goodwill Account is usually written off over a number of years, the Profit and Loss Account being debited and the Goodwill Account credited. In this way the new partner contributes out of his share of the profits to writing off the amount of Goodwill which was credited to the Capital Accounts of the existing partners when he entered the partnership.

EXERCISES 33

1. Budd and Benson, each with a capital of £2,000 and sharing profits and losses in equal proportion, decide to admit Bentley as partner on condition that he brings in £1,000 in cash as capital and pays £1,000 as premium for admission. The premium is paid directly by Bentley to Budd and Benson. The profits in future are to be shared as follows:—Budd and Benson, each $\frac{2}{5}$, Bentley $\frac{1}{5}$.

Show the effect of the admission of the new partner on the partnership accounts.

2. Thomas and James are in partnership with capitals respectively of £2,500 and £1,500, sharing profits and losses in equal proportions. They decide to admit Jackson as partner on condition that he brings into the business £2,000 of which £1,000 is Jackson's capital contribution and £1,000 is the premium for his admission to the partnership. The sum of £2,000 is paid into the firm's Banking Account, and the premium of £1,000 is paid out to Thomas and James in the proportions in which they are entitled to share it. The profits in future are to be shared, Thomas $\frac{2}{5}$; James $\frac{2}{5}$; Jackson $\frac{1}{5}$.

Record the new partner's admission and the payment out of the premium in the firm's accounts.

3. Wise and Wisdom are in partnership, sharing profits and losses in proportion to their capitals which are £3,000 and £2,000 respectively. They agree to admit Woolley as partner on condition that he pays into the firm £2,500 of which £1,500 is to be Woolley's capital contribution, and £1,000 the premium he is to pay for his admission.

The cash is paid into the firm's Banking Account, and the premium is paid out to Wise and Wisdom.

The profits are to be shared in future, Wise and Wisdom, $\frac{3}{8}$ each; Woolley $\frac{1}{4}$.

Record Woolley's admission to the firm and the payment out of the premium.

4. West and Wilson are equal partners, each with a capital of £3,000. They agree to admit Williams as partner provided he pays in £4,000 of which £3,000 is to be his capital contribution and £1,000 the premium he pays for his admission. Williams paid in the cash which was paid into the firm's Banking Account. The premium is to remain in the business. The profits are to be shared in future equally between the three partners, but 5% interest is to be allowed on capital.

Record the admission of the new partner.

5. Acton and Ascott, trading in partnership, share profits and losses in proportion to their capitals, which are £2,000 and £1,500 respectively. They admit Bennett as partner on his contributing in cash £1,000 as capital and £700 as premium.   The premium is to remain in the business, and profits in future are to be shared, Acton, $\frac{4}{9}$, Ascott $\frac{1}{3}$, and Bennett, $\frac{2}{9}$.

Record Bennett's admission to the partnership.

6. Caton and Coulter are in partnership, sharing profits and losses equally. Each has a capital of £4,000 in the firm.   They agree to admit Denton as partner, who, however, can command only £2,000 as his cash contribution.   It is arranged that this sum shall be his capital, that a Goodwill Account shall be raised for £2,000, and that Caton's and Coulter's Capital Accounts shall be credited with £1,000 each.

Give the entries to carry these decisions into effect.   The partners are to share profits in future in proportion to their capitals.   State the ratio in which the profits will be shared.

7. Dunn and Dugald, trading in partnership each with a capital of £2,000 and sharing profits and losses equally, decide to admit Everton as a partner on condition that he brings in £1,000 in cash as capital and pays them a premium of £1,000 as premium for his admission.   Everton cannot find sufficient cash to carry out these terms.   It is agreed, therefore, that in lieu of the cash premium a Goodwill Account for £3,000 shall be raised, and that a similar sum shall be credited to Dunn and Dugald in the proportion in which they formerly shared profits and losses.

Record Everton's admission under these terms.

8. A and B are partners sharing profits in the same proportion as their capital, which is £6,000 and £3,000 respectively.   They agree to admit their Manager C. into partnership.   Under the original agreement C. was to pay £3,000 to A and B by way of premium for admission to the firm, and was to pay in a further £3,000 as his capital in the business.

C, however, is only able to raise £4,000; it is, therefore, agreed that a Goodwill Account of £8,000 is to be created, and £1,000 only paid to A and B by way of cash premium.

Prepare the necessary entries to record these transactions.   *R.S.A.*

CHAPTER 34

PARTNERSHIP ACCOUNTS: THE AMALGAMATION OF EXISTING BUSINESSES. DISSOLUTION OF PARTNERSHIPS

Independent traders engaged in the same kind of business, or persons practising the same profession, may agree to amalgamate and merge their assets and liabilities in a partnership concern with a view, possibly, to the reduction of overhead charges or the elimination of competition.

The decision to amalgamate will involve the fixing of the date on which the amalgamation is to take place, and agreement on the terms under which it shall be carried out. Each trader must be prepared to make full disclosure of the financial position of his business, and there must be some assessment of the relative values of the businesses as going concerns. A satisfactory plan is the preparation of a Balance Sheet by each trader as at the amalgamation date, and mutual agreement upon the adjustments that may be necessary in the value of the assets or the extent of the liabilities. If the Goodwill of the businesses be unequal, then it may be more equitable to make allowance for this in the amalgamation by compensating the owner of the more valuable concern. The Balance Sheet of each concern is re-drafted, taking into consideration the adjustments agreed upon, and these re-drafted Balance Sheets are then combined to form the initial Balance Sheet of the partnership.

Example 45.—Butcher and Baker decide to amalgamate their businesses as from 1st January, 19.., their respective Balance Sheets at 31st December, 19.., preceding, being as follows:—

Butcher's Balance Sheet
31st December, 19..

	£			£
Capital	20000	*Fixed Assets—*		
Current liabilities—		Freehold property ..		4000
Sundry creditors	2900	Fixtures and fittings ..		900
		Current assets—		
		Stock		10000
		Sundry debtors		7000
		Cash at bank		1000
	£22900			£22900

318

Baker's Balance Sheet
31st December, 19..

	£			£
Capital	5000	*Fixed Assets—*		
Current Liabilities—		Fixtures and fittings	..	500
Bills Payable	1500	*Current Assets—*		
Sundry creditors	3000	Stock		4200
		Sundry debtors		4000
		Cash		800
	£9500			£9500

The agreement provides that both stocks are to be reduced in value by 10%; that a provision for bad debts of 5% is to be made on the sundry debtors: that Baker's fixtures and fittings are to be kept by him and disposed of as he thinks best; that Butcher's fixtures and fittings are to be re-valued at £800, and that Butcher is to be credited with £3,000 for Goodwill.

Show the initial Balance Sheet of the partnership as at 1st January, 19.., after taking into account the above adjustments.

Butcher and Baker will make the necessary adjustments in their books so that these show the financial position immediately prior to amalgamation. In Baker's case the Journal entries required will be:

Journal

19..		£	£
Jan. 1	Capital Account .. .. .. Dr.	1120	
	Stock		420
	Provision for bad debts		200
	Fixtures and fittings		500
	being reductions on revaluation and by amalgamation agreement.		

Baker's Balance Sheet
1st January, 19..

	£	£		£	£
Capital	5000		*Current Assets—*		
less Loss on revaluation	1120		Stock		3780
		3880	Sundry debtors ..	4000	
Current Liabilities—			*less* Provision for bad		
Bills Payable		1500	debts	200	
Sundry creditors ..		3000			3800
			Cash at bank		800
		£8380			£8380

Similar procedure by Butcher will involve the following entries in his books:—

Journal

19..		£	£
Jan. 1	Capital Account .. .. .. Dr.	1450	
	Stock		1000
	Provision for bad debts		350
	Fixtures and fittings		100
	being reductions on revaluation of assets.		
,, 1	Goodwill Account .. .. .. Dr.	3000	
	Capital Account		3000
	being agreed value of Goodwill on amalgamation.		

It is now possible to draw up a Balance Sheet to show the new position:

Butcher's Balance Sheet
1st January, 19..

	£	£		£	£
Capital	20000		Goodwill		3000
add Goodwill ..	3000		*Fixed assets—*		
	———		Freehold property..		4000
	23000		Fixtures and fittings		800
less Loss on revaluation	1450		*Current assets—*		
	———	21550	Stock		9000
Current liabilities			Sundry debtors ..	7000	
Sundry creditors ..		2900	*less* Provision for bad		
			debts	350	
				———	6650
			Cash at bank ..		1000
		£24450			£24450

It remains to combine the re-drafted Balance Sheets to provide the initial Balance Sheet of the new firm—

BUTCHER & BAKER
Balance Sheet.   1st January, 19..

	£	£		£	£
Capital—			Goodwill		3000
Butcher ..	21550		*Fixed Assets—*		
Baker	3880	25430	Freehold property ..		4000
			Fixtures and fittings		800

Balance Sheet. *Continued*

	£	£		£	£
Current liabilities—			*Current assets—*		
Bills Payable ..		1500	Stock		12780
Sundry creditors ..		5900	Sundry debtors ..	11000	
			less Provision for bad debts	550	
					10450
			Cash at bank ..		1800
		£32830			£32830

Dissolution of Partnerships

A partnership is a voluntary association of persons, and just as its inception is by mutual agreement, so it may be dissolved at any time by the mutual consent of the partners.

The Partnership Act, 1890, enacts that, subject to any agreement between the partners, a partnership is dissolved:—

(a) If entered into for a fixed term, on the expiration of that term.

(b) If entered into for a single adventure or undertaking, on the termination of that adventure or undertaking.

(c) If entered into for an undefined time, on any partner giving notice to the other member or members of his intention to dissolve the partnership.

(d) On the death or bankruptcy of a partner.

(e) At the option of the other partners, if a partner suffers his share of the partnership property to be charged under the Act for his separate debt.

Also, on application of a partner, the Court may decree a dissolution when a partner is found lunatic or permanently incapable of performing his part of the partnership agreement or is guilty of such conduct as may be prejudicial to the carrying on of the partnership business. The Court may also decree dissolution, on application of a partner, when the business can only be carried on at a loss.

On dissolution the assets of the partnership are realised, and Section 44 of the Partnership Act, 1890, decrees that, in settling the accounts between partners on dissolution, the following rules shall be observed:—

(*a*) Losses, including capital losses, shall be paid first out of profits, next out of capital and, if necessary, by the partners individually in the proportion in which they shared profits.

(*b*) The assets of the firm, including any contribution by the partners as above to make up losses, are to be applied in the following order:—

1. Firstly, to the payment of outside debts and liabilities; then

2. To the repayment, rateably, of loans from partners.

3. To repayment of the partners' capital.

4. The surplus, if any, after the satisfaction of these claims, to be divided among the partners in the proportion in which they shared profits.

It follows from this that any losses are first to be charged against any undrawn profits shown in the partners' Current Accounts. If this is insufficient or no such undrawn profits exist, then the losses are to be charged against the partners' Capital Accounts. Should undrawn profits and capital be together insufficient to meet the losses then the partners must contribute in actual cash sufficient to make good the remaining deficiency. After such adjustments the distribution of the assets must proceed according to the above rules subject to any agreement otherwise between the partners. Such agreement, however, cannot affect the first rule which grants to outside creditors the first claim upon the assets.

Closing the Partnership Books on Dissolution

Where there are no complicating circumstances the procedure adopted to close the partnership books is as follows:—

1. Open a Realisation of Assets Account in the Ledger for the purpose of ascertaining the financial result of the realisation of the partnership assets.

2. Close all the asset accounts, except the cash, by transfer to the debit of the Realisation Account.

3. When the assets are realised, debit the Cash Book with the proceeds and credit the Realisation Account.

   If a partner takes over an asset at an agreed value, debit the value to the partner's Capital Account and credit Realisation Account.

4. Credit the Cash Book and debit the Realisation Account with the expenses of the dissolution.

The balance of the Realisation Account now shows a profit or a loss on realisation of the assets which is divisible among the partners in the proportion in which they shared profits. In the event of a loss, credit Realisation Account and debit the partners' respective Capital Accounts with the appropriate shares of the loss. In the event of a profit—debit Realisation Account and credit the partners' respective Capital Accounts with the appropriate shares of the profit.

5. Discharge the liabilities, crediting cash and debiting the various liability accounts.

The balance of cash in hand, after payment of the outside liabilities, should now exactly equal the aggregate of the balances of the partners' Capital Accounts if they are in credit, and the entries consequent on the payment to the partners of the capital sums will close the Cash Book and the partners' Capital Accounts.

Example 46.—F. Lynch and B. Finch decide to dissolve partnership as on 30th June, 19... Profits and losses are shared equally. The firm's Balance Sheet as at date of dissolution was as follows:—

Balance Sheet. 30th June, 19. .

LIABILITIES		£	ASSETS			£
Capital—			Premises	..	..	1200
F. Lynch	.. ..	2500	Fittings	..	..	250
B. Finch	..	2000	Stock	..	..	2500
Sundry creditors	..	1500	Sundry debtors		..	1750
			Cash	..	..	300
		£6000				£6000

The results of the realisation were: Premises, £1,400; Stock, £2,700; Debtors, £1,700; B. Finch took over the fittings at an agreed price of £200. The expenses of dissolution amounted to £100. Prepare the necessary accounts.

The solution is given below:—

1

Dr.				F. Lynch.	Capital Account				Cr.
			£	19..				£	
19..				June 30	Balance	..	b/d	2500	
June 30	Balance	c /d	2600	,, 30	Realisation				
					A/c.	..	J.	100	
			£2600					£2600	
June 30	Cash ..	C.B.	2600	June 30	Balance	..	b/d	2600	

Journal

19..					£	£
June 30	Realisation Account .. .. Dr.	8	5700	
	Sundry assets—			
	Premises	4		1200
	Fittings	5		250
	Stock	6		2500
	Sundry debtors	7		1750
	being transfer of assets on dissolution.			
„ 30	B. Finch. Capital Account .. Dr.	2	200	
	Realisation Account	8		200
	being agreed value of fittings taken over.			
„ 30	Realisation Account .. .. Dr.	8	200	
	F. Lynch. Capital Account.. ..	1		100
	B. Finch. Capital Account	2		100
	being profit on realisation transferred.			

2

Dr.			B. Finch.	Capital Account			Cr.
19..			£	19..			£
June 30	Fittings	J.	200	June 30	Balance ..	b/d	2000
„ 30	Balance..	c/d	1900	„ 30	Realisation A/c. ..	J.	100
			£2100				£2100
June 30	Cash ..	C.B.	1900	June 30	Balance ..	b/d	1900

3

Dr.			Sundry Creditors				Cr.
19..			£	19..			£
June 30	Cash ..	C.B.	1500	June 30	Balance ..	b/d	1500

4

Dr.			Premises				Cr.
19..			£	19..			£
June 30	Balance..	b/d	1200	June 30	Realisation A/c. ..	J.	1200

5

Dr.			Fittings				Cr.
19..			£	19..			£
June 30	Balance ..	b/d	250	June 30	Realisation A/c. ..	J.	250

6

Dr.			Stock				Cr.
19.. June 30	Balance ..	b/d	£ 2500	19.. June 30	Realisation A/c. ..	J.	£ 2500

7

Dr.			Sundry Debtors				Cr.
19.. June 30	Balance ..	b/d	£ 1750	19.. June 30	Realisation A/c. ..	J.	£ 1750

8

Dr.			Realisation Account				Cr.
19.. June 30	Sundry assets .. Cash— (Dissolution expenses) Balance ..	J. C.B. c/d	£ 5700 100 200	19.. June 30 " 30	Cash— (Proceeds of sale of assets) .. B. Finch (Fittings)	C.B. J.	£ 5800 200
			£6000				£6000
June 30	F. Lynch.. B. Finch ..	J. J.	100 100	June 30	Balance ..	b/d	200
			200				200

9

Dr.			Cash Book				Cr.
19.. June 30 " 30	Balance .. Proceeds of sale of assets ..	b/d 8	£ 300 5800	19.. June 30	Dissolution expenses Sundry creditors F. Lynch.. B. Finch ..	8 3 1 2	£ 100 1500 2600 1900
			£6100				£6100

Loss on Realisation

In the above example a profit is made on realisation of the assets. If the assets realise less than their book values and a loss results, such loss will appear as a debit balance in the Realisation Account, and the contra entry is made to the debit of the partners' Capital Accounts. The loss is shared by the partners in the proportions in which they agreed to share the profits or losses of the partnership. If each partner's Capital Account is still in credit the final settlement in cash will follow the lines shown in the above worked example. The cash balance will exactly equal the aggregate of the credit balances of the Capital Accounts.

Partner's Capital Account in Debit

If realisation of the assets results in a loss and a partner's Capital Account is already or is thereby placed in debit, the partner must pay in sufficient cash to clear the balance as otherwise the remaining partners cannot be paid the sums shown to their credit. This point is illustrated in the following example:—

Example 47.—T. More and W. Morris are trading in partnership, sharing profits two-thirds and one-third respectively. They decide to dissolve partnership and realise the assets. The firm's Balance Sheet at the date of dissolution was as follows:—

Balance Sheet
31st December, 19. .

LIABILITIES			£	ASSETS			£
Capital—				Sundry assets ..	..	..	1800
T. More ..	..	..	3000	Stock	..	..	2450
W. Morris	..	..	500	Cash at bank ..	..	..	450
Sundry Creditors	..	..	1200				
			£4700				£4700

The sundry assets realised £1,400 and the stock £1,450.

The expenses of realisation amounted to £190.

Prepare the necessary accounts to show the results of the realisation as they should appear in the books of the firm, and the position of the two partners after satisfying the firm's liabilities.

The solution to the example is given below, where it will be observed that there is a loss on realisation. The share of the loss to be borne by W. Morris places him in debt to the firm, and he has to pay in cash to enable More to be paid the sum due to him.

Dr.			Realisation Account				Cr. [1]
Dec. 31	Sundry Assets .. Stock .. Cash— (Dissolution expenses)	C.B.	£ 1800 2450 190	Dec. 31	Cash— Proceeds of sale of assets .. Balance carried down ..	C.B.	£ 2850 1590
			£4440				£4440
Dec. 31	Balance brought down ..		1590	Dec. 31	T. More $\frac{2}{3}$ share of loss .. W. Morris $\frac{1}{3}$ share of loss ..		1060 530
			£1590				£1590

Dr.			Cash Book				Cr.
19.. Dec. 31	Balance Proceeds of sale of assets .. W. Morris, Cash paid in ..	b/d 1 3	£ 450 2850 30	19.. Dec. 31	Sundry creditors Expenses of dissolution .. T. More	1 2	£ 1200 190 1940
			£3330				£3330

Dr.			T. More. Capital Account				Cr. [2]
19.. Dec. 31 „ 31	Realisation Account, share of loss .. Balance ..	1 c/d	£ 1060 1940	19.. Dec. 31	Balance ..	b/d	£ 3000
			£3000				£3000
Dec. 31	Cash ..	C.B.	1940	Dec. 31	Balance ..	b/d	1940

3

Dr.			W. Morris.	Capital Account			Cr.
19..			£	19..			£
Dec. 31	Realisation Account, share of loss ..	1	530	Dec. 31 „ 31	Balance .. Balance ..	b/d c/d	500 30
			£530				£530
Dec. 31	Balance ..	b/d	30	Dec. 31	Cash ..	C.B.	30

The Ledger Accounts for the assets and liabilities other than capital, are not shown in this worked example.   One of the partners has a credit balance on Capital Account, and the payment in of cash by the partner in debit makes it possible to extinguish the credit balance and to close the books.   It may happen that the loss on realisation is so great that all the partners are placed in debit, which would mean that the cash balance would be insufficient to discharge the Sundry Creditors.   Each partner would, in that case, have to pay in sufficient cash to extinguish his debit balance and so to provide enough cash to pay the outside creditors.

A further possibility is that a partner may be insolvent, and unable to make good the debit balance on his Capital Account. This deficiency is regarded as a further loss which has to be borne by the remaining partners, but in this case it is important to note that the loss is not divided among the solvent partners in the ratio in which they shared profits and losses.   In accordance with the decision in the English case of *Garner* v. *Murray* (1904) this deficiency must be borne by the solvent partners in the ratio which their individual capital accounts, before adjustment for their respective shares of the realisation loss, bear to the total capital of all the remaining solvent partners.   This is a ruling of the English Courts which might not be upheld by the Scottish Courts should a similar case arise for decision, and the ruling has caused considerable controversy among accountants.   The points involved belong, however, to the advanced stage of Bookkeeping.

EXERCISES 34

1. The Balance Sheets shown below are those of two independent traders who have agreed to amalgamate their businesses as from 1st January on the basis of these Balance Sheets, subject to the adjustments mentioned.

Barnett's Balance Sheet
31st December, 19..

LIABILITIES	£	ASSETS	£
Capital	9000	Premises	2000
Creditors	840	Fittings	300
Bills Payable	500	Stock	5250
		Debtors	1750
		Bills Receivable	200
		Cash at bank	840
	£10340		£10340

Marsden's Balance Sheet
31st December, 19..

LIABILITIES	£	ASSETS	£
Capital	3000	Furniture and fittings ..	180
Creditors	1200	Stock	3100
		Debtors	800
		Cash at bank	120
	£4200		£4200

The adjustments are: Marsden to retain the furniture and fittings and to dispose of them privately; Marsden to write off £150 of the sundry debtors as a bad debt, and to reduce his stock valuation to £2,500. Barnett's stock valuation is to be reduced to £5,000, and he is to be credited with £1,000 for the Goodwill of his business. Subject to these adjustments the new firm is to take over all the assets and liabilities.

Show the opening Balance Sheet of the partnership as at 1st January.

2. Lucas and Cave agree to amalgamate their businesses from 1st January on the basis of the following Balance Sheets, subject to the adjustments mentioned below:—

Lucas's Balance Sheet
31st December, 19..

LIABILITIES	£	ASSETS	£
Capital	6500	Plant and machinery ..	3000
Sundry creditors	850	Stock	2000
		Fittings	400
		Sundry debtors	1050
		Cash at bank	900
	£7350		£7350

Cave's Balance Sheet
31st December, 19..

LIABILITIES	£	ASSETS	£
Capital	2200	Plant and machinery ..	1200
Creditors	700	Stock	1510
Overdraft	450	Fittings	140
		Sundry debtors	500
	£3350		£3350

Prepare the opening Balance Sheet of the partnership as at 1st January, taking the following adjustments into consideration:—Lucas is to be credited with £1,000 for Goodwill. Cave's machinery and plant is to be reduced in value to £1,000. Both stocks are to be reduced in value by 10%. Cave is to pay off his overdraft from his private funds. Each trader is to create a provision for bad and doubtful debts at 5% of the sundry debtors.

3. X and Y are independent traders in the same line of business, their respective Balance Sheets on 31st December, 19.., being as follows:—

X. Balance Sheet
31st December, 19..

	£			£
Capital	22400	Goodwill		2000
Sundry creditors	2047	Freehold property		2400
		Fixtures and fittings ..		530
		Stock		10854
		Debtors		7591
		Cash at bank		1072
	£24447			**£24447**

Y. Balance Sheet
31st December, 19..

	£			£
Capital	4660	Fixtures and fittings ..		180
Bills Payable	1200	Stock		5171
Sundry creditors	2318	Debtors		3146
Bank overdraft	319			
	£8497			**£8497**

X and Y decided to amalgamate their businesses as from 1st January, the firm taking over all the assets and liabilities at the figures stated except Y's fixtures and fittings, which he was to retain and dispose of, and Y's stock which is to be written down by £280. The Goodwill of Y's business was agreed to be valued at £600.

Draw up the opening Balance Sheet of the partnership. *R.S.A.*

4. McArthur and Dickson are partners sharing profits as to $\frac{3}{5}$ and $\frac{2}{5}$ respectively. They agree to dissolve partnership and realise the business assets.

Upon the conclusion of the realisation the position was as follows:—
McArthur, Capital Account, £5,000; Loan Account, £1,000.
Dickson, Capital Account, £3,000; Sundry creditors, £1,456.
Net amount realised by the assets, £11,441.

Submit a statement showing how you would deal with the amount realised.
R.S.A.

5. A. Adams and B. Bates were in partnership, sharing profits and losses two-thirds and one-third respectively. On 31st January, 19.., their Balance Sheet showed as follows:—

LIABILITIES		£	ASSETS		£
Sundry creditors	.. ..	1800	Cash in hand	.. ..	70
Capital Accounts—			Sundry debtors	.. ..	3600
A. Adams	.. ..	2300	Stock in hand	.. ..	1580
B. Bates ..	.. ..	1150			
		£5250			£5250

On this date they decided to dissolve partnership and realise the assets. The stock realised £1,200, and the sundry debtors £3,150. The sundry creditors were paid, and discount to the amount of £40 was received. The expenses of realisation amounted to £18. Make the entries necessary to complete the above, and show the Ledger Accounts of the partners in their final form. *N.C.T.E.C.*

6. Brown and Green are in partnership, sharing profits and losses two-thirds and one-third respectively, and on the 31st January, 19.., their Balance Sheet shows as follows:—

LIABILITIES		£	ASSETS		£
Sundry creditors	.. ..	2800	Cash in hand	.. ..	700
Capital Accounts—			Sundry debtors	.. ..	2100
A. Brown..	.. ..	3800	Stock in hand	.. ..	4200
W. Green..	.. ..	1900	Furniture, etc.	.. ..	1500
		£8500			£8500

On this date they decided to dissolve partnership, and the assets realised as follows:—The furniture was taken over by Brown at an agreed price of £1,450; sundry debtors realised £2,025; and the stock, £4,500. The expenses of realisation amounted to £91. Make the entries necessary to close the books of the firm, and show the Ledger Accounts in their final form. *N.C.T.E.C.*

7. A and B, trading in partnership, decide, as on March 31st, 19.., to dissolve partnership and to liquidate their business.

Their Balance Sheet as on that date was as follows:—

Balance Sheet

31st March, 19..

		£				£
Capital Account: A ..	..	2000	Cash	..	..	1800
Capital Account: B ..	..	1500	Sundry debtors	..	..	2800
Sundry creditors	..	2750	Other assets ..	..	..	850
			Goodwill ..	..	..	800
		£6250				£6250

Profits and losses are shared equally.

The debtors realised £2,700, other assets £950, and the Goodwill of the business was sold for £400. The expenses of liquidation amounted to £100.

Prepare the necessary accounts to show the result of the realisation as it would appear in the books of the firm, and the position of the two partners as regards the disposal of the balance of cash remaining after satisfying the firm's liabilities. *R.S.A.*

CHAPTER 35

CONCERNING LIMITED LIABILITY COMPANIES

(Except where specifically stated sections of the Companies Acts referred to in this chapter refer to the Companies Act 1948).

Companies have been the subject of legislation since the first Companies Act of 1855, and are now governed by the provisions of the Companies Act, 1948, as amended and extended by the Companies Act, 1967. A company as a form of business ownership differs from the sole trader or partnership in that it is a corporate body sanctioned by Act of Parliament, and has a legal entity distinct from the persons comprising it. The company may sue and be sued upon in its own name in an action at law, and neither the death or bankruptcy of any of its members nor any change in the personnel of the membership affects its existence. Many thousands of companies have been formed, and they are a popular form of business ownership as, with certain rare exceptions, the members are limited in their liability for the debts contracted by the company. The most that a member can lose is the amount he has contributed or has agreed to contribute towards the capital of the company. This principle of limited liability has attracted investors who are willing to become part owners of a business under such conditions, and has made possible the formation of companies with very large capitals to carry on large-scale businesses. At the other extreme, many sole trading and partnership concerns have been converted into companies to take advantage of the limitation of liability.

Companies may be incorporated by special Act of Parliament, as were the British Railways; by Royal Charter, like the Hudson Bay Company; or under the Companies Acts 1948 and 1967.

The reader must not assume that the word "Company" as part of a firm name indicates that the concern is an incorporated company. A sole trader or partnership may adopt a title such as "John Brown & Company" for trading purposes.

Three kinds of companies may be formed under the Companies Act, 1948, namely:—

(a) Companies limited by shares.

332

(*b*) Companies limited by guarantee.

(*c*) Companies, with or without share capital, the liability of whose members is unlimited.

The first kind is the most appropriate for business undertakings, and is the subject-matter of this chapter.

Under the Companies Acts any seven or more persons may apply to be registered as a public company, and any two or more may apply to be registered as a private company. The application is made in writing to the Registrar of Companies, and is in the form of a Memorandum of Association signed by the applicants, who are known as the "signatories," and is accompanied by certain other documents required by the Act.

The Memorandum must state—

(*a*) *The name of the company with "Limited" as the last word of its name.* The purpose of this is to inform all persons having dealings with the company of the fact that it is a limited liability company.

(*b*) *Whether the registered office of the company is to be situate in England or in Scotland.* Later the company must register its address with the Registrar, and its registered office is the address for all notices and communications. The company's name must be affixed or painted in a conspicuous position on the outside of every place where the company carries on its business, and must be on all notices, advertisements, bills of exchange, cheques, orders, invoices, and receipts under a penalty for default.

(*c*) *The objects of the company.* These must be carefully stated, as a company cannot legally undertake any business other than that set out in this clause of its Memorandum.

(*d*) *That the liability of its members is limited.*

(*e*) *The amount of share capital with which the company proposes to be registered and the division thereof into shares of a fixed amount.* The capital as stated is known as the authorised, nominal, or registered capital of the company. The capital may be, say, £10,000. The shares of fixed amount into which this is divided may be £1 shares or £0·25 shares or whatever value is agreed upon. If they are to be £1 shares then the capital, if £10,000, is made up of 10,000 shares of £1 each. The signatories to the memorandum must state opposite their names how many shares they propose to take up. It is seldom that more than one share each is stated, and it is also very infrequent that the number of signatories exceeds the minimum of seven, or two for a private company, required by the Act.

Usually another document, called the Articles of Association, is filed with the Registrar. This contains the regulations for the internal management and organisation of the company. If no such Articles are filed then the company is bound by the model set of regulations contained in the first schedule to the Companies Act, 1948, and known as Table A, except that a private company, as defined below, cannot adopt Table A without the amendment that is necessary to comply with the statutory definition of a private company.

These documents, duly stamped for fees and stamp duty, are lodged with the Registrar of Companies, who on accepting the registration, issues a Certificate of Incorporation. A private company may then commence business, but a public company has only power to issue a prospectus. Certain other formalities are necessary before a public company may commence to trade.

Private Companies

A "private company" is a company which by its articles—

1. Restricts the right to transfer its shares.

2. Limits the number of its members to fifty, excluding employees who may be members and ex-employees who became members whilst so employed and continue to be members.

3. Prohibits any invitation to the public to subscribe for any shares or debentures of the company.

As mentioned above, two or more persons as against seven or more in the case of a public company, may apply to form a private company. Private companies are a popular form of ownership, especially for small businesses and family concerns, and many sole trading and partnership firms have been converted into private companies in order to take advantage of the limitation of liability.

Except for the restrictions above mentioned the remarks hereafter apply equally to public and private companies.

Directors

The members of a company, as such, have no right to any share in the management of the company and cannot bind the company or fellow members in any way. The business is conducted by

Directors whose activities are governed by the provisions of the company's Articles of Association. The first directors are appointed by the signatories to the Memorandum of Association or by being declared as such in the Articles of Association. The articles of Association usually fix a minimum share qualification for the directors but unless the Articles so provide a director need not hold any share qualification. The directors are known, collectively, as the Board of Directors and usually have power to fill any casual vacancies in their number. The Articles usually contain a clause to the effect that one or more of the Board shall retire annually but shall be eligible for re-election for a further period. Many boards are composed of four or five directors, but large companies may have many more. The Articles state the maximum number and also fix their remuneration.

Common Seal

Under Section 108 of the 1948 Act a company must have its name engraved in legible characters on its common seal. The seal is impressed upon the share certificates and deeds as the company's official signature, and the Articles usually provide that it shall be affixed only in the presence of two directors and the company secretary who shall sign that the seal was so affixed.

Annual Meeting and Directors' Report

Under Section 131 of the Act every company must hold a general meeting of its members once at least in every calendar year, and not more than fifteen months after the holding of the last preceding general meeting. At the general meeting the directors, by Section 148, must lay before the company a Profit and Loss Account made up to a date not earlier than the date of the meeting by more than nine months, and also a Balance Sheet as at the date to which the Profit and Loss Account is made up. To every Balance Sheet must be attached a report by the directors on the state of the company's affairs, and the amount, if any, which they recommend should be paid as dividend, and the amount, if any, they propose to carry to reserve, together with the auditors' report. The dividend is the distribution of the profits of the company which is made to the members in proportion to their holdings in the share capital and in accordance with the provisions of the Articles of Association.

It is at this annual meeting that the election or re-election of directors takes place.

The Prospectus and the Kinds of Capital

Immediately after formation the directors have to consider the question of obtaining capital. A public company may invite subscriptions from the public, and the invitation takes the form of a prospectus in which general particulars regarding the company are set out and a formal offer is made of the shares for subscription. Private companies and small public companies may obtain capital from relatives, friends, or business acquaintances, or the capital may be contributed by the signatories only, but private companies may not offer shares for public subscription.

The Act contains very strict provisions regarding prospectuses to safeguard the public as far as possible from fraud as the prospectus is the basis of the contract between the company and the shareholder. A copy of the prospectus, dated and signed by the directors, must be filed with the Registrar of Companies on or before the date of publication.

The prospectuses are distributed to possible subscribers and among banks and stockbrokers for their clients. As a further means of publicity, press advertising of abridged copies may be made. The full prospectus must contain a copy of the company's Memorandum of Association.

For the use of subscribers an application form for the shares accompanies each prospectus. The required particulars are to be filled in, and the form, together with the first instalment on each share, known as the application money, is to be handed in to the company's bankers.

The capital of the company mentioned in the Memorandum of Association is the maximum amount it has authority to issue. The directors may decide that not all the capital authorised is wanted immediately, and may offer part only for immediate subscription. The shares applied for may exceed or may be less than the number offered. In the former case an issue is said to be over-subscribed, and the directors have to find some way of reducing the applications. If less is subscribed than offered the issue is said to be under-subscribed. It is obvious that unless a certain minimum, varying according to circumstances, at least is subscribed the company may be handicapped for want of funds and may find it impossible to commence trading or, having commenced, to continue to trade. The prospectus of any offer of shares must state the minimum subscription on which the directors will proceed to allotment and each subscriber makes his application for shares on the assumption that such minimum will be obtained before allotment. The Companies Acts impose penalties on directors for allotments made where the minimum subscription has not been received, and such allotments may be repudiated by the subscribers within one month after the statutory meeting of the company. Section 47 provides that where the minimum subscription has not been received within forty days after the first issue of the prospectus the directors must refund the application money without interest, and after forty-eight days the directors are personally liable for the repayment with interest at five per cent. per annum.

It follows that the uncertainty which this possibility creates constitutes a severe handicap to genuine business propositions. Consequently a third party, known as an underwriter, is usually approached to guarantee that the minimum subscription shall be at the disposal of the directors. The underwriter is a financier who undertakes to subscribe for all shares in the offer not otherwise subscribed in consideration of a commission based on the number of shares underwritten. If 100,000 shares of £1 each are underwritten, and only 90,000 are subscribed, the underwriter must personally subscribe for 10,000 shares. Against the cost of these shares he will receive his commission on the whole 100,000 shares underwritten by him.

In most instances the shares applied for are payable by instalments. The first instalment, which must not be less than five per cent. of the nominal value of the share, is paid on application. The second instalment is paid on allotment of the shares to the applicant, and the remainder, if any, at times decided by the directors, which may or may not be specifically mentioned in the prospectus. Such remaining instalments are known as Calls, and it is usual to give shareholders fourteen days' notice by a Call Letter that a call is due.

The total amount paid up on the shares at any given date is referred to as the *paid-up capital* of the company, and the shares are *fully-paid* shares when all the instalments have been paid.

The directors may decide not to call up the final instalment until such time that further working capital is required. Meanwhile the paid-up capital will be less than the subscribed capital by the amount of *uncalled capital*. The paid up capital may not, however, agree with the actual amount of *called-up* capital. Not all the calls may be met at due date by shareholders, and such outstanding instalments are referred to as *Calls in arrear*. Other instances arise where the shareholder pays the instalments before the due date, and such are known as *Calls in advance*.

The following example illustrates the various terms referred to above as applied to the capital of a company:—

> Brown & Fox Limited are registered with a nominal capital of £120,000 divided into 120,000 shares of £1 each. 80,000 shares were offered to the public, and were fully subscribed. By June 30th, 19..., £0·50 per share on application and allotment, and the first call of £0·25 per share had been paid up except the call of £0·25 on 2,000 shares, held by L. T. Green, which remained unpaid.

From this example, therefore,

		£
The Authorised or Nominal or Registered Capital is		120000
The Issued Capital		80000
The Subscribed Capital		80000
The Called-up Capital		60000
The Paid-up Capital		59500
The Uncalled Capital		20000
The Calls in Arrear...		500

Various Classes of Shares

Though the capital of a company is divided into shares of fixed amount, the capital may comprise groups or classes of shares according to the rights and privileges attaching to each class. The three principal classes are Preference Shares, Ordinary Shares, and Deferred Shares.

Preference Shares usually carry the right to a fixed dividend from the profits each year before any other class is paid a dividend. In some cases preference shares have prior right to dividend and also first claim to return of capital in the event of liquidation.

Ordinary Shares usually have no special dividend rights, and the holders are entitled to the surplus profits remaining after the fixed dividend has been paid on the Preference Shares, subject to the right of the Deferred Shares, if any, to participate in any distribution above a given amount or percentage.

Deferred Shares rank for dividend only after the other classes have received payment of dividend. Where deferred shares exist the dividend payable on the ordinary shares may be fixed or the ordinary shares may be given prior right up to a certain amount and thereafter be entitled to share in any balance with the deferred shareholders.

Preference shares may be cumulative or non-cumulative. With Cumulative Preference Shares the arrears of dividend, if any, consequent on insufficient profits to pay the dividend in any year, are carried forward. The current dividend and the arrears must be paid before any distribution may be made to the subordinate classes of shares. Non-cumulative Preference Shares carry no right to payment of arrears of dividend. Unless the Articles of Association state otherwise, Preference Shares are assumed to be cumulative.

Participating Preference Shares carry an additional right to a fixed share in the profits over and above the fixed dividend, after the payment of a fixed dividend on the subordinate classes of shares.

There are also many instances of gradations of Preference Shares, such as First Preference and Second Preference Shares. In all cases, the basis is the order in which dividend is payable. An example is the Preferred Ordinary Shares which rank for dividend after the Preference Shares but before the Ordinary Shares. The classification is made to encourage investors of all temperaments since some wish for safety and a fixed rate of dividend from year to year, and others are less anxious and are attracted by the larger dividend that is usual on the Ordinary Shares.

Redeemable Preference Shares are a class permitted to be issued under the Companies Act. By Section 58 a company may issue redeemable Preference Shares, if so authorised by its Articles, but the shares may be redeemed only if fully paid and only out of profits which would otherwise be available for dividend or out of the proceeds of a fresh issue of shares made for the purpose of the redemption. If redemption is to be made from the profits of the company, a sum equal to the amount to be applied in redeeming the shares must be set aside out of profits to a reserve fund called the "Capital Redemption Reserve Fund." Any premium on redemption must also be provided for out of the profits before redemption.

Distinguishing Numbers and Share Certificates

Each share in a company having a share capital is usually distinguished by its appropriate number. Where shares are numbered consecutively, the numbers must be stated on the Share Certificates to which each shareholder is entitled. The share certificate is usually signed by two directors and the secretary, and bears the seal of the company. It certifies that the person named therein is the registered proprietor of the stated number of shares, and mentions the distinguishing numbers of such shares. The company must have such certificates ready for delivery within two months after the shares have been allotted, unless the conditions of issue otherwise provide.

The shareholder may transfer his shares to another person who then takes over all the rights and obligations, including the liability for outstanding calls, of the previous holder. Such transfer must be in writing and in proper form. Printed forms of transfer are obtainable from law stationers. The transferor completes and signs the form and passes it to the transferee, together with his share certificate. The latter signs the transfer form and lodges both the form and the share certificate at the company's office, paying the transfer fee of, usually, two shillings and sixpence. The company must have the new certificate made out in the transferee's name ready for delivery within two months from the date on which the transfer was lodged with the company.

Most shares are marketable, and those of many companies may be bought and sold on the Stock Exchange. In other cases the shares can be disposed of only by private treaty, and if the prospects of the company are not bright it may be difficult to find a purchaser. A shareholder can realise his investment only by sale. He cannot demand the return of his invested capital from the company, and only under rigid and special conditions may a company make any return of capital to shareholders.

The price which a shareholder may obtain for his shares depends upon the prospects of future dividends, the financial standing of the company, and the value the intending purchaser places upon these. The holder may have subscribed £1 for each £1 share, but that does not wholly determine the selling value. The shares may be worth more or less in the market than their nominal value. The selling price concerns only the buyer and seller. The company is not affected and has only to record the change in the ownership of shares bearing certain distinguishing numbers.

It will be seen that a person may become a member of a company by signing the Memorandum on its formation, by applying for and being allotted shares, or by the transfer of shares to him by an existing shareholder.

The Statutory Books of a Company

Every company must keep certain books of record in addition to the proper books of account relating to its trading activities. In addition, many periodical returns to the Registrar of Companies have to be made.

THE REGISTER OF MEMBERS.—Under Section 110 of the Act every company must keep in one or more books a register of its members, and enter therein the following particulars:—

The names and addresses of the members.

A statement of the shares held by each member, distinguishing each share by its number (as long as the shares are numbered), and of the amount paid or agreed to be considered as paid on the shares of each member.

The date at which each person was entered as a member in the register.

The date at which any person ceased to be a member.

Every company having more than fifty members must keep an index of the names of the members unless the register of members is in a form as to constitute in itself an index. It may be a card index, and any necessary alteration in the index consequent on an alteration in the register must be made within fourteen days.

The register of members and the index must be kept at the company's registered office or office where the work is done and be available for inspection for not less than two hours each day during business hours.

There is no special form of register. It is sufficient if the ruling permits of the entry of the above information. In practice it is usual to find the Register of Members combined with the Share Ledger to which reference is made in a later chapter.

The register may be closed for a period not exceeding thirty days in the year on giving notice by advertisement. The purpose is to allow time for the preparation of the dividend lists. Most companies close their register for fourteen days prior to the date of the Annual General Meeting. Where there are different classes of shares, it is usually more convenient to have separate registers of each class of shareholders.

ANNUAL RETURN.—Under Section 124 of the 1948 Act, every company having a share capital must once at least in every year make a return containing a list of all persons who, on the fourteenth day after the first or only ordinary general meeting in the year, are members of the company, and of all persons who have ceased to be members since the date of the last return.

The list must state the names and addresses of all the past or present members therein mentioned, the shares held by them, the shares transferred since the last return, and the date of transfer. The company's registered address must be stated, and a complete summary of the company's capital must be given. The particulars required are given in Section 124 of the 1948 Act as extended/ amended by the 1967 Act, and in Schedules to these Acts. Forms suitably printed containing all the particulars required may be purchased from company or law stationers, and are used for the purpose of making the copy required to be forwarded annually to the Registrar of Companies. The actual return itself must be contained in a separate part of the Register of Members. The return must include a Profit and Loss Account and Balance Sheet, and Directors' Report, all conforming to the requirements of the Companies Acts.

MINUTE BOOK.—Under Section 145 of the Act every company shall cause minutes of all proceedings of general meetings and all proceedings of directors' meetings to be entered in books kept for that purpose. Members have the right to inspect the minutes of the general meetings of the shareholders and to copies of the minutes at a specified charge.

REGISTER OF DIRECTORS OR MANAGERS.—Under Section 200 every company shall keep at its registered office a register of its directors or managers containing full names, residential address, nationality, and occupation of each director or manager, and shall notify the Registrar of any change within fourteen days.

REGISTER OF MORTGAGES AND CHARGES.—Under Sections 95 to 106 every limited company shall keep at its registered office a register of charges and enter therein all charges specifically affecting the company's property and all floating charges and the names of the persons entitled thereto. Every such mortgage or charge and all releases therefrom must be registered with the Registrar of Companies.

The keeping of the above books is compulsory under the statute but, in addition, it is usual to find a Register of Transfers, a Register of Debenture holders, if debentures[1] have been issued, and a Register of Probates. Much depends upon the size of the company's capital

---

[1] The nature of debentures is explained in Chapter 38.

and the frequency of the changes in ownership of the shares as to how many additional books are required for efficiency in this branch of a company's office.

EXERCISES 35

1. State briefly the difference between (*a*) The Authorised Capital and the Issued Capital of a Limited Liability Company; (*b*) Preference Shares and Ordinary Shares in a Limited Liability Company.

2. What is meant by:—

(*a*) The Memorandum of Association;
(*b*) The Articles of Association

of a Joint Stock Company?

3. In what ways does a *Private* Limited Liability Company differ from a *Public* Limited Liability Company?

CHAPTER 36

COMPANY ACCOUNTS. SHARE CAPITAL AND THE ISSUE OF SHARES

The prospectus makes an offer of shares for subscription, and contains particulars regarding the number and kind of shares offered, and the way in which the shares may be paid for. The usual method is to accept payment by instalments through the company's bankers with whom it may be arranged that a special temporary account shall be opened to keep the payments separate from the ordinary banking account. The special Bank Statement is a help in checking the receipts, and the work of the share department does not affect the routine of the counting house.

The period during which applications may be received is limited— and for a first issue is fixed by Section 47 of the 1948 Act to forty days, so that the response to the offer may be known and the applications dealt with as a whole. The application forms are first checked against the Bank Statement and the total number of shares applied for is ascertained. If the offer is over-subscribed the directors must decide the method to adopt to reduce the applications to the limits of the offer. A proportionate reduction of all applications may answer the purpose, or applications for a small number of shares may be declined.

The next step is to allot the shares to the applicants. Allotment is the formal act of the directors expressed in a resolution that the shares be allotted to the applicants in accordance with the allotment list which is prepared and submitted to the meeting. The allotment list shows the names, addresses, and occupations of the applicants, the number of shares allotted to each of them, and the balance due on the shares. The applicants are notified by an Allotment Letter that the shares have been allotted to them, and the posting of these letters signifies the acceptance by the company of the offer of the applicants to take the shares. The contract between the applicant and the company is then complete, and the applicants, once allotment is made, become shareholders in the company and are liable for the balance due on the shares.

The allotment letter states the number of shares allotted, the sum already paid, the sum due upon allotment, and concludes with a request that the latter sum be paid forthwith.

The applicants for shares to whom no allotment is made have their application money returned in full. Applicants who are allotted a smaller number of shares than they applied for do not have part of their money returned to them. The amount they have overpaid on application is carried forward towards the amount due from them on allotment.

The company must make within one month a return of allotments to the Registrar of Companies, giving full particulars of the allottees, the number and nominal value of the shares allotted, and the amount paid or due and payable on each share.

If no allotment can be made to an applicant he is notified to this effect by a Letter of Regret, and his application money is returned.

Entries in the Accounts

The financial aspect of the issue of shares must be recorded, and the entries required are illustrated by the following example:—

The issue of Ordinary Shares only is illustrated. If the capital of a company is divided into several classes of shares, for example, Ordinary, Preference, and Deferred Shares, and a public issue was made of each, then separate accounts in the following form would be required for each class of shares. The company would have separate Registers of Members and Share Ledgers for each class of share.

Example 48.—Redman & Butcher Limited was registered with a nominal capital of £100,000 divided into 100,000 ordinary shares of £1 each. 80,000 shares are offered for public subscription on June 1st, 19.., payable by instalments as follows:—

£0·25 a share on application;
£0·25 a share on allotment;
£0·25 a share one month after allotment;
£0·25 a share two months after allotment.

All the shares offered were subscribed and allotted, and the application and allotment money received.

Show the entries required in the company's books to record the issue and allotment.

The first financial effect of the offer and subscription is the receipt of the application money. This is debited to the Cash Book. Often it is more convenient to have a temporary Shareholders' Cash

Book in use. The credit entry is made to an Application and Allotment Account in the Ledger as shown below.

The allotment is made and the allotment letters are posted. The instalments due on allotment are received and the entries required are similar to those for the application money. These also are shown below.

Dr.				Cash Book				Cr.
19..			£	19..				£
June 1	Application and Allotment Account being instalments of £0·25 a share on application	1	20000					
„ 8	Application and Allotment Account being instalments of £0·25 a share on allotment	1	20000					

1

Dr.			Application and Allotment Account				Cr.
19..			£	19..			£
				June 1	Cash— Application instalments	C.B.	20000
				„ 8	Cash— Allotment instalments	C.B.	20000

As the contract to take shares is completed by the posting of the allotment letters, the allottees are then actual shareholders, and the instalments paid by them are contributions towards the company's capital. At this point it is necessary to record that fact, which is done by transferring the balance of the Application and Allotment Account to a Share Capital Account in the Ledger. The effect is to close the Application and Allotment Account, which has served the purpose of a temporary resting place for the items, and to open, for the first time, a Capital Account in the Ledger. The transfer is made by Journal entry.

Journal

19.. June 5	Application and Allotment Account Dr. Ordinary Share Capital Account, being £0·25 a share on application, and £0·25 a share on allotment on 80,000 ordinary £1 shares by resolution of directors on 5th June, 19...	1 2	£ 40000	£ 40000

2

Dr.	Ordinary Share Capital Account					Cr.
19..		£	19.. June 5	Application and Allot- ment A/c.	J.	£ 40000

1

Dr.	Application and Allotment Account						Cr.
19.. June 5	Ordinary Share Capital Account	J.	£ 40000	19.. June 1 „ 8	Cash— Application instalments Cash— Allotment instalments	C.B. C.B.	£ 20000 20000
			£40000				£40000

It is, of course, essential to keep a record of the liability of the company to its members for the contributions each has made towards the capital of the company. The Ordinary Share Capital Account, as above, represents the total of the individual contributions; details are entered in the Share Ledger.

The Register of Members, mentioned in the preceding chapter, is usually ruled to contain Ledger Accounts as well as the particulars required as a register proper. Actually the Register is a combined Share Ledger and Register of Members, and it is in these Shareholders' Ledger Accounts that the individual contributions towards the company's capital are recorded. The Share Capital Account in the Ledger is a totals account, the details of which are to be found in the Share Ledger. It would be inconvenient to have a large number of individual Capital Accounts in the general Ledger, as the changes may be frequent and the Ledger would then be in constant demand for this purpose alone, to the exclusion of its use for general purposes.

Calls

The third and fourth instalments in the above example are due on certain dates. If no dates are given in the prospectus for the payment of the remaining instalments, they are payable at the discretion of the directors who are said to "make a call" on the shareholders. It is usual for the Articles to provide that any one call should not exceed 25 per cent. of the nominal value of the share, and for calls to be made at an interval of not less than one month.

The procedure in making a call is that the directors pass a resolution to the effect that a call be made, and send a Call Letter to the shareholders, giving, usually, fourteen days notice to pay the instalment due on their shares.

First Call

The passing of the resolution creates a liability on the part of the shareholders for the amount, and an entry is made through the Journal to the credit of the Share Capital Account and to the debit of a new account, the First Call Account.

As the cash is received from the shareholders the Cash Book is debited and the First Call Account is credited. The Call Account will show at any time whether all the calls have been received.

The combined entry in the Share Capital Account must be entered in detail in the shareholders' accounts in the Share Ledger so that the position of each shareholder is on record.

The entries for the first call are shown below:—

Journal

19..				£	£
July 5	First Call Account .. .. .. Dr.	3		20000	
	Ordinary Share Capital Account ..	2			20000
	being first call of £0·25 a share on 80,000 Ordinary £1 shares by the terms of the issue.				

2

Dr.				**Ordinary Share Capital Account**			*Cr.*
19..			£	19..			£
				June 5	Application and Allotment A/c.	J.	40000
				July 5	First Call Account ..	J.	20000

Dr.				First Call Account				3 Cr.
19..			£	19..				£
July 5	Ordinary Share Capi- tal A/c.	J.	20000	July 10	Cash	..	C.B.	20000

Dr.				Cash Book				Cr.
19..			£	19..				£
June 1	Application and Allot- ment A/c., being instal- ments of £0·25 a share on applica- tion ..	1	20000					
„ 8	Application and Allot- ment A/c., being instal- ments of £0·25 a share on allotment	1	20000					
July 10	First Call A/c., being first call of £0·25 a share ..	3	20000					

Final Call and Calls in Arrear

At due date of subsequent instalments, or on the directors resolving that a second or final call be made, the full amount is debited to a Second or Final Call Account, and is credited to the Share Capital Account.

For the final call of the above example the entries would be—

		Journal			£		£
19..							
Aug. 5	Second and Final Call Account .. Dr. Ordinary Share Capital Account .. .. being second and final call of £0·25 a share on 80,000 shares by the terms of the issue.			4 2	20000		20000

By way of illustration it may be assumed that a holder of 500 shares fails to pay the final call of £0.25 per share. The cash receipts will be £125 less in consequence, and the amount outstanding

2

Dr.				Ordinary Share Capital Account			Cr.
19..			£	19..			£
				June 5	Applications and Allotment A/c.	J.	40000
				July 5	First Call A/c.	J.	20000
				Aug. 5	Second and Final Call A/c. ..	J.	20000

will appear as a balance on the Call Account, remaining as such until payment is made or the directors decide to forfeit the shares.

The Call Account is given below.

As and when the call money is received the Cash Book is debited and a contra credit entry is made in the Call Account.

4

Dr.			£	19..			£
19.. Aug. 5	Ordinary Share Capital A/c. ..	J.	20000	Aug. 15 „ 15	Cash .. Balance ..	C.B. c/d	19875 125
			£20000				£20000
Aug. 16	Balance	b/d	125				

Second and Final Call Account

Dr.			£	19..			£
19.. June 1	Application and Allotments A/c., being instalments of £0·25 a share on application ..	1	20000	19..			£
„ 8	Application and Allotment A/c., being instalments of £0·25 a share on allotment	1	20000				
July 10	First Call A/c., being first						

Cash Book

Dr.   **Cash Book.** *Continued*   Cr.

19..			£	19..			
	call of £0·25 a share ..	3	20000				
Aug. 15	Second and Final Call Account, being final call of £0·25 a share ..	4	19875				

If the calls are still in arrear at the date of the preparation of the Balance Sheet it will be necessary to take them into account as debts due to the company, but the practice is to show them in the Balance Sheet as a deduction from the liability to which they relate and not as an asset.

The capital in the above example will therefore appear in the Balance Sheet as below. It should be observed that the Balance Sheet presents to the shareholders full information regarding the capital of the company. The issued capital is the only actual capital liability of the company. The authorised or nominal capital is ruled short as it is given for information only.

Balance Sheet, Redman & Butcher, Limited
(Showing left-hand side only)

	£	£
AUTHORISED CAPITAL		
100,000 Ordinary Shares of £1 each	100000	
ISSUED CAPITAL		
80,000 Ordinary Shares of £1 each fully called ..	80000	
less Calls in arrear	125	79875

The Balance Sheet of a company having different classes of shares should show each class of share separately.

Uncalled Capital

The directors may decide not to make calls until such times that the extra capital is needed, but as shares with a liability for calls are not popular as investments, the practice is now less frequent than formerly. Section 60 of the Act, however, provides that a company may, by special resolution, determine that the uncalled portion of its share capital shall not be capable of being called up except in the event and for the purposes of the company being wound up.

Calls in Advance

A company may be empowered by its Articles to accept calls in advance, and to pay a fixed rate of interest thereon. Such calls paid in advance of the general call being made are loans to the company at interest, and the interest is payable though the company may have made no profits.

Example 49.—A shareholder, Thomas Haynes, when making payment on 1st July of the first call, paid in advance the remaining instalment of £0·25 a share on 2000 £1 shares.

The payment in advance of £500 is debited to the Cash Book and credited to a Calls in Advance Account.

Dr.			**Calls in Advance Account**			*Cr.*
19..		£	19.. July 1	Cash— T. Haynes	C.B.	£ 500

When the directors make the call, the payment ceases to be in advance and becomes the shareholder's current instalment. A debit entry is then made to the Calls in Advance Account, which is thereby closed, and a corresponding credit entry is made in the Share Capital Account.

Should a Balance Sheet be prepared before the call is made, the call paid in advance will appear under that heading on the liability side.

The interest is usually paid half-yearly and should be recorded as follows:—

Journal

19.. Jan. 1	Interest Account .. .. Dr. Thomas Haynes .. .. being interest at 5% per annum on calls paid in advance for half-year to 31st December. (Income Tax is ignored.)	£ 12·5	£ 12·5

These entries will be posted to the respective Ledger Accounts. The payment by cheque will be credited to Cash and debited to Thomas Haynes's Account. The payment closes the shareholder's account and the balance of the Interest Account is transferred to the Profit and Loss Account on closing the books for the financial year.

EXERCISES 36

1. The Manchester Goods Company Limited, whose registered capital is 80,000 Ordinary Shares of £1 each, offered on 1st July 50,000 shares for public subscription, payable £0·12½ a share on application and £0·87½ on allotment.

All the shares were applied for and allotment was made on 16th July, and all the money was received by the company.

Make the entries to record the issue of the shares in the company's books, and show the statement of the company's capital in its Balance Sheet.

2. Godfrey & Co. Limited, registered with a capital of £120,000, comprising 120,000 Ordinary Shares of £1 each, offered 100,000 shares on 1st April for public subscription, payable £0·25 a share on application and £0·75 on allotment. All the shares were applied for and were allotted on 15th April. The cash was duly received.

Show the entries required to record the issue in the books of the company, and show how the capital would appear in the company's Balance Sheet.

3. Godfrey & Co. Limited, whose registered capital consists of £120,000 divided into 120,000 Ordinary Shares of £1 each, of which 100,000 shares have been issued, decide to issue the balance of its shares for public subscription on 1st October. The shares were payable, as to £0·12½ a share on application, £0·37½ a share on allotment, and £0·50 a share one month after allotment.

Record the issue in the company's books, all the shares being subscribed and allotted, and all instalments being paid at their due dates.

Show also the capital of the company as it would appear in its Balance Sheet.

4. Gilbert's Stores Limited was registered with a nominal capital of £75,000 divided into 75,000 Ordinary Shares of £1 each. Of these shares, 60,000 were offered for public subscription on 1st November, payable as to £0·12½ a share on application, £0·25 a share on allotment, and the balance one month after allotment. Show the entries required to record the issue in the books of the company on the basis that the whole of the issue was subscribed and allotted and all the cash received. Show also the capital as it would appear in the company's Balance Sheet.

5. Richard's Stores Limited, registered with a nominal capital of £50,000 consisting of 50,000 Ordinary Shares of £1 each, make a public issue on 15th March of 40,000 shares, payable as below:—

On application, £0·12½ a share.
On allotment, £0·37½ a share.
On 30th April, £0·25 a share.
On 30th June, £0·25 a share.

All the shares were applied for and allotted on 30th March, and all cash was received on allotment and for the two calls. Make the entries required to record the issue in the company's books, and show the capital as it should appear in the company's Balance Sheet.

6. Richmond & Co. Limited, registered with a capital of £60,000 in 60,000 Ordinary Shares of £1 each, offer for public subscription on 1st June, 50,000 shares payable as follows:—

£0·12½ a share on application.
£0·37½ a share on allotment.
£0·25 a share one month after allotment.
£0·25 a share two months later.

All the shares were subscribed for and allotted on 15th June, and all the cash received on allotment and for the two calls. Give the entries that are necessary to record the issue in the company's books, and show the company's capital as it should appear in its Balance Sheet.

7. Richmond & Kew Limited, registered with a capital of £150,000 divided into 150,000 Ordinary Shares of £1 each, offer, on 1st January, 120,000 shares for public subscription, the terms of payment being—

£0·12½ a share on application.
£0·37½ a share on allotment.
£0·25 a share on 15th February.
£0·25 on 15th March.

All the shares on offer were subscribed for and allotted, and all the money on application, allotment, and for both calls was received with the exception of the final call of £0·25 a share on 2,000 shares allotted to Henry Watson.

Give the entries required to record the issue in the books of the company, and show the capital as it would appear in the company's Balance Sheet.

8. Gillingham & Sons Limited was registered with a capital of £40,000, consisting of 40,000 shares of £1 each. An offer of 30,000 shares was made for public subscription on 1st May, payable, as to £0·12½ a share on application, £0·37½ a share on allotment, and £0·50 a share one month after allotment.

All the shares were subscribed for and allotted on 15th May, and all the cash due on allotment and for the final instalment was received with the exception of the call of £0·50 a share on 1,500 shares allotted to James Chatham.

Record the issue in the company's books, and show the capital as it should appear in the company's Balance Sheet.

9. Bedford & Luton Limited was registered with a capital of £100,000, comprising 40,000 6% Preference Shares of £1 each, and 60,000 Ordinary Shares of £1 each. All the Preference Shares and 50,000 Ordinary Shares were offered for public subscription on 1st October, payable in each case as follows:—

£0·12½ a share on application.
£0·37½ a share on allotment.
£0·50 a share on 1st December.

All the shares were subscribed for and allotted on 15th October, and the allotment money and the first call paid on due date.

Make the required entries in the books of the company, and show the company's capital as it would appear in the Balance Sheet.

10. Kent & Essex Limited, registered with a capital of £50,000 in 40,000 Ordinary Shares of £1 each and 10,000 6% Preference Shares of £1 each, offer for public subscription all the Preference Shares and 30,000 Ordinary Shares on 1st March, payable in each case to £0·12½ a share on application, £0·37½ a share on allotment, and £0·50 a share on 1st May.

All the shares offered were subscribed for and allotted on 15th March, and the allotment money received. In addition, B. Bryson and W. Tanner who subscribed for 400 Ordinary Shares and 600 Ordinary Shares respectively, paid the final instalment of £0·50 a share with their allotment instalment. Make the entries in the company's books as at allotment, and show how the capital of the company would then appear in its Balance Sheet.

11. Explain the difference in treatment in the books of account between (a) a Partner's Capital Account, and (b) a Share Capital Account of a company limited by shares. *R.S.A.*

CHAPTER 37

THE ISSUE OF SHARES. THE PURCHASE OF A BUSINESS BY A COMPANY

The Issue of Shares at a Premium

Where the market price of a company's shares is above par, the amount by which the market price exceeds the nominal value of the share is termed the premium.

When new shares of the same class are issued, they are very often issued at a premium equal to the premium at which the already issued shares stand. This would bring to the company a sum over and above the nominal value of the issue, which would increase its financial resources but cannot be regarded as part of its issued capital. The premiums are in the nature of a capital profit, and under the Companies Acts must be transferred to an account called the "Share Premium Account."

This account is considered part of the company's capital and may only be reduced under the following circumstances:—

(a) In writing off the preliminary expenses[1] of the company.

(b) In writing off any expenses or commission paid, or discount allowed on, the issue of any shares or debentures[2] of the company.

(c) In providing for the premium payable on redeeming any of the company's redeemable preference shares or debentures.[2]

If not used in any of the foregoing ways the Share Premium Account may be used for issuing bonus shares.

So long as there is any balance left in the Share Premium Account it must be shown as a separate item in the Balance Sheet.

Should the premium be used for writing down any of the items allowed in the Act the writing down is effected by a credit entry to the Expense Account and a corresponding debit entry to the Share Premium Account, the entry being first passed through the Journal.

Example 50.—Redman & Butcher Limited, whose nominal capital is 100,000 Ordinary Shares of £1 each, of which 80,000 shares have been issued and fully paid up, decide to offer the unissued capital for subscription

---

[1] The nature of these expenses is explained on page 362.
[2] The nature of debentures is explained in Chapter 38.

at £1·50 a share, payable as to £0·25 a share on application, £1·00 a share (including the premium of £0·50 a share) on allotment, and £0·25 a share two months after allotment.

All the shares were subscribed and were allotted on 5th July. The allotment money was paid by 8th July and the calls by 8th September.

In the example, as is usual in practice, the premium is payable with the instalment due on allotment and a combined Journal entry is made for the allotment instalment and the premium.

The entries for the application and allotment instalments and the final call follow the procedure already illustrated. The new point is the treatment of the premium on the shares.

The following are the entries required:—

Journal

19..				£	£
July 5	Application and Allotment Account Dr.	2		25000	
	Ordinary Share Capital Account	1			15000
	Premium on Ordinary Shares Account ..	3			10000
	being £0·25 a share on application and £1·00 per share, including £0·50 premium a share, on allotment on 20,000 Ordinary £1 shares allotted by resolution of Directors dated 5th July, 19...				
Sept. 8	First and Final Call Account .. Dr.	4		5000	
	Ordinary Share Capital Account	1			5000
	being first and final call of £0·25 a share on 20,000 shares by terms of issue.				

Below are the Ledger Accounts for the new issue, the new account being the Premium on Ordinary Shares Account in which the premium is recorded.

1

Dr.   Ordinary Share Capital Account   Cr.

19..			£	19..			£
Sept. 8	Balance	c/d	100000	Jan. 1	Balance (original issue)	b/d	80000
				July 5	Applications and Allotments A/c. (New issue)	J.	15000
				Sept. 8	First and Final Call A/c. (new issue) ..	J.	5000
			£100000				£100000
				Sept. 8	Balance ..	b/d	100000

Dr. **Application and Allotment Account** *Cr.* 2

19..			£	19..				£
July 5	Ordinary Share Capital Account	J.	15000	July 6	Cash— Application instalment	C.B.		5000
	Premium on Shares A/c. ..	J.	10000	,, 8	Cash— Allotment instalment and premium ..	C.B.		20000
			£25000					£25000

Dr. **Premium on Ordinary Shares Account** *Cr.* 3

19..			£	19..			£
				July 8	Application and Allotment A/c.	J.	10000

Dr. **First and Final Call Account** *Cr.* 4

19..			£	19..			£
Sept. 8	Ordinary Share Capital Account	J	5000	Sept. 8	Cash ..	C.B.	5000

Dr. **Cash Book** *Cr.*

19..			£	19..		£
July 6	Application and Allotment A/c.	2	5000			
July 8	Application and Allotment A/c., being £0·50 a share on allotment and £0·50 a share premium ..	2	20000			
Sept. 8	First and Final Call Account ..	4	5000			

The capital of the company and the premium will appear in the Balance Sheet as below:—

Balance Sheet, Redman & Butcher Limited
(Showing left-hand side only)

	£		£
AUTHORISED CAPITAL			
100,000 Ordinary Shares of £1 each	100000		
ISSUED CAPITAL			
100,000 Ordinary Shares of £1 each, fully paid ..			100000
Premium on Ordinary Shares Account			10000

The Issue of Shares at a Discount

Section 57 of the Companies Act, 1948, makes it possible for companies to issue shares at a discount. This provision is of value to a company whose issued shares stand at a discount as often in such circumstances it is difficult to obtain subscriptions to a further issue of shares at par value. The section, however, imposes the following restrictions:—

The proposed issue must be of a class already issued, and must be authorised by resolution passed in general meeting of the company, and must be sanctioned by the court.

The resolution must specify the maximum rate of discount.

The issue may be made only after the expiration of one year from the date on which the company was entitled to commence business.

The shares must be issued within one month of the date of sanction by the court or within such extended time that the court may allow.

Every prospectus and balance sheet issued subsequent to the issue of such shares must state the discount allowed or so much thereof that has not been written off.

Example 51.—Redman & Butcher Limited, whose nominal capital is 100,000 Ordinary Shares of £1 each, of which 80,000 shares are issued and fully paid up, decide to offer the unissued capital for subscription at a discount of 10%, payable as to £0·25 a share on application, £0·25 a share on allotment, and £0·40 a share two months after allotment.

All the shares were subscribed and were alloted on 5th July. The allotment money was paid on 8th July and the final instalment on 8th September.

Show the entries for the issue in the company's books and how the capital would appear in the company's Balance Sheet.

The entries for the applications and allotment follow the procedure already illustrated. The final instalment is affected by the discount, and the following entries are required on the call being made:—

Journal

19..				£	£
Sept. 8	First and Final Call Account Dr.	2		8000	
	Discount on Ordinary Shares Account Dr.	3		2000	
	Ordinary Share Capital Account ..	1			10000
	being first and final call of £0·40 a share on 20,000 Ordinary £1 shares and the discount of 10% thereon.				

1

Dr.   **Ordinary Share Capital Account**   *Cr.*

19..			£	19..				£
				Jan. 1	Balance (original issue)	b/d	80000
				July 5	Application and Allotment (new issue) ..		10000
				Sept. 8	First and Final Call Account (new issue)	J.	8000
				„ 8	Discount on Shares A/c.	J.	2000

2

Dr.   **First and Final Call Account**   *Cr.*

19..			£	19..			£
Sept. 8	Ordinary Share Capital Account	J.	8000	Sept. 8	Cash ..	C.B.	8000

3

Dr.   **Discount on Ordinary Shares Account**   *Cr.*

19..			£	19..			£
Sept. 8	Ordinary Share Capital Account —10% discount on 20,000 £1 shares ..	J.	2000				

Dr.			Cash Book			Cr.
		£	19..			£
19..						
Sept. 8	First and Final Call of £0·40 per share on 20,000 £1 shares	2	8000			

The discount appears in the Balance Sheet as below, but steps should be taken to write off the amount as soon as possible.

Balance Sheet. 8th September, 19..

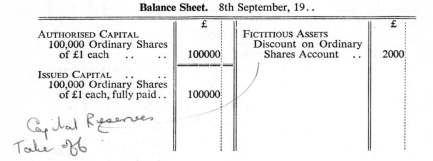

	£		£
AUTHORISED CAPITAL 100,000 Ordinary Shares of £1 each	100000	FICTITIOUS ASSETS Discount on Ordinary Shares Account . .	2000
ISSUED CAPITAL . . . . 100,000 Ordinary Shares of £1 each, fully paid. .	100000		

Capital Reserves

Take off

Stock

Under Section 62 of the 1948 Act a company, if so authorised by its Articles, may, in general meeting, decide (*a*) to increase its share capital by new shares; (*b*) to consolidate and then divide its capital into shares of larger amount than its existing shares; (*c*) to subdivide its shares into shares of smaller amount; (*d*) to convert all or any of its paid up shares into stock and to reconvert the stock again into shares; and (*e*) to cancel that part of its authorised capital represented by unissued shares.

To convert shares into stock is to convert an aggregate of shares into one mass or block of capital. The holder of 100 shares of £1 each then holds, not 100 separate shares each bearing a distinguishing number, but a £100 portion of the total block of stock forming the company's capital.

Stock is usually transferable in units, of, *e.g.*, £5 or multiples thereof. In some cases smaller units are permitted and even fractions of a pound as with Government stocks. The same procedure for transfer applies to stock as for shares.

The Purchase of Business by a Company

An existing company may buy an additional business or a company may be formed for the express purpose of taking over a going concern. The purchase price may be paid wholly in cash or partly in cash and partly in shares in the company, or as in some cases, wholly in shares. The method of payment is arranged between the company and the vendor of the business. If the company makes a public issue of shares to obtain capital to make the purchase, the statement in the prospectus that the vendor is to be paid either wholly or in part in shares encourages investors, as it may be taken as a sign that the vendor has himself faith in the future prospects of the concern under the new ownership. The shares allotted as consideration for the purchase become part of the issued capital of the company.

It is essential to know the terms of the contract under which the business is to be acquired. It is probable that the purchase price will include payment for Goodwill and for the assets, which may or may not include the cash balance. If the liabilities are taken over it is usual for the vendor to guarantee that they shall not exceed the figures in the agreed Balance Sheet.

The entries in the company's books to record the purchase of a business will be similar to those discussed in Chapter 27, with the possible addition of the allotment of shares as part of the purchase price. In some instances a special issue of shares, part of the company's unissued capital, is made to finance the purchase. The procedure for the issue and allotment will follow the usual course already described.

The following example illustrates the purchase price being paid partly in cash and partly in shares.

Example 52.—Weston & Sons Limited was registered with a capital of £150,000 divided into 100,000 Ordinary Shares of £1 each and 50,000 6% Preference Shares of £1 each. The company was formed to acquire an existing business as from 1st January, taking over the following assets and liabilities:—

	£
Freehold Premises	25000
Plant and Machinery	22000
Stock	19000
Sundry Debtors	11000
Sundry Creditors	7000

The purchase price, including Goodwill, was £80,000, payable as to £30,000 in cash and as to £50,000 in fully paid Ordinary Shares.

The directors subscribed for 10,000 Ordinary Shares and paid in full on allotment. The whole of the Preference Share capital was offered for public subscription and was fully paid up. Preliminary expenses amounted to £2,000.

Give the Journal entries and the Cash Book entries to record these transactions, and show the opening Balance Sheet of the company.

Journal

19..		£	£
Jan. 1	Business Purchase Account .. Dr.	80000	
	Vendor's Account		80000
	being purchase price by contract dated..		
	Freehold Premises.. .. .. Dr.	25000	
	Plant and Machinery .. .. Dr.	22000	
	Stock .. .. Dr.	19000	
	Sundry Debtors .. .. .. Dr.	11000	
	Goodwill .. .. Dr.	10000	
	Business Purchase Account		87000
	being assets taken over by contract dated..		
	Business Purchase Account .. Dr.	7000	
	Sundry Creditors		7000
	being liabilities as by contract dated..		
	Vendor's Account .. .. .. Dr.	50000	
	Ordinary Share Capital Account ..		50000
	being 50,000 £1 Ordinary Shares allotted fully paid as part purchase price.		
	Ordinary Shares Application and Allotment Account .. .. .. Dr.	10000	
	Ordinary Share Capital Account ..		10000
	being 10,000 £1 Ordinary Shares allotted by Directors' resolution dated..		
	Preference Shares Application and Allotment Account .. .. .. Dr.	50000	
	Preference Share Capital Account ..		50000
	being application and allotment money on 50,000 £1 Preference Shares alloted by resolution of Directors dated ..		

The preliminary expenses incurred cover such items as the legal charges, stamp duty, and printing costs on the formation of the company. For present purposes it is sufficient to remark that they are treated as capital expenditure, and as such appear among the assets in the Balance Sheet. Such an item included in the assets is sometimes referred to as a "fictitious asset" and it is usual for this item to be written off out of profits over a series of years.

Dr.				Cash Book				Cr.
19..			£	19..				£
Jan. 1	Preference Shares Application and Allotment Account		50000	Jan. 1	Vendor ..			30000
				„ 1	Preliminary Expenses			2000
				„ 1	Balance ..	c/d		28000
„ 1	Ordinary Shares Application and Allotment Account		10000					
			£60000					£60000
Jan. 2	Balance ..	b/d	28000					

Balance Sheet, Weston & Sons, Limited

	£	£		£	£
AUTHORISED CAPITAL			FIXED ASSETS		
50,000 6% Preference Shares of £1 each	50000		Goodwill	10000	
100,000 Ordinary Shares of £1 each	100000		Freehold Premises ..	25000	
		150000	Plant and Machinery	22000	
					57000
ISSUED CAPITAL			CURRENT ASSETS		
50,000 6% Preference Shares of £1 each ..	50000		Stock..	19000	
60,000 Ordinary Shares of £1 each.. ..	60000		Sundry Debtors ..	11000	
		110000	Cash	28000	
					58000
CURRENT LIABILITIES			FICTITIOUS ASSETS		
Sundry Creditors ..	7000		Preliminary Expenses	2000	
		7000			2000
		£117000			£117000

In some instances debentures may be issued and allotted by a company in payment of the purchase price. Entries similar to those for shares would be required. The nature and issue of debentures form the subject-matter of the next chapter.

EXERCISES 37

1. York & Lancaster Limited, whose authorised capital is £100,000 in 100,000 Ordinary Shares of £1·00 each, of which 60,000 have been issued, offer the remaining 40,000 shares for public subscription on 1st June at a premium of £0·25 a share, payable as follows:—

£0·12½ a share on application.
£0·62½ a share, including the premium, on allotment.
£0·50 a share one month after allotment.

All the shares offered were subscribed for and were allotted on 15th June, and all the cash due on allotment and for the final instalment was received at due date.

Make the necessary entries in the company's books, and show the capital and the premium as it would stand in the company's Balance Sheet.

2. A company issued 40,000 Ordinary Shares of £1 each at a premium of £0·05 per share. The amounts due upon the shares were payable as follows: £0·55 per share on application (including the premium); £0·25 per share on allotment; and £0·25 per share three months after allotment. All the shares were duly applied for and the cash paid with the exception of the final call on 1,000 shares. Show the entries necessary to record the above transactions in the books of the company, and draw up a Balance Sheet.   *N.C.T.E.C.*

3. A limited company was registered with a nominal capital of £150,000, divided into 50,000 6% Preference Shares of £1 each, and 100,000 Ordinary Shares of £1 each. The Preference Shares were offered for subscription at par, and the Ordinary Shares at a premium of £0·12½ per share. On February 1st, 19.., the public subscribed for 45,000 Preference Shares and 80,000 Ordinary Shares, payable as follows:—

On application, £0·12½ per share in both cases; on allotment (February 10th) £0·25 per share on the Preference Shares, and £0·37½ per share (including the premium) on the Ordinary Shares. On March 15th, £0·62½ per share in both cases.

On March 20th, all moneys due on the shares had been received except the final call on 100 Preference Shares which remained outstanding.

Submit the entries necessary to record the above issue in the books of the company.   *R.S.A.*

4. On January 1st, 19.., Blanks Limited offered for public subscription 100,000 Ordinary Shares of £1 each at £1·50 per share, payable as to £0·50 per share on application, and £1·00 per share (including premium) on January 15th. The public applied for 115,000 shares, and duly paid the application moneys. 100,000 shares were allotted on January 17th, and application moneys were returned to the unsuccessful applicants. The final call was duly paid on or before the due date.

Give the entries necessary to record the above share issue in the company's books.   *R.S.A.*

5. Townley & Sons Limited, whose registered capital is £120,000, consisting of 120,000 Ordinary Shares of £1 each, of which 80,000 have been issued and are fully paid, have received the sanction of the Court to issue the remainder of its capital at a discount of 5%, payable £0·25 a share on application, £0·25 a share on allotment, and £0·45 a share two months after allotment. All the shares offered were subscribed for and were allotted on 15th June. All the cash due on allotment and for the final instalment was received. Show the entries for the issue in the books of the company, and show the capital of the company as it should appear in its next Balance Sheet.

6. Beauval & Woodwarde Limited obtained the sanction of its shareholders in general meeting and of the Court to offer its unissued capital of 50,000 £1 Ordinary Shares for public subscription at a discount of 10%. The shares were payable £0·12½ on application, £0·37½ on allotment, and £0·40 two months after allotment.

All the shares were subscribed for and were allotted on 15th May, and all the cash due on allotment and on 15th July was received.

Show the entries for the issue in the company's books, and how the capital would appear in the company's Balance Sheet.

7. The Balance Sheet of Grace and Robins at 31st December 19.. is as follows:—

Balance Sheet, Grace and Robins, 31st December, 19...

	£			£
Grace, Capital Account ..	4750	Goodwill		250
Robins, ditto	7236	Land and buildings		3100
Bank Overdraft	464	Machinery and plant		2720
Bills Payable	300	Fixtures and fittings		416
Sundry creditors	1250	Stock		4891
		Debtors	2340	
		Less Reserve for bad		
		debts	117	
				2223
		Bills Receivable ..		400
	£14000			£14000

On 31st December, 19.., the business was acquired by Grace & Co. Ltd., specially formed for that purpose, with a nominal capital of 15,000 Ordinary Shares of £1 each, and 15,000 6% Preference Shares of £1 each.

The company took over all the assets except the Bills Receivable, and undertook to pay off the sundry creditors, but not the Bank Overdraft nor the Bills Payable. The purchase consideration was £15,000 consisting of 10,000 £1 Ordinary Shares and 4,000 £1 Preference Shares and the balance in cash.

The company revalued the land and buildings at £3,800, and the machinery and plant at £2,500.

On the 31st January the balance of the Ordinary Shares was issued to the public, and by the 28th February all moneys due had been received. On the 28th February, the purchase consideration was discharged. The preliminary expenses paid were £436.

You are required to give—

(1) The Journal entries in the books of Grace & Co. Ltd.
(2) All the Ledger Accounts affected in the books of Grace & Co. Ltd.
(3) The Balance Sheet as on the 28th February, 19... *U.E.I.*

8. Enterprise Limited was registered in 19.. with a nominal capital of £500,000, divided into 250,000 7% Preference Shares of £1 each, and 500,000 Ordinary Shares of £0·50 each.

The company was formed to acquire an established business, the purchase price, £300,000, including Goodwill, being payable as follows: £50,000 in Preference Shares, £50,000 in Ordinary Shares (both fully paid), £100,000 in 4½% Debenture Stock[1], and the balance in cash.

The balance of the Preference Shares were subscribed by the public and fully paid up, and 200,000 Ordinary Shares were subscribed by the Directors and fully paid up.

---

[1] This is dealt with in Chapter 38.

The assets and liabilities taken over (at agreed values) were—

	£			£
Freehold works	75000	Plant and machinery ..		31000
Stock	66000	Sundry debtors		112000
Patents and trade marks ..	8000	Sundry creditors		12000

Give the Journal entries necessary to record the above transactions in the books of the Company, and show its initial Balance Sheet.   *R.S.A.*

9. Chatenays Limited was registered with a nominal capital of £200,000 (100,000 Ordinary Shares of £1 each and 100,000 6% Preference Shares of £1 each), to purchase the old-established business of Abel Chatenay. The purchase price was agreed at £120,000, payable as to £30,000 in cash, £40,000 in Ordinary Shares of £1 each, and £50,000 in 6% Preference Shares of £1 each.

The company was to discharge the liabilities of the old firm.

The Balance Sheet of Abel Chatenay as on the date of purchase was as follows:—

Balance Sheet

	£			£
Capital	100000	Freehold works		36000
Creditors	14040	Machinery and plant ..		37860
Bank loan	2000	Sundry debtors		18764
		Stock		22440
		Cash in hand		976
	£116040			£116040

The balance of the Ordinary and Preference Shares was issued to the public and fully subscribed and paid up.

Prepare the accounts necessary to record the above purchase in the company's books, and give the initial Balance Sheet of the new company.   *R.S.A.*

10. A. Alpha carried on business as a manufacturer and his position at 31st December, 19.., was as follows:—Freehold property, £5,000; loan from J. Alpha, £1,200; machinery, £3,250; debtors, £3,786; creditors, £1,100; balance at bank, £254; and cash in hand, £10.

It had been arranged that a limited company should be formed to take over all the assets and liabilities of the business as shown for the purchase price of £15,000 and the price was to be satisfied by the issue of 15,000 shares of £1 each.

A. Alpha Limited was duly formed with an authorised capital of £20,000 divided into shares of £1 each, and the transfer took place on 1st January, 19.., when the remaining 5,000 shares were allotted to J. Alpha, as to £3,800 in consideration of cash and as to the balance in consideration of the cancellation of his loan.

Draft the Balance Sheet of the company on the completion of these transactions.   *R.S.A.*

CHAPTER 38

COMPANY ACCOUNTS. LOAN CAPITAL. DEBENTURES

The legal process of increasing the share capital of a company is not difficult, and many companies take this step to increase the working capital. Other companies may require the use of additional cash resources for developments but, owing to the state of the market for their shares, they may be able to obtain further cash only by offering greater security to the investor. Moreover an increase in the share capital involves a wider spread of the profits by way of dividend, and, unless profits increase in proportion, this may lead to diminution in the dividend percentage. In such cases a company may raise money by means of loans which are often referred to as the loan capital of the company.

As security for the money lent, the company may charge to the lender certain of the company's assets or may give a floating charge over the whole of the company's assets including its stock and book debts.

The document issued to the lender acknowledging the debt and creating a charge in his favour on the company's property, is called a Debenture.

A debenture issue may be made for public subscription and, in such circumstances, the terms of payment of interest and of repayment of the capital will be included in the debentures. Property specifically charged to the debenture holders cannot be disposed of or otherwise dealt in by the company to the detriment of the debenture holders. In the event of default in regard to any covenant entered into, the debenture holders may take possession and deal with the property charged to them. A floating charge covering all the property of the company, including its stock, cash, and book debts, does not, however, prevent the company dealing with these in the ordinary course of business. It gives the debenture holders priority to all other creditors should they have to intervene owing to the company's default in payment of interest or in repayment of capital.

Debentures containing a specific charge are often referred to as Mortgage Debentures. They must be registered, as must be all charges on the company's property, with the Registrar of Companies.

Debentures are usually of £100 each, and the issue of a series involves entries in the books of account similar to those for an issue of shares. A sum is payable on application and the remainder by periodical instalments, but usually the balance is payable in full on allotment.

Debenture interest is usually paid half-yearly, and as it is a debt due from the company secured by the terms of the debenture, it is payable whether profits have been made or not, and outstanding debenture interest must be brought into account as an accrued liability at the close of an accounting period. This point should not be overlooked by students as the fact that interest is outstanding is sometimes purposely omitted from the items in an examination test.

Debentures are transferable and the common form of transfer is used. Debentures also may be converted into debenture stock so that a holder of one £100 debenture of a series of fifty such debentures would, under the conversion, become the holder of £100 of debenture stock, or in other words, of a one-fiftieth portion of the total block of £5,000 of stock.   Debentures may be transferred only as units. Debenture stock may be transferred in multiples or fractions of a pound. Debenture stock must be fully paid where debentures may be partly paid. Debentures may be issued at par, at a discount, or at a premium, and there are no restrictive conditions on the issue of debentures at a discount as there are for shares.

Debenture holders are merely loan creditors of the company. They are not members of the company, though Section 158 of the 1948 Act states that a copy of the last Balance Sheet and a copy of the last Profit and Loss Account, together with the auditor's report, must be sent to all holders of debentures of a public company.

The Issue of Debentures

The following example illustrates the record required for an issue of debentures.

Example 53.—Redman & Butcher Limited offered for public subscription on 1st July, 19. ., 500 5% Debentures of £100 each, payable as to £20 a debenture on application, £30 a debenture on allotment, and £50 a debenture two months after allotment. The whole of the debenture issue was subscribed and allotment was made on 6th July. The final instalment was paid on 6th September.

Show the entries for the issue in the company's books and how the debentures should appear in the company's Balance Sheet.

It will be observed from the working of the example shown below that the entries in the books of account for a debenture issue are similar to those for an issue of shares as discussed in an earlier chapter.

Journal

19..			£	£
July 6	5% Debenture Application and Allotment Account .. .. Dr.	2	25000	
	5% Debentures Account	1		25000
	being £20 a debenture on application and £30 a debenture on allotment on 500 5% debentures allotted on resolution of directors, dated 6th July, 19...			
Sept. 6	Call Account (5% Debentures) .. Dr.	3	25000	
	5% Debentures Account	1		25000
	being final instalment of £50 each on 500 5% Debentures by the conditions of issue.			

1

Dr.   **5% Debentures Account**   *Cr.*

19..			£	19..			£
				July 6	Application and Allotment A/c.	J.	25000
				Sept. 6	First and Final Call Account	J.	25000

2

Dr.   **5% Debentures Application and Allotment Account**   *Cr.*

19..			£	19..			£
July 6	5% Debentures A/c.	J.	25000	July 3	Cash ..	C.B.	10000
				„ 10	„ ..	C.B.	15000
			£25000				£25000

3

Dr.   **First and Final Call (Debentures) Account**   *Cr.*

19..			£	19..			£
Sept. 6	5% Debentures A/c.	J.	25000	Sept. 6	Cash ..	C.B.	25000

Dr.				Cash Book			Cr.
19..			£	19..			£
July 3	Application A/c.		10000				
,, 10	Allotment A/c. ..	2	15000				
Sept. 6	First and Final Call	3	25000				

The 5% Debentures Account is a total account comprising the sundry amounts subscribed by the debenture holders. The details appear in a Register of Debenture Holders which contains a Ledger Account for each debenture holder.

The debenture issue is shown in the Balance Sheet as a liability. The issue is usually placed immediately below the share capital, as in the following illustration. It is assumed, for the purpose of illustration, that the share capital is as shown in the Balance Sheet on page 351.

Balance Sheet, Redman & Butcher Limited
(Showing left-hand side only)

	£	£
AUTHORISED CAPITAL		
100,000 Ordinary Shares of £1 each	100000	
ISSUED CAPITAL		
80,000 Ordinary Shares of £1 each, fully called ..	80000	
Less Calls in arrear	125	
		79875
LOAN CAPITAL		
5% DEBENTURES		
500 Debentures of £100 each, fully paid		50000

Issue of Debentures at a Discount

A company may be authorised by its Articles of Association to issue debentures at a discount. Had the company, in the above example, doubted the success of an issue at par, they may have sought to make the issue more attractive by offering £100 debentures at £98 each. The interest is payable on the par value so that the investor obtains a higher return on the money he actually invests. Further, the debenture for which £98 is subscribed may contain an undertaking to repay at par value or even higher at a later date.

Example 54.—Redman & Butcher Limited offer for public subscription on 1st July, 19.., 500 5% Debentures of £100 each at a price of £98 each payable as to £20 a debenture on application, £30 a debenture on allotment, and £48 a debenture two months after allotment. The whole issue was subscribed and allotted on 6th July. The final instalment was paid on 6th September.

The full face value of the issue is £50,000 which is the extent of the company's liability to the debenture holders. Only £49,000 is received in actual cash as there is a discount of £1,000 on the issue. The full liability must be recorded in the books and shown in the Balance Sheet. The discount is posted to a separate account and shown on the assets side of the Balance Sheet. In effect it is part of the cost of the debenture issue. The amount is written off against profits during the life of the debentures.

The Journal and Ledger entries for the example are as shown below:—

Journal

19..				£	£
July 6	5% Debentures Application and Allotment Account .. .. Dr.	2		25000	
	5% Debentures Account ..	1			25000
	being £20 a debenture on application and £30 a debenture on allotment on 500 5% Debentures allotted on resolution of Directors, dated 6th July, 19..				
Sept. 6	Call Account (5% Debentures) .. Dr.	3		24000	
	5% Debentures Account	1			24000
	being final instalment of £48 a debenture on 500 5% Debentures issued at £98 by the conditions of issue.				
Sept. 6	Debenture Discount Account .. Dr.	4		1000	
	5% Debentures Account	1			1000
	being discount of £2 a debenture on 500 5% Debentures issued at £98.				

1

Dr.				£	5% Debenture Account			*Cr.*
19..					19..			£
					July 6	Application and Allotment A/c. ..	J.	25000
					Sept. 6	First and Final Call A/c. ..	J.	24000
					„ 6	Debenture Discount A/c.	J.	1000

2

Dr.	5% Debentures Application and Allotment Account								Cr.
19..			£	19..					£
July 6	5% Debentures A/c.	J.	25000	July 3	Cash	..	C.B.		10000
				„ 10	„	..	C.B.		15000
			£25000						£25000

3

Dr.	First and Final Call (Debentures) Account								Cr.
19..			£	19..					£
Sept. 6	5% Debentures A/c.	J.	24000	Sept. 6	Cash	..	C.B.		24000

4

Dr.	Debenture Discount Account						Cr.
19..			£	19..			£
Sept. 6	5% Debentures A/c.	J.	1000				

Dr.	Cash Book						Cr.
19..			£	19..			£
July 3	Application A/c. (Debentures)	2	10000				
„ 10	Allotment Account (Debentures)	2	15000				
Sept. 6	First and Final Call (Debentures) ..	3	24000				

Balance Sheet

	£			£
LOAN CAPITAL— 5% DEBENTURES 500 Debentures of £100 each, fully paid ..	50000		FICTITIOUS ASSETS Debenture Discount	1000

Issue of Debentures at a Premium

Debentures, like shares, may be issued at a premium to take full advantage of the popularity of the company's securities and the demand for them in the investment market.

Example 55.—Redman & Butcher Limited offer for public subscription on 1st July, 19.., 500 5% Debentures of £100 each at a price of £102 each, payable as to £20 a debenture on application, £32 a debenture on allotment, including the premium, and £50 two months after allotment. The whole issue was subscribed and allotted on 6th July. The final instalment was paid on 6th September.

Show the entries required in the company's books and how the debenture issue and the premium should appear in the Balance Sheet.

The entries for the applications and allotment will follow the usual procedure. The premium is treated similarly to the premium on shares, requiring the opening of a "Premium on Debentures Account".

The entries for the example are shown below:—

Journal

19..
July 6
	5% Debentures Application and Allotment
	Account .. .. Dr.
	   5% Debentures Account .. .. ..
	   Debentures Premium Account .. ..
	being £20 a debenture on application and £32 (including premium of £2) a debenture on allotment on 500 5% Debentures allotted on resolution of Directors, dated 6th July.
		£
		26000
			£
			
			25000
			1000

Sept. 6	Call Account (5% Debentures) .. .. Dr. 5% Debentures Account .. .. .. being final instalment of £50 a debenture on 500 5% Debentures by the terms of issue.	25000	 25000

1

Dr.   **5% Debentures Account**   *Cr.*

19..			£	19.. July 6	Application and Allotment A/c.	J.	£ 25000
				Sept. 6	First and Final Call Account ..	J.	25000

2

Dr.   **5% Debentures Application and Allotment Account**   *Cr.*

19.. July 6	5% Debentures Account ..	J.	£ 25000	19.. July 3 „ 10	Cash .. „ ..	C.B. C.B.	£ 10000 16000

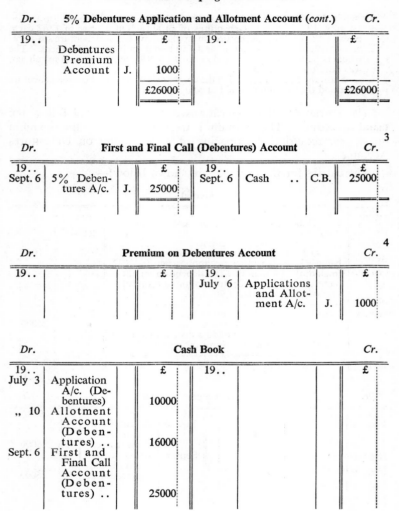

Dr.	5% Debentures Application and Allotment Account (*cont.*)		Cr.

19..	Debentures Premium Account	J.	£ 1000	19..			£
			£26000				£26000

3

Dr.	First and Final Call (Debentures) Account					Cr.

19.. Sept. 6	5% Debentures A/c.	J.	£ 25000	19.. Sept. 6	Cash ..	C.B.	£ 25000

4

Dr.	Premium on Debentures Account				Cr.

19..			£	19.. July 6	Applications and Allotment A/c.	J.	£ 1000

Dr.	Cash Book			Cr.

19.. July 3	Application A/c. (Debentures)		£ 10000	19..			£
„ 10	Allotment Account (Debentures) ..		16000				
Sept. 6	First and Final Call Account (Debentures) ..		25000				

    The premium on debentures is not part of the loan capital but is a gain to the company. Though the premium may be treated as ordinary revenue, the usual policy is to regard it as capital reserve and to retain it to strengthen the financial resources. As such it must be shown separately as a liability in the Balance Sheet.

Balance Sheet
(Showing left-hand side only)

	£
LOAN CAPITAL	
5% DEBENTURES	
500 Debentures of £100 each, fully paid	50000
Premium on Debentures Account	1000

Debentures as Collateral Security

Sometimes debentures are issued as security for a loan. The company's bankers may make an advance by loan or overdraft and debentures for a nominal value of 10% to 15% above the amount of the loan may be deposited with them. The company's liability to the bankers is the amount of the loan or overdraft and not the value of the debentures. The bankers do not receive interest on them or exercise any powers under them unless the company makes default on the loan. No entries are made in the books for the debentures, but the fact that they have been issued and given as collateral security should be noted against the heading of the Loan Account in the Ledger, and must be disclosed in the Balance Sheet as below:—

Balance Sheet
(Left-hand side only)

	£
LOAN CAPITAL	
Loan from Bankers	4500
(Secured by an issue of £5,000 5% Debentures)	

Expenses of Debenture Issues

The expenses involved by a debenture issue have been ignored in the above examples. With every issue, printing, advertising, and law costs as well as stamp duty, filing fees, and, possibly, underwriting commission have to be paid. These will be debited to a Debenture Issue Expenses Account in the Ledger, the balance of which represents the total expense of the debenture issue. The balance of the account must be shown as a temporary asset in the Balance Sheet in so far as it is not written off. The amount may be written off by instalments during the life of the debenture issue. By this method the cost of the issue is spread over the period of the debentures instead of being charged in one sum against the profits of the year of issue.

EXERCISES 38

1. The authorised capital of Newton & Co. Limited is £150,000, consisting of 50,000 6% Preference Shares of £1 each and 100,000 Ordinary Shares of £1 each, all of which have been issued and are fully paid. It is decided to offer for public subscription on 1st June, 1,000 5% Debentures of £100 each, payable £20 on application and £80 on allotment. The issue was fully subscribed and allotment made and the cash received by 9th June.

Show the entries for the debenture issue in the company's books and set down the company's share capital and the debenture issue as it should appear in the Balance Sheet.

2. Give the entries to record in the books of the Essex Ironworks Ltd., the issue of 1,000 5% Debentures of £100 each. The issue was made on 1st January, and the debentures were payable—

£20 for each debenture on application.
£30 for each debenture on allotment.
£50 for each debenture one month after allotment.

The issue was fully subscribed and the Directors went to allotment on 5th January. The cash was received for the remaining instalments on the due date.

3. Riverhead Mills Limited offered for public subscription on 1st February 1,000 5% Debentures of £100 each at the price of £105, payable £20 on application, and £85, including the premium, on allotment. The whole issue was subscribed and allotted and the cash was paid by 8th February.

Show the entries for the issue as in the company's books.

4. Kemsing Cotton Mills Limited offered for public subscription on 1st May 500 5% Debentures of £100 each at a price of £102, payable £25 on application and £77 on allotment, including the premium.

The whole issue was subscribed and allotted and the cash due was received by 9th May.

Record the issue as in the books of the company.

5. Record in the books of Remington & Sons Limited the issue of 500 5% Debentures of £100 each at a price of £98 a debenture, the costs of the issue being £500. Show the particulars of the issue as it would appear in the company's Balance Sheet.

6. Give the entries in the books of Jennings Stores Limited necessitated by the issue of 500 5% Debentures of £100 each at a price of £102 a debenture. The costs of the issue amounted to £600. Show also how the issue would be recorded in the company's Balance Sheet.

7. The Woodside Manufacturing Company Limited offered for public subscription on 1st March, 1,000 5% Debentures of £100 each at a price of £98 a debenture, payable £20 on application, £40 on allotment and £38 one month after allotment. The issue was fully subscribed and allotted on 9th March, and final instalment was paid by 9th April.

Show the entries for the issue as in the company's books.

8. Lawson's Limited offered for subscription on 1st January, 500 5% Debentures of £100 at a price of £95, payable £20 on application and £75 on allotment. The issue was fully subscribed and allotted and the cash received.

Give the entries to record the issue in the books of the company and show how the issue would appear in the Balance Sheet of the company.

9. A limited company borrowed from its bankers a sum of £4,000, and by way of security issued to the bank 50 6% debentures of £100 each. How should this transaction appear in the next Balance Sheet of the company? *U.L.C.I.*

10. Woodcraft, Ltd., was registered to take over the business of Joseph Andrews at 31st December 19.., whose Balance Sheet at that date was as follows:—

LIABILITIES	£	ASSETS	£
Capital 14917		Goodwill, Patents, etc. .. 3330	
Creditors 3276		Plant 3311	
		Furniture, etc. 1809	
		Stock.. 5491	
		Debtors 4107	
		Cash at bank 145	
	£18193		£18193

The purchase price was fixed at £13,500, payable as to £5,000 in cash, and £5,000 in fully paid Ordinary Shares, and the balance in 7½% debentures of £100 each.

The company took over all the assets and liabilities with the exception of the cash, debtors, and creditors, and agreed to collect the debtors for the vendor and remit him the proceeds less 2½% collecting commission.

The shares and debentures were allotted on 1st January, 19.., on which date 20,000 Ordinary Shares of £0·50 each were offered to the public, payable as to £0·25 per share on application and £0·25 per share on allotment.

Applications were received for 19,600 shares by 16th January, and these were duly allotted and the allotment money received by 30th January on which date the balance of the purchase money was paid over to the vendor. On 31st January the vendor's debtors had all been collected, and the amount due to the vendor paid over. The formation expenses of the company, £642, were also paid on that date.

Open the books of Woodcraft, Ltd., record the above transactions in Cash Book and Ledger Accounts, and prepare a Balance Sheet as at 31st January 19...

Journal entries are not required, but all accounts should be presented. *U.E.I.*

11. Draw up the Journal entries in proper form to record the following in the books of A. B. Company, Ltd., when preparing the accounts for the year ending 31st March, 19..:—

(*a*) It was decided that £300 of the Bad Debts Provision of £675 was no longer required.

(*b*) The interest on an issue of £10,000 6% Debentures had been paid to 30th September, in the previous year of account. (Ignore tax.)

(*c*) Included in purchases is £750 and in wages £650 relating to expenditure which was incurred in building an extension to the company's factory.

R.S.A.

CHAPTER 39

THE FINAL ACCOUNTS OF A COMPANY

That a business is owned by a limited company does not affect the ordinary trading records. These do not differ whether the business is owned by a company, an individual, or a partnership firm. The form of ownership affects the proprietorship accounts, and the preceding chapters make clear the material differences in form of the Capital Accounts of a company from those of the sole trader and partners. Another point of difference in company accounts is in the treatment of the profit. A company may not increase its capital except under the conditions laid down in the Companies Act, 1948. Any profit, therefore, that remains after payment of dividends and transfers to Reserve Accounts cannot be transferred to the Capital Accounts but must remain on the books as the balance of the Profit and Loss Account. Further, the Companies Act makes certain provisions regarding the contents of a company Balance Sheet and Profit and Loss Account, and usually, certain adjustments, peculiar to company accounts, may be necessary in the final accounts at balancing time.

Reserves and Provisions

It has been explained in Chapter 19 that a company may set aside part of the profits to meet known liabilities and such allocations of profit are known as "Provisions." If, however, an appropriation of profit is made for the general or specific purpose of strengthening the financial position of the business such appropriations would be known as Reserves.

The creation of a Dividend Equalisation Fund by a company would also come under this category, the purpose of such a fund being to provide a reserve of profits in good years that may be drawn upon in bad years to maintain dividends at a certain level.

The reserve, being an appropriation of profit, is debited to Profit and Loss Appropriation Account. The corresponding credit entry is made in the special account opened in the Ledger for the particular reserve. Such accounts remain open at the date of balancing, and the balances appear in due course as liabilities in the Balance Sheet under their appropriate headings.

378

Example 56.—Before closing the books for the financial year, create an Employees' Superannuation Fund by the transfer of £15,000 to such fund, the amount to remain invested in the business.

Debit £15,000 to the Profit and Loss Appropriation Account and *Credit* Employees' Superannuation Fund Account with the like sum.

The profit available for distribution will be less by £15,000, and the balance of the Superannuation Fund Account will be shown as a liability in the Balance Sheet separately and under its own appropriate heading.

In such a case as this the firm becomes answerable for the reserve of profits, and the sum appears as a liability in the Balance Sheet. As it is left in the business it becomes part of the capital employed and no specific asset may be regarded as representing the investment of the reserve of profit. Another method is to invest the amount outside the business, but there must be sufficient cash in hand to invest in securities. The entries would be as above, and in addition, cash is credited and Investment Account debited for the investment made. The balance on the Investment Account will appear among the assets in the Balance Sheet. The total assets will not be increased as the investment will take the place of the cash withdrawn, but the reserve liability will be represented by a specific asset, and not by an unidentified portion of the general assets. Such an invested reserve is sometimes referred to as a Reserve Fund.

Example 57.—Machines Ltd., finding that very heavy charges for repairs occur every few years, has created a Repairs Equalisation Provision by appropriating £500 each year out of profits, and charging the actual cost of repairs against the fund. The balance to the credit of the Provision Account on 1st January was £800. Repairs cost £700 during the year. Show the Provision Account as at 31st December, and the necessary entries charging the repairs and making the appropriation of profit to the Provision for the current year.

Dr.			Repairs Equalisation Provision Account			Cr.
19..		£	19..			£
Dec. 31	Transfer from Repairs A/c.	700	Jan. 1	Balance brought down		800
„ 31	Balance carried down	600	Dec. 31	Profit and Loss A/c.		500
		£1300				£1300
			Jan. 1	Balance brought down		600

Dr.			£		Repairs Account			Cr.
19..	Cash— Repairs for the year..	C.B.	700	19.. Dec. 31	Transfer to Repairs Equalisation Provision A/c. ..			£ 700

Dr.			£	19..	Profit and Loss Account			Cr. £
19.. Dec 31	Repairs Equalisation Provision A/c.		500					

The balance of the Repairs Equalisation Provision Account is shown in the Balance Sheet as a liability. The above balance would appear as below:—

Balance Sheet
(Left-hand side only)

	£
Repairs Equalisation Provision ..	600

The annual instalment to be placed to the Repairs Provision is usually based on the average cost of repairs in past years, but it must be adequate, otherwise the account may be placed in debit. The creation of such a provision equalises the charge against profits year by year for repairs, and if the fund appears inadequate in course of time the annual appropriation is increased accordingly.

The Appropriation Account

The net trading profit of a company is carried down to a second section of the Profit and Loss Account. This second section is called the Appropriation Account and contains all the appropriations of the net profit. The separation of the Profit and Loss Account into two sections increases its value for purposes of comparison from year to year and for the information it affords. The first part contains the gross revenue for the year and the expenses incurred in earning it. The second part shows the disposal of the profit. It follows that the first part should contain all charges against profits such as directors' fees, debenture interest, depreciation, interest, rent, rates, and similar expenses, and that the Appropriation Account should contain only the appropriations of the profit that the first section shows available for distribution.

Examples of such appropriations are transfers to reserve, the payment of preference share dividends and interim dividends, allocations to pension funds, and any sums written off Goodwill and preliminary expenses.

The balance remaining after the appropriations have been made is available for distribution as dividend to the shareholders.

The directors set out the net trading profit in their report to the shareholders at the Annual General Meeting and include a statement of their recommendations for its disposal by way of dividend, transfers to reserve, etc. A resolution is proposed that the dividend specified shall be paid on a certain date, and, if the resolution is carried, the dividend becomes a debt due from the company to the shareholders. Only when the dividend has been declared is the entry for it made in the Appropriation Account. The shareholders cannot authorise the distribution of a larger dividend than that recommended by the directors, but they may recommend less.

The Appropriation Account is closed after the entry of the various allocations of profit and the final dividend. Any balance, whether a profit or a loss, is carried forward to the next period. The Appropriation Account is treated as a continuous account. It follows that after the first year's working the Account will show the balance brought forward from the preceding financial year and the balance to be carried forward to the next. In a company Balance Sheet the profit or loss is shown as a separate item—a profit on the liabilities side, a loss on the assets side.

The balance brought down to the Appropriation Account for the new trading period appears in the Trial Balance extracted at the close of that period. In a Trial Balance given as an examination test it usually appears under the heading of "Profit and Loss Account Balance" and in the preparation of the final accounts, the item should be carried to the Appropriation Account (which should directly follow the Profit and Loss Account), first ensuring whether the Trial Balance item represents a profit or a loss brought forward.

Example 58.—A typical example of the appropriation section of a Profit and Loss Account is given below.

Profit and Loss Account
for the year ended 31st December, 19..

19.. Dec. 31			£	19.. Dec. 31		£
	Total Expenses		20000		Gross Profit	38000
	Balance carried down		18000			
			£38000			£38000

Appropriation Account

19.. Dec. 31			£	19.. Dec. 31			£
	Interim dividend on 100000 Ordinary Shares ..		5000		Trading Profit brought down		18000
„ 31	Transfer to Reserve Account		3000	„ 31	Balance brought forward from last year		1500
„ 31	Goodwill written off		1500				
„ 31	Preliminary expenses written off		2000				
„ 31	Balance ..	c/d	8000				
			£19500				£19500
				Dec. 31	Balance	b/d	8000

The contra entries in the Ledger for the debit entries in the Appropriation Account would be as follows:—

The interim dividend would be credited to the Ordinary Shares Dividend Account.

The transfer to reserve would be credited to the Reserve Account.

The sums written off Goodwill and preliminary expenses would be credited respectively to the Goodwill Account and the Preliminary Expenses Account.

The balance on the Appropriation Account (£8,000) is sufficient to allow the directors to declare a final dividend on the Ordinary Shares of 5% per annum. This would absorb £5,000, leaving £3,000 to be carried forward to next year.

The final dividend would be credited to the Ordinary Shares Dividend Account. The payment out of the dividend would be credited in the Cash Book and debited to the Ordinary Shares Dividend Account. The payment is made by special forms of cheque known as dividend warrants. If all the warrants are cashed the Dividend Account is closed, but a balance would remain should any dividends not be claimed. Such balance must be shown on the liability side of the Balance Sheet under the heading of Unclaimed Dividends.

Interim Dividends

The Articles usually give the directors power to pay interim dividends. These are dividends paid during the financial year before the annual accounts are made up. They are usually paid at the end of the first half-year, but the directors must take care that the profits justify the payment.

Transfer Fees and Preliminary Expenses

The transfer fees paid by transferees on the lodging of transfers of shares are credited to the Profit and Loss Account as a gain.

Preliminary expenses are usually written off against profits by instalments over a period of three to five years.

The Companies Acts and the Final Accounts of a Company

Companies are required by law to publish their final accounts at least once a year. This takes the form of a published Profit and Loss Account and Balance Sheet. They are required to do so by law so that all shareholders, debenture holders, and any member of the general public who may be interested may have necessary information about the company. Copies of such published accounts are sent annually to all shareholders and debenture holders, on the registers of the company at the date of publication. Other interested parties may inspect a copy of these accounts at the office of the Registrar of Joint Stock Companies.

These published accounts may differ in form from the accounts as made up for the purpose of ascertaining the profit or loss of the company. The 1948 and 1967 Companies Acts lay down certain requirements on the items which must be shown in the published accounts of a company and matters which must be dealt with in the Directors' Report. These requirements were greatly extended by the 1967 Act and it is not proposed to go fully into them at this stage. A detailed study of these requirements must be left to a more advanced stage of study. Students who are interested will find full details in the Companies Acts and, in particular, in Schedule 2 of the Companies Act 1967 which deals with the legal requirements for the published Profit and Loss Accounts and Balance Sheets of Joint Stock Companies.

The Published Profit and Loss Account

The published Profit and Loss Account is required to show certain items such as charges for depreciation and renewals, debenture interest, aggregate amount of directors' emoluments and other items as laid down in Schedule 2 of the 1967 Companies Act. To show these items, the aggregate amount of them is written back to the figure of net profit as arrived at in the accounting records of the company. The amount so arrived at is shown on the credit side of the published Profit and Loss Account. On the debit side each item required by law to be published is shown and the final figure of net profit will be the same as that shown in the company's accounts. This profit, reduced by provisions for taxation, will be the amount shown in the Appropriation Account as available for appropriation as reserves or dividends.

Taxation

Companies must provide for payment of Corporation Tax at a rate determined in the annual budget presented to Parliament by the Chancellor of the Exchequer and are also responsible for deducting tax, at the standard rate ruling at the time, from all payments of dividends and interest to shareholders and debenture holders. The total amount so deducted is paid by the company to the Inland Revenue Authorities. In the Appropriation Account such dividends are shown at the gross amount but the amount paid to shareholders is the gross amount less tax at the standard rate in force at the time of payment, the amount of tax being passed by the company to the Income Tax Authorities. Further treatment of this subject must be left to a more advanced stage of study.

The Balance Sheet

Schedule 2 of the 1967 Companies Act lays down many requirements relating to the published Balance Sheets of Companies. While it would be unwise to enter into a full discussion of these requirements at this stage, students should, when preparing the Balance Sheet of a Limited Liability Company observe the following rules as a preliminary stage to more advanced study.

On the *liabilities side*:

1. The Authorised Share Capital, the Issued Share Capital, Reserves, Provisions (other than provisions for depreciation which are normally shown by way of deduction from the asset to which they relate) and Current Liabilities should be shown under separate headings.
2. Share premiums must be shown separately under the heading "Share Premium Account".
3. The aggregate amount of bank loans and overdrafts must be shown.
4. The aggregate amount (before deduction of tax) recommended for distribution as dividends.

Assets Side

1. Fixed assets, current assets, and assets that are neither fixed nor current must be separately identified.
2. Fixed assets and current assets should be grouped and the total of each group should be shown.
3. The basis of valuation of fixed assets must be shown. These will generally be shown "at cost" less the aggregate amount of depreciation written off to date.
4. Investments should be shown separately. Trade, quoted and unquoted investments should be separately identified. The market value of quoted investments must be shown if different from the Balance Sheet valuation.
5. The following should be shown under separate headings:
   (*a*) Goodwill and Trade Marks in so far as the amount is ascertainable and has not been written off.
   (*b*) Preliminary expenses not written off.
   (*c*) Expenses, commission and discount on any issue of shares or debentures in so far as it has not been written off.

At this stage of study students will not usually be called upon to prepared the *published* Profit and Loss Account of a limited liability company. In doing exercises and in examination work the Profit and Loss Account and its Appropriation Section will be prepared as explained on pages 380-82. In preparing a company Balance Sheet students should observe the rules set out above.

The Companies Acts provide that every Balance Sheet of a company must be signed on behalf of the board by two directors or by the sole director, and that the auditor's report must be attached and be read before the company in general meeting.

A company must appoint an auditor or auditors at its annual general meeting to hold office until the next annual general meeting. The auditors have right of access at all times to the company's books, accounts, and vouchers, and shall be entitled to require from the officers of the company such information and explanations as they think necessary for the performance of their duties as auditors. They must report to the members on the accounts examined by them.

This report is usually confined to statements as to whether, in the opinion of the auditors:

(*a*) the Balance Sheet and Profit and Loss Account have been properly prepared in accordance with the provisions of the Companies Acts;

(*b*) the Balance Sheet and Profit and Loss Account give a true and fair view respectively of the state of affairs and the profit or loss of the company.

Simplified Appropriation Account and Balance Sheet of a company

Appropriation Account

for year ended 31st December, 19..

		£			£
Dec. 31	Pref. share dividend paid	1400	Dec. 31	Net trading profit b/d	28960
	Interim Ord. share dividend paid ..	5000		Balance brought forward from last	
	Transfer to Reserve	5000		year	4280
	Final Ord. share dividend recommended	15000			
	Balance carried forward	6840			
		£33240			£33240

Balance Sheet as at 31st December 19. .

Capital employed

	Authorised £	Issued £
SHARE CAPITAL—		
7% Preference shares of £1 each ..	50000	20000
Ordinary shares of £1 each ..	200000	100000
REVENUE RESERVES at 1st Jan., 19.. (35000)		
Add transfer this year .. (5000)	40000	
Balance of Profit and Loss A/c.	6840	46840
		£166840
LOAN CAPITAL—		
1,000 7% Debentures of £10 each		10000
Capital employed ..		£176840

Net value of assets

	£	£	£	£
Goodwill			10500	
FIXED ASSETS				
Freehold premises, at cost ..			120000	
Machinery and plant, at cost ..		51000		
less provision for depreciation ..		21700	29300	
Furniture and fittings, at cost ..		2600		
less provision for depreciation ..		1400	1200	161000
Investments (quoted), at cost (Market value £10,210) ..				8080
CURRENT ASSETS				
Sundry debtors		4200		
less provision for bad debts ..		210	3990	
Stocks			6840	
Amounts prepaid			90	
Cash in hand and balance at bank			19920	
			£30840	
Less CURRENT LIABILITIES—				
Sundry creditors:—				
Trade	7960			
Expense	120	8080		
Recommended dividend on ordinary shares		15000	23080	
				7760
Net value of assets				£176840

This form of Balance Sheet is the form now usually adopted by limited liability companies. It shows clearly the capital employed, the working capital and the net book value of the assets. Students are advised to adopt this form of Balance Sheet when working exercises and in examination work.

EXERCISES 39

1. If you were the accountant to a limited company and had drawn up a Trial Balance as at 31st December, 19.., prior to preparing the accounts, state how you would deal with the following items appearing therein, giving reasons for your replies—

(a) Premium on an issue of Shares £5,000.

(b) Cash at bank £6,800 (including proceeds of £2,500 Bills Receivable, discounted with the Company's Bankers and falling due during January and February).

(c) Discount on an issue of Debentures £4,000.

(d) Reserve for Bad and Doubtful Debts (previously made) £2,000.

(e) Preliminary (or Formation) Expenses, £950.   *U.L.C.I.*

2. The Crystal Glass Works, Ltd., having made a profit of £9,448 during the year decided to appropriate it, together with a balance of profit of £3,329 brought forward, as follows:—

(a) In payment of a dividend of 6¼%, less tax, on 56,400 Preference Shares of £1 each, fully paid.

(b) In payment of a dividend of 7%, free of tax, on 94,600 Ordinary Shares of £1 each, £0·50 paid.

(c) In transfer of £1,000 to a Reserve Fund Account with a corresponding investment of cash in securities.

(d) In writing off the figure of Goodwill, £1,600.

The balance of profit remaining was to be carried forward. The cash balance at the date prior to the payment of the dividends and the investment stood at £8,628.

Show the Profit and Loss Appropriation Account and the entries in all the other accounts necessary to give effect to the above resolution, allowing for unclaimed dividends £219 on the ordinary shares.   *U.E.I.*

3. The A.B. Engineering Co. Ltd. has an authorised capital of £50,000 divided into 100,000 shares of £0·50 each.

On 31st December, 19.., the following balances appear in the books of the company.

	£
Share capital (fully paid)	30000
General reserve	5000
Profit and Loss Account (credit balance)	10480
Machinery and plant (at cost)	34000
Furniture and fittings (at cost)	3000
Provisions for depreciation:—	
Machinery and plant	9700
Furniture and fittings..	800
Sundry debtors	4780
Sundry creditors	2340
Cash in hand and balance at bank	9140
Stocks	7400

For the year ended 31st December 19.. the directors decided to transfer £2,000 to reserve and to recommend a dividend of 20% on the ordinary shares.

Prepare the Appropriation Account of the company for the year ended 31st December, 19.., and a Balance Sheet as at that date.

The Balance Sheet is to be prepared in such a way as to show clearly *within the Balance Sheet*:—

    (i) The total of fixed assets;
    (ii) the total of current assets;
    (iii) the total of current liabilities;
    (iv) the total of revenue reserves;
    (v) the working capital;
    (vi) the net book value of the assets.

Note:—Ignore Taxation.   *A.E.B., G.C.E. "O" Level.*

4. You are required to prepare the Balance Sheet of a limited company as on the 31st December, 19. ., from the following information:—The Alma Manufacturing Company Limited was formed in the previous December, with a nominal capital of £80,000 in ordinary shares of £1 each. Up to and including December 31st, 50,000 shares had been issued and fully paid with the exception of 2,000 shares on which £0·12½ per share was still unpaid. Cash in Hand, £100, Cash at Bank, £3,400, Investments, £4,000, Sundry Debtors, £16,071, Leasehold Property, £6,700, Stock in Hand, £36,297, Plant and Machinery £7,800, Goodwill, £10,000, Provision for Bad and Doubtful Debts, £800, Sundry Creditors, £29,000, Interim Dividend paid, £4,975, Profit for the year ending December 31st, 19. ., £9,793.   *N.C.T.E.C.*

5. A. B. Ltd., was formed and commenced trading on 1st January, 19. . The authorised capital was £20,000 divided into 20,000 Ordinary Shares of £1 each, all of which were issued at £1·50 each and fully paid.

The following balances remained on the books after the revenue accounts had been closed at 31st December, 19. . :—

Share Capital Account, £20,000; preliminary expenses, £500; sundry creditors, £4,820; freehold premises, £9,800 (cost £10,000 *less* depreciation £200); cash in hand, £120; Profit and Loss Account (*Cr.*), £2,000; Share Premium Account, £10,000; Goodwill at cost, £10,000; machinery, £6,800 (cost £8,500, *less* depreciation £1,700); general reserve, £1,000; sundry debtors, £7,975; stocks as valued by officials of the company, £2,270; provision for dividend, £1,000; provision for bad debts, £50; and balance with bank, £1,405.

Draft the Balance Sheet as at 31st December, 19. ., for presentation to the members of the company.   *R.S.A.*

6. C. D. Ltd., manufacturers, had an Authorised Capital of £150,000 of which £100,000 was in Ordinary Shares of £1 each and the balance in 5% Preference Shares of £1 each.

From the following list of balances at 30th June, 19. ., prepare the Balance Sheet of the company at that date for presentation to the members:—

Formation expenses, £2,050; Ordinary Share Capital Account, £100,000; cash in hand, £255; sundry creditors, £14,326; General Reserve Account; £30,000; leasehold premises at cost, £42,000, less depreciation £8,000; stocks on hand as valued by officials of the company, £15,826; Profit and Loss Account —undistributed profits, £23,739; machinery at cost, £126,056, less depreciation £16,056; equipment and tools at cost, £10,763, *less* depreciation £5,382; Preference Share Call Account (*Dr.*) £150; Preference Share Capital Account, £50,000; office furniture at cost, £2,978, *less* depreciation £952; sundry debtors, £37,377; balance at bank, £11,000.   *R.S.A.*

7. Beta Gamma Limited was formed to take over as from 31st March, 19.. the business of a private trader whose Balance Sheet on that date was as follows:—

	£		£
Capital	46000	Plant and machinery ..	17300
Sundry Creditors	5471	Vans and lorries	3940
		Fixtures and fittings ..	600
		Stock	19731
		Debtors	7978
		Cash	1922
	£51471		**£51471**

The company took over all the assets, including cash, at the book values and assumed responsibility for the liabilities. The Goodwill was valued at £9,000.

The authorised capital of Beta Gamma Limited consisted of 40,000 6% Preference Shares of £1 each, 236,000 Ordinary Shares of £0·25 each, and 20,000 Deferred Shares of £0·05 each. The vendor took the whole of the Deferred Shares and the balance of the purchase consideration in Ordinary Shares, all at par, and on 30th April, 19.., 20,000 of the Preference Shares were subscribed privately at a premium of £0·05 per share and fully paid. £15,000 was spent on new machinery, the balance being retained as working capital.

Six months' dividend on the Preference Shares was paid on 31st October, 19...

On closing the books on 30th December, 19.., £3,000 was provided for depreciation of plant and machinery, £440 for depreciation of vans and lorries, and £30 for depreciation of fixtures and fittings, and £620 was provided as a reserve for bad and doubtful debts. The remaining balances, after closing the Profit and Loss Account, in addition to those already indicated, were—

	£
Sundry Creditors	4597
Stock, 31st December	29388
Sundry Debtors	11396
Cash	5605
Net Profit for the period	8142

You are required to draw up the Company's Balance Sheet as on 31st December, 19...   *R.S.A.*

8. The Chromium Steel Company, Ltd., having a nominal capital of £50,000 divided into 30,000 Ordinary Shares of £1 each and 20,000 6% Preference Shares of £1 each, was formed to acquire the business of C. Barnby & Sons as from January 1st, 19...

The purchase consideration was fixed at £20,000 for which tangible assets to the value of £15,000 were acquired.

On the following 31st December the purchase price had been discharged by the issue of £10,000 in fully paid Ordinary Shares, £5,000 in 7% Debentures of £100 each, and the balance in cash. 7,500 Ordinary Shares had been taken up by the public and fully subscribed, with the exception of £62 calls in arrear, and 10,000 Preference Shares had been issued and fully subscribed.

The following balances stood in the books of the company on 31st December, 19.., in addition to those indicated by the above transactions:—

	£
Plant and machinery	6150
Salaries	1938
Directors' fees	1000
Investments	3010
Fixtures and fittings	250
Carriage inwards	397
Fuel, light, and heating (factory)	382
Freehold factory	3946
Wages	15473
Manufacturing expenses	965
Stock at 1st January	21,421
Rates and Insurance	968
Purchases	54930
Sales	78226
Returns inwards	471
Returns outwards	521
Discount Account (*Cr.*)	214
Bank loan	2412
Cash in hand	4294
Creditors	20353
Debtors	14480
Office expenses	647
Repairs to buildings	686
Transfer fees	6
Apprentices' premiums (P. and L. Account)	250
Bad debts	231
Provision for bad and doubtful debts	400
Interest and bank charges (*Dr.*)	98
Solicitors' fees	125
Bills Payable	5142
Motor lorries	2200
Loose tools	900

Prepare Trading and Profit and Loss Accounts for the year ended 31st December, 19.., and a Balance Sheet at that date.

Make provision for the following:—

(i) Motor lorries were re-valued at £1,760, and loose tools at £960.
(ii) Depreciation—plant and machinery, $7\frac{1}{2}\%$, fixtures and fittings, 5%.
(iii) Unexpired rates and insurance, £119.
(iv) Provision for bad debts to be made up to 5% on the debtors.
(v) Debentures interest due (12 months).
(vi) Closing stock, £14,419.   *U.E.I.*

9. Derry, Ltd., a company with an authorised share capital of £25,000 in shares of £1 each, had the following balances at 31st December, 19..:—

Trial Balance

	£	£
Share Capital Account (15,000 shares of £1 each, £0·75 called)		11250
Debtors	5500	
Rent received		400
Rent paid	600	

	£	£
Bank balance	4250	
Purchases and returns	28500	150
Sales and returns	650	35000
Stock at 1st January	3000	
Bad debts written off	400	
Bad debts provision		450
Cash in hand	260	
Rates	240	
Salaries	3520	
Profit and Loss Account at 1st January		5150
Fixtures and fittings	1530	
Creditors		2150
Discount (net)		200
Advertising	300	
Interim dividend paid (ignore income tax)	750	
General expenses	250	
Goodwill	5000	
	£54750	£54750

You are required to prepare the Trading and Profit and Loss Accounts for the year ending 31st December, 19.., and Balance Sheet at that date, taking into consideration the adjustments required by the following:—

(a) The stock at 31st December, 19.., was valued at £4,500.
(b) Depreciate fixtures and fittings at the rate of 10% of cost (£1,700).
(c) Set aside £1,000 for General Reserve.
(d) Included in the rate account is £40 paid in respect of the following year.
(e) The sum of £50 is due to the company for the rent owing at 31st December, 19...
(f) Included in the Advertising Account is the sum of £100 paid in December for advertising abroad, but the advertisements did not appear until the following year. *R.S.A.*

10. The Loamshire Garage, Ltd., is a company with an authorised share capital of £5,000 in shares of £1 each.

The following Trial Balance is extracted from the books of the company at 31st December, 19..:—

	£	£
Share Capital Account		5000
Calls in arrear	25	
Plant and machinery	2250	
Petrol pumps	850	
Purchases of spares	1326	
Purchases of petrol	5268	
Stock at 1st January—Spares	591	
Petrol	127	
Sales—Repairs Department		8011
Petrol Department		5970
Wages—Repairs Department	2948	
Petrol Department	316	
Premises	4200	
Creditors		266
Debtors	572	

	£	£
Rates	63	
Salaries	924	
Insurance	72	
Light, heat, and power	97	
Office expenses	48	
Bank balance	850	
Cash in hand	91	
Profit and Loss Account at 1st January ..		1420
General expenses	49	
	£20667	£20667

You are required to prepare separate Trading Accounts for each department and a general Profit and Loss Account for the year ending 31st December, 19.., together with the Balance Sheet at that date, after making such adjustments as are necessary in respect of the following:—

(*a*) The plant and machinery to be depreciated at the rate of 10% on cost £2,500.

(*b*) The petrol pumps to be depreciated at the rate of 15% on cost £1,000.

(*c*) Provide £20 in respect of doubtful debts.

(*d*) Included in the Insurance Account is £12 in respect of the following year.

(*e*) The stock on hand at 31st December, 19.., was valued at spares £467; and petrol £22.

(*f*) Provide for a dividend of 5% on the called up capital (ignore taxation).

R.S.A.

11. A manufacturing firm found that the cost of repairs to the machinery varies greatly from year to year, and to equalise the charge against profits for such repairs, created four years ago a Repairs to Machinery Provision by crediting to it a sum of £900 each year. The actual expenditure on repairs was charged against the Provision each year.

Write up the Provision Account for the four years, taking into consideration the following sums actually expended on repairs:—

First year £350, Second year £1,050, Third year £1,200, Fourth year £250.

Show also how the balance on the Provision Account each year would be shown in the firm's Balance Sheet.

APPENDIX 3

ADDITIONAL EXERCISES

1. A. Back and B. Bite started up in partnership on 1st April, 19.., contributing capitals of £5,000 and £10,000 respectively but without any formal agreement as to profit sharing. On 1st October, 19.., Bite made available an additional £6,000 as a loan but without any agreement as to interest.

The accounts for the year ended 31st March, in the following year, disclose a profit of £3,150, but the partners are unable to agree as to its allocation. Bite contends that interest at 6% ought to be brought into account and Back for his part that the technical knowledge which he made available ought to be remunerated by way of a salary allowance of £2,000 per annum which he reckons he could have earned in outside employment.

You are asked to show the distribution of the profit between the partners: the partners' accounts are not, however, required.

London Chamber of Commerce—Intermediate.

2. **Balance Sheet of A. Bishop, Grocer.** 31st March, 19...

LIABILITIES	£	ASSETS	£
Capital	8800	Premises	5200
Creditors	230	Furniture and equipment	1240
Expenses accrued	30	Stock	1800
		Debtors	88
		Cash at bank	732
	£9060		£9060

(*a*) On 31st March, 19.., Bishop sells the business to Canon and Dean for £9,500, it being agreed that Bishop retains cash at bank and pays outstanding liabilities—which he does the same day. The purchase price is paid into Bishop's banking account.

Prepare Bishop's Realisation Account and show his Capital Account at the end of the day, when he closes his business accounts.

(*b*) On 31st March, 19.., Canon and Dean enter into partnership on equal terms to purchase Bishop's business. Canon pays £6,000 into the new firm's banking account, Dean £4,000, and Dean also brings into the firm stock valued at £2,000. They draw cheque for £9,500 payable to Bishop and take over his assets (other than his cash at bank).

As agreed between them, the partners write up the value of the premises to £6,500, revalue Bishop's stock at £1,500, and write down the furniture and equipment to £1,000.

Prepare Canon and Dean's opening Balance Sheet on 31st March, 19.., after effect has been given to the foregoing. *W.J.E.C.—G.C.E. "O" Level.*

3. Pheasant and Partridge are in partnership sharing profits and losses equally. Pheasant's capital is £8,000 and Partridge's £7,000. On January 1st, 19.., they admit Grouse to partnership. The Goodwill of the existing partnership is to be capitalised at £4,000 and Grouse is to bring in cash £4,000 as his capital. Pheasant is to be allowed to withdraw £5,000 of his capital.

394

The terms of the new partnership provide that before division of the profits each partner is entitled to 5% per annum interest on his capital and that the remaining profits be divided: Partridge, one-half, Pheasant and Grouse, one-quarter each.

(*a*) Show, *by means of Journal Entries*, the records necessary to give effect to the above.

(*b*) At the end of the first year of trading the following details are available *in addition* to those arising from the above.

You are required to prepare a Balance Sheet as at the end of the first year of the new partnership.

	£
Net trading profit *before* charging interest on capital and *before* writing £500 off Goodwill	6400
Cash in hand and at bank	1772
Freehold premises	10000
Mortgage on freehold premises	6000
Stock	4950
Sundry debtors	5800
Provision for bad debts	290
Sundry creditors:—	
Trade	4450
Expenses	350
Machinery and equipment at cost	9790
Furniture and fittings	670
Depreciation Fund for machinery and equipment	6980
Current Accounts at January 1st, 19..:—	
Partridge: Balance at January 1st. Cr.	29
Drawings during year	2800
Pheasant: Balance at January 1st. Dr.	17
Drawings during year	1350
Grouse: Drawings during year	1350

College of Preceptors—Senior.

4. The following are the Balance Sheets of John Smith as at December 31st, in two successive years.

	YEAR 1	YEAR 2		YEAR 1	Year 2
	£	£		£	£
Capital, January 1st	5000	4700	Premises	1500	1500
Profit for year	1200	2000	Fixtures	400	350
Proceeds from sale			Motor vehicles		700
private investment		600	Stock	1100	1500
			Debtors	2600	2900
	6200	7300	Bank	900	
Deduct:—					
Drawings	1500	1800			
	4700	5500			
Mortgage on premises	500				
Bank		650			
Sundry creditors	1300	800			
	£6500	£6950		£6500	£6950

Smith looks at his overdraft of £650 and says that he cannot understand how he can have made a profit of £2,000 in year 2.

You are asked to prepare a statement showing Smith where his profit has "gone". *London Chamber of Commerce—Intermediate.*

5. Explain the following in relation to the accounts of a Limited Liability Co., and state exactly where you would look in the Ledger for information on the amount of the item:—

    (*a*) Preference Share Capital;
    (*b*) Reserve;
    (*c*) Preliminary expenses;
    (*d*) Depreciation Fund. *College of Preceptors—Senior.*

6. Record the following by way of Journal entries:—

    (*a*) The purchase of a new motor vehicle for £1,800 after bringing into account an allowance of £400 for the one which it replaced and which cost £1,600. The depreciation element has been passed through a separate Depreciation Provision Account and £1,000 of the balance on this account at the date of the purchase of the new vehicle related to the vehicle sold.

    (*b*) The sale of goods on behalf of I. Trust for £1,500 cash. No entries with regard to the goods had previously been passed through the books. The sellers' remuneration is on a commission basis—3% of the gross sale proceeds.

    (*c*) The adjustment, at the financial year end, of the existing balance on a Bad Debts Provision Account of £750 to 5% of the total of the debtor's balances which amounted to £18,000.

    (*d*) The directors' allocation of their company's available profit, viz.,

    (1) Transfer to Reserve, £5,000.

    (2) Proposed final dividend of £0·1 per share on an issued capital of 100,000 shares of £1 each fully paid. *London Chamber of Commerce—Intermediate.*

7. Distributors Ltd. own a fleet of lorries which are depreciated on the fixed instalment system at the rate of 25% on the basis that lorries in existence at the end of the financial year are depreciated for a full year irrespective of the date of purchase, depreciation on lorries sold during the year not being brought into account.

The lorries are maintained in the books at cost, the depreciation provision being disposed of in a separate Depreciation Provision Account.

On 1st January, 19. ., the total cost of the lorries held and the aggregate sum provided as depreciation thereon were £35,000 and £18,500 respectively. On 1st April, 19. ., a new lorry was acquired at a net cost of £1,500 after bringing into account an allowance of £300 for the one which it replaced, which latter had been acquired 2 years and 7 months previously at a cost of £2,000.

An addition to the fleet was acquired on 1st November, 19. ., at a cost of £2,200. You are required to write up the accounts concerned for the financial year ended 31st December, 19... *London Chamber of Commerce—Intermediate.*

8. Omega Ltd. made an issue of 50,000 ordinary shares of £1 each at a premium of £0·40 per share, payable £0·20 on application, £0·80 on allotment (including premium) and £0·40 on call.

60,000 shares were applied for and allotment made as follows:—

Applicants for 45,000 shares in full.
,,   ,,   10,000   ,,   50% of number applied for.
,,   ,,   5,000   ,,   Nil allotment and application money returned.

    60,000

You are required (*a*) to show, by way of Ledger Accounts only, the entries arising out of the issue (cash transactions included) on the basis that the shares are fully called and that all moneys are duly received save the call money on 200 shares.

(*b*) What do the Companies Acts say about share premiums?
London Chamber of Commerce—Intermediate.

9. H. Jackson, Ltd. has as Capital, Authorised, Issued and Paid-up:—

	£
160,000 Ordinary Shares of £0·25 each	40000
120,000 6% Preference Shares of £1 each	120000

Its Profit and Loss Account on 31 December, 19.., had a credit balance of £35,600.

The Net Profit for the following year was £29,500 and the directors decided to:—

(*a*) pay one year's dividend on the Preference Shares;
(*b*) transfer £10,000 to General Reserve;
(*c*) recommend a dividend of £0·07½ per share on the Ordinary Shares.

Prepare Profit and Loss Appropriation Account for the year ended 31st March, 19...   *W.J.E.C.—G.C.E. "O" Level.*

10. *Either*, (*a*) Giving appropriate examples, *briefly* distinguish between the two terms in any *three* of the following:—

(i) Capital Expenditure and Income Expenditure;
(ii) Reserve and Provisions;
(iii) Capital and Working Capital;
(iv) Nominal Capital and Authorised Capital;
(v) Receipts and Payments Account and Income and Expenditure Account.

Or, (*b*) Consider the following: the X.Y. Company decides to alter the basis of the valuation of its Stock for the year 1958–9.

	Old basis	New basis
	£	£
Stock, 1st April, 1958	2400	3000
Stock, 31st March, 1959	3240	4010

What will be the effect of the alteration on its apparent gross profit?
W.J.E.C.—G.C.E. "O" Level.

11. The following are the balances of A. Watson, Ltd., on 31st December· 19..:—

	Dr.	Cr.
	£ thousands	
Capital: Authorised, Issued, and Fully Paid up:—		
200,000 5% Preference Shares		200
500,000 Ordinary Shares, £0·20 each		100
General Reserve		285
Profit and Loss Account, 1st Jan., 19..		90
Preference Dividend Account	11	
Trade creditors and accrued charges		50

	Dr.	Cr.
	£ thousands	
Customers' unpaid balances	340	
Motor vehicles		2
Furniture, fixtures, and equipment	21	
Premises	99	
Stock in trade	158	
Investments at cost	56	
Dividends received on investments		5
General expenses	118	
Directors' remuneration	22	
Cash in hand and at bank	88	
Gross trading profit for the year ended 31st December, 19..		185
	£915	£915

You are required to prepare Profit and Loss Account for the year ended 31st December, 19.., and Balance Sheet as at that date, taking into account the following:—

(a) Fixed assets, as shown, are valued at cost less depreciation written off to the end of the previous year of account.

(b) The Auditors' fee of £1,000 is outstanding.

(c) The Board of Directors decide to (i) write off a further £1,000 from the book value of the motor vehicles and to write down the value of the furniture, fixtures, and equipment to £19,000; (ii) make a provision for doubtful debts equal to 5% of customers' unpaid balances; (iii) appropriate a further £18,000 to the General Reserve; (iv) recommend the payment of a year's dividend on the Ordinary Shares of £0·075 per share.   *W.J.E.C.—G.C.E."O" Level.*

12. The following are the balances of F. Williams & Co., Ltd., on 31st December, 19...

	Dr.	Cr.
	£ thousands	
Capital: Authorised, Issued, and Fully Paid up:—		
150,000 6% Preference Shares, £1 each		150
640,000 Ordinary Shares, £0·25 each		160
General Reserve		75
Profit and Loss Account, 31st December (previous year) ..		59
Trade creditors and accrued charges		273
Freehold property	166	
Plant and equipment	19	
Office furniture and equipment	12	
Motor-vehicles	16	
Investment at cost	10	
Stock in hand	405	
Debtors	350	
Bad debts	5	
Bank loan		172
Cash in hand and at bank	3	
Interest on bank loan	9	
Directors' remuneration:—		
Fees	5	
Salaries	14	
Gross trading profit for the year ended 31st December, 19.. ..		125
	£1014	£1014

You are required to prepare Profit and Loss Account for the year ended 31st December, 19.., and Balance Sheet as at that date, taking account of the following:—

(*a*) A dividend of £1,000 on investment received on 31st December, has not been entered in the books.

(*b*) The Auditors' fees for the year amount to £1,000.

(*c*) Fixed assets, as shown, are valued at cost less depreciation written off to 31st December, in previous year.

The Board of Directors decides to (i) write off a further 25% on the book value of the motor vehicles and write down the value of the plant and equipment to £16,000; (ii) make a provision of £10,000 for doubtful debts; (iii) appropriate £20,000 to increase the General Reserve; (iv) recommend the payment of a year's dividend on the Preference Share Capital and one of 20% on the Ordinary Share Capital. *W.J.E.C.—G.C.E. "O" Level.*

13. The following list of balances was extracted from the books of Workshops Limited *after* the completion of the Manufacturing Account for the year ended 31st December, 19...

You are required to prepare Trading and Profit and Loss Accounts for the year and Balance Sheet at that date.

	£	£
Cost of goods manufactured	59800	
Stocks—		
Raw materials, 31st December, 19..	5650	
Work in progress, 31st December, 19..	1190	
Finished goods, 1st January, 19..	9750	
Sundry factory expenses accrued		80
Sundry office and administration charges	7750	
Sundry selling and distribution charges	13800	
Interim dividend paid 30th June, 19..	1500	
Debenture interest, half year to 30th June, 19.., paid ..	100	
Preference dividend, half year to 30th June, 19.., paid ..	600	
Plant and machinery at cost	32500	
Provision for depreciation on plant (1st January, 19..) ..		10750
Plant depreciation, provision for current year		3250
Freehold premises at cost	29000	
Trade creditors		5220
Trade debtors	9100	
Transfer fees		90
Share Capital—		
50,000 Ordinary Shares of £1 each fully paid		50000
20,000 6% Preference Shares of £1 each fully paid ..		20000
5% Debentures..		4000
Reserve		5000
Provision for bad debts, 1st January, 19..		520
Sales		87200
Cash in hand and at Bank	16100	
Bad debts	420	
Profit and Loss Account, 1st January, 19....		1150
	£187260	£187260

In preparing the accounts the following matters are to be brought into account—

(a) The company's authorised capital is fully issued.

(b) Debenture interest is payable half yearly, the half year to 31st December, 19.., being due on that date.

(c) At 31st December, 19.., office and administration charges were prepaid £120 and selling and distribution charges due and not yet paid amounted to £350.

(d) Provision for bad debts is to be reduced by £60.

(e) The directors recommend that the current year's profit be appropriated as follows—

    (i) Transfer to Reserve £2,000.

    (ii) Payment of half-year's dividend on Preference Shares.

    (iii) Payment of a final dividend of 6% on the Ordinary Share Capital.

(f) Stock of finished goods at 31st December, 19.., was valued at £11,950

Notes.—

    (i) Income tax to be ignored.

    (ii) Candidates are advised to pay particular attention to the set out of assets and of liabilities in the Balance Sheet.

London Chamber of Commerce—Intermediate.

14. Summum Bonum Ltd. was formed to take over the business formerly carried on by A. Summum and B. Bonum in partnership, whose Balance Sheet just prior to the take over was as follows:—

	£		£	£
Capital—		Premises		5000
A. Summum	10000	Plant		7500
B. Bonum	6000	Stock and work in pro-		
	———	gress		4000
	16000	Debtors		3500
Contingency Reserve	1500	Cash—		
Creditors	3100	At bank	500	
		In hand	100	
			———	600
	———			———
	£20600			£20600

The company took over all the partnership assets and assumed responsibility for all the liabilities subject to the following:—

(1) It was decided that the contingency in respect of which the reserve was built up would not materialise.

(2) The following revaluations were made—

	£
Premises	8000
Plant	10000
Stock	3000
Debtors	3000

(3) The purchase price was £25,000 to be discharged by way of an issue at par of ordinary shares of £1 each in the company.

Since it was considered likely that the business would expand, an issue of 10,000 6½% cumulative preference shares of £1 each was made and subscribed for by certain friends of Summum and Bonum at a premium of £0·05 per share payable as follows:—

On application ..	..	£0·25 per share.
On allotment ..	..	£0·55 per share including the premium.
On call	..	£0·25 per share.
		£1·05

The issue was fully called and paid except for 1,000 shares on which the call moneys have not yet been received.

You are asked to record the foregoing by way of Journal entries on the basis that:—

(1) The company has carried on with the partnership books.

(2) The ordinary shares have been allotted to the vendors.

London Chamber of Commerce—Intermediate.

APPENDIX 4

ASSOCIATED EXAMINING BOARD
for the General Certificate of Education

Ordinary Level

PRINCIPLES OF ACCOUNTS

THREE HOURS ALLOWED

Answer TWO *questions from Section A* (30 *marks per question*).
Answer TWO *questions from Section B* (20 *marks per question*).

PAPER I

SECTION A

Answer TWO *questions from this Section.*

1. Hare and Line are in partnership. Their agreement provides that partners are entitled to interest on capital at 7% per annum and thereafter share profits and losses equally.

The following balances were extracted from the books of the partnership at 31st March, 1968.

	£	£	£
Capital: Hare			6500
Line			4500
Current Accounts:		£	
Hare: Credit balance at 1st April, 1967 ..		120	
Drawings during year of account		3000	
			2880
Line: Debit balance at 1st April, 1967		10	
Drawings during year of account		2800	
			2810
Stock (1st April, 1967)			6200
Purchases			62180
Sales			77210
Rent, rates, and insurance			1340
Selling expenses			3490
Administrative expenses			3570
Furniture and fittings			240
Trade debtors			5520
Trade creditors			6190
Goodwill			2000
Cash in hand and balance at bank			4170
		£94400	£94400

Prepare—
(*a*) the Partnership Trading and Profit and Loss Account for the year ended 31st March, 1968,
(*b*) the Partners' Current Accounts for the year ended 31st March, 1968, as they would appear when balanced for the year,
(*c*) the Balance Sheet as at 31st March, 1968.

(*Note:* The balances only of the Current Accounts are to be shown in the Balance Sheet. Details are *not* necessary.)

In preparing the accounts the following matters are to be taken into consideration.

(i) On 31st March, 1968, stock was valued at £6,750.

(ii) During the year Line had taken from stock goods valued at £80 but no entry had been made in the books.

(iii) The firm's premises belong to Hare who is entitled to a rent of £1,200 per annum. On 31st March, 1968, six months' accrued rent was due to Hare.

(iv) After ascertaining the net trading profit for the year it was decided to write £400 off goodwill.

2. On 1st April, 1967, F. Roe had the following assets and liabilities: cash in hand and balance at bank £1,556, stock £2,460, trade debtors £756, trade creditors £2,409, furniture and fittings £400, motor vans £1,350.

Roe does not keep proper books of account. On 31st March, 1968, the following information is available.

(i) *Summary of receipts and payments.*

Receipts	£	Payments	£
Receipts from trade debtors	6307	Payments to trade creditors	12273
Cash sales	10520	Business expenses	730
Sale of old motor van ..	290	Rent, rates, and insurance	1540
		Drawings	1900
		Furniture and fittings ..	150

(ii) On 31st March, 19.., stock was valued at £2,120; trade debtors were £609; trade creditors were £2,106 and £200 was written off motor vans.

(iii) The book value of the motor van sold during the year was £250.

(*a*) Prepare Roe's trading and profit and loss account for the year ended 31st March, 1968, and a balance sheet as at that date.

(*b*) If the only information available had been—
(i) Roe's assets and liabilities at 1st April, 1967,
(ii) Roe's assets and liabilities at 31st March, 1968,
(iii) Roe's drawings for the year,

how would you have proceeded to find Roe's profit for the year. Use the details given above to illustrate your answer.

3. J. Bentley is a manufacturer. The following balances were extracted from his books on 31st December, 1967.

	£	£
Stocks (1st January, 1967):		
Raw materials	904	
Finished goods	2436	
Purchases of raw materials	10842	
Sales of finished goods		33409
Wages and salaries: Factory	11250	
Offices	3200	
Rates and insurance (⅘ factory; ⅕ offices) ..	1820	
Manufacturing expenses	836	
Trade expenses	646	
Sundry general expenses	327	
Plant and machinery (at cost)	8000	
Provision for depreciation on plant and machinery		
(1st January, 1967)		3200
Freehold premises	10500	
Trade debtors	3724	

	£	£
Trade creditors		183
Cash in hand and balance at bank	2307	
Drawings	3000	
Capital (1st January, 1967)		23000
	£59792	£59792

Prepare:—
(a) Bentley's manufacturing account for the year 1967;
(b) his Trading and Profit and Loss Account for the year 1967, and
(c) his Balance Sheet as at 31st December, 1967.
The following matters are to be taken into account:—
On 31st December, 1967—
   (i) stocks of raw materials were valued at £816 and stocks of finished goods at £2,312;
   (ii) factory wages outstanding amounted to £210;
   (iii) rates and insurance prepaid amounted to £320;
   (iv) depreciation is to be written off plant and machinery at 10% of cost.

SECTION B
Answer TWO *questions from this Section.*

4. (a) The following Trial Balance was extracted from the books of T. Stevens on 31st May, 1968.

	£	£
Capital (1st January, 1968)		2750
Drawings	1800	
Stock (1st January, 1968)	1160	
Sales		7330
Purchases	5380	
Trade debtors	2130	
Trade creditors		2735
Business expenses	810	
Furniture and fittings	750	
Cash in hand and balance at bank ..	820	
	£12850	£12815

The Trial Balance did not agree and the following errors were discovered.
   (i) A purchase of fittings £62 had been included in the Purchases Account.
   (ii) A cheque for £87 received from a customer had been correctly entered in the Cash Book but posted to the customer's account as £97.
   (iii) A page of the Sales Book was correctly totalled at £987 but had been carried forward as £897.
   (iv) Cash £12 paid out for Stevens' private expenses had been included in business expenses.
   (v) An invoice for £127 received from a supplier had been correctly entered in the Purchases Book but had been posted to the Supplier's Account as £172.
Show the Trial Balance as it would appear *after* the above errors had been corrected.
(b) If a sale of goods £47 to J. Carr was posted to the wrong side of his account and a discount allowed to Carr £14 was omitted from his account (but was included in the Cash Book) by how much would the Trial Balance disagree? State which side of the Trial Balance would be the greater and by how much.

5. (*a*) On 31st December, 1967, the balances on the following accounts in L. Ray's Ledger were:—

	£
Provision for bad debts (Credit Balance at 1st January, 1967)	262
Provision for depreciation on machinery (Credit Balance at 1st January, 1967)	4870
Packing materials (Debit Balance)	276

When preparing final accounts for the year ended 31st December, 1967
(i) provision for bad debts was adjusted to 4% of trade debtors (£7,300),
(ii) machinery, at cost £9,000, was depreciated by 15% of cost,
(iii) the stock of packing materials was £47.

Make entries for these items in the above accounts and balance the accounts as on 31st December, 1967, bringing down balances where appropriate.

(*b*) What information can be derived from *each* of the entries in the following accounts?

Dr.			**F. Percy**				*Cr.*
1967		£	1967				£
May 5.	Bank ..	361	May 1.	Balance b/d	..	380
„ 5.	Discount ..	19	„ 17.	Purchases	..	296
„ 21.	Returns ..	14				
„ 31.	Balance c/d ..	282				
		£676				£676

				June 1.	Balance b/d	.	282

Dr.			**Insurance Account**				*Cr.*
1967		£	1967				£
July 1.	Balance b/d ..	14	Dec. 31.	P & L A/c	..	27
Nov. 1.	Bank	24	„ 31.	Balance c/d	..	11
		£38				£38

19..
Jan. 1. Balance b/d .. **11**

6. (*a*) On 1st March, 1967, J. L. Fox rented premises at £1,200 per annum and paid three months' rent in advance.

On 1st April, 1967, he sub-let part of the premises at £240 per annum and received one month's rent in advance.

By 31st December, 1967, Fox had paid three further quarterly instalments of rent and had received seven further monthly instalments from his sub-tenant.

Fox prepared his Final Accounts at 31st December, 1967.

Write up Fox's rent payable account and his rent receivable account for the ten months ended 31st December, 1967, making any necessary adjustments at that date and bringing down balances where appropriate.

(*b*) F. James started business on 1st July, 1967. During the ensuing six months he transacted the following business.

				£
Purchased goods on credit	..	..	..	31209
Returned goods to suppliers	..	..	..	314
Paid cheques to suppliers ..	..	..	..	23545
Sold goods on credit	..	..	..	43607
Customers returned goods	..	..	..	405
Received cheques from customers		..	..	36890
Received cash discount from suppliers	..	..	1146
Allowed cash discount to customers		..	..	1603

Construct control accounts to ascertain the amount owing by James to trade creditors and the amount owing by trade debtors to James at 31st December 1967.

PAPER II
SECTION A

Answer TWO *questions from this Section.*

1. J. Bale is a manufacturer. The following balances were extracted from his books on 31st March, 1968, *after* the Manufacturing Account had been prepared.

	£	£
Capital		21500
Drawings	3600	
Cost of goods manufactured	82340	
Stocks: raw materials (31st March, 1968)	2320	
finished goods (1st April, 1967)	8730	
Sales		102940
Carriage on sales	1335	
Advertising	3720	
Salesmen's commission and expenses	5450	
Office salaries	4500	
Office expenses	825	
Bank charges and interest	55	
Factory wages		420
Machinery and plant (at cost)	18500	
Provision for depreciation on machinery and plant ..		9250
Trade debtors	6850	
Trade creditors		714
Provision for bad debts (1st April, 1967)		296
Bad debts	310	
Bank overdraft		3415
	£138535	£138535

Prepare Bale's Trading and Profit and Loss Account for the year ended 31st March, 1968, and a Balance Sheet as at that date.

Bring into account the following matters.

At 31st March, 1968:—
  (i) stock of finished goods was valued at cost £9,165;
  (ii) during the year finished goods, valued at cost £800, had been given away as free samples but no entries had been made in the books;
  (iii) salesmen's expenses £266 were outstanding;
  (iv) the provision for bad debts is to be adjusted to 4% of trade debtors;
  (v) bank charges and interest £72 had not been entered in the books.

2. The following Trial Balance was extracted from A. Carr's books at 31st May, 1968.

	£	£
Capital (1st July, 1967) ..		7000
Drawings	1600	
Stock (1st July, 1967) ..	2650	
Sales		18720
Purchases	14310	
Motor vans	1350	
Trade debtors	3630	
Trade creditors		2310
Business expenses	3080	

				£	£
Bad debts	..	..	..	160	
Cash at bank		..	..	1250	
				£28030	£28030

(*a*) Open account for *each* of the above items and enter the opening balances.
(*b*) During June, 1968, the following transactions took place. Make the entries which arise from these transactions *direct* into the Ledger Accounts opened in part (*a*). Ignore dates.

	£
Sold a motor van for cash at book value..	.. 350
Sales on credit for the month	 3930
Purchases on credit for the month	 1920
Receipts from trade debtors for the month	.. 3220
Payment to trade creditors for the month	.. 2190
Business expenses paid during the month	.. 720
Bad debts written off during the month ..	.. 84
Cash drawn for personal use during the month ..	250

Note: All receipts are paid into bank and all payments are made by cheque.

(*c*) Prepare A. Carr's Trading and Profit and Loss Account for the year ended 30th June, 1968, and balance the Ledger Accounts as at that date.
The following adjustments are to be brought into account.
(i) Stock at 30th June, 1968, was valued at £2,710.
(ii) Motor vans are to be depreciated by £220.
(iii) Business expenses include rates £240 for the half-year 1st April, 1968, to 30th September, 1968.
(iv) Business expenses outstanding at 30th June, 1968, amounted to £106.
Note: A Balance Sheet is not required.

3. F. Exton owns a small hotel. On 1st January, 1967, his assets and liabilities were as follows:—
Cash at bank £450; stocks of provisions, wines, spirits, etc., £1,050; charges due from visitors £310; freehold premises £10,500; furniture, fittings, and equipment £4,250; glassware and china £920; trade creditors £610.
Exton does not keep complete records. He pays all receipts into bank and makes all payments by cheque.
On 31st December, 1967, the following information is available.
(i) The bank statement for the year 1967 showed—

Amounts Paid into Bank	£	Cheques Drawn	£
Balance (1st January, 1967)	450	Payment to trade creditors ..	6840
Receipts from visitors ..	14260	Repairs and maintenance ..	205
		Office expenses	95
		Wages and salaries	2480
		Rates and insurance ..	490
		Heat and light	260
		Drawings	3000
		Glassware and china ..	200
		Balance 31st December, 1967	1140
	£14710		£14710

(ii) Charges due from visitors at 31st December, 1967, amounted to £240.

(iii) Trade creditors at 31st December, 1967, amounted to £840.

(iv) Stock of provisions, wines, and spirits, etc., at 31st December, was valued at £1,320.

(v) A demand for rates £260 for the half-year ending 31st March, 1968, had been received but had not been paid.

(vi) The loss on glassware and china for the year is estimated at £230.

(vii) Furniture, fittings, and equipment are to be depreciated by 10%.

(viii) Exton and his wife live in the hotel and a charge of £800 per annum is to be made for hotel services.

Using the above information prepare Exton's Profit and Loss Account for the year ended 31st December, 1967, and a Balance Sheet as at that date.

SECTION B

Answer TWO *questions from this Section.*

4. (*a*) L. Brown is a trader. What is meant by saying that Brown's capital in his business is £5,000 and how is this amount calculated?

(*b*) On 1st January, 1968, L. Bee started a business with a stock of goods valued at £1,600, furniture and fittings valued at £400 and £650 in a business Bank Account.

During the following six months he withdrew £780 from the business.

On 30th June, 1968, his business assets were cash at bank £770, stock £1,920, sundry debtors £310, furniture and fittings £380, and the business owed sundry creditors £560.

Prepare a statement to show Bee's net profit for the half year ended 30th June, 1968.

(*c*) The following are the Balance Sheets of L. Martin as at 31st December, 1966, and 31st December, 1967.

	1966 £	1967 £		1966 £	1967 £
Capital (1st Jan.)..	4000	4400	*Fixed Assets:*		
Add: Net profit	1800	1600	Furniture and fittings	750	850
	5800	6000	*Current Assets:*		
Less: Drawings	1400	1400	Stock..	3040	3110
	4400	4600	Trade debtors ..	1220	1280
Trade creditors ..	950	800	Cash in hand and balance at bank ..	340	160
	£5350	£5400		£5350	£5400

Martin is rather puzzled that, although he has made a profit in 1967 he has less in the bank than in 1966.

Draw up a statement to explain to Martin where his profit has "gone".

5. (*a*) On 24th March, 1965, V. Tee started business as a carrier. He purchased a motor vehicle for £900.

On 4th April, 1966, he purchased another motor vehicle for £1,000.

On 10th February, 1967, he sold the vehicle he purchased on 24th March, 1965, for £570 and purchased a new motor vehicle for £1,100.

Tee makes up his final accounts at 31st December in each year. On that date he depreciates each motor vehicle by 20% of the cost of the vehicle.

(i) Write up Tee's Motor Vehicles Account for the years 1965, 1966, and 1967.

(ii) What is the book value of each of the two vehicles in Tee's possession at 31st December, 1967?

(*b*) L. Large owns property and employs an agent to collect the rents. The agent makes disbursements on the property out of the rents collected.

Prepare the agent's account in the books of L. Large from the following details relating to the year 1967.

	£
Rents collected	4650
Rates paid	540
Repairs paid	345
Commission charged by agent	465
Amounts received from agent	3000

Note: Nothing was owing to or by the agent at 1st January 1967.

(*c*) On 4th October, 1968, F. Richards purchased 20 boxes of goods at £10 per box from Suppliers Ltd. Boxes were charged in addition, at 10s. each and were returnable. When returned an allowance of 10s. per box is made.

On 15th October, 1968, Richards returned two boxes of the goods purchased on 4th October together with 10 empty boxes.

Make the entries relating to the above in the account of Suppliers Ltd, in Richards' ledger and balance the account at 31st October, 1968.

6. (*a*) In a burglary at S. Turner's premises on the night of 21st October, 1968, the petty cash balance and part of the stock were stolen.

A claim was made on the insurance company for the amount of the loss.

(i) Estimate the amount of this claim from the following particulars.

The petty cash imprest is £20 and expenses are refunded at the end of each month. The petty cash book for October, 1968, showed disbursements of £14 from 1st to 21st October, 1968.

Stock, at cost, on 30th September, 1968, was £3,420.

Purchases from 1st to 21st October, 1968, were £2,340.

Sales from 1st to 21st October, 1968, were £3,780.

Stock remaining after the burglary was valued at cost, £1,810.

Turner's average mark up on cost to ascertain selling price is 20%.

(ii) Make a Journal entry to pass this claim through the books.

(*b*) A and B are in partnership. A's capital is £5,000 and B's capital is £3,000. A has made a loan to the firm of £2,000.

Show, by means of Journal entries, how to deal with the following matters in the books of the partnership.

(i) B had surplus office furniture in his private possession. This furniture was transferred to the partnership at a valuation of £500.

(ii) A's private residence was repaired and decorated by the firm at a cost of £300, which the firm paid by cheque.

(iii) B took stock-in-trade from the firm valued at £50.

(iv) The partnership net trading profit for the year 1967, after entries for the above matters had been made but before allowing one year's interest on A's loan was £7,600. Apportion this net trading profit between the partners, assuming that the provisions of the Partnership Act, 1890, are applicable.

ROYAL SOCIETY OF ARTS

SINGLE-SUBJECT EXAMINATIONS

STAGE II (Intermediate)—BOOKKEEPING

[TWO AND A HALF HOURS ALLOWED]

ALL *questions in Section A and* ONE *question from Section B are to be attempted.*

PAPER I

SECTION A

ALL *questions in this section are to be attempted.*

1. B. Gally, a trader, did not keep a proper set of books but you were able to obtain the following data about his business:

Balance Sheet 31st December 1966

	£	£		£	£
Capital		9471	Fixed assets ..		7250
Creditors:			Current assets:		
Goods	2148		Stock	2181	
Expenses ..	121		Debtors.. ..	1392	
		2269	Bank	917	
					4490
		11740			11740

Details at 31st December 1967: £

				£
Stock in trade	..	..	..	3198
Debtors	..	..	..	1281
Bank balance..	..	..	..	1422
Creditors: Goods	..	..	..	2210
Expenses		..	..	102

No fixed assets were bought or sold during the year.

Included in payments by cheque during the year was £848 for expenses and £1,500 for drawings. All receipts were paid into the bank and there were no cash expenses. Gross profit throughout the year is at the rate of 25% on sales.

You are asked (1) to calculate Gally's net profit for 1967, (2) to reconstruct the trading and profit and loss account for 1967, and (3) prepare his Balance Sheet at 31st December, 1967.

Note: Ignore depreciation of fixed assets.

2. Bush and Mill are partners sharing profits in the ratio of 3:2. The following trial balance is extracted from their books as at 31st December 1967:

Trial Balance

				£	£
Capital: Bush ..	..	..	..		8823
Mill ..	..	..	..		6132
Drawings: Bush	..	..	..	1800	
Mill	..	..	..	1420	
Debtors and Creditors		..	..	2401	1869
Sales ..	..	..	..		22718

		£	£
Purchases		15226	
Discounts received			249
Discounts allowed		418	
Motor expenses..		326	
Rent and rates		940	
Salaries		2461	
Lighting and heating		322	
Bad debts		298	
Provision for doubtful debts			450
General expenses		649	
Balance at bank		492	
Stock in trade, December 31st, 1966..		4288	
Delivery vans at cost			
Less depreciation		2200	
Freehold building at cost		7000	
		£40241	£40241

You are given the following additional information:—
(i) Stock in trade December 31st, 1967, amounts to £5,263.
(ii) Rent due at 31st December, 1967, amounted to £200. A bill for £160 for rates for the half year to 31st March, 1968, was paid on 1st November, 1967.
(iii) Lighting and heating due at 31st December, 1967, amounted to £39.
(iv) The balance on delivery vans account represents three vans each costing £1,000, two were purchased on 1st January, 1965, and the third on 1st July, 1967. Depreciation has been charged at the rate of 20% per annum on cost and the same rate is to be continued for 1967.
(v) Provision for doubtful debts is to be increased to £500.
(vi) Bank charges, £28, were debited by the bank on 30th December, 1967, but have not yet been entered in the books.
You are asked to prepare a Trading and Profit and Loss Account for the year ended 31st December, 1967, and a Balance Sheet as at that date.

3. Tullymurray Ltd operated its own delivery service and maintained a fleet of vans for this purpose. The vans were carried forward at cost in the books, until sold or traded in, and the annual depreciation charge was credited to a Depreciation Provision Account.
The firm commenced business on 1st January, 1964, when 10 vans each costing £800 were purchased. On January 1st, 1965, 2 further vans, each costing £900, were purchased and on 31st December, 1966, two vans purchased in 1964 were traded in for £300 each and were replaced by two vans each costing £1,000. No further changes took place. The annual depreciation charge is at the rate of 20% of cost.
You are asked to prepare the Vans Account and the Depreciation Provision Account for each year to 31st December, 1967, and show the entry in the Balance Sheet at that date for the delivery vans.
Accounts are prepared annually at 31st December.

SECTION B

Answer EITHER *Question* 4 OR *Question* 5.

4. Dunmow Ltd, property owners, agreed to sell for £70,000 to Braintree Ltd, one of their tenants, the property which the latter occupied at an inclusive annual rental of £6,000. The completion date for the transfer was 1st November, 1967, by which date Braintree had already paid the rent to the end of December, 1967,

and Dunmow had paid rates to the end of March, 1968, at an annual charge of £1,200. Water rates for the half year to 31st March, 1968, £30, were paid in November by Braintree who had agreed to do this. The original cost of the property was £48,000 and it appeared in Dunmow's books at that amount. The profit on sale is to be transferred to the Profit and Loss Account.

You are asked to:

(a) prepare a statement to show the amount of cash to be paid to Dunmow Ltd on 1st November, 1967, and

(b) show the Journal entries in the books of Dunmow Ltd to record the receipt of cash on sale and the other relevant adjustments to the Freehold Property Account.

5. In June, 1967, Broad consigned 100 articles to Oak in Australia. The total cost of the goods to Broad was £4,000 and he incurred charges for freight and insurance amounting to £200. Oak paid £160 customs and clearance charges in Australia. Oak was entitled to 5% commission on gross sales.

Oak sold 75 articles for £3,872 by 31st December, 1967, and paid £88 for delivery charges to his customers. By arrangement with Broad he put the remainder of the consignment into storage for the following season and paid in advance storage charges of £50. He reported to Broad that the prospects for a profitable sale in 1968 were quite satisfactory. He then remitted £3,300 on account to Broad.

You are asked to show the accounts recording these matters, including the appropriate transfer to Profit and Loss Account, in the books of Broad.

PAPER II

SECTION A

ALL *questions in this section are to be attempted.*

1. Sheering Ltd maintained a system of self-balancing Ledgers. You are asked to prepare the Sales Ledger Control Account from the following figures:—

	£
Debit balance 1st January, 1968	4296
Credit balance 1st January, 1968	26
Sales	51264
Cash received from customers	48629
Discount allowed	824
Returns and allowances	968
Bad debts	426
Increase in provision for doubtful debts	122
Credit balance 12th December, 1968	32

2. The following information was extracted from the books and records of the Herring Bone Club:

Bank Account for 1968

	£		£
Balance 1st January, 1968	762	Bar supplies	17146
Subscriptions for 1968 ..	1864	Cost of social events.. ..	722
Subscriptions for 1969 ..	21	Wages	2468
Bar takings	22184	General expenses	1962
Receipts from social events	794	Repairs and decorations to	
Balance 31st December, 1968	573	premises	1400
		New furniture purchased	
		July 1, 1968	2500
	£26198		£26198

Note: All bar takings and other receipts are banked intact.
The buildings belonging to the Club appeared in the 1967 Balance Sheet at
£15,000. The written down value of the furniture reported therein was £1,600.
Subscriptions in advance amounting to £26 were received in 1967.
Depreciation on furniture is to be provided at the rate of 10% per annum on
the written down value of the old furniture and on the cost of the new purchases.
The following additional details are given:

	31st December, 1967	31st December, 1968
	£	£
Bar stock	861	928
Creditors for bar supplies	1241	1266

You are asked to give the Club's bar Trading Account and Income and
Expenditure Account for 1968 together with the Balance Sheet as at 31st December,
1968.

3. The Trial Balance extracted from the books of Wormley, a trader, as at
31st December, 1968, was as follows:—

Trial Balance

	£	£
Capital		11219
Furniture and equipment (cost £2,100)	1640	
Motor vans (cost £1,700)	1120	
Purchases	36291	
Rent and rates	800	
Salaries	3969	
Bad debts	281	
General expenses	1062	
Bank balance	308	
Sales		45622
Provision for doubtful debts as at 1st January, 1968		269
Stock in trade as at January 1st, 1968	8726	
Debtors	4289	
Creditors		3164
Drawings	1788	
	£60,274	£60,274

You are given the following additional information:—
(a) Stock in trade 31st December, 1968, £9,428.
(b) Rates paid in advance at 31st December, 1968, £60.
(c) General expenses unpaid at 31st December, 1968, £166.
(d) Provision for doubtful debts is to be adjusted to £241.
(e) A motor van purchased on 1st January, 1967, at a cost of £800 was traded
    in for £350 on 31st December, 1968, and a new van purchased at a cost
    of £1,000 on the same day. The amount due on the new van was
    payable on 1st January, 1969. No entries had been made in the books
    in respect of this transaction when the Trial Balance at 31st December,
    1968, was extracted.
(f) Depreciation is to be charged on furniture and equipment at the rate of
    5% per annum on cost and on the vans at the rate of 25% per annum
    on cost.

You are asked to prepare Wormley's Trading and Profit and Loss Account for 1968 and his Balance Sheet as at 31st December, 1968.

SECTION B

Answer EITHER *question 4* OR *question 5, not both.*

4. Clacton and Jaywick are in partnership, sharing profits in the ratio of 2 : 1. Their Balance Sheet on 31st March, 1968 is as follows:—

Balance Sheet

	£		£
Capitals:		Investment at cost	
Clacton	6422	(market value £13,000)	10000
Jaywick	7168	Cash	3590
	£13590		£13590

Clacton and Jaywick dissolved partnership on 31st March, 1968, and the investments were sold at the market price. State the amount of cash which would be paid to Clacton on dissolution. Explain how you calculate the amount and justify the procedure you adopt.

5. Explain briefly the distinction between capital and revenue expenditure. State with reasons how you would classify each of the two following items:—

(a) Wages of own workmen on building an extension to a firm's factory, and
(b) Cost of rebuilding the wall of a factory.

THE LONDON CHAMBER OF COMMERCE

(Incorporated)

INTERMEDIATE

Instructions to Candidates:

(a) *All questions should be attempted.*

(b) *Marks may be lost by lack of neatness.*

1. The Top Dressing Co. Ltd, leases from T. Ulph the right to extract sand from his quarries. The conditions of the lease are:—

1. Royalty to be £0·1 per ton of sand extracted.
2. Minimum rent £1,200 per annum.
3. Shortworkings recoverable for two years after the year in which they arose.

The output for the first four years was:—

Year 1	6000 tons
Year 2	10000 tons
Year 3	15000 tons
Year 4	20000 tons

You are required to show the necessary accounts in the books of the Top Dressing Co. Ltd for the four years in question.

(23 marks)

2. Kleenwick Ltd, which manufactures detergents, makes up its account to 31st December in each year. At the 31st December, 1967, the books contained amongst others, the following balances:—

	£		
Office expenses	5100	Stocks—1st Jan., 1967—	
Rates and insurance	2168	Finished goods	13622
Carriage inwards	1999	Work in progress	6081
Manufacturing wages	37186	Raw Materials consumed	67444
Fuel and power	8121	Heat and light	984
Factory expenses	4001	Carriage outwards	2162
Selling expenses	6204	Sales	181622
		Profit and Loss A/c (*Cr.*)	13161

You are required to prepare the Company's Manufacturing Account for the year ended 31st December, 1967, bearing in mind that the Company desires such account to show the Prime Cost and the Factory Cost as separate figures, and that the manufactured output is charged to Trading Account at a profit loading of 12½% on factory cost.

Thereafter you are to prepare the Company's Trading Profit and Loss and Appropriation Accounts for the same year, taking into account the following matters:—

1. Rates and insurance and heat and light can be regarded as chargeable seven-eighths to factory and one-eighth to office expenses whilst one-sixth of the office expenses are properly chargeable to the factory (excluding the apportionment from rates and insurances and heat and light).

415

2. Closing stocks are:—

	£
Work in progress ..	7174
Finished goods	13829

3. Depreciation on plant and machinery amounts to £3,910 and on office furniture £121.

4. The directors propose to transfer £8,000 to Dividend Equalisation Fund and also to pay a final dividend of 20% on the Issued Capital of £80,000, having paid an interim dividend of 10%.

(30 marks)

3. From the following particulars you are required to prepare an Income and Expenditure Account for the year ended 31st December, 1967, and a Balance Sheet at that date, for the Tanglewood Home for the Aged and Infirm.

	£		£
Cash in hand	816	Donations received	150
Cash on deposit	5000	Medical and surgical supplies ..	316
Furniture and fittings ..	1500	Interest on deposit (ignore tax) ..	250
Salaries—Nursing staff ..	7161	Rates, taxes, and insurances ..	387
Other staff ..	3630	Repairs and maintenance ..	114
Premises at cost	6000	Printing and stationery ..	217
Fees received from residents	19418	Fuel, light, and cleaning ..	665
Sundry creditors	912	Miscellaneous expenditure ..	57
Food purchased	1216	Fund balance, 1st Jan., 1967 (*Cr.*)	6349

In preparing the accounts regard must be paid to the following matters:—
1. Stock of food at 31st December, 1967, was £97.
2. Bills are outstanding for printing the prospectus amounting to £53 whilst the stock of stationery, etc., totalled £31.
3. Depreciation to be written off premises at 5% and furniture and fittings as 20%.
4. Fees outstanding from residents amount to £961.
5. Salaries amounting to £812 are outstanding for the nursing staff, and £79 for the other staff.
6. Interest on deposit is taken to Revenue Account.

(30 marks)

4. The following particulars relate to the plant and machinery of the Creda Company, Ltd:—

	£
Value of plant and machinery owned at 1st January, 1967, at cost	15121
Amount of depreciation provision at 1st January, 1967	9666
New plant and machinery purchased 1st September, 1967 ..	1500
Old machine sold 1st August, 1967, for	715
(This machine cost £1,262)	
Depreciated book value of old machine sold	860
Provision for depreciation for the year ended 31st December, 1967	1381

You are requested to prepare the Plant and Machinery Account and the Depreciation Provision (Plant and Machinery) Account for the year ended 31st December, 1967, and to show the appropriate entries in the Company's Profit and Loss Account.

(17 marks)

INDEX

417

Printed at The Burlington Press, Foxton, Royston, Herts SG8 6SA.
Telephone: Cambridge (0223) 870266